DICTIONARY
OF WORD ORIGINS

Linda Flavell completed a first degree in modern languages and has subsequent qualifications in both secondary and primary teaching. She has worked as an English teacher in England and overseas, and more recently as a librarian in secondary schools and as a writer. She has written three simplified readers for overseas students and co-authored, with her husband, *Current English Usage* for Papermac and several dictionaries of etymologies for Kyle Cathie. She lives in York.

Roger Flavell's Master's thesis was on the nature of idiomaticity and his doctoral research on idioms and their teaching in several European languages. On taking up a post as Lecturer in Education at the Institute of Education, University of London, he travelled very widely in pursuit of his principal interests in education and training language teachers. In later years, he was concerned with education and international development, and with online education. He also worked as an independent educational consultant. He died in December 2005.

DICTIONARY
OF WORD ORIGINS

Linda and Roger Flavell

Kyle Cathie Ltd

First published in Great Britain in 1993 by
Kyle Cathie Limited
23 Howland Street
London W1T 4AY
general.enquiries@kyle-cathie.com
www.kylecathie.com

Published in paperback 1994

Revised edition published 2008

This completely revised and updated edition published 2010

10 9 8 7 6 5 4 3 2 1

ISBN 978 1 85626 861 5

A Cataloguing in Publication record for this title is available
from the British Library.

Printed and bound in Great Britain by Cox & Wyman

· Introduction ·

With a book of this kind it is always tempting to ignore the introduction. The browser plunges into the text at random, while the reference reader confines his or her reading to the index and the relevant entries. In this case we hope that both types of reader will take a moment to read these few pages. They provide background information about the development of the English language that will increase your enjoyment and understanding of the rest of the book.

Indo-European

Nearly all European languages, together with languages spoken in the Middle East and northern India, show a number of striking similarities which point to a common prehistoric source. This is assumed to be a language spoken thousands of years ago, possibly in the region of eastern Ukraine and southern Russia, and is referred to as **proto-Indo-European**. Languages deriving from it belong to the Indo-European family. The term Indo-European describes the extent of the geographical distribution of the different languages.

The dispersal of the people who spoke proto-Indo-European caused various linguistic branches to spring from the parent stock. Among them are:

Balto-Slavic: Lativian, Polish, Czech, Russian, etc.
Germanic: Swedish, English, Dutch, Gothic, etc.
Celtic: Irish Gaelic, Welsh, Breton, etc.
Italic: Latin and the modern Romance languages – Italian, Spanish, Portuguese, French, etc.
Hellenic: ancient Greek, modern Greek.
Indo-Iranian: Sanskrit (giving Bengali, Hindi, Urdu, etc.) and Iranian (giving Farsi, etc.).

Within the Germanic branch, the original prehistoric tongue, now referred to as **proto-Germanic** or **Common Germanic**, eventually divided into North Germanic, East Germanic and West Germanic.

Modern Scandinavian languages developed from North Germanic, Gothic, now extinct, is from East Germanic, and English, along with Frisian, Flemish, German and Dutch, evolved from West Germanic.

Old English

During the fifth and sixth centuries Britain was invaded and settled by the Angles, the Saxons and the Jutes, Germanic peoples from Jutland and southern Denmark. The Germanic dialects they spoke were very similar to each other and from them the language known as Old English gradually evolved. A wave of Viking invasions, which began in the middle of the ninth century, introduced a stock of North Germanic (**Old Norse**) words into the language, particularly in northern England (see VIKING CONQUESTS, page 303). Old English was written and spoken from around the middle of the fifth century until the end of the eleventh.

Middle English

The Middle English period lasted from about 1100 to 1500. English changed considerably as a result of the Norman Conquest in 1066. The conquerors were of Viking origin (Norman being 'Norseman') but had been granted lands in northern France. They spoke **Anglo-Norman**, a dialect of Old French, and **Anglo-French** became the language of government and law. English survived as the language of the masses but naturally began to absorb Anglo-Norman and Old French words.

During the thirteenth century, however, following decades of hostility and the loss of territories on the continent, the kings of England and the nobility began to identify more closely with the country and to express themselves in English. In doing so, they made use of Old French words that were familiar to them, so that an even greater influx of foreign terms poured into every area of English vocabulary. Where an Old English word and an Old French word had the same meaning, the Old English was often discarded in favour of the French.

The plague known as the Black Death (1349–50) was also significant in promoting the use of English. The death toll was so great that the surviving labourers and merchants achieved a new economic importance, and so did the language that they spoke.

Significant fourteenth-century markers in the progress of Middle English are the poetic works of Geoffrey Chaucer (c. 1340–1400) and the Statute of Pleading (1362), which required the use of English in law courts, so that the common people could understand what was happening. Also in 1362 Parliament was for the first time opened with a speech made in English.

Modern English

Modern English, which dates from about 1500, continued to assimilate a huge number of foreign terms.

The Renaissance excited the spirit of discovery. The invention of printing with movable type sparked the desire to break the restriction of Latin as the language of scholarship and to communicate in the vernacular to a wider readership. Where English was inadequate for this purpose, classical terms were introduced and naturalised. Translations were made from modern languages such as French and Italian, as well as from classical Greek and Latin, thus introducing more foreign words into English.

New continents and peoples were discovered and English vocabulary extended through the adoption of strange terms descriptive of exotic landscapes, life and customs. (Some of the essays in this book explore borrowings from individual languages such as Malay, Chinese, Hindi and Arabic.) Trade flourished and new commodities were made avail-able, from different fabrics to beverages such as tea and cocoa. Medical and scientific knowledge increased and was expressed in terms coined from Latin and Greek.

English continues to grow and change rapidly as it reflects the concerns, interests and needs of its speakers. Technological advances in the twentieth century, for instance, introduced a wealth of new terms while, at the close of the century, the adjective *green* developed a new meaning that reflects present-day preoccupation over the welfare of our planet.

Notes on other languages mentioned throughout the book

Vulgar Latin. The lively everyday Latin dialects of the Roman Empire (as opposed to formal or literary Latin) from which the Romance languages eventually evolved by the ninth century.

Late Latin (c. 200–600). The Latin of the late Western Roman Empire and the works of early Christian writers.

Medieval Latin (c. 600–1300). The language of letters, of government and of the church.

Modern Latin. Latin in use since the beginning of the sixteenth century. The language of Renaissance classical scholarship, of science, religion and diplomacy.

Old French. The French language written and spoken c. 900–1550. (See Vulgar Latin above.)

Provençal. A Romance language spoken in the southern regions of France before the sixteenth century. (See Vulgar Latin above.)

Modern English. The English spoken and written from the sixteenth century onwards.

How to use this book

This dictionary seeks to trace the origins of particular words and to provide a historical context for them. These 'headwords' are arranged in alphabetical order. Often, however, other words from the same source are referred to within the entries and so, for ease of reference, a comprehensive index has been included. Here headwords appear in italic type while their etymological relatives, together with words which feature in the essays, are printed in plain type. The essays and boxes scattered throughout the book expand on themes that are relevant to a number of entries or are of general interest in the development of the language.

It is rarely possible to be exact about when a word appeared in English. SERENDIPITY and ROBOT are exceptions. Where a word is set in a particular century it usually means only that the first known written record of the term appeared then. There is no way of knowing how long a word featured in spoken English before it occurred in written form.

Sometimes a word is traced back to an 'unattested' term or root. This means that although there is no written evidence that the particular form ever existed, linguistic scientists have been able to draw upon their understanding of how words in that family develop and are confident that it did.

In selecting words for inclusion, we have chosen those which have a story to tell. While we have striven for scholarly accuracy (without, we hope, falling into academic pedantry), we have also aimed to show something of the richness and diversity of the English language, and to include sufficient that is plain curious to satisfy the browser motivated by nothing more than a quest for knowledge and a love of words.

LINDA FLAVELL,
YORK, SEPTEMBER 2009

MAIN ESSAYS

accolade

the conferment of a knighthood; an expression of praise or high honour

'I like Ed. I'm so glad you brought him. He's going to make everyone feel better.'
Marcus didn't seem to approve of this **accolade**. *'I hope he's going to be my first mate.'*
(KATIE FFORDE,
GOING DUTCH, 2007)

*SOUTH AFRICAN AIRWAYS CLAIMS ANOTHER **ACCOLADE!***
The airline was named Africa's Leading Airline during the World Travel Awards in June, the seventh award the carrier has picked up this year.
(FRIENDSHIP NEWS,
SEPTEMBER 2008)

The Frankish emperor Charlemagne, who reigned over central and western Europe in the eighth century, rewarded his mounted warriors with grants of land in exchange for a certain number of men-at-arms to be supplied in times of conflict. The warriors, in turn, secured the services of such men by granting them benefices on condition that they pledged themselves to be available for military duties when required. Later, the warriors' lands were declared hereditary and an elect order of professional fighting men was established. These became the knights of the Middle Ages.

Only those born into a knightly family could become knights. At the age of seven or eight the eldest son in such a household would be sent to another household, or to court, where he would become a page, the servant of a knight, and then a squire, learning fighting skills in order to accompany his lord into battle. When the training was complete the ceremony to bestow knighthood would take place.

Initially the ceremony was a simple one but, during the eleventh century, as knights prepared to fight the Crusades, the Church made it more elaborate. It centred round a blow to the neck with an open hand or the flat of a sword. This was known as a dubbing or a *colee*, the latter a word borrowed from Old French and derived from Latin *collum*, 'neck'.

The word *accolade*, 'dubbing', did not appear in English until the seventeenth century, by which time knighthoods were bestowed as a reward for service to the sovereign. Its etymology suggests that, at some time, bestowal of a knighthood involved an embrace. Its source is the unattested Vulgar Latin verb *accollāre*, 'to embrace round the neck', from Latin *ad-*, 'to', and *collum*, 'neck'. In Provençal this became *acolar*, and the derived noun *acolada*, 'embrace', was taken into French as *accolade* and from there into English.

The present-day British monarch still confers knighthoods upon servants of the realm by means of a sword, and the attached customs and ceremonies ensure that *accolade* is still used in its original sense. Since around the middle of the nineteenth century, however, the word has been used more often figuratively as an expression of great honour or praise in other areas; an actor might receive an *accolade* for an outstanding performance, for instance, or a particular award might be considered the highest *accolade* in a profession.

aftermath

a second crop of hay; the after-effect of an event or action

Several hundred people sat on the sea wall, staring south into the late afternoon sky. It was a bruised, feverish red, flaring like the ***aftermath*** *of an explosion, and it induced a sombre mood among the spectators.*
(ALEXANDER FRATER, CHASING THE MONSOON, 1990)

There have been more than 20 such raids since August, said Richard Beeston in The Times, *and the* ***aftermath*** *always follows a familiar pattern: 'Washington refuses to comment, Pakistan denounces the action and Britain sits somewhere uncomfortably between the two.'*
(THE WEEK, 29 NOVEMBER 2008)

The story is told of a teacher of mathematics who called his retirement home Aftermath. However, *aftermath* originated as an agricultural term, in use since at least the early sixteenth century. It is a combination of *after* and *math*, from an Old English word *mæth*, 'a mowing', and denotes a second crop of grass in the same season (*aftercrop* follows the same pattern).

Aftermath has been used figuratively since around the mid-seventeenth century. The action of mowing is brutal and the second crop of grass generally weaker than the first. *No aftermath*, writes Robert Southey, *has the fragrance and sweetness of the first crop* (THE DOCTOR, 1862). And so the term is now used to describe the unpleasant consequences that are reaped after a disaster – a second crop of misery.

agnostic

someone who claims the existence of God cannot be known

If I am asked, as a purely intellectual question, why I believe in Christianity, I can only answer, 'For the same reason that an intelligent ***agnostic*** *disbelieves in Christianity.' I believe in it quite rationally upon the evidence.*
(G K CHESTERTON, ORTHODOXY, 1909)

He formed his verses as a series of reflections from dawn to dusk about life and the universe, ending in a boozy, ***agnostic*** *resignation.*
(ROBERT IRWIN IN THE LONDON LIBRARY MAGAZINE, WINTER 2008–09)

An *agnostic* is not simply someone who doubts the existence of God, but one who believes that only the finite can be known and made sense of, so that God and the infinite are unknowable. The word was coined in 1869 by Thomas Henry Huxley, a biologist and vigorous exponent of Darwin's evolutionary theory. In the February 1889 issue of THE NINETEENTH CENTURY, Professor Huxley explained the reasoning behind the new word:

When I reached intellectual maturity and began to ask myself whether I was an atheist, a theist, or a pantheist, a materialist or an idealist, a Christian or a free-thinker, I found that the more I learned and reflected, the less ready was the answer, until at last I came to the conclusion that I had neither art nor part with any of these denominations except the last. The one thing in which most of these good people agreed was the one thing in which I differed from them. They were quite sure they had attained a certain 'gnosis', had more or less successfully solved the problem of existence; while I was quite sure I had not, and had a pretty strong conviction that the problem was insoluble.

This was my situation when I had the good fortune to find a place among the members of that remarkable confraternity of antagonists, long since deceased, but of green and pious memory, the Metaphysical Society. Every variety of philosophical and theological opinion was represented there, and expressed itself with entire openness; most of my colleagues were ists of one sort or another; and, however kind and friendly they might be, I, the man without a rag of a label to cover himself with, could not fail to have some of the uneasy feelings which must have beset the historical fox when, after leaving the trap in which his tail remained, he presented himself to his normally elongated companions. So I took thought, and invented what I conceived to be the appropriate title of 'agnostic'. It came into my head as suggestively antithetic to the 'Gnostic' of Church history who professed to know so much about the very things of which I was ignorant, and I took the earliest opportunity of parading it at our society, to show that I, too, had a tail like the other foxes.

Other accounts as to exactly when Huxley announced his new word differ slightly. According to R H Hutton, editor of THE SPECTATOR and fellow founder member of the Metaphysical Society, he aired it not after debate with the society's members but at a party held before its formation, at James Knowles's house on Clapham Common on 21 April 1869. The first written record of the word occurred just a few weeks later in THE SPECTATOR of 29 May 1869. Perhaps Huxley had used the party as an opportunity to test the waters with his new tag.

As for the form of the word, Hutton claimed that Huxley's inspiration was St Paul's mention in Acts 17: 23 of the altar to the Unknown God: in Greek *agnōstō theō*. Whether this account is true or not, *agnostic* is a simple coinage.

The term Gnostic referred to a member of an early Christian sect who believed that salvation was achieved by the very few who were capable of transcending the material world by embracing esoteric spiritual truths. As Huxley states, he had simply taken the noun, a derivative of Greek *gnōsis*, 'knowledge', and added the negative prefix *a-*, 'not'.

Today the scope of the word has been extended to refer to someone who questions the wisdom of an opinion or course of action.

For other words where the precise date of coinage can be demonstrated, see ALTRUISM, AMMONIA and PRECISE TIMING (page 241). See AMETHYST for a classical Greek example of the prefix *a-*.

agony
acute mental or physical torment; intense emotion

*Cramp seized her tired feet, knotting her toes into twisted shapes, moving up to her calves until she gasped with pain. Stamping and trying to tread away the **agony**, she drew the curtains, switched on the light. There was no river, no fish, no child.*
(MARY WESLEY,
AN IMAGINATIVE EXPERIENCE, 1994)

*Much of the subsequent days and nights was spent in an **agony** of emotions and opinions and discussions. It is truly a terrible thing when questions of love and family and home are no longer answerable.*
(JOSEPH O'NEILL, NETHERLAND, 2008)

The ancient Greeks took athletic contests very seriously, believing that the gods took pleasure in strong, well-toned bodies in competition. The Olympic Games, for instance, were held every four years in honour of Zeus and Hera. From the verb *agein*, meaning 'to drive, to bring', the Greeks derived the noun *agōn*. Originally this meant 'a bringing together of competitors for the games', but gradually came to mean the contest, the fight itself. From this a new noun *agōnia* was derived to describe the 'mental anguish' involved in the competitive struggle. This word was subsequently borrowed into Late Latin as *agōnia*.

The route into Middle English is unclear. *Agony* in the sense of 'mental distress' appears in Chaucer's 'Miller's Tale' (c. 1387):

> *This man is falle, with his astromye,*
> *In som woodnesse [madness] or in som*
>   *agonye...*

It may have been borrowed from Old French *agonie* or from Wycliffe's translation (1382, from the Latin of the Vulgate) of Luke's Gospel, where he uses *agonye* to describe the mental anguish of Christ in the Garden of Gethsemane. Wycliffe himself is known to have been a strong influence on Chaucer. Today the sense of 'mental suffering' lives on in letters to *agony aunts*; the *agony column* feature in magazines dates back to just after the middle of the nineteenth century.

The early eighteenth century saw the emergence of a new, connected sense where *agony* was used to describe an intense sensation of delight:

> *Then he thought of his flower. He got it*
> *out, rumpled and wilted, and it mightily*
> *increased his dismal felicity. He wondered*
> *if she would pity him if she knew? Would*
> *she cry?... This picture brought such an*
> *agony of pleasurable suffering that he*
> *worked it over and over again in his mind*
> *and set it up in new and varied lights,*
> *till he wore it threadbare.*
> (MARK TWAIN, THE ADVENTURES OF
> TOM SAWYER, 1876)

Pain and pleasure may well be the reverse sides of the same coin; current usage, nonetheless, emphasises the former over the latter. The agony usually wins out over the ecstasy.

Agony was used to describe 'death pangs' from the mid-sixteenth century but it was not until the early seventeenth century that it was also applied to extreme physical pain.

For another painful word, see EXCRUCIATING. For another word from ancient Greek athletics, see GYMNASIUM.

alarm
a warning; a feeling of fear or anxiety

> *Portia jumped up and stalked about for a*
> *bit, testing out potential sleeping spots with*
> *her claw. She committed, finally, to lying*
> *heavily – and hotly – across my calves.*
> *I set my **alarm** and turned out the light.*
> *Through a gap in the curtains, a moonbeam*
> *shone glamorously on Portia, like a spotlight.*
> (ZOE HELLER,
> NOTES ON A SCANDAL, 2003)

> *A toddler who drove his battery-powered*
> *toy truck into a river was swept eight miles*
> *downstream and emerged unshaken.*
> *Demetrius Jones, three, was camping with his*
> *family near their home in British Columbia,*
> *Canada, when he slipped out of the tent for*
> *a morning drive, wearing just his nappy*
> *and a T-shirt. When his parents awoke they*
> *sounded the **alarm**: three hours later rescuers*
> *found him drifting happily downstream,*
> *using the upturned car as a boat.*
> (THE WEEK, 25 JULY 2009)

The Old Italian phrase *all'arme* was a warning cry meaning 'to arms!'. It was often written as a single word *allarme*. As such it was borrowed into Old French as *alarme*, and from there into Middle English in the fourteenth century, still as a call to arms.

In the late sixteenth century the word was applied to any loud noise or cry made to alert people to imminent danger, and also to mechanisms which sounded the alarm. This sense is best noted today in the *alarm clock*, with its warning that it's time to get up. *Alarm* was also used to describe the sense of disquiet or fear felt at the approach of danger or uncertainty, again in the late sixteenth century. Today one increasingly finds signs on doors that read *This door is alarmed*. Clearly, doors have no sense of fear: 'equipped with a burglar alarm' is a new meaning.

An alternative spelling *alarum* dates from medieval times. It probably arose through the marked pronunciation of the letter *r* in a drawn-out last syllable when the call to arms was made, and is now obsolete.

album

a book with blank pages for the collection of like items: stamps, photographs, etc.; a collection of songs on a CD

*My dad opens an **album** of ancient black-and-white photographs from before he was born, and although he sees the faces of his mother and his father and his aunts and uncles, their grown-up faces smiling through the smiles of when they were children, many of the people in the album are complete strangers to him, people he never met, with names he will never know. Not now.*
(TONY PARSONS,
ONE FOR MY BABY, 2001)

[Hayley Westenra] has released a 'Best of' compilation, River of Dreams. *Listening to the **album**, which roves seamlessly from classical to Celtic-inspired folk to pop, is a good way to sample the breadth of her work. Filing her under 'classical' only tells part of her story.*
(YORKSHIRE LIVING, APRIL 2009)

Album is the neuter form of *albus*, a Latin adjective meaning 'white'. The word was used as a noun in ancient Rome to refer to a white tablet upon which a praetor's edicts were written and which would be displayed in an open place such as the Forum so that its contents could be made public. Anyone changing or erasing wording in the album was severely punished. Later the word *album* came to signify a list of public bodies; the *album senatorium* contained a list of senators, while the *album judicum* was a list of judges.

The word came into English by way of the *album amicorum* or 'album of friends'. This concept originated in Germany among students who collected inscriptions in blank books from their friends and professors as souvenirs of their student days. Some of the contributions ran to several pages, others were illuminated like medieval manuscripts, the illustrations carefully expressing the true meaning of the text. References to this custom began to appear in English texts in the mid-seventeenth century and in 1755, in his DICTIONARY OF THE ENGLISH LANGUAGE, Dr Samuel Johnson defined *album* as *a book in which foreigners have long been accustomed to insert the autographs of celebrated people*.

In England, the *album* became popular during the nineteenth century. The Victorians applied the word to any book with blank pages which was used to collect like items together; photographs or pressed flowers, for instance. In the 1950s it was taken up by the world of recorded music, when a collection of songs on a long-playing gramophone record became known as an *album*; the term is now similarly applied to a CD.

FROM ALL POINTS OF THE COMPASS

English collects words from other languages like a magpie. Apart from obvious sources such as Latin, Greek, Arabic and the Romance languages of Western Europe, just in this book are included:

Chinese: *tea, kowtow*
Czech: *robot*
Tahitian: *tattoo*
Tongan: *taboo*

Even a cursory glance at a large dictionary shows how many other languages from around the world have enriched English over the centuries. The biggest dictionary of them all, the Oxford English Dictionary, lists more than 500 foreign languages and dialects that have influenced its entries, from Abnakei and Aboriginal to Zulu and Zuñi.

See also WORDS FROM ARABIC (page 20), WORDS FROM THE MALAY ARCHIPELAGO (page 65), WORDS FROM CHINESE (page 170), A TASTE OF INDIA (page 272).

alcohol
intoxicating drink

*I could smell the settler he had had before he came in the hospital door, I could smell his lunch-time wine and last night's beer. But there was also some metabolic shift, a sweetness to his blood and breath that I did not recognise. He didn't eat much, those last years, his body already cycling on **alcohol**. And sitting on the train to Brighton I wonder if he had diabetes, if that was what was wrong.*
(ANNE ENRIGHT, THE GATHERING, 2007)

*Researchers defined a low-risk lifestyle as including above-average physical activity, a healthful diet, light or moderate **alcohol** consumption, not smoking, a BMI (body mass index, a relation of height to weight) of less than 25, and a waist circumference of 34.6 inches or less for women or 36 inches or less for men.*
(FOCUS ON HEALTHY AGEING, 1 JULY 2009)

Few would guess the connection between this word and the make-up box. *Alcohol* is an Arabic borrowing: *al-* meaning 'the' and *khul*, 'kohl'. It was the custom in the Middle East and beyond to darken the eyelids with kohl, finely crushed antimony. Originally, this was done to repel tiny insects, which transmitted disease, as well as to protect the eyes from the glare of the sun. Women soon discovered, however, that the application of kohl had a cosmetic effect, making the whites of their eyes look brighter and the pupils darker. In the Old Testament of the Bible, the prophet Ezekiel (born around 621 BC) gives God's judgement on Oholah and Oholibah (allegorical figures representing Israel and Judah) for their provocative behaviour: *You bathed yourself; you painted your eyelids, and put on your finest jewels for them* (THE LIVING BIBLE, Ezekiel 23: 40). In the early seventeenth century, the English traveller and colonist George Sandys, on a visit to Egypt, Mount Sinai and Palestine, wrote that *the people put betweene the eye-lids and the eye a certaine black powder... made of a minerall brought from the kingdom of Fez, and called Alcohole* (THE RELATION OF A JOURNEY, 1615).

However, when the word *alcohol* was first borrowed into English in the mid-sixteenth century, probably by way of Medieval Latin, it was in the realm of alchemy, its use in Arabic having been extended to apply not just to ground antimony but to any solid substance refined into the finest powder by sublimation. In Europe, this notion of purity and refinement was extended to fluids in the late sixteenth century, hence *alcohol of wine* (*alcohol vini*), the purest essence of wine obtained by distillation. (Distillation, coincidentally, was a skill learnt from Arab alchemists several centuries earlier.) Edward Phillips, nephew of the poet John Milton, clearly shows the development of the word in his NEW WORLD OF ENGLISH WORDS (1658):

Alcahol or Alcool, the pure Substance of anything separated from the more Gross. It is more especially taken for a most subtil and highly refined Powder, and sometimes for a very pure Spirit: Thus the highest rectified Spirit of Wine is called Alcohol Vini.

By the mid-eighteenth century, *alcohol of wine* was being shortened to *alcohol* to refer to 'the intoxicating element in fermented liquors'. Its popular use for 'any intoxicating liquor or brew' dates from the second half of the nineteenth century, when it was already recognised that those who abstained from strong drink enjoyed a longer life:

Life assurance offices have found that the average length of life of total abstainers is greater than that of drinkers of alcohol.
(JOHN JAMES RIDGE, THE TEMPERANCE PRIMER, 1879)

☛ There are quite a number of other borrowings from Arabic that begin with *al-*. This is the Arabic definite article, which was borrowed into most European languages along with its following noun. It is obviously present in *alchemy*, ALGEBRA, *almanac* and a number of other words, and less clearly so in *azimuth* and *lute* (for a fuller discussion, see WORDS FROM ARABIC, page 20).

For more on strong drink and temperance, see ALE and TEETOTALLER.

ale
a fermented, intoxicating drink

*Daddy and some of the other fellows found the alcohol ban intolerable. 'That filthy fake beer, No-**Ale**, is the only aspect of Fabianism I can't swallow,' he said.*
(JILL DAWSON, THE GREAT LOVER, 2009)

*It's not only a cosy pub in the richest tradition…but also a mini-beer festival all by itself, offering as many as eight different **ales**, always changing and usually superb.*
(THE TIMES, 2 MAY 2009)

A Germanic root, *alut-*, possibly from proto-Indo-European *al-*, 'bitter', gave rise to Old English *ealu*, 'ale', and related words in Scandinavian languages: Swedish has *öl*, for instance, and Danish *øl*. The Old English word *bēor*, 'beer', also existed. This may have sprung from an unidentified Germanic root or, as some etymologists now claim, from the Latin noun *biber*, 'drink', a derivative of *bibere*, 'to drink'. Whatever the source, it was also responsible for *bier*, the word for 'beer' in both German and Dutch. In Saxon and medieval England the two words were synonymous, although *ale* was much more commonly used, *beer* being reserved for more formal poetic contexts.

Ales of varying strength were drunk daily in great quantities by men, women and children. Water was generally contaminated and unsafe to drink but the fermentation processes used to make ale killed off the harmful bacteria. Ale was a strong, sweetish drink made from barley malt, water and yeast with the addition of herbs such as wood sage, costmary (*alecost*) or ground-ivy (*alehoof*) to preserve and flavour it. Indeed, at various times in the history of ale, an amazing variety of ingredients has been used to lend it flavour, as this tasty seventeenth-century recipe shows:

To make Cock Ale. Take eight gallons of Ale; then take a March Cock and boil him well; and take four pounds of raisins well stoned, two or three nutmegs, three or four flakes of mace and half a pound of dates. Beat all these in a mortar, and put to them two quarts of the best sherry-sack. Put all this into the Ale, with the Cock, and stop it close six or seven days, and then bottle it: and after a month you may drink it.
(THE CLOSET OF SIR KENELM DIGBY OPENED, 1669)

In the late fifteenth century, however, Flemish immigrants introduced the practice of adding hops to the malted grain; this drink was then called *beer* to distinguish it from ale. Beer consumption grew because it was cheaper and kept better than ale. In his DYETARY OF HELTH (1542), Andrew Boorde describes the brew, and laments the harmful effects of its popularity: *Bere is made of malte, of hoppes, and water: it is a naturall drynke for a Dutche man. And nowe of late dayes it is moche vsed in Englande to the detryment of many Englysshe men.* But just under a century later, in John Gerard's revised HERBALL (1633), beer is found to be a nourishing beverage: *The manifold virtues of Hops so manifestly argue the wholesomeness of beer above ale: for the hops rather make it a physical drink to keep the body in health, than an ordinary drink for the quenching of our thirst.* Beer and ale are now used more or less interchangeably, with beer being the generic term for all malt liquors.

In the Middle Ages and through to the seventeenth century, ale was not only a drink but a term given to a 'festivity where ale was drunk'. Sometimes this would be a family occasion (*bride ale, dirge ale*). Often an ale would be held on a saint's day or Christian festival (*Whitsun ale*) to benefit church funds. The congregation would donate malt from which the church wardens brewed ale to sell back to them at the celebration. Or an ale might mark out the agricultural or working year (*lamb ale, scythale*). These festivities were sometimes at the expense of the lord of the manor, but often peasants were ordered to contribute malt and then forced to buy the brew (L F Salzman, ENGLISH LIFE IN THE MIDDLE AGES, 1926). Whatever the excuse for the ale, it was generally marked by revelry and drunkenness.

See also BRIDAL and DIRGE. See CIDER for the etymology of another alcoholic drink.

algebra
a generalised type of mathematics that uses letters and symbols to represent numbers

*For many students, **algebra** has become the most daunting obstacle to graduation. 'Algebra triggers more dropouts than any other single subject – especially in at-risk schools,' said Glynn Willett, CEO of Learn Without Limits. And it's not just high school students. Over 50% of college students taking algebra fail each year.*
(BUSINESS WIRE, 20 FEBRUARY 2008)

*At school we encounter a few basic concepts in arithmetic, **algebra**, geometry, calculus, probability and not much else. The professional community recognises about 100 branches of mathematics with names such as 'algebraic topology' and 'stochastic processes'. They represent the hidden world of frontier research and they are as unlike school mathematics as composing a symphony differs from playing scales on a piano.*
(THE TIMES, 22 NOVEMBER 2008)

Derived from the Arabic verb *jabara*, 'to restore to a state of wholeness, to reunite', the term *al-jebr* meant 'the bringing together or reunion of broken parts' and was therefore used for 'the setting of fractured bones' and also for 'a fracture'. The word was taken into Italian, Spanish and Medieval Latin as *algebra* and borrowed into English from one of these languages in the sixteenth century. In his HISTORICALL EXPOSTULATION AGAINST THE ABUSES OF CHYRURGERIE AND PHISICKE (1565), John Halle informs his readers that *This Araby worde Algebra sygnifyeth as well fractures of bones, etc. as sometyme the restauration of the same*. In this sense, the word was relatively short-lived in English; the Spanish term *algebrista*, 'bone-setter', is more recently obsolete.

In the ninth century, however, the term *al-jebr* began to be used by Arabian mathematicians investigating algebraic computation. It first appeared in an early ninth-century work by Mahommed ibn Musa al-Khwarizmi, ILM AL-JEBR WA'L-MUQABALAH, 'The Science of Completion and Equation'. In this mathematical sense *al-jebr* was borrowed into Italian as *algèbra* through the work of Leonardo Fibonacci at the beginning of the thirteenth century. In the first half of the sixteenth century, other Italian mathematicians began to investigate algebraic problems, and by the middle of the century the term *algebra* to denote this branch of mathematics had been borrowed into English. It was initially spelt *algeber*, possibly influenced by the French *algèbre*, but also certainly a confusion with the name of the Arab chemist Geber, who was erroneously held by some to be its inventor. By the late sixteenth century, however, the Italian spelling had become the accepted form.

See also ALCOHOL and WORDS FROM ARABIC (page 20).

alibi
evidence to demonstrate that the accused was elsewhere at the time of the crime

*Providing illicit lovers with **alibis** has become a lucrative industry that is spreading across Europe and is now heading for Britain. Despite criticism from the Catholic Church, German 'alibi agencies' are faking the evidence needed to convince suspicious spouses that their clients have been at seminars or late-night meetings, not with their lovers.*
(THE SUNDAY TELEGRAPH, 11 JULY 2004)

'I know he was drunk last night – too drunk to do anything in cold blood.'
*'Unless he was putting it on, Sir. Alcohol's a great **alibi** if you do it convincingly enough.'*
(NICOLA UPSON, ANGEL WITH TWO FACES, 2009)

Alibi translates as 'in another place'. It is the locative case (denoting place) of Latin *alius*, 'other', and was originally an adverb, coined in the early eighteenth century as a legal term meaning 'elsewhere when the crime took place', so the accused had to prove that he was *alibi*. By the middle of the century, however, the word had begun to be used as a noun denoting 'a plea or a form of defence in which the accused tries to prove that he was in another place when the crime took place'. It has retained this sense ever since.

Developments in America in the early twentieth century made the word a synonym for 'an excuse', a usage that soon crossed the Atlantic: *Low spirits make you seem complaining.... I have an alibi because I'm going to have a baby* (L P HARTLEY, FELLOW DEVILS, 1951).

Still later it fell victim to the American habit of creating verbs out of nouns, so that there is now a verb *to alibi* someone, meaning 'to provide an

WORDS FROM ARABIC

Arabic has provided English with a store of common words. Some of them are listed here, others are given fuller treatment as separate entries (see ALGEBRA, ALCOHOL, ASSASSIN, COFFEE, GIRAFFE, HAZARD, MAGAZINE). There are also entries for several words which were strongly influenced by Arabic (see APRICOT, CHESS, SERENDIPITY). A number of these words begin in *al-*. This is the definite article 'the' which, in Arabic, is not easily separated from its noun, so that the whole is often borrowed as a single item. In the list below, *alcove, alkali* and *lute* show this tendency (see also the entries for ALCOHOL, ALGEBRA and APRICOT). In some instances, *chemist*, for example, the prefix *al-* was lost. This was doubtless because there was a growing etymological awareness that *al-* was simply the definite article.

The effects were patchy, however. For example, the English *magazine*, originally meaning 'storehouse, depot', and Spanish *almacén*, with the same meaning, share the one Arabic root, yet only the latter shows evidence of the definite article. The same is true for the English/Spanish pairs *mattress/almadraque* and *cotton/algodón*. The reasons why the definite article is lost in some cases and not in others are as obscure as the reasons why, out of several hundred words in English that come from Arabic sources, only a small percentage were borrowed with the article integrated in the first place.

alcove (17th cent): from French *alcôve*, from Spanish *alcoba*, 'a recess for a bed', from Arabic *al-qubbah*, 'the vaulted space'.

alkali (14th cent): Middle English *alcaly*, from Medieval Latin *alcali*, from Arabic *al-qali, al-qaly,* 'the ashes (of the saltwort plant)', from *qalay*, 'to fry'. The original alkali was soda, obtained from the ashes of the saltwort, a plant which grew on alkaline soil.

carafe (18th cent): from French *carafe*, from Italian *caraffa*, from Spanish *garaffa*, from Arabic *gharāffa*, from *gharafa*, 'to draw water'.

chemist (16th cent): from New Latin *chimista*, taken from Medieval Latin *alchymista* with the definite article *al-* removed, from Medieval Latin *alchymia*, 'alchemy', from Arabic *al-kimiya*, 'science of transmutation', from Greek *khēmia*.

cipher (14th cent): Middle English *cifre*, 'the symbol for zero', from Old French, from Medieval Latin *cifra*, from Arabic *sifr* 'empty', the adjective being used as a noun. Originally, then, *cipher* was the symbol for 'nought', but by the sixteenth century was freely applied to any numeral and then to codes, many of which substituted numbers for letters.

cotton (14th cent): Middle English *cotoun*, from Old French *coton*, from Spanish Arabic dialect *qoton*, from Arabic *qutn*. The Spanish/Arabic *alqoton*, which includes the definite article *al-*, is responsible for modern Spanish *algodón* and Portuguese *algodāo*.

crimson (15th cent): Middle English *cremesin*, from Old Spanish, from Arabic *qermazí*, 'red colour, crimson'; from *qirmiz*, 'kermes', a species of scale insect from which the dye was made.

gazelle (16th cent): from Old French *gazels*, from Arabic *ghazāl*, perhaps via Spanish *gacela*.

jar (16th cent): from French *jarre*, from Provençal *jarra*, from Arabic *jarrah*, 'earthenware water pot'.

lute (14th cent): from Middle French *lut* (earlier *leut*), from Old Provençal *laut*, from Arabic *al-'ud*, 'the oud' (literally 'the wood') where *al-* is the definite article. The article is still present in the Romance borrowing, being represented by the initial *l*. The lute was descended from the oud, a similar Arabic instrument.

mask (16th cent): from French *masque*, from Italian *maschera*, probably from Arabic *maskharah*, 'buffoon, clown'.

mattress (13th cent): Middle English *materas*, from Old French, from Italian *materasso*, from Arabic *al-matrah*, 'the place where something is thrown down', hence 'mat or cushion', from *taraha*, 'to throw'.

monsoon (16th cent): from early modern Dutch *monssoen* (now obsolete), from Portuguese *monção*, from Arabic *mausim*, 'season' and hence 'monsoon season'.

racket (16th cent) [tennis]: through French *raquette*, from Italian *racchetta*, from Arabic *rāhat*, 'palm of the hand'. Tennis was originally played with the hand.

safari (19th cent): from Swahili, 'journey', from Arabic *safar*, 'journey'.

sash (16th cent): Originally *shash* in English, from Arabic *shāsh*, 'turban' and also the 'band of cloth', such as muslin, from which the turban was made.

sequin (17th cent): from French *sequin*, from Italian *zecchino*, from *zecca*, 'the mint', from Arabic *sikkah*, 'die for stamping coins'. The zecchino was a Venetian gold coin and *sequin* was originally used in this sense in English. The term was applied to an 'ornamental spangle' in the last quarter of the nineteenth century.

sofa (17th cent): from Arabic *soffah*, 'a raised part of the floor scattered with carpets and cushions'. Originally used in this sense in English but then, from the early eighteenth century, to denote a piece of drawing-room furniture.

syrup (14th cent): Middle English *sirop*, from Old French, from Medieval Latin *siropus*, from Arabic *sharāb*, 'beverage' (heavily sweetened), from *shariba*, 'to drink'. Used since medieval times in cookery as a sweetener or preservative and in medicine as a vehicle for remedies.

tariff (16th cent): from French *tarif*, from Italian *tariffa*, from Turkish *ta'rifa*, from Arabic *ta'rif*, 'notification, explanation', from *'arafa*, 'to notify'. Originally an 'arithmetical table', then a 'list or table of customs duties' and finally, from the mid-eighteenth century, a 'list of charges'.

excuse or alibi'. There is also the rather neat expression *alibi artist*, someone who is 'an expert at making excuses'.

☛ Latin *alius*, 'other', is also responsible for:

alias (16th cent): Latin *aliās*, 'otherwise', was borrowed into sixteenth-century English as an adverb with the sense 'otherwise called or named'. Like *alibi* it subsequently became a noun meaning 'an alternative name', in particular one adopted for nefarious purposes.

alien (14th cent): Latin *aliēnus* meant 'belonging to another'. Borrowed into Middle English through Old French in the fourteenth century it meant 'belonging to another person or place'. The word's use in science fiction dates from just before the mid-twentieth century.

See ALTRUISM for words stemming from the related *alter*.

alligator
a large reptile

'Surely these are only crocodiles?'
 'Alligators! Alligators! There is hardly such a thing as a true crocodile in South America....'
(SIR ARTHUR CONAN DOYLE,
THE LOST WORLD, 1912)

*The woman's sun-cooked skin resembled that of an **alligator**. She pulled her orange lips back in a smile.*
(BARBARA NADEL, HAREM, 2003)

Early Spanish explorers in the Americas, struck by the alligator's similarity to the lizards in their home-land, referred to the creature as *el lagarto*, 'the lizard', a word from Latin *lacerta*, a common form of *lacertus*, 'lizard'. The English borrowed the Spanish term and modified it, running the two words (the definite article and the noun) into one and substituting English vowel sounds. The English naval commander Sir John Hawkins, who led expeditions to the Spanish-American coast in the second half of the sixteenth century, came close to the Spanish, using *ala-gartoes* in his descriptions of his voyages. But Shakespeare's ROMEO AND JULIET shows how the word was evolving. While the First Quarto of 1597 has:

> *And in his needy shop a tortoyrs hung,*
> *An Aligarta stuft,*

the First Folio of 1623 has *allegater*. Ben Jonson favoured the spelling *alligarta* and, according to Nares, in a still credulous age seems to hint at a superstition that the reptile would make any plant it urinated upon poisonous: *And who can tell, if before the gathering and making up thereof, the alligarta hath not piss'd thereon* (BARTHOLOMEW FAYRE, 1614).

Aligator, *alegator* and *allegator* are other seventeenth-century forms but the spelling had more or less settled into *alligator* by the eighteenth century. The word has the distinction of being one that was borrowed from English into French, rather than the other way round.

To discover how *alligator* ultimately means 'forearm', see LIZARD. For the etymology of its relative the CROCODILE, see that entry.

aloof

withdrawn, reserved, keeping at a distance

He left thinking how much he disliked aloof, remote, self-contained women who couldn't even bring themselves to engage in pleasantries never mind any more meaningful social contact.
(MARGARET FORSTER, KEEPING THE WORLD AWAY, 2006)

[Peter O'Toole] certainly revels in his role in Dean Spanley *as Horatio Fisk, a cold-hearted patriarch who has lost his wife to illness and a son to the Boer War – and remains aloof from his remaining offspring, the long-suffering Henslowe.*
(THE TIMES, 6 DECEMBER 2008)

Britain has always been a great seafaring nation, and the English language has been enriched by the figurative use of many nautical words and phrases. *Aloof* is one such and dates from the sixteenth century. The word may be split into two parts, *a-* and *loof*. *A-* is an Old English prefix meaning 'on' and is found in other words such as *afoot*, *aground*, etc. The *loof* element is an alternative form of *luff*, from Old French *lof*, perhaps from Middle Dutch *loef*, and denotes a 'windward direction'. Thus, when a sixteenth-century sea captain commanded his crew to *steer aloof*, he wanted the head of the ship brought into the wind. The word is obsolete in this sense today, although *luff* is still current; Admiral William Smyth in his SAILOR'S WORD-BOOK (1867) defines *aloof* as *The old word for 'Keep your luff' in the act of sailing to the wind.*

A ship would sail into the wind in order to avoid the coast or any obstacle on the leeward, the side away from the direction the wind was blowing. In the first half of the sixteenth century, this nautical sense gave rise to the more general one of 'steer-

ing clear, keeping at a distance'. Shakespeare in ROMEO AND JULIET (1597), for instance, has Paris command his page, *Give me thy torch, boy. Hence, and stand aloof*, and Milton uses the word similarly in PARADISE REGAINED (1671):

They at his sight grew mild,
Nor sleeping him nor waking harmed;
*   his walk*
The fiery serpent fled and noxious worm;
The lion and fierce tiger glared aloof.

From this, in the last quarter of the sixteenth century, came the further sense of holding oneself at an emotional distance, so that *aloof* also came to mean 'detached, uninvolved, unsympathetic'. Thus it was applied to a person who remains with the company and yet holds back, keeping himself to himself.

The original morphological division of the word is at odds with the humorous efforts of one folk etymologist. A well-known graffito begins with *Be alert!* Underneath another hand had written: *No, don't be a lert, be a loof. We've got enough lerts.*

altruism

consideration and regard for the well-being of others without expectation of reward

Pharmagene has more than 250,000 bits of human body in its compact laboratory, which would test the stomach of even the most devoted fan of horror films. The company provides a unique service – it tests drugs on human tissue, reducing the need to use animals.

'Our whole business relies on altruism,' says chief executive Alistair Riddell. 'The goodwill that makes people give blood, or donate their organs.'
(THE GUARDIAN, 8 FEBRUARY, 2001)

*Reading the report had certainly made him
feel something, but it wasn't for revenge or
confrontation. He just wasn't a radical.
His only response was of humanitarianism
and **altruism**, of a priest-in-waiting.
Priests didn't hurl bombs.*

(MARY CAVANAGH,

A MAN LIKE ANY OTHER, 2007)

Like AGNOSTIC, this word was
invented to encapsulate a philosophical principle, that of seeking to
promote and taking satisfaction from
the well-being of others. *Altruisme* was
coined by the French philospher
Auguste Comte, in his COURS DE
PHILOSOPHIE POSITIVE (1830–42),
as the antithesis of *egotism*, the principle of self-advancement. Where
egotism has its roots in Latin *ego*,
meaning 'I', *altruism* is derived from
Italian *altrui* (French *autrui*), meaning
'belonging to others'. This, in turn,
derives from Latin *alter*, meaning
'other'. Inspiration for the word is
believed to have come from the French
law terms *le bien d'autrui*, 'the good of
others', and *le droit d'autrui*, 'the right
of others'.

Altruism was readily embraced in
Europe and America by those who,
having reasoned themselves out of
belief in God, found in the philosophy
a motive for practising unselfish morality. However, many a promising philosophy has foundered on the sharp rock
of basic human nature. Walsh quotes
the following New York newspaper
report on the demise of the Altruist
Society of St Louis:

*Those to whom experiments for a
remodelling of society appeal must be
saddened by the last phase in the history
of the Altruist Community of St Louis.
'We find it necessary,' says Mr Alcander
Longley, its late president, in the columns
of its organ, the* Altruist, *'to announce
to our readers that the Altruist*

*Community is dissolved by mutual
consent of all the members. The reasons
for the dissolution are some of them as
follows. Since Mr Smith withdrew, late
last fall, there have been but two male
members of the community, George E
Ward and myself; and our natures and
our methods of doing things are so
different that there has been more or less
discord at different times since, and not
at any time real harmony.'*

*One of the causes of disagreement was
Mr Ward's ambition to be 'appointed or
elected as one of the editors and managers
of the* Altruist', *which Mr Longley had
decided views about controlling himself,
'saying that he would not own and manage
a paper with Mr Ward or any one else.'
This led to the calling of a special meeting
to elect a president in Mr Longley's place,
and the success of Mr George E. Ward and
two Mrs Wards, who formed a majority of
the community.*

*Meanwhile, Mr Longley admits, 'I
have, during our dissensions, said some
very uncomplimentary and disrespectful
things to Mr Ward, for which I have told
him I am sorry. Among them was, I
charged him with being an anarchist and
with bullying his wife to get her to vote as
he desired in the community, and with
having acted fraudulently in keeping the
record of the community as secretary and
in the election of himself as president, all
of which I hereby retract and apologize
for.' Mr Longley and the remaining
members of the pentagonal community,
except Miss Travis, withdrew when Mr
Ward's journalistic aspirations were
about to be gratified.*

(NATION, APRIL 10, 1890)

☛ Latin *alter*, 'other', surfaces today
in the sixteenth-century borrowing of
Cicero's Latin phrase *alter ego*, 'other
self, close friend', and a little more
obliquely in a number of English
words, such as *to alter* (14th cent),
'to make something other, different';

altercation (14th cent), 'dispute with another'; *alternate* (16th cent), 'to do one thing after another by turns'.

See ALIBI for words from the related Latin *alius*.

ambition
a strong desire to achieve an objective

*...George V was a model constitutional monarch. His **ambitions** did not soar beyond his stamp collection and his shoots. He was a country gent whose tastes were lower middle class and who preferred the workers to the aristocracy.*
(PAUL JOHNSON,
WAKE UP BRITAIN!, 1994)

*These are not bums, mind you. This is a very high grade of people, multinational, talented and clever. But it seems to me that everyone I meet here used to be something once (generally 'married' or 'employed'); now they are all united by the absence of the one thing they seem to have surrendered completely and forever: **ambition**. Needless to say, there's a lot of drinking.*
(ELIZABETH GILBERT,
EAT PRAY LOVE, 2006)

*Yes, he was full of contempt, he told me, but most of it was for himself – he'd had a breakdown when an undergraduate at Oxford, an emotional and intellectual breakdown, as a result of which he'd got an inferior degree, but more crucially, had lost his **ambition**, his will to act in life.*
(SIMON GRAY,
THE LAST CIGARETTE, 2008)

This word is one which rests easily on a politician's shoulders and, indeed, its origins are political. It comes from the Latin *ambitiō*, meaning 'a going round' (from the verb *ambīre*, 'to go around', from '*ambi-*, 'around' and *īre*, 'to go'), a word which was particularly applied to political candidates doing the rounds in Rome to solicit support. The candidates were highly motivated and so, not surprisingly, the word gradually came to mean 'a determination to achieve success'.

The term came into English in the fourteenth century by way of Old French *ambition*. Initially it denoted 'an excessive desire for distinction or success' and was classed as a vice; in the sixteenth century, Thomas Nashe defined *ambition* as *any puft vp greedy humour of honour or preferment* (CHRIST'S TEARS OVER JERUSALEM, 1593). Not for another three hundred years or so did an inordinate craving for preferment moderate to a strong but more acceptable urge.

☛ The two Latin elements of *ambition* are quite productive in English. There are nearly twenty words (most of them obscure) that contain *ambi-*, 'around'. Common examples are:

ambidextrous (17th cent): an adjective from Medieval Latin *ambidexter*, from *ambi-* and *dexter*, 'right-handed'. The literal sense, therefore, is 'right-handed on both sides'.
    ambiguous (16th cent): from Latin *ambiguus*, 'driving here and there' and hence 'uncertain, doubtful', from *ambigere*, 'to move from place to place', from *ambi-* and *agere*, 'to drive, to lead'.

There are more than twice as many words derived from *īre*, 'to go'. These include:

☛ *exit* (16th cent): from Latin *exīre*, 'to go out', from *ex-*, 'out', and *īre*. First used as a stage direction in the sixteenth century to indicate that one of the characters was to leave the set.
    perish (13th cent): Middle English *perisshen*, from Old French *perir*, from Latin *perīre*, 'to pass away, to die', from *per*, 'away', and *īre*.
    sedition (14th cent): from Old French *sedition*, from Latin *sēditiō*, 'a going apart', from *sē*, 'apart', and *itiō*, 'a going', from *īre*.

transit (15th cent): from Latin *transīre*, 'to go across', from *trāns-*, 'across', and *īre*.

Just *ambit* and *ambient* contain both elements. The former made its appearance at the end of the fourteenth century, the latter two hundred years later.

For another word arising from Roman elections, see CANDIDATE.

ambrosia
delectable food; anything of fine taste or flavour

If you want to become fabulously wealthy, live in a mansion, drive a Rolls and have servants cater to your every wish, all you have to do is invent a new fishing lure that 30 million American bass fishermen will rush to buy...the Senko [is] a soft, plastic worm that looks like a dead slug. It's fat, ungainly and roughly the same size at either end. It in no way resembles the lifelike, almost elegant slitherers and tapered, curly-tailed, plastic wonders that all of us own by the bagsful in enough colors to make a rainbow blush with envy.

No, this thing looks like a clogged injection molding machine suddenly burped and what came out was a chubby, unappetizing mistake as far as humans are concerned. To a bass, however, it's **ambrosia***, a veritable magnet that says, 'Taste me. Take a bite.'*
(THE WASHINGTON TIMES, 22 JUNE 2003)

According to Greek and Roman mythology, *ambrosia* was the food of the gods and was the source of their immortality, although ordinary mortals would surely die if they tasted it. *Ambrosia* was derived from Greek *ambrotos*, 'immortal', from *a-*, 'not' and *mbrotos*, 'mortal'. The word was borrowed into English in the sixteenth century by way of Latin *ambrosia*.

Initially it referred to 'the fabled food of the gods' but was soon applied to 'something that is a delight to taste or smell'.

When Jill complains to Jack for want of meate,
Jack kisses Jill, and bids her freely eate:
Jill sayes, of what? sayes Jack, on that sweet kisse,
Which full of Nectar and Ambrosia is,
The food of poets; so l thought sayes Jill,
That makes them looke so lanke, so Ghost-like still.
Let Poets feed on aire, or what they will;
Let me feed full, till that I fart, sayes Jill.
(ROBERT HERRICK, 1591–1674)

In modern usage, the word is still applied to anything which tastes or smells particularly delicious; in Britain a brand of creamed rice, for instance, is called Ambrosia. Perhaps it makes those who eat it wax lyrical, in line with the poetic feel of the word. That said, a strange recent usage has taken the term into new territory by applying it to anything at all that gives great pleasure, as this sports writer shows:

...spilling ball and then becoming punchy would have been ambrosia for the Wasps backroom staff.
(DAILY TELEGRAPH, 7 JULY, 2008)

Not quite poetry, then.

Ambrosia takes care of the gods' food. For what they drank, see NECTAR.

ambulance

a vehicle for transporting injured people

*She looked behind her; there was activity at the front door and then, against the wall, the flashing blue light of the **ambulance** outside.*
(ALEXANDER MCCALL SMITH, THE SUNDAY PHILOSOPHY CLUB, 2004)

*The last time I was stung by a wasp, on a small boat in Greek waters about ten years ago, I went into shock, and had to be carried, on the point of death I was subsequently told, in a slow, unresponsive **ambulance** over mountains and through flocks of goats and herds of wild horses to a hospital which was in its hygienic arrangement more lethal than a wasp sting.*
(SIMON GRAY, THE LAST CIGARETTE, 2008)

In the early Middle Ages, men were sometimes paid a small fee for carrying wounded soldiers off the battlefield, and during the Crusades in the eleventh century the Knights of St John offered medical care. In 1487, at the Siege of Malaga, the Queen of Spain allowed a cart to bring the wounded away from the battle line, and her son Charles V gave similar permission during the Siege of Metz in 1553. In the centuries that followed, however, the wounded were often left where they fell until after the battle.

In the first half of the seventeenth century, French had the term *hôpital ambulatoire*. This literally meant 'hospital adapted to moving about', *ambulatoire* coming from the Latin verb *ambulāre*, 'to move about, to walk'. It denoted a field hospital, a temporary unit set up behind the battlefield to give initial treatment to the wounded. This term was later replaced by *hôpital ambulant*, 'walking hospital', and by the end of the eighteenth century this had become *ambulance*. After the Campaign of the Rhine in 1792 Dominique-Jean Larrey, surgeon-in-chief in Napoleon's army, wrote:

I now first discovered the inconveniences to which we were subjected in moving our ambulances or military hospitals. The military regulations required that they should always be one league distant from the Army. The wounded were left on the field, until after the engagement, and were then collected at a convenient spot, to which the ambulances speeded as soon as possible; but the number of wagons interposed between them and the Army, and many other difficulties so retarded their progress that they never arrived in less than 24 or 36 hours, so that most of the wounded died for want of assistance.
(MEMOIRES OF MILITARY SURGERY, AND CAMPAIGNS OF THE FRENCH ARMIES, 1814)

Larrey's answer to this problem was the *ambulance volante*, 'flying ambulance', a wheeled cart especially designed and equipped to take medical aid directly to the battlefield and promptly evacuate the seriously wounded to the field hospitals. His inspiration was the swift, manoeuvrable carts used by the light artillery units. Thus the term *ambulance* was transferred to a vehicle. It was taken into English at the beginning of the nineteenth century.

☛ Latin *ambulāre*, 'to walk', is also responsible for:

amble (14th cent): a word initially used for the easy movement of a horse which walks by lifting two feet on one side and then two on the other. It therefore came to mean 'to move at a regular, easy pace'.

perambulate (15th cent): a compound of Latin *per-*, 'through', and *ambulāre*, 'to walk'. Initially used in Scotland with the sense 'to travel through an area of land in order to survey it'.

somnambulist (18th cent): a compound of Latin *somnus*, 'sleep', and *ambulāre*, 'to walk', hence 'a sleepwalker'.

amethyst
a stone of purple quartz

One of Scotland's most senior churchmen has appealed for the safe return of a ceremonial ring… The ring has a large **amethyst** *stone inset and bears the Latin motto* 'nec tamen consumebatur', *which means 'yet it is not consumed' – a reference to the burning bush witnessed by Moses.*
(DAILY MAIL, 5 SEPTEMBER 2006)

Another lot is a stunning 20th-century collar necklace with a row of oval-cut **amethysts**, *which graduate slightly in size from the centre towards a hexagonal amethyst clasp. Suspended from this row is a fringe of seven similarly-set amethyst drops spaced by filigree floral motifs. The whole fringe is embellished with spherical bead drops. Its estimate is £1,500–2,000.*
(WESTERN DAILY PRESS,
3 DECEMBER 2008)

According to Brewer's DICTIONARY OF PHRASE AND FABLE, Roman ladies of a certain age treasured this gemstone in the belief that it would prevent their husbands' affections from wandering. The stone was chiefly prized, however, by those who loved carousing, for it was believed that it had the power to prevent intoxication. A classical myth tells how Bacchus, the god of wine, was angry with the chaste Diana, goddess of the hunt. In revenge he vowed to unleash his fierce tigers against the first maiden who came his way. At that moment, the sweet Amethyst came into view. Bacchus carried out his threat and, in terror, the girl called out to Diana, who swiftly changed her into a statue of beautiful crystal. Bacchus, feeling somewhat remorseful, anointed it with wine so that the exquisite statue was stained the colour of the grape. From then on, the fortunate possessor of a charm or drinking vessel fashioned in the purple quartz could drink as much as he liked and feel no ill effects. That, at least, was the theory – the learned Greek biographer and moralist Plutarch knew better, it seems:

As for the amethyst, as well the herb as the stone of that name, they who think that both the one and the other is so called because they withstand drunkennesse, miscount themselves, and are deceived. (MORALIA, TR. PHILEMON HOLLAND, 1603)

The ancient belief is reflected in the word itself, which is a compound of Greek *a-*, meaning 'not' and *methuskein*, 'to intoxicate' (from *methu*, 'wine'). The Greek adjective *amethustos*, 'anti-intoxicant', was applied to both the gemstone and a herb that was thought to possess the same qualities. From this came the Latin name for the quartz, *amethystus*. Old French borrowed the word as *ametiste*, and it was taken into Middle English as *ametist* in the thirteenth century. It was only in the sixteenth century that the *-th-* was reintroduced, after the Latin.

ammonia
a colourless, pungent gas

A man and a woman and a child huddled together on the floor, rocking and moaning as if they shared an injury among them. There was the smell of sweat and other humors mixed with **ammonia**, *as if humanness itself had been made into medicine.*
(MICHAEL CUNNINGHAM,
SPECIMEN DAYS, 2005)

*They passed through poorly lit hallways where barefoot children stepped aside and watched. They had dishevelled hair or shaved scalps... Laila smelled soap and talcum, **ammonia** and urine, and rising apprehension in Aziza, who had begun whimpering.*
(KHALED HOSSEINI,
A THOUSAND SPLENDID SUNS, 2007)

The origin of this word is both heavenly and very down to earth. The supreme Egyptian god Amen was known as Ammōn by the Greeks, who recognised him as Zeus. He was worshipped at his desert oracle, which was situated by the oasis of Jupiter Ammon in Lybia. It was near this same oasis that a substance the Romans called *sal ammōniācus*, 'salt of Ammon' (from Greek *ammōniakos*, from *Ammōn*), was processed from the dung and urine of camels collected, presumably, while they were watered there. *Ammonia*, the term for the colourless gas obtained from *sal ammoniac* (better known today as *ammonium chloride*), derives its name from that of the compound. This New Latin term was coined by the Swedish chemist Torbern Bergman in 1782. Today *ammonia* is obtained through the Haber-Bosch process for ultimate use in fertilisers, explosives and nitric acid.

For another word where the precise time of coining can be fixed, see AGNOSTIC. See also PRECISE TIMING (page 241). For another nineteenth-century scientific term that finds its origin in myths of the ancient world, see TANTALISE.

ampersand
an abbreviation (&) denoting 'and'

*The WGA [Writers Guild of America] negotiations are so complex that they have resulted in a strange code in which the difference between the word 'and' and an **ampersand** can be measured in millions of dollars and years of glory. A screenplay by, say, 'Christopher Marlowe & Thomas Middleton' means that the two men are a writing team but, if it says 'Christopher Marlowe and Thomas Middleton', the pair might never have met and may well have spent months in litigation.*
(THE GUARDIAN, 17 SEPTEMBER 2005)

*In the rarefied world of high-level diplomacy, potentially ground-breaking progress can be measured by an **ampersand**. In 2006, under George W Bush, Beijing and Washington embarked upon the Strategic Economic Dialogue. Under Obama, that has been recast as the Strategic & Economic Dialogue. Biannual meetings will become annual and will encompass much more than trade.*
(THE TELEGRAPH, 2 JUNE 2009)

An *ampersand* is the sign &, used to represent *and*. The symbol was Roman shorthand for *et*, 'and', which was subsequently borrowed by western scribes, calligraphers and, with the invention of printing in the mid-fifteenth century, printers. In Old English the ampersand was included among letters of the alphabet by Byrhtferth in 1011, and so the ampersand came to be recognised as the twenty-seventh symbol after *z*. Children obliged to recite the alphabet would chant the Latin *per se*, that is 'by itself', after letters that could stand alone as a complete word. Including & these numbered four: 'A per se, A', 'O per se, O', 'I per se, I' and '& per se, &'. Eventually, by the nineteenth century, the contracted drawling of '& per se, &', gave rise to the name of the symbol, *ampersand*.

The other stand-alone letters took on lives of their own also. From the fifteenth to the seventeenth centuries the phrase *A per se, A* was used figuratively to describe 'the most admirable' person or thing. In his poem IN

HONOUR OF THE CITY OF LONDON (1501) William Dunbar writes: *London, thowe arte of townes A per se*. On the other hand, *I per se, I* extolled the uniqueness of a person: *I only was compleat; I was I per se I; I was like a Rule, without exception* (James Mabbe, THE ROGUE, tr. 1622).

For more information on the schoolroom and an example of an ampersand in a sixteenth-century quotation, see CRISS-CROSS.

anathema
something despised and abominated

No matter how immoral, no matter how lascivious the behaviour of his clients, he would never think of allowing his own ethical standards, or his standards in anything, to affect his professional behaviour.... To do so would be both unprofessional and sinful, and both of those things were anathema to him.
(DONNA LEON, SUFFER THE LITTLE CHILDREN, 2007)

The neighbours are gossipin', you have to agree,
And the waggin' of tongues is anathema to me.
(ROGER MCGOUGH, ADAPTATION OF TARTUFFE BY MOLIÈRE, 2008)

This Greek word originally denoted 'a thing offered up to a god'. It comes from the verb *anatithenai*, 'to set up', a compound of *ana-*, 'up', and *tithenai*, 'to place'. From 'a votive offering' *anathema* came to mean 'a thing devoted to evil' and, by the time it was borrowed into Latin, 'a cursed thing'.

The word was much used in the early church as a term of utter condemnation, consigning the offender to hell. When in AD 428, for instance, Nestorius was appointed Bishop of Constantinople, he began to expound heretical views on the duality of Christ as both God and man. These were disputed by Cyril of Alexandria who, empowered by the Pope, demanded that Nestorius accept no fewer than twelve anathemas denouncing his doctrine. Nestorius, not to be outdone, replied with twelve of his own. He was deposed in 431 and died in exile.

In the Roman Catholic church *anathema* became an extreme form of excommunication, a formal act severing a communicant from the Christian community and handing him over to the Devil. In a solemn ceremony ordained by the Roman Pontifical (a papal or episcopal court), the following would be repeated:

We separate him, together with his accomplices and abettors, from the precious body and blood of the Lord and from the society of all Christians; we exclude him from our Holy Mother, the Church in Heaven, and on earth; we declare him excommunicate and anathema; we judge him damned, with the Devil and his angels and all the reprobate, to eternal fire until he shall recover himself from the toils of the devil and return to amendment and to penitence.

A bell was then rung, a book (the Bible) was closed and a candle was snuffed to signify the spiritual darkness of a person *condemned to eternal fire with Satan and his angels and all the reprobate, so long as he will not burst the fetters of the demon, do penance, and satisfy the Church*.

By the second half of the seventeenth century, however, *anathema* was no longer found exclusively in religious contexts but was being used more generally to denote something objectionable. Robert Herrick dared to use the word in a quasi-religious way in HESPERIDES (1648):

Who read'st this Book that I have writ,
And can'st not mend, but carpe at it:
By all the muses! thou shalt be
Anathema to it, and me.

So it went on until, by the nineteenth century, the impact of the word had weakened considerably: *Apple-green papers in bedrooms have long been anathema to nervous men* (LITTELL'S LIVING AGE, 5 April 1862). And its devaluation continues:

*Matt Whyman takes a reflective sip of Becks. 'My ideal boys' night out,' he says, 'would be a night in. Going out with a bunch of blokes is **anathema** to me. Who wants to talk about football or whine on about your partner with a load of grumpy bastards?'*
(EVENING STANDARD, 14 JUNE 2001)

May such trivialisation of a mighty word be anathema.

For other words concerning temple or sacrifices, see FANATIC, HOLOCAUST, MINT and SCAPEGOAT.

antelope
a deer-like creature

*It would suit me just fine if every year, for the rest of my life, I had the chance to hunt **antelope** somewhere, sometime with a black-powder rifle. In general, antelope are plentiful to the point that if you blow a stalk, you just turn 180 degrees and start glassing for another buck.*
(J GUTHRIE IN PETERSEN'S HUNTING, 1 SEPTEMBER 2008)

*The rangeland southwest of Loa is, many agree, some of the best **antelope** habitat in the country, as good as any found in Wyoming. There is an abundance of flowering non-woody plants to eat, water to drink and wide-open country to watch for and elude predators. Because of these conditions, there are lots of antelope.*
(DESERET NEWS, 15 JANUARY 2009)

The PHYSIOLOGUS was a Greek collection of tales about animals that dated back to the third or fourth century. The purpose of the work was to explore the moral and theological lessons contained in nature. The original text is now lost, but revised versions survive and these were translated into Latin and various European vernacular languages in the Middle Ages, becoming the inspiration for the medieval bestiaries.

The word *antelope* comes from Late Greek *antholops*. This became *ant(h)alopus* in Medieval Latin, and English acquired it via Old French *antelop* in the fifteenth century. The antelope described in the PHYSIO-LOGUS and the bestiaries bore no resemblance to the creature we call *antelope* today. Instead we read of a fabulous animal with saw-like horns capable of cutting through tree branches, which roamed the banks of the Euphrates. The creature was so wary and savage that it was impossible for any hunter to approach it. Occasionally, however, when the antelope pranced among the trees by the river on its way to drink, its horns would become entangled in the branches, leaving it vulnerable to the hunter. Two morals were drawn from this particular treatise. The first likened the antelope's sharp horns to the Old and New Testaments of the Bible, which could be used to attack sin. The second warned people against playing in places of moral danger where momentary pleasure leads to spiritual death.

The *antelope* was used as a heraldic emblem, sometimes shown with tusks as well as serrated horns and the tail of a lion. The poet John Lydgate describes

Twoo antelopis stondyng on outher syde,
Withe the armys of Englond and of Fraunce.
(MINOR POEMS, C. 1430)

WORDS FROM CLASSICAL MYTHOLOGY AND LITERATURE

Classical mythology and literature have inspired many common English words. Hector, the hero of Homer's ILIAD, for instance, was the champion of the Trojans in their war against the Greeks. The embodiment of every virtue both on and off the battlefield, *Hector* was first used in Middle English to personify 'a valiant warrior'. His reputation remained intact until the second half of the seventeenth century when his name was uncharacteristically applied to well-off yobs who, for amusement, intimidated folk as they went about their business on the streets of London. How the Greek hero fell to these depths is a mystery, but his name lives on in English in the form of the verb *to hector*, 'to behave in a blustering and intimidating fashion', which was coined at this time.

Panic finds its source in a divine bully. As the dangerous brooding god of forests and shepherds, Pan roamed the valleys and mountains. Travellers were terrified of him and believed him to be the source of any eerie sound issuing from remote regions of the countryside. The Greeks accordingly described an attack of fear where there was no obvious reason for it as *pānikos*, 'of Pan'. The adjective *panic* (as in *panic groan*) came into English at the beginning of the seventeenth century by way of French *panique* and Modern Latin *pānicus*, and was used as a noun in the modern sense from the early eighteenth century.

Pan was also a fertility god who forced his attentions upon either sex. On one occasion the beautiful nymph Syrinx escaped his lustful advances when she was changed into a bed of reeds. It was from these reeds that the god made his pan-pipes, traditionally played by shepherds. The instrument was known as *surigx* in

---

In 1607 the English curate Edward Topsell published his HISTORIE OF FOURE-FOOTED BEASTES. The book was intended to describe *the True and Lively Figure of Every Beast* and drew upon an earlier work by the Swiss naturalist Konrad Gesner. Topsell is credited with the application of the word *antelope* to the animal that resembles a deer, although the woodcut illustration, with its pointed nose, sharp teeth and lion's tail, still bears little resemblance to the creature we know today, and much of the information he supplies echoes that of the bestiary. Nevertheless, by 1662 the diarist John Evelyn was grouping the *antelope* with stags and elks.

antimacassar
a chair-back cover

...I remember every evening in the holiday, sitting with my dad in the tiny lounge at the front of the boarding-house, with its **antimacassars** *and 'Magicoal' fire, having milk and biscuits before going to bed.*
(ALAN TITCHMARSH,
TROWEL AND ERROR, 2002)

In here everything was covered up, like a scandal in a thriller, the floor with layers of white sheepskin rugs, the surfaces of chairs and tables with throws, **antimacassars,** *piles of embroidered cushions and chenille cloths, the TV with a shawl.*
(MICHÈLE ROBERTS,
READER, I MARRIED HIM, 2004)

Greek, a word which also denoted 'tube'. This was borrowed into Latin as *syrinx* and the altered Late Latin form *syringa* ultimately became English *syringe*. The nymph's name is also perpetuated in the Latin term for the lilac and mock-orange bushes, *syringa*, since shepherds' pipes were once made from them.

In spite of Pan's high libido, it was the Greek god Eros who was the personi-fication of sexual love. Said to be the son of Ares, god of war, and Aphrodite, goddess of love, his nature reflected that of both parents. Early classical litera-ture emphasises both his power over people and his cruelty towards them. In early visual art, his facial features and athletic physique are physical perfection. From *erōs*, 'sexual desire', the Greeks derived *erōtikos*, 'pertaining to sexual love', and this adjective came into English in the mid-seventeenth century as *erotic*. The derivatives *erotica* and *eroticise* date from the mid-nineteenth and early twen-tieth centuries respectively.

Aphrodite was a faithless wife and a bad example to her son. She had the power of making others as sexually irresistible as herself. From her name, Greek derived the adjective *aphrodisiakos*, 'lustful', from which English derived *aphro-disiac* in the early eighteenth century.

Eros was, in fact, born of illegitimate passion, for Aphrodite was married to Hephaestos, the god of fire and smelting, whom the Romans knew as Volcānus or Vulcan. Italian borrowed his Latin name as *volcano* to denote a 'mountain which discharges fire and molten matter', and this term was taken into English in the early seventeenth century.

See also OTHERWORLDLY INFLUENCES (page 156), AMETHYST, ATLAS, MINT and TANTALISE.

Fashionable and well-groomed nine-teenth-century gentlemen would slick their hair into place with an application of Rowland's Macassar Oil, imported from *Makasar*, Indonesia. It was pro-duced by Rowland and Son, and widely advertised: in 1809 the younger Rowland, Alexander, wrote an ESSAY ON...THE HUMAN HAIR, WITH REMARKS ON THE VIRTUES OF THE MACASSAR OIL. The product made such an impact that it even made its way into Byron's DON JUAN (1819):

In virtues nothing earthly could surpass her,
Save thine 'incomparable oil', Macassar!

By the second half of the century there were complaints of an adulterated product containing none of the natural ingredients of the original oil. Perhaps that in part explains why the oil rubbed off on to the parlour upholstery, leaving a greasy stain. In consequence practical Victorian housewives took to draping pieces of embroidered or lace-trimmed fabric known as *antimacassars* over the chair backs to protect them. Appropriately, the prefix *anti-* means 'against, to prevent the effects of'; it is found in other compounds such as *anti-corrosion* and *antibiotic*. *Antimacassar* is first recorded in 1852 – where else but in the LADY'S NEWSPAPER?

The fall from favour of Macassar oil towards the end of the century did not bring the demise of the antimacassar, however. The oil's successor in the 1880s was Brilliantine, which gave men hair as smooth and shiny as a bil-liard ball but was no kinder to the upholstery. Indeed, the antimacassar lingered on in sitting rooms until the early 1960s when, for the first time, fashion dictated clean, natural-looking hair for men. And where antimacassars exist today, they lend the décor a dated appearance:

Hoteliers have boned up on interior design but holiday cottages still threaten death by antimacassar.

(EVENING STANDARD, 27 MARCH 2002)

apology
an acknowledgement of fault and a request for pardon for it

Val Scott wrote to me and later told me on the telephone of her regret about the part she had played in the saga. She blamed herself as much as anyone for what had happened, and wanted to offer me her regrets and **apologies**.
(JONATHAN AITKEN, PRIDE AND PERJURY, 2000)

First let me **apologise** *for my long silence, Mary Ann. In answer to your question – I think I just needed a break. A few days in my own shoes.*
(MAUREEN FREELY, ENLIGHTENMENT, 2007)

In 1529 Sir Thomas More unwillingly succeeded Cardinal Wolsey as Lord Chancellor of England. He struggled, however, with those policies of the king which challenged papal authority. In 1532 Henry VIII accepted his Chancellor's resignation but More continued to be a thorn in Henry's side when he refused to attend the coronation of Anne Boleyn. In 1533 he wrote a work entitled APOLOGIE OF SYR THOMAS MORE, KNYGHT; MADE BY HIM, AFTER HE HAD GEUEN OUER THE OFFICE OF LORD CHANCELLOR OF ENGLANDE. The word *apologie* in the title meant 'formal defence'. More was offering a robust explanation of his political and spiritual stance.

Apology comes from Greek *apologiā*, 'speech given in one's own defence', a compound formed from *apo-*, 'away, off', and *logos*, 'speech'. The word came into English either directly from Latin *apologia* or by way of French *apologie*. Many other works of firm defensive argument were subsequently termed *apologies*; in 1796, for instance, Bishop Watson wrote a book entitled AN APOLOGY FOR THE BIBLE.

By the second half of the sixteenth century, however, *apology* was circulating in everyday speech with the less formal sense of 'an explanation of an incident', that is to say an excuse for it. The modern meanings 'an excuse offered for a perceived offence to placate the offended person' and 'an acknowledgement of fault and expression of regret for it' were evolving at about the same time. These shifts in sense are recorded by Shakespeare, who is remarkable for his free use of new vocabulary and idiom.

All this meant, of course, that *apology* in its original sense of 'a formal justification' could no longer be used for fear of misunderstanding. In the late eighteenth century, therefore, Latin *apologia* was borrowed again, this time retaining its Latin form. Acceptance of the word was boosted by Cardinal John Henry Newman's autobiographical APOLOGIA PRO VITA SUA ('A Defence of One's Life', 1864), written to counter Charles Kingsley's attack on Newman and the Catholic priesthood.

apricot
a fruit shaped like a plum with flesh and skin texture similar to a peach, yellow-orange in colour

*To make cream ice. Peel, stone and scald twelve **apricots**, beat them fine in a mortar, and put to them six ounces of sugar and a pint of scalding cream...*
(ELIZABETH RAFFALD,
THE EXPERIENCED ENGLISH
HOUSEKEEPER, 1769)

*Another, a man of indeterminate age with a great rust-colored curl of mustache and a chin slightly smaller than an **apricot**, hobbled his big square head and said, 'Welcome, friends, welcome, friends, welcome, friends.'*
(MICHAEL CUNNINGHAM,
SPECIMEN DAYS, 2005)

*The addition of a little honey to a madeleine is delightful. Combine that with some **apricots** poached with vanilla and a little more honey, served together with vanilla ice cream, and you have the sort of dessert that the French are justly famous for.*
(RICK STEIN, FRENCH ODYSSEY, 2005)

Peaches and apricots both originated in China and were successfully cultivated in Persia and Armenia respectively. The Greeks and Romans clearly thought the fruits originated from their source of supply; the peach was known to both as the 'Persian apple' (*Persicum mālum* in Latin) and the apricot as the 'Armenian plum' (*prūnum armeniacum*) or the 'Armenian apple' (*mālum armeniacum*).

The Romans regarded the apricot as a kind of peach, and since supplies were available earlier in the year, they called it *praecoquum*, 'early ripening', (from *praecox*, 'ripening before its time', from *praecoquere*, 'to ripen early', from *prae-*, 'before' and *coquere*, 'to ripen, to cook'). This was taken into Greek as *praikokion*, into Byzantine Greek as *berikokkon* and from there into Arabic as *al-birqūq* (*al-* being the definite article). Arab influence in the Iberian peninsula brought the word into Spanish, Portuguese and Catalan, where it became *albaricoque*, *albricoque* and *abercoc* respectively. English probably picked it up from Catalan in the sixteenth century as *abrecock*:

There be two kindes of peaches. The other kindes are soner ripe, wherefore they be called abrecox or aprecox.
(HENRY LYTE, DODOENS, NIEW
HERBALL OR HISTORIE OF PLANTES,
TR. 1578)

Within half a century this early English spelling was subject to two important changes. Firstly, a final *t* was gradually assimilated from French *abricot* – itself a product of Catalan influence – although the old *-ck* ending persisted until at least the mid-eighteenth century. Secondly, a spelling with an initial *apr-* instead of *abr-* started to emerge. In Shakespeare's RICHARD II (1595), for instance, a gardener bids a servant *Go, bind thou up yon dangling apricocks*. The answer to this puzzle is provided by the seventeenth-century language teacher and lexicographer John Minsheu. He explains the word as deriving from the Latin *in aprico coctus*, 'ripened in a sunny place', an erroneous etymology which was obviously widely believed at the time.

By the time *apricot* made its appearance in English, *peach* had been long established. From Latin *Persicum mālum* came the elliptical form *persicum*, which became *persica* in Late Latin. This was taken into Old French as *pesche*, becoming *peche* before it was borrowed directly into Middle English in the fourteenth century. The modern spelling *peach* dates from the late sixteenth century.

For another word from the same source see PRECOCIOUS. For more information about Arabic words see WORDS FROM ARABIC (page 20).

arena

a forum for combat or competition; a field of interest

*Facebook may be a great way to maintain contact with people to whom you would not entrust your email address, but to me it merely represented an additional **arena** of social obligation in which I was bound to disappoint.*
(THE GUARDIAN, 29 NOVEMBER 2008)

*That was when the dancing started. Not just dancing, but small plays, songs and comedy sketches: the acts played out in our headlight-illuminated **arena** as the hours flew by.*
(THE TIMES, 13 DECEMBER 2008)

Arena has a more gruesome history than might be imagined. Mankind has developed a number of ways of soaking up spilt blood; in previous centuries, when royalty and nobility were beheaded, straw was spread: in butchers' shops past and present, sawdust is strewn. Similarly with the Roman amphitheatre, where a thick layer of sand would be scattered upon the ground to absorb the gore as the gladiators fought. *Arēna* is Latin for 'sand' and so the central area of the amphitheatre where the combats took place became known by that name. It was borrowed into English directly from Latin in the seventeenth century.

Since the late eighteenth century, the word has also been applied figuratively to any scene of conflict (*arena of war*, *controversy*, etc.) or sphere of action (*political arena*).

arrant

downright, out-and-out, utter

> *One morning, very early, before the*
> *sun was up,*
> *I rose and found the shining dew on*
> *every buttercup;*
> *But my lazy little shadow, like an **arrant***
> *sleepy-head,*
> *Had stayed at home behind me and was*
> *fast asleep in bed.*
> (ROBERT LOUIS STEVENSON,
> A CHILD'S GARDEN OF VERSES, 1885)

In addition to all the other people that she has displeased with her seedy memoirs, Cherie Blair has irked senior courtiers at Buckingham Palace with her claim that the Queen's servants went through her bags without her permission when she stayed at Balmoral.
*'The woman is talking **arrant** nonsense,' one tells me. 'All female guests of Her Majesty are assigned a maid – and, in the case of a man, a valet – who will always offer to unpack their bags. It is never done, however, without the guest's explicit consent.'*
(THE TELEGRAPH, 12 MAY 2008)

Malory's LE MORTE D'ARTHUR (c. 1470) has familiarised us with the exploits of the *knights errant* of earlier centuries who travelled about the countryside seeking out opportunities to demonstrate the virtues of courage, loyalty, courtesy and charity. *Arrant* is a variant of *errant*, 'wandering, roving', from Old French *errant*, 'wandering', from *errer*, 'to wander'. This came from Late Latin *iterāre*, 'to travel', a verb derived from *iter*, 'journey'.

Knights were not the only ones to roam, however; others did so with evil intent. Chaucer's CANTERBURY TALES (1387) mentions a *theef erraunt*, 'an outlawed robber', and *arrant*, a sixteenth-century variant, was regularly used in this sense. From here the meaning of 'utter, unmitigated' began to evolve as the adjective was used to emphasise just how unacceptable a person really was by intensifying the noun that followed it: *an arrant coward* (an unmitigated coward), *an arrant traitor* (an utter traitor). In the seventeenth century, this use was extended to include vices and undesirable qualities : *arrant hypocrisy* (out-and-out hypocrisy).

arrive

to reach a destination; to achieve success

*Evans had frostbite to fingers and nose, and Wilson was grappling with the agonies of snow blindness, according to entries in Scott's diary dated 25 January – the same day that Amundsen and his men **arrived** safely back at the Bay of Whales, having covered almost 3,000km (1,860 miles) in 99 days.*
(JONATHAN & ANGELA SCOTT, ANTARCTICA, 2007)

This is the house Jay Gatsby would have bought if he had mysteriously turned up in Boston rather than Long Island. Huge and showy, it has everything but the green light at the end of the dock, left on waiting for Daisy. It all but shouts, 'I HAVE ARRIVED!' Ultimately, this is the house of an insecure man. John Henry is not an insecure man.
(BOSTON GLOBE, 26 SEPTEMBER 2007)

A manuscript dating from around 1300 tells *Hou Seint Thomas the holi man at Sandwych aryved was*. Thomas Becket, the Archbishop of Canterbury in the reign of Henry II, had angered the king by refusing to agree to all his policies regarding the church and had been forced into exile in France. In an attempt at reconciliation Becket returned, stepping ashore at Sandwich in Kent. Like any thirteenth-century traveller disembarking from a ship, Becket had literally *arrived*. The verb

ultimately comes from Latin *ad rīpam*, 'towards the shore', a phrase which gave rise to the unattested Vulgar Latin verb *arripāre*, 'to come ashore, to land'. This passed into the Romance languages, eventually coming into Middle English as *ariven* by way of Old French *ariver*. Only gradually did the wider sense of 'coming to the end of a journey' take hold from the time of Chaucer onwards. The notion of 'achieving success' dates from the late nineteenth century.

For a word from the same source, see RIVER.

assassin

a murderer, usually of an important person for political or religious ends

*Surely, I thought, no **assassin** would be so bold as to make an attempt on the life of a consul in broad daylight, with dozens of bodyguards and thousands of witnesses all around.*
(STEVEN SAYLOR, A GLADIATOR ONLY DIES ONCE, 2005)

*The **assassin** of Prime Minister Yitzhak Rabin has said in telephone interviews from prison that he was influenced by Israeli military leaders who had criticized Rabin's land-for-peace deal with the Palestinians.*
(WASHINGTON POST, 1 NOVEMBER 2008)

In late eleventh-century Persia (now Iran), the missionary Hasan-i Sabbah founded a sect of Islamic fundamentalists with the intention of controlling the Muslim world through acts of violence. His base was the hilltop fortress of Alamut. The sect opposed the Seljuk dynasties of central and western Asia and later also directed its efforts against the Crusaders in northern Syria. During the next two hundred years the sect established a chain of hill forts in Syria as bases for terrorist attacks. One of the leaders of the Syrian branch of the sect in the twelfth century was famously known as the Old Man of the Mountain.

The sect members were called *hashshāshīn*, 'hashish-eaters', because it was said that they prepared themselves for their atrocities by eating hashish (cannabis). *Hashshāshīn* is the plural of *hashshās*, 'hashish-eaters', from *hashāsh*, 'hemp, an intoxicating preparation from the hemp plant'. The English singular noun *assassin*, which appeared in the seventeenth century through French *assassin* or Late Latin *assassinus*, is therefore an Arabic plural.

There are objections to this etymology, however. It is argued that Hasan-i Sabbah was a strict and principled religious leader and would never have condoned the use of hashish. Objectors try to derive the name of the sect from Hasan-i Sabbah's name. It is indeed unlikely that the sect members took the drug but they were, nevertheless, known as hashish eaters. The story of drug use is usually attributed to Marco Polo's fictional account of his visit to Alamut in 1273.

Crusaders returning to Europe brought back reports of the sect's murderous exploits, and historians such as William of Tyre recorded details of their operations in Latin. Frank M Chambers, a scholar of medieval French poetry, has advanced a theory that *assassin* entered the popular vocabulary of Western Europe after a rumour was circulated by the French king Philip Augustus in 1192. This stated that Richard the Lion-Heart had persuaded the Old Man of the Mountain to send some assassins to France to murder him (MORE ABOUT THE WORD ASSASSIN IN PROVENÇAL, 1950).

The rumour was, apparently, widespread in France, and was just the sort of gossip likely to bring the word into popular use. Mr Chambers points out that, just after that date, Provençal troubadours became fascinated by the Old Man of the Mountain. They used him and the absolute allegiance borne by his followers to give expression to their theme of courtly love. Aimeric de Peguilhan, for instance, declared that his lady had him *more in her power than the Old Man of the Mountains his Assassins, who go to kill his mortal enemies*, and Bernart de Bondeilhs claimed *just as the Assassins serve their master unfailingly, so I have served Love with unswerving loyalty*.

atlas
a book of maps of the world

*The world was in a state. Everybody could see that. The north and south poles, always reliably blue in every **atlas**, now had flecks of yellow in them. He knew that these flecks were not printers' errors…The idea of everything getting hotter and dirtier made Badger Newbold feel faint.*
(ROSE TREMAIN, PEERLESS, 2005)

According to Greek mythology, when the Titan Atlas was punished for joining a war against Zeus he was condemned to stand upon the western edge of the earth and to bear the weight of the heavens upon his shoulders. It is a popular error that Atlas was forced to support the earth: in classical art he holds a celestial sphere showing the stars and planets upon his shoulders.

Pictures of the Titan in this posture were a feature on the title pages of sixteenth-century map books, hence the term *atlas*. The respected Flemish carto-grapher Gerardus Mercator (1512–94) is generally credited with the first use of the word in the Latin title of a map book in the late sixteenth century: ATLAS, SIVE COSMOGRAPHICAE MEDITATIONES DE FABRICA MUNDI (1585). The volume was published in English in 1636 as ATLAS; OR A

GEOGRAPHIC DESCRIPTION OF THE WORLD. The term *atlas* was extended to cover other sizeable volumes of illustrative plates or charts in the second half of the nineteenth century.

☞ Another myth tells how Perseus asked Atlas for refuge. When Atlas refused, Perseus used the head of the Gorgon Medusa to turn him into Mount Atlas (in northwest Africa), upon which the heavens were then said to rest. The Greek stem of Atlas was *Atlant-*, which gave the adjective *Atlantikos*, 'belonging to Atlas'. The Greeks called the ocean immediately beyond the mountain *pelagos Atlantikos*, 'the sea of Atlas', and the Romans *mare Atlanticum*. Now, of course, the full expanse of the sea is known and it bears the name *Atlantic Ocean*.

See also WORDS FROM CLASSICAL MYTHOLOGY AND LITERATURE (page 32) and the individual entries for AMETHYST, MINT and TANTALISE.

atone
make amends for

Turned from the house, and in such a way! Without any reason that could justify, any apology that could **atone** *for the abruptness, the rudeness, nay, the insolence of it.*
(JANE AUSTEN,
NORTHANGER ABBEY, 1803)

When they'd got to Peterborough she'd imagined staying for a few days, a week maybe, just her and Jacob. Keep an eye on Dad and make sure he wasn't planning to hack something else off. Give Mum a hand. Be a better daughter and **atone** *for the guilt about disappearing last time.*
(MARK HADDON,
A SPOT OF BOTHER, 2006)

From the thirteenth century, Middle English had the adverbial phrase *at one* to denote 'a state of harmony, of concord'. The phrase may have been based on Latin *adunīre*, 'to unite', from *ad-*, 'to, at', and *unum*, 'one'. The context often carried an implication that unity had been achieved only after a time of disagreement and conflict: *And went and kist his brother, and than they were at oon* (THE TALE OF GAMELYN, c. 1400). Thus, *to bring, to set at one* meant 'to reconcile, to bring together'.

Increasingly, however, *at one* was written as a single word. And so, in Chaucer's CANTERBURY TALES (c. 1387), we find:

> *If gentil men, or othere of hir contree*
> *Were wrothe, she wolde bringen*
> *hem atoon.*

When the two words were run together in this way, the old pronunciation was preserved (just as it is in *alone* and *only*).

The verb *atone* dates from the sixteenth century: *Since we cannot attone you, you shall see Iustice designe the Victors Chiualrie* (Shakespeare, RICHARD II, 1595). *To atone for*, which has the sense of 'to expiate, to make amends' arose in the seventeenth century.

The noun *atonement*, influenced by Middle English *onement*, 'reconciliation', and *to be atone*, dates from the early sixteenth century. Thomas More writes of *those hauyng more regarde to their olde variaunce then their newe attonement* (HISTORY OF KING RICHARD III, 1513). This new word also met a religious need. William Tyndale chose it for his translation of the Bible into English in 1526. In *atonement* he found a term that perfectly encapsulated the reconciliation of man to God through the sacrifice of Jesus Christ upon the cross: *God...hath geven unto us the office to preache the atonement* (2 Corinthians 5: 18). Other translators followed Tyndale's lead, using *atonement* in contexts where Wycliffe had used *recouncilyng* or *accordyng*, and the term thus entered theological vocabulary. Indeed Tyndale (1533) and then Coverdale (1548) even described Christ as an *atonemaker* between God and man, a word that is now obsolete.

auspicious
marked by the promise of success

It's unclear whether July 7, 2007, will be the luckiest wedding day of the century, but it will certainly be one of the busiest this year.... The date is popular for many reasons, as seven is considered an **auspicious** *number in a variety of cultures.*
(WASHINGTON POST, 30 JUNE 2007)

A news report in Myanmar says professional astrologers in Myanmar plan to launch a web site to advise expectant mothers on the most **auspicious** *time to give birth. It will be the first online tool to enable parents to pick the luckiest time to have their babies through a Caesarean section.*
(DAILY EXAMINER, AUSTRALIA, 15 APRIL 2009)

In Roman times, leaders needing to make a decision or generals wanting to know the outcome of a campaign would consult an *auspex*, an augur who would predict the future by observing the behaviour of birds, or even their entrails spread upon the ground. Indeed, *auspex* is a combination of *au-* from *avis*, 'bird', and *-spex* from *specere*, 'to look'. The emperor Augustus was both a high priest and a politician, so was presumably able to make his own infallible decisions.

The stem of *auspex* was *auspic-*, hence the Latin derivation *auspicium* for 'bird divination'. This was borrowed into English by way of French *auspice* in the sixteenth century, initially with reference to the Roman practice of augury. In modern English the noun is usually found in the plural in the phrase *under the auspices of*, to denote 'with the propitious support or influence of', and dates from the late eighteenth century. The adjective *auspicious* dates from the early seventeenth century.

Augur (earlier *auger*) was another Latin term for an auspex and is probably similarly derived from *avis*. This time the word is a combination of *au-* from *avis*, 'bird', and *gerere*, 'to perform', with reference to the contemplation of the birds' behaviour for the purpose of establishing omens. The derived Latin verb *inaugurāre* meant 'to predict the future by means of birds' and then 'to induct someone formally into office having properly consulted all omens'. The verb was borrowed into English as *inaugurate* in the early seventeenth century in the latter sense, though without reference to augury.

For other words involving signs and portents in the Roman period, see CONSIDER and TEMPLE. See also DISASTER and INFLUENCE.

· B ·

bankrupt
insolvent and unable to continue
trading

*Many years previously, my father-in-law
had been the Rolls-Royce-driving financial
director of a British conglomerate that had
collapsed in notorious circumstances. He
had never entirely resurfaced from his
consequent* **bankruptcy** *and, in the old-
fashioned belief that he'd shot his bolt, he
lurked about the house with a penitent,
slightly mortified smile on his face.* ·
(JOSEPH O'NEILL, NETHERLAND, 2008)

*Lord Mandelson is drawing up plans to
choose which businesses and industries are
important enough to be saved in the event
of their going* **bankrupt** *as the recession
bites, the Guardian can reveal.*
(THE GUARDIAN, 29 NOVEMBER 2008)

Medieval Venice was a prosperous
trading centre where a lot of money
changed hands. Men in the business of
lending money and exchanging cur-
rencies would set up simple counters
in the main squares. The term for one
of these tables was *banca* (from unattested Germanic *bangk-*, 'shelf', hence
'bench'), the Italian for 'bench' and
the origin of our word *bank*. Many
authorities, including Dr Johnson,
have it that when one of these money-
lenders was insolvent and could no
longer trade he was legally obliged to
break up his counter and was then
declared *banca rotta*, literally 'broken
bench' (from Latin *ruptus*, from
rumpere, 'to break'.

There are two very significant
authorities which suggest that the story
is not only unfounded but also needless.
Skeat points out that Late Latin already
had a figurative application of *ruptus*,
'broken', to refer to 'a broken man, a
bankrupt'. The OED adds the further
argument that Italian *rotto* (feminine
rotta) could also be applied to a ship to
mean 'wrecked' and then, figuratively,
'defeated, stopped'. Probably, then, the
rupt element in *bankrupt* is used in a
figurative sense and does not imply the
actual breaking of a bench.

As for the route of the word into
early sixteenth-century English, it
came by way of French *banqueroute* but
was soon modified along the lines of
Latin *ruptus*, the spelling *bankrupt*
occurring as early as the 1540s.

☛ Latin *rumpere*, 'to break', is also
evident in *abrupt* (16th cent), *interrupt*
(15th cent) and *rupture* (15th cent).
Corrupt (14th cent) comes from
Old French, from Latin *corruptus*, from
corrumpere, 'to break in pieces, to
spoil', from *cor-*, 'altogether', and
rumpere, 'to break, to destroy'.
The initial sense, 'totally rotten,
decomposed', was used figuratively
in the fourteenth century to signify
'morally depraved'.

barbarous, barbaric
uncivilised; cruel, brutal

*I knew what Mark had 'done' out there,
why he was in Longdale, because he told
me. It was serious and inexplicable, but not*

barbaric. I never knew what crime Gerry had committed and it didn't seem to be important to our friendship.
(SEBASTIAN FAULKS, ENGLEBY, 2007)

When Julius Caesar had landed near Dover two thousand years earlier he was venturing beyond civilization to a backward, **barbaric** *island on the edge of the world.*
(JOHN O'FARRELL, AN UTTERLY IMPARTIAL HISTORY OF BRITAIN, 2007)

When confronted by something in a foreign language that he does not understand, the stereotypical Englishman might well use that common idiom *It's all Greek to me*, accompanied by a dismissive shrug. Ironically, this is very much the attitude the ancient Greeks had towards the varied languages of the surrounding peoples. The Greek term for 'alien, foreign' was *barbaros*. It is thought that this word, with its strong overtones of 'not Greek and therefore not civilised', was originally intended to imitate the unintelligible babbling of foreign tongues (Latin has *balbus* and Sanskrit *barbaras*, both meaning 'stammering').

When the word was adopted into Latin as *barbarus* it, too, had derogatory connotations; it was particularly applied to the fierce northern tribes who eventually overthrew the Empire and so came to mean 'totally uncultured, rude'. Later, the term was used by Christians to describe any who were not of the faith and were therefore 'heathen'. *Barbarous* was borrowed into English from Latin in the early sixteenth century.

Greek derived the adjective *barbarikos*, 'like a foreigner', from *barbaros*. This was taken into Latin as *barbaricus* and into Old French as *barbarique*. It was borrowed into Middle English as *barbaric* in the fifteenth century.

For information on a barbarous plant, see RHUBARB.

bastard

an illegitimate child; an unpleasant person; a particular kind of person (*lucky bastard, miserable bastard*)

She doesn't tolerate bad language in the school canteen. She doesn't even let the little **bastards** *scrap with each other....*
(TONY PARSONS, ONE FOR MY BABY, 2001)

'The Chauci, I remember, dwelt on high wooden platforms to escape the treacherous tides of that region. They gathered mud with their bare hands, which they dried in the freezing north wind, and burnt for fuel. To drink they consumed only rainwater, which they collected in tanks at the front of their houses – a sure sign of their lack of civilisation. Miserable bloody **bastards**, *the Chauci.' He paused. 'Leave that last bit out.'*
(ROBERT HARRIS, POMPEII, 2003)

At the time, Mariam did not understand. She did not know what this word 'harami' – **bastard** *– meant.... Later, when she was older, Mariam did understand...that she, Mariam, was an illegitimate person who would never have legitimate claim to the things other people had, things such as love, family, home, acceptance.*
(KHALED HOSSEINI, A THOUSAND SPLENDID SUNS, 2007)

William the Conqueror, the illegitimate son of Robert, Duke of Normandy, and Herleve, a tanner's daughter, was also known as William the Bastard. The epithet that described him is Old French in origin and came into Middle English in the thirteenth century. It seems to originate in the phrase *fils de bast*, 'packsaddle son', which was popularly used for a child born as a result of a passing liaison. Apparently, muleteers would use their saddles as pillows and it was thus not unknown for children to be conceived against a packsaddle.

Pierre Vidal was a muleteer in the early fourteenth century who transported grain and was based in the little mountain village of Montaillou. When an Inquisition questioned him on his morals he was of the opinion that it was not wrong to make love outside marriage if the man had paid for his pleasure or if the act had been mutually agreed and pleasing (Emmanuel Le Roy Ladurie, MONTAILLOU, 1978). With views like these and a cosy saddle, the results were inevitable – and not only for muleteers, as Robert, Duke of Normandy, proved.

Old French *bast* comes from Medieval Latin *bastum*, 'pack saddle', which may derive from the unattested Vulgar Latin verb *bastāre*, 'to carry', from Greek *bastazein*, 'to lift, to carry'. The suffix *-ard* was often used pejoratively in Old French: *coward* is another example.

Calling William the Conqueror *the Bastard* was not regarded as particularly derogatory at the time, just a statement of fact. The popular use of *bastard* as a term of abuse for a 'contemptible, objectionable person' dates from the early nineteenth century; in THE HISTORY OF MORLEY IN YORKSHIRE (1830), Norrisson Scatcherd defines *bastard* as *a term of reproach for a mischievous or worthless boy*.

bedlam

a state of disorder and confusion

*From then on it was **bedlam**. We separated our mob into two groups, luggage and all. Distributing them into separate hotels took us over an hour. Two people had not arrived on the plane and we had hell's own job persuading the second hotel we hadn't sold them into slavery, or – worse – to another hotel.*
(JONATHAN GASH,
THE GONDOLA SCAM, 1984)

*On your application, you must write an essay, gather references and answer questions about your mental and physical health, about any possible history of drug or alcohol abuse and also about your financial stability. The Guru doesn't want people to use her Ashram as an escape from whatever **bedlam** they have created in their real lives: this will not benefit anyone.*
(ELIZABETH GILBERT,
EAT PRAY LOVE, 2006)

*All the drivers go very fast, and very noisily, and if you come in July and August, as Victoria and I used to do, the island is a **bedlam**, and dangerous.*
(SIMON GRAY,
THE LAST CIGARETTE, 2008)

In 1247 Simon FitzMary founded a priory at Bishopsgate, London. By 1330, this had a hospital attached to it, the Hospital of St Mary of Bethlehem, which was originally devoted to the medical needs of the poor. The admission of some mentally ill patients began around 1357, though their care probably amounted to nothing more than keeping them chained out of harm's way and beating them or dousing them with water if they became too disturbed. By 1402, however, the hospital was specialising in the care of the mentally ill and in 1547, after the dissolution of the monasteries under Henry VIII, the priory buildings were granted to the City of London and incorporated as a royal foundation to continue the work of the asylum.

Records show that by the middle of the fifteenth century the hospital was known as *Bedlam*, a contraction of *Bethlehem*, and by the sixteenth century both the hospital and its patients, or potential patients, were referred to by this name:

But his wife (as he had attired her) seemed indeede not to be well in her wittes, but, seeyng her housbandes maners, shewed herself in her conditions to bee a right bedlem.
(BARNABY RICHE, FAREWELL TO MILITARIE PROCESSION, 1581)

Bedlam also came to be used adjectivally to mean 'mad'. In a book on falconry (Turbery, 1575), restless falcons are described as being *impatient and bedlam* and Shakespeare speaks of *bedlam and ambitious humour* (HENRY VI PART II, 1593).

In 1676 the hospital was moved to a new site. John Evelyn, who went to see it *most sweetly placed in Moorfields*, was deeply impressed by the elegant new building, which he compared to the Louvre in Paris. Magnificent architecture was not the only attraction, however. People were generally fascinated by the insane and this curiosity was tapped for revenue. During the eighteenth century, for a small entrance fee, visitors were admitted to ogle and jeer at the inmates, chained in their cells in galleries. Such sport was disruptive and noisy bouts of disorder must have been commonly witnessed, so that *bedlam* came to be used figuratively to describe scenes of commotion and uproar, the sense it retains today.

At the beginning of the nineteenth century the building was declared unsafe and the hospital was moved to Lambeth. After the First World War it was in Addington, Surrey and at present is in Beckenham, Kent. The name of the Bethlehem Royal Hospital has changed little, but patients now receive the highest standard of care.

In Hebrew *Bethlehem* means 'house of bread', being a compound of *bayit*, 'house', and *lehem*, 'bread' or more generally 'food'.

For another word arising from a corruption of a biblical name, see MAUDLIN.

beer
a bitter-tasting alcoholic brew

*He drew the **beer** to a foaming head and set it down delicately on the bar where the foam rocked and then slopped gently over the glass's side.*
(SALLY VICKERS, MR GOLIGHTLY'S HOLIDAY, 2003)

See ALE.

biscuit
a dry, crisp cake or pastry

*I pick up one of the **biscuits** and nibble it, grateful to have something to do and some object to look at. Silence.*
(MICHAEL FRAYN, SPIES, 2002)

*Cora's strident voice was then heard calling up the stairs, to tell them that she was off to Mr Bhatti's, because they were clean out of milk and **biscuits**, and you had to offer tea and biscuits to all the people who would be coming round to pay their respects, and actually it would be a very good idea if Mr Fuller could do a full shop at Sainsbury's when he could find the time.*
(MARY CAVANAGH, A MAN LIKE ANY OTHER, 2007)

In modern British English the word *biscuit* conjures up a plateful of custard creams or chocolate digestives. Originally, however, *biscuits* were thin,

---

WORD MYSTERIES

Q What do *balderdash*, *bludgeon*, *boffin* and *bunch* all have in common, apart from the fact that they all begin with the letter *b*?

A They are just four among thousands of English words whose origins remain a mystery.

See BISTRO.

flat discs made of unleavened bread dough which were baked twice until they were hard and dry. In this form they kept well and were useful for lengthy journeys or military campaigns; *ship's biscuit* was a staple ration for sailors on a long voyage:

> *As drie as the remainder bisket*
> *After a voyage.*
> (SHAKESPEARE, AS YOU LIKE IT, 1600)

There was once probably an unattested Medieval Latin term *biscoctus (panis)*, 'twice-cooked (bread)', a compound of Latin *bis*, 'twice' and *coctus*, past participle of *coquere*, 'to cook'. This was taken into Old French as *bescoit*, *bescuit*, and from there into Middle English as *besquite* in the fourteenth century.

Although the original biscuits were unappetising, creative cooks began to experiment with different ingredients to make a variety of twice-cooked treats that could be offered on social occasions. The ACCOMPLISH'D FEMALE INSTRUCTOR of 1719 gives the following recipe for biscuits with full instructions for the important second cooking:

To make Queen's Bisket, Genoua Bisket, etc. – Take as much fine flower, a loaf-sugar finely beaten, nine yolks and twelve whites of eggs, to a pound of flower, and a pound of sugar, corriander-seeds, and anni-seeds, of each three quarters of an ounce finely beaten and sifted; rose-water and ale-yest very new, of each two or three spoonfuls, then boil up as much fair water as will make it into a convenient thin past something like batter; take it up with a spoon or ladle, and drop it on fine paper on which fine sugar is strewed, or put it into tin coffins four or five inches long, and an inch and a half broad, and put them into an oven not too hot; and when sufficiently baked, take them out and lay them on a paper to cool; after that, harden them in a stove or warm oven, to keep long: and thus you may make Genoua-bisket.

There has been a remarkable variety of spellings over the centuries, from *bysqwyte* to the contemporary *biscuit*. The latter is a rather precious borrowing of the modern French word. It supplanted *bisket*, which had been the regular spelling for three hundred years up to the eighteenth century, and had reflected the common pronunciation.

bistro

a restaurant in French style

A place like Le Blanc was Simon's idea of unchallenging because it wasn't cool anymore. Three years ago it had been a Laundromat, just a dingy hole on Mott Street, and then somebody cleaned the hundred-year-old tile walls, put up yellowed mirrors, installed a zinc-topped bar, and poof, it was a perfect Parisian **bistro**.
(MICHAEL CUNNINGHAM, SPECIMEN DAYS, 2005)

Meals in restaurants were 'off-ration', although there were strict limits as to what could be served. During the war the government set up 'British Restaurants': local authority cafés that provided basic low-cost meals to the general public. For who better to run your favourite **bistro** *than the council?*
(JOHN O'FARRELL, AN UTTERLY IMPARTIAL HISTORY OF BRITAIN, 2007)

Bistro is an etymological mystery. It has been suggested that the word was introduced into France after the fall of Napoleon in 1815, when Russian troops entered Paris. Details of the story differ. Some say that impatient soldiers chivvied harassed restaurant owners with cries of *bistro*, 'hurry'. Others maintain that it was the owners themselves who shouted *bistro* from the doors of their establishments to advertise the fact that a good, cheap meal was instantly available – a nineteenth-century fast-food gimmick. The theory is supported by the fact that there is a similar-sounding Russian word meaning 'quickly'; it is cast into doubt by the fact that *bistro* did not appear in print until seventy years after the cossack invasion.

There are alternative theories, however. One is that *bistro* derives from *bistouille* or *bistrouille*, a term for the hot coffee and shot of cheap brandy sold in modest cafes in northern France. Another suggests an origin in *bistraud*, a word from the Poitou dialect of southwest France, possibly meaning either 'lesser servant' or 'small household'. Emilie Carles, describing her impoverished childhood in the early 1900s in the High Alps of southeastern France, has this to say about the hard drinking that took place in village bistros:

The bistro was all there was, the only entertainment around, and those peasants certainly did not deny themselves. Bored and worn out...they believed that their hard labor gave them the right to drink wine. 'A liter in the morning, one at noon, and another at night,' they'd say, 'that doesn't make me drunk, and I can still drink a glass or two in the bar'.
(EMILIE CARLES, TR. AVRIEL H GOLDBERGER, A WILD HERB SOUP, 1991)

The term was borrowed into English in the first quarter of the twentieth century when, as in France, it was used of a modest wine-shop or restaurant. In the 1960s and 1970s, however, it became a vogue word for an intimate little restaurant with a French flavour. Suddenly there was a bistro in every town, with prices far removed from the original humble French tariffs.

See WORD MYSTERIES (page 44).

blackguard
a rogue, a scoundrel

*'At least,' said Flambeau, 'the wretched constable who caught the **blackguard** then sent him on into the party will be dismissed, and I hope sentenced to a generous term in prison!'*
'On the contrary,' replied his friend. 'I hope that he will be spared, for he is the only man in this sad sequence of events to emerge with any credit.'
(SIMON HOGGART IN THE GUARDIAN, 25 JUNE 2003)

*'One has met and indeed entertained many visiting heads of state, some of them unspeakable crooks and **blackguards** and their wives not much better.'*
This at least raised some rueful nods.
(ALAN BENNETT, THE UNCOMMON READER, 2007)

In early sixteenth century, *black guards* were menial kitchen servants who had care of pots, pans and utensils blackened by the flames and who turned the spits over the fires. It was grimy and back-breaking work. When a wealthy family travelled with full retinue or a royal progress was underway, these drudges travelled with the greasy pots and pans, their filthy condition exposed to full view. In his play THE WHITE DEVIL (1612), John Webster speaks of *a lousy slave, that within these twenty years rode with the black guard in the Duke's carriage, 'mongst spits and dripping pans.*

Servants and camp followers in the army train were similarly known as the *black guard*, and there also seems to have been a real guard of attendants who were dubbed the *Black guard*, probably because they dressed in black.

By the eighteenth century the *black guard* had come to describe destitute children scratching a living on the streets. In his DICTIONARIUM BRITANNICUM of 1736, Nathan Bailey defines *black-guard* as *dirty tatter'd*

Boys, who ply the Streets to clean shoes.
Such children were what Francis Grose
called *dirty tattered and roguish boys*
(DICTIONARY OF THE VULGAR
TONGUE, 1785) and so it is unsurpris-
ing that, in the first half of that century,
the term was extended to denote 'an
out-and-out scoundrel, a rogue'.

For other words with a similar
meaning, see CAD and VILLAIN.

blackmail
money or favours obtained by
extortion

*The young hero was in love with his
father's ward, an heiress. The father's
former mistress, Mrs Vibert, turned up
unexpectedly with their grown-up
illegitimate son, and a villainous tutor, in
tow. Mrs Vibert tried to attach the ward to
her son, and the tutor sought to exploit the
situation through **blackmail**. In the end
his bluff was called by a morally reborn
Mrs Vibert and all ended happily. It was
a comedy.*
(DAVID LODGE,
AUTHOR, AUTHOR, 2004)

*'What do you think?' Montalbano asked
Fazio.
    'Inspector Augello's explanation could be
right. But, and I can't really say why, I'm
not convinced. I would lean more towards
blackmail.'
    'Blackmail over what?'
    'I dunno, maybe Pellegrino threatened to
tell everyone they had a relationship – that
Gargano was gay...'*
(ANDREA CAMILLERI,
THE SCENT OF THE NIGHT, 2000)

This word has nothing to do with the
exploits of the Black Prince or with
knights in armour who have behaved
dishonourably. *Mail* was a Scottish
word for 'rent' or 'tax' (from Old Norse
māl meaning 'speech, agreement').

Burrow-mails, for example, were the
dues payable within boroughs during
the reign of James I of Scotland
(1394–1437). Such tributes were
usually paid in silver coin, or *white
money*.

During the sixteenth and seventeenth centuries, marauders plagued
farmers in the border country between
England and Scotland by demanding
protection payments. If a farmer
refused to comply, they would lay his
property waste. *Black* has always carried
overtones of evil, and so this demand by
extortion, usually made for cattle, was
known as *blackmail* to contrast with
white money payments, which were in
coin and were lawful. Protection rackets
are obviously no new thing.

In the nineteenth century the term
was extended to denote 'any payment
exhorted by threat', particularly the
threatened exposure of a secret. The
terms *moral* and *emotional blackmail* date
from the second half of the twentieth
century.

blanket
a warm woollen covering for a bed;
all-inclusive, indiscriminate

*One other obstacle to understanding is the
use of such **blanket** terms as 'the West'
and 'Muslim world'. However convenient
such phrases are, in reality, such places
do not exist.
    The Muslim world of which we speak
consists of 72 Islamic sects.*
(RICHARD SEYMOUR IN
THE MIDDLE EAST, 1 MARCH 2002)

*He ran along the side of the ship towards
the stern and Attilius followed, his head
lowered, his feet sinking into the heavy
blanket of white pumice that covered
the deck like snow.*
(ROBERT HARRIS, POMPEII, 2003)

It wasn't just aristocrats who had a sense of the quirky. The Reverend Robert Hawker...had a pet pig and wore a pink hat with a poncho made from a yellow horse **blanket**.
(GOOD HOUSEKEEPING, OCTOBER 2008)

A popular etymology for this word states that a man named Thomas Blanket wove fine bed covers and that his name was given to the finished articles. The story is widespread. It appears, for instance, in THE THREE EDWARDS (1958), a book by Thomas Costain, a prolific Canadian author of historical novels. Sadly this is a case of suppositon being taken for fact for, although it is common for words to be coined from people's names (see BLOOMERS, GUILLOTINE and SAND-WICH), *blanket* is not one of them.

The word's origins lie not with the apocryphal Mr Blanket but in the whitish colour of raw wool. Indeed, when the word first appeared in Middle English at the very beginning of the fourteenth century, it simply denoted 'white woollen cloth' that was used for clothing. It was a borrowing of Old French *blanquet*, *blanchet*, a diminutive form of *blanc*, meaning 'white'. Not until the middle of the fourteenth century was the word applied to 'a bed covering'. The adjectival use meaning 'all-inclusive' or 'indiscriminate' dates from the second half of the nineteenth century.

blindfold

to place a bandage over a person's eyes so that they cannot see; the bandage or other material used for this purpose

She becomes anxious again when he is stressing how careful they must be.

'But we are allowed to kiss one another?' she asks, as if verifying the terms of a contract she has signed while happily **blindfolded**.
(JULIAN BARNES, ARTHUR AND GEORGE, 2005)

We came to a halt and were told we could remove the **blindfolds**. *I have no memory of the outside. Just the usual melee of men with keffiyeh and guns.*
(BOB GELDOF, GELDOF IN AFRICA, 2005)

Middle English had the verb *blindfellen*, 'to strike blind'. The second element *fellen*, from Old English *fellan*, is the source of the verb *to fell*, and meant 'to cut or strike down' as one would a tree, for instance, or a foe in battle. In the thirteenth century *blindfellen* also came to mean 'to cover the eyes with a cloth'. The past participle was *blindfelled*, but by the fifteenth century the letter *d* was assumed to be part of the stem of the verb, hence the CATHOLICON ANGLICUM of 1483 has *To Blyndfeyld [blyndfelle]*. By the sixteenth century the verb was frequently corrupted to *blindfold*, the folding of the cloth to make the bandage for the eyes obviously triggering the change.

For another example of a word influenced by an etymologically unrelated one, see UPROAR.

blitz

an intensive air bombardment, specifically that of London during the Second World War; an energetic, concentrated effort

It was part of family lore that as the country prepared to face Hitler's invasion, Edward's birth was considered by the local authority to be an emergency, a crisis in hygiene. Men with picks and shovels came, rather elderly men, and mains water was

*channelled to the house from the Northend
road in September of that year, just as
the London **Blitz** was beginning.*
(IAN MCEWAN,
ON CHESIL BEACH, 2007)

*Still can't get used to the brevity of the
night up here in northern Europe.
Scarcely has the sun gone down than
it's up again. Morning sunshine **blitzes**
through the fragile curtains from four
o'clock onwards.*
(MICHAEL PALIN, NEW EUROPE, 2007)

When Hitler launched Germany into
open conflict in 1939 he did so with
confidence, believing that he held
superiority both on land and in the air.
His key strategy, which proved very
effective in Poland, was the *Blitzkrieg*,
or 'lightning war' (from *Blitz*, 'lightning' and *Krieg*, 'war'), a sudden, sharp
attack that would swiftly overwhelm
the enemy. The short form *Blitz*
entered English vocabulary early in the
war when major British cities were
subject to sudden, heavy air raids.
Referring to this period, the word is
now written with an initial capital
letter: *Blitz*. Since the war, *blitz* has
been used figuratively to describe a
sudden, energetic endeavour to complete a task.

bloomers
voluminous knee-length knickers

*The men pushed the punts to the sides,
the two sexes disappeared behind their
own bushes and emerged, the women in
bloomers and camisoles, the men in
underpants if anything at all and 'had
a good bathe'.*
(FRANCES OSBORNE,
THE BOLTER, 2008

*A pair of fine cotton **bloomers** that Queen
Victoria once wore have fetched 4,500
pounds at auction. The 'exciting' knickers*
*bearing a VR monogram were actually
expected to fetch 500 pounds. The pants
are open-crotch with separate legs joined
by a draw-string at the waist, a popular
style in the late Victorian era.*
(HINDUSTAN TIMES, 31 JULY 2008)

Bloomers are the type of knickers one
imagines one's maiden aunt to be
wearing under her tweed skirt. They
may be out of vogue today but at one
time they were ahead of fashion and
caused no small upset in polite society.
The word derives from the name of
Amelia Jenks *Bloomer* – not because she
invented the garment but because she
associated herself with it.

Mrs Bloomer ran a paper called
THE LILY, for which she wrote articles
on temperance, social reform and
women's rights. In 1850 she wrote in
support of a group of women who
turned up in her home town of Seneca
Falls, New York State, wearing knee-
length skirts over baggy trousers that
were gathered at the ankle. This costume was favoured by members of the
Women's Rights Movement who
argued that the fashionable crinoline,
which skimmed the ground, was both
cumbersome and unhygienic.

The new outfit was very decent by
modern standards but mid-nineteenth-
century society reacted unfavourably to
women in trousers. Mrs Bloomer,
however, was persuaded that it was a
practical way to dress and said so in
THE LILY. She also took to wearing the
costume herself. Her spirited defence
was noted by the national press and
brought instant notoriety. Before long
those plunging into the controversy
were referring to the outfit as *the
Bloomer*. Mrs Bloomer had plenty of
opportunity to publicise her way of
dressing, for she was soon in demand as
a speaker. In 1852 she toured the
northern cities of the United States as a
lecturer, doubtless hoping that her

GARMENTS

What has a saint to do with underwear? *San Pantaleone* or *Pantalone* was a much-loved Venetian saint in whose honour boys of the city were frequently baptised. Among Italians, therefore, the name often denoted a Venetian and was accordingly given to a Venetian character in the *commedia dell'arte*. He appeared as a scrawny, bespectacled dotard wearing slippers and tight trousers. The word *pantaloon* came into English via French *pantalon* to describe a similar kind of tight trouser-cum-hose, which was fashionable during the reign of Charles II (1660–85). Over the years the word was applied to other styles of fashionable trouser. To this day French retains *pantalon* to mean 'trousers'; American English did the same with *pantaloon*, shortening it to *pants* in the nineteenth century. In British English, however, *pants* are strictly underwear.

Like San Pantaleone and the character Pantalone, a number of figures who were once well-known are now remembered chiefly by the garments named after them. Amelia *Bloomer*, whose story is told in detail elsewhere in this book, is one of them (see BLOOMERS). Another is Jules *Léotard*, a famous nineteenth-century French acrobat and inventor of the flying trapeze. He was also the designer of the *leotard*, the figure-hugging one-piece garment that was adopted by others of his profession and subsequently by dancers and gymnasts.

A more substantial garment bears the name of the Scottish chemist Charles *Macintosh*, who in 1823 patented a type of cloth layered with rubber to form an impermeable material from which heavy-weather cloaks and coats were made. Later the word *mackintosh* (a variant spelling of the inventor's name) was used to denote any type of raincoat and, at the beginning of the twentieth century, became subject to the inevitable abbreviation *mack* or *mac*.

The dress of military commanders seems to have been much noted and copied in the nineteenth century. Arthur, first Duke of *Wellington*, was such a prominent and popular figure through his decisive military triumphs in the Peninsular War and his victory over Napoleon at Waterloo (1815) that coats, hats, trousers and boots were named in his honour. Today he is remembered only for *wellington boots*, which were originally long and loose topped, the fronts coming above the knee. The unglamorous rubber variety were an invention of the first quarter of the twentieth century, and the affectionate abbreviation *welly* dates back to the early 1960s.

audiences were there to inform themselves of her many worthy convictions rather than simply to gawp at her attire.

In fact, Mrs Bloomer was not particuarly happy with this type of celebrity – she would have preferred to be known for her work on behalf of women's suffrage. So at one time she suggested that, as the idea for the apparel originally came from Elizabeth Smith Miller, the garments should really be called *millers*. However, her protestations got her nowhere. Over a century later, she is remembered, if at all, for her dress sense rather than as a feminist.

Towards the end of the century, improved bicycles made cycling a pleasure and many cycling clubs were formed. Women were as eager to participate as men and so, naturally,

But military success was not a prerequisite of sartorial prominence. Two figures responsible for the ill-fated Charge of the Light Brigade, as a result of which British troops sustained heavy losses during the Crimean War (1854–6), are also remembered for their style. Lord *Raglan* was responsible for the ambiguous order which initiated the Charge. He wore a sensible overcoat without shoulder seams, which was named after him. Later his name was given to the *raglan sleeve*, which continues seamless up to the neck. His name is often found in knitting patterns, as is that of his fellow officer James Thomas Brudenell, seventh Earl of *Cardigan*, who is remembered by his title for his woolly button-through jackets as well as for leading the disastrous Charge. Indeed, the Crimean campaigns did much for knitting. *Balaclava caps* or *helmets* were named after the town of *Balaclava*, site of the British base, where soldiers wore them to weather the freezing temperatures. After the war, the cosy winter headgear was worn by the civilian population also.

The adoption by civilians of garments issued to soldiers was nothing new. During the Thirty Years' War (1618–48), Croatian mercenaries pressed into service for France wore linen bands round their necks. French men and women of fashion copied the garment in fine fabrics trimmed with lace, bestowing on it the name *cravate*, 'a Croatian', from German *Krabate* and Flemish *Krawaat*, from Serbo-Croatian *Hrvat*.

Balaclava was not the only place to lend its name to an article of clothing. *Jodhpurs*, the breeches commonly worn for riding, come from the city of that name in Rajasthan, India, and were brought to England in the nineteenth century. Also from India come *dungarees*. *Dungri* is a district of Bombay where a rough kind of calico was made in the seventeenth century. Stout trousers made of the fabric have been known as *dungarees* since the nineteenth century.

Closer to home *duffle* (or *duffel*) *coats* take their name from the heavy woollen fabric from which they have been made since the seventeenth century. Of course, the fabric is named for its place of manufacture, the Belgian town of *Duffel*. Knitted goods have been produced on the island of *Jersey* since at least the sixteenth century. In the nineteenth century the knitted fisherman's *jersey* tunic became fashionable and the same century saw the emergence of the sporting *jersey*, originally made of close-knit woollen cloth.

For various fabrics called after their place of origin, see FABRICS (page 263).

more practical clothing for women was required. The historian Christopher Hibbert (THE ENGLISH, 1987) quotes an account of those days by the daughter of the Plumian Professor of Astronomy at Cambridge, who says:

And soon after that everyone had bicycles and [they] became the smart thing in society... We were then permitted to wear baggy knickerbockers, horridly improper, but rather grand... I only once saw a woman (not, of course, a lady) in real bloomers.

Even as the century closed, it seems, *bloomers* were not quite the thing in polite circles.

For more articles of clothing named after their wearers, see GARMENTS (above).

bonanza
a tremendous opportunity for gain,
a source of sudden great wealth

*Vegetarian mountain gorillas live among
a vegetable **bonanza** where there is
absolutely no food restriction that might
prevent gregariousness.*
(CYRIL RUOSO & EMMANUELLE
GRUNDMANN, THE GREAT APES, 2007)

*It was quickly my impression...that making
a million bucks in New York was essentially
a question of walking down the street – of
strolling, hands in pockets, in the cheerful
expectation that sooner or later a bolt of
pecuniary fire would jump out of the
atmosphere and knock you flat. Every third
person seemed to have been happily struck
down: by a stock-market killing, or by a
dot-com **bonanza**, or by a six-figure
motion-picture deal for a five-hundred-word
magazine article about, say, a mystifying
feral chicken which, clucking and pecking, had
been found roosting in a Queens backyard.*
(JOSEPH O'NEILL, NETHERLAND, 2008)

A newspaper headline proclaims
HOLIDAY CASH BONANZA, and goes
on to tell how *Keith Crummack
of Kirkburton won £1,000 in Thomas Cook
holiday vouchers at the Halifax's branch
in Cloth Hall Street* (HUDDERSFIELD
EXAMINER, 13 September 2008);
Vogue.com tempts readers with *The Great
Handbag Bonanza* (27 May 2008); and a
glance at the internet reveals that *bonanza*
is the chosen name for companies selling
everything from greenhouses to holidays.
Bonanza is a word that hits advertising
and promotions from time to time,
usually when a competition carrying a
great deal of prize money is announced
or a sale is advertised. There is no such
razzmatazz about its origins, however.
Bonanza is a Spanish word and simply
meant 'good sailing weather'. It derives
from Latin *bonus*, 'good', via the unattested Vulgar Latin *bonacia*. The word
was modelled on Latin *malacia*, which

actually meant 'calm at sea' but was erroneously supposed to derive from *malus*,
'bad', and to mean 'bad weather'. From
this sense of 'fair weather' and presumably, therefore, a good voyage, *bonanza*
came to mean 'good luck' or 'prosperity'.

The word then took another metaphorical turn, as the Spanish exploited
the abundant mining deposits they
found in Mexico. Here *bonanza* became a
familiar term for 'a rich seam of ore or
minerals', and so when the western
states of America were probed for gold
in the nineteenth century, *bonanza* was
borrowed into the vocabulary of
American prospectors: earliest records of
the borrowing go back to the 1840s. To
this day there are towns, mountains,
lakes and rivers called Bonanza throughout the North American continent.

The gold fever of nineteenth-
century America sometimes gave the
word unfavourable connotations. So
often apparently great riches failed to
materialise or the bubble of Stock
Market speculation led to ruin. In the
late 1870s, for example, the Big
Bonanza near Virginia City fuelled
wild investment that rapidly came to
nothing. There is no hint of ruin in the
British 'bonanza' advertising campaigns, however. You can't lose; everyone is a winner.

For another word originating in fair
weather, see OPPORTUNITY.

bonfire
a large fire to burn rubbish or for
public celebration

*Why did she bother with these diaries?
She and her sister made a **bonfire** of their
diaries the night before their double
wedding, and it was a custom she kept up
throughout her life. Why set words down
just to destroy them?*
(MARGARET ATWOOD,
MORAL DISORDER, 2006)

*...and then fireworks erupted from the field next to the restaurant, fizzy white snakes, purple sea urchins, yellow starbursts, weeping willows of incandescent green light. And those whumps like someone hitting cardboard boxes with a golf club that took her straight back to **bonfires** and baked potatoes in silver foil and the smell of sparkler smoke.*
(MARK HADDON,
A SPOT OF BOTHER, 2006)

Large bonfires, not the garden-rubbish variety, are usually lit for public celebration. This has led some etymologists to seek out a happy origin for the word: they attempt to derive it from the French *bon feu*, 'good fire', but do not take into consideration the facts that this term does not exist in French and that the expression for a celebratory bonfire in that language is, in fact, *feu de joie*. Rather the word is English, its true origins being a little grisly but still festive.

In past times piles of clean cattle bones were burnt to commemorate certain anniversaries, a practice which probably had pagan origins. In England, for instance, the mid-summer feast of St John (24 June) was marked by the pagan practice of kindling a chain of bonfires. In pre-Christian times the sun was recognised as the source of life, and people sought to prevent the gradual diminishing of its intensity after Midsummer's Day. Dr Brewer's DICTIONARY OF PHRASE AND FABLE quotes from the FESTWALL of 1493 (printed in 1515):

In the worship of St John the people made three manner of fires: one was of clean bones and no wood, and that is called a bone fire; another of clean wood and no bones, and that is called a wood-fire and the third is made of wood and bones, and is called St John's fire.

Festivities apart, *bone fires* were a regular feature of agricultural life in medieval times. A thirteenth-century verse which states the fact that *Of the sheep is cast away nothing* goes on to say *to ashes goeth his bones*. In WATER IN ENGLAND (1964), Dorothy Hartley discusses the value to the medieval community of the huge annual markets; all the byproducts of the fair, ranging from animal dung to the waste from the butchers' stalls, benefitted the land. *Bone fires* burned continually, with the further advantage that the smoke from them acted as an insect-repellent.

Over time the stressed syllable of *bone-fire* was contracted, first in speech and then in written form. By the sixteenth century *bonfire*, though still occasionally written as *bone-fire*, was more generally applied to a large prepared blaze of any sort, whether lit for a special occasion or just to burn rubbish. Even so, some of these were fuelled with bones – the burning of saints' relics during the dissolution of the monasteries, for instance, or of heretics at the stake.

book
printed pages joined along one edge and protected by a cover

*Over and over I read the pages of the **book** I'd written as a young man. It was so long ago. I was naïve. A twenty-year-old in love.*
(NICOLE KRAUSS,
THE HISTORY OF LOVE, 2005)

See WRITE.

boom

a loud, resonant noise; a surge of growth and activity, often economic

*The number of landlords falling into arrears with their banks has soared by 50 per cent as the **boom** in getting poor people to pay off your mortgage while you jet-ski in Barbados withers like a petrol station carnation.*
(THE TIMES, 13 DECEMBER 2008)

*The birds live scattered lives, seldom coming together. They have adapted for a life in the best of New Zealand's wild wet habitats, places that, in the times when its only mammals flew, occasionally echoed to the apologetic **boom** of the male kakapo in its rare amorous moods.*
(THE TIMES, 28 FEBRUARY 2009)

Boom is an onomatopoeic word to describe 'a deep, sonorous sound which disturbs the air'. It could be of English origin but may be a borrowing from German or Dutch, both of which have similar words. In any event, *boom* was used, as noun and verb, from the fifteenth century on and applied to anything from the buzzing of a bee to cannon fire, crashing billows or any other loud, resonant noise.

Since the seventeenth century, the word has also encapsulated a sense of the rushing motion required to generate the sound; a ship sailing at full speed, for instance, was said to be *booming: We are booming along all night* (C D Warner, MY WINTER ON THE NILE, 1876). It is probably with this in mind that the meaning of *boom* was given a new twist in nineteenth-century America when it was applied to a rush of political activity during Ulysses S Grant's bid for a third term as Republican president.

The St Louis GLOBE DEMOCRAT first used the word in this context in 1879; other newspapers were more cautious because of its 'slangy' nature.

Nevertheless, before long it had been unreservedly adopted and was soon on everyone's lips. For a month or two *boom* circulated in the political sphere until the press recognised its potential as a punchy term to describe 'a spurt of economic growth'. The INDIANAPOLIS JOURNAL of October 1879 quoted a frustrated businessman who remarked, *Nearly everything has had a boom except soap, and I'm looking for a soap boom every day*.

Since then *boom* has been applied to many areas of business and investment and, in more recent times, to population figures when the large number of babies born after the Second World War was termed the *baby boom*. But the word's popularity was almost stillborn. Towards the end of 1879, in a mood of sour grapes, some of the Democratic press condemned the term and tried to suppress it, obviously to no avail: the same edition of the INDIANAPOLIS JOURNAL reported:

Since the Ohio election one or two Democratic papers have suggested that the word has an unpleasant sound, and ought to be done away with, but it is evident this suggestion springs from base partisan motives. It is a good word, and answers a great many purposes. Let it boom.

bridal

connected to a bride or a wedding

*Beside me walks Rashid, a slim figure in a long white gown, white backless slippers and a small cap. We move as though we were a **bridal** couple parading up the aisle; we tell each other bad jokes in appalling French and from time to time join in singing the* Marseillaise.
(JOHN MORTIMER, SUMMER OF A DORMOUSE, 2000)

*'We took down all your measurements and then you lost eight pounds, remember? We got to Baltimore the day of the wedding and found you just a shadow of your former self. Right up till time for the ceremony we had to baste and pin and tuck...You'd turned into a skeleton. I guess it was **bridal** jitters.'*
(ANNE TYLER, BACK WHEN WE WERE GROWNUPS, 2001)

Old English had the compound noun *brydealu*, literally 'bride-ale' (more recognisable in its Middle English form *bridale*), for a 'wedding feast'. The *bride-ale* was a rowdy affair, obviously helped along by the consumption of copious amounts of ale. This was especially brewed for the festivities and was sold to the guests for the benefit of the couple. Nevertheless, participation was wholehearted and generous. Christopher Hibbert (THE ENGLISH, 1987) quotes Bishop Richard Poore of Salisbury who, in the first quarter of the thirteenth century, felt moved to remind his flock that marriages should be *celebrated reverently and with honour, not with laughter or sport or at public potations or feasts*. The Bishop's plea had little effect, however, for not until the last quarter of the sixteenth century does the learned clergyman William Harrison report a reduction in the *heathenish rioting at bride-ales* (DESCRIPTION OF ENGLAND, 1587). Indeed, a sermon delivered some twenty-two years later suggests more sober ingredients as a recipe for a joyful celebration and subsequent wedded bliss:

How happy are those in whom faith and love, and godlinesse are maried together, before they marry themselves? For none of these martiall, and cloudy, and whining mariages can say, that godlines was invited to their bride-ale; and therefore the blessings which are promised to godlinesse, doe flue from them.
(SMITH, SERMONS, 1609)

These sentiments would have gladdened Bishop Poore's heart.

The spelling *bridale* to denote the celebrations occurs as early as 1200, though *bredeale*, *biydale* and *brydeale* are found in the fifteenth and sixteenth centuries. From the second half of the fourteenth century the word was often applied not just to the feast but to the ceremony as well. By the seventeenth century *bridal* was being used attributively, the word being erroneously influenced by adjectives of Latin origin such as *cordial*, *circumstantial*, *natal* and *mortal*. This gave rise to couplings such as *bridal bed*, *bridal cake*, *bridal house*, *bridal knot* and *bridal lace*. By the eighteenth century *bridal* was understood to be an adjective, surviving as a noun only in the form *bride-ale* where the writer was intent upon historical effect.

For further discussion of ALE as a feast, see that entry.

brogue
a strong leather shoe

*Does he lie in bed while he listens? Hard to picture him there in his thick grey woollen socks, twiddling his toes, his tie off and shirt collar agape and hands clasped behind that stringy old neck of his. Out of his room he is vertical man itself, from the soles of his much-mended glossy brown **brogues** to the tip of his conical skull.*
(JOHN BANVILLE, THE SEA, 2005)

*To her surprise, [Florence] Welch has become something of a style icon, by virtue of her skill in mixing, for example, old silk dresses and 1980s suit jackets (today, it is brown **brogues** with white ankle socks, turquoise cotton skirt and white T-shirt).*
(THE TELEGRAPH, 4 JUNE 2009)

Modern-day brogues are stout leather shoes, embellished by perforated patterning, for country wear. They have even become stylish fashion items from time to time. All this, however, is a twentieth-century development. *Brogues* were originally crude heavy footwear made of untanned leather which were worn in remote parts of Scotland and Ireland. Sometimes they were strengthened with clouts or nails, as this reference from Shakespeare's CYMBELINE (c. 1610) shows:

> I thought he slept, and put
> My clouted brogues from off my feet, whose
> rudeness
> Answer'd my steps too loud.

The word is from Scottish and Irish Gaelic *brõg*, which comes from Old Irish *brõc*, 'shoe', and ultimately from Old Norse *brok*, 'trousers'. Leggings, it seems, often covered the top of the foot as well as the leg, hence the derivation from the Old Norse word. This link is further reflected in *brogue* being used not only for 'shoe' but also for 'trousers' in the English of the seventeenth to the nineteenth centuries. In THE FAIR MAID OF THE INN (John Fletcher, 1625), for instance, Forobosco tells the Clown: *Then will I conveigh thee stark naked to Develing to beg a pair of brogs, to hide thy mountainous buttocks.*

The term *Irish brogue* denotes the particularly strong accent of some Irish speakers of English and has been current since at least the early eighteenth century. Its derivation is a mystery, although some have suggested that it refers to 'the accent of one who wears brogues'.

brusque

rough-mannered, curt, sharp

Dora waited a tactful moment before saying, 'Has Marcus been here long?'
  'Not terribly. Long enough to have a cup of tea.'

'And it's been OK? I still find Marcus a bit scary. He's so knowledgeable and a bit **brusque**. *I feel I might make a mistake when he's around.'*
(KATIE FFORDE, GOING DUTCH, 2007)

When the celebrity world has exhausted the possibilities of naming their children after countries (India, China, Ireland), cities (Slash's son is London Emilio, and I think we know Brooklyn Beckham) and fruits, flowers and plants (Apple Paltrow Martin, Bluebell Halliwell, Sage Moonblood Stallone), days of the week might just be the way to go. They sound familiar but **brusque** *('Don't pick your nose, Thursday!'). And of course, you can't call anyone Wednesday, because that was the name of the daughter in* The Addams Family.
(THE INDEPENDENT, 9 JULY 2008)

The source of *brusque* is thought to be the unattested Vulgar Latin word *bruscum*, the name commonly given to the very spiky plant 'butcher's broom'. This became *brusco* in Italian, which then used the name of the disagreeable shrub as an adjective to describe unpleasantly sharp-tasting wine or tart fruit. The adjective was borrowed into other Romance languages in the sixteenth century with the figurative sense of 'rough-mannered, rude'. It came into English by way of French *brusque* in the seventeenth century. Initially it was spelt *brusk* but the French spelling and pronunciation were adopted in the mid-eighteenth century.

☛ It is probable that *brisk* was an earlier sixteenth-century borrowing of French *brusque*. In the late sixteenth and the seventeenth centuries it was often used in contexts where *brusque* would serve just as well, and in his DICTIONARIE OF THE FRENCH AND ENGLISH TONGUES (1611), Randle Cotgrave uses *brisk* to define *brusque*:
BRUSQUE: briske, liuely, quicke, etc.

buccaneer
pirate, adventurer

'You have heard of this Flint, I suppose?'
*'Heard of him!' cried the squire. 'Heard
of him, you say! He was the bloodthirstiest
buccaneer that sailed. Blackbeard was a
child to Flint. The Spaniards were so
prodigiously afraid of him that, I tell you,
sir, I was sometimes proud he was an
Englishman.'*
(ROBERT LOUIS STEVENSON,
TREASURE ISLAND, 1883)

*The prime objective of these early explorers
and **buccaneers** was to seek trade for their
countries, so they were often reluctant to
reveal the exact location of where they
had seen land, making life difficult for
geographers and mapmakers.*
(JONATHAN & ANGELA SCOTT,
ANTARCTICA, 2007)

In the sixteenth century many
Europeans who had fallen foul of the
law in their own countries ended up in
the New World colonies. Some were
contracted there as indentured servants
to supply much-needed labour on the
plantations, others simply fled and
ended up living wild. The word *buccaneer* originated among French outlaws
who settled in the West Indies. These
men lived by hunting and adopted the
native custom of drying or smoking
meat by laying it upon a raised framework of sticks placed over a pit fire.
The Brazilian Tupi word for the
wooden frame was *mukem*, a term which
had been taken to the West Indies by
Europeans. The French hunters corrupted this to *boucan* (*boucan* in seventeenth-century English). From this they
derived the verb *boucaner*, which meant
'to dry meat on a boucan', and also the
noun *boucanier*, to denote a person who
cured meat like this. *Boucanier* was borrowed into English as *buccaneer* in the
seventeenth century, originally to refer
to such a hunter.

The woodsmen soon found a more
profitable means of existence, however.
The islands and coves in the Caribbean
provided excellent cover for surprise
attacks on shipping and settlements
along the Spanish main. Their success
encouraged many Dutch and English to
join them in raiding Spanish shipping
so that, by the second half of the seventeenth century, the term *buccaneer* had
become synonymous with 'pirate'. Far
from frowning upon these dishonest
dealings, from the middle to the end of
the seventeenth century the French and
English governments sanctioned them
as a way of keeping Spain in check. One
of the most notorious buccaneers was a
Welshman, Henry Morgan, who was
knighted by Charles II.

In modern English *buccaneer* is used
in the world of business to describe
unscrupulous business men, particularly
those involved in private equity firms:

*'BUCCANEERS' BLAMED FOR
BIRD'S EYE CLOSURE*
*Captain Birds Eye is setting sail from Hull
after hundreds of workers were told the
factory where its famous frozen fish fingers
are made will close. The GMB union
blamed 'buccaneering venture capitalist
asset strippers' for the closure, which comes
five months after private equity firm
Permira bought the iconic frozen food
company from Unilever for £1.16bn.*
(THE GUARDIAN, 12 JANUARY 2007)

☛ In Haiti a wooden framework for
curing meat, similar to the *boucan*, was
barbacoa, a name originally derived from
a Taino word. Spanish borrowed the
term, which passed into English in the
late seventeenth century as *barbecue*.

For a word with a similar meaning
see PIRATE.

budget

an allocated sum of money; a plan for spending money; offering basic value for money

*It was teatime when we arrived, and…the room was full of visitors. One (a former student) was a physicist, now working in Denmark. Another (also a former student) had just purchased a **budget** airline in the American Southwest.*
(MAUREEN FREELY,
ENLIGHTENMENT, 2007)

*We settled on a longer period to film the peak of the dry season (or so we hoped) from early August into November; and the best of the rains in January, February and March, with an extension into April if the **budget** allowed.*
(AMANDA BARRETT,
NATURE'S GREAT EVENTS, 2009)

*The first and most important thing Judith and Gordon need to do is to establish their requirements in monetary terms. This means setting a **budget**, and reviewing it regularly.*
(GOOD HOUSEKEEPING, JULY 2009)

Although the mention of *budget* brings the thorny question of finance to most minds, the word had already had a very long history before such considerations became part of it. The Romans had the term *bulga* for 'a leather bag' which, according to the Latin lexicographer Festus, was derived from a Gallic source. (The Romans also used the word humorously for 'a womb'.) Old French borrowed it as *bouge* and formed the diminutive *bougette*, which was taken into Middle English as *bouget*, 'bag, wallet, pouch', in the fifteenth century.

Towards the end of the sixteenth century *budget* referred not only to the pouch but also to its contents, whatever they might be. In an extension of this use, the word was later applied to 'a package of papers containing the annual financial statement presented to the British Parliament by the Chancellor of the Exchequer'. The first recorded use in the context of government finance was in a satirical pamphlet of 1733 entitled THE BUDGET OPENED, in which the First Minister Sir Robert Walpole was likened to a quack doctor opening his bag of fake remedies. Its next appearance, in THE GENTLEMEN'S MAGAZINE in 1764, shows that *budget* had since become established as a political term. In this financial sense the word remained linked to government but in the second half of the nineteenth century it was also applied to more modest domestic accounts.

The verb *to budget* has come to mean 'to plan one's expenditure' or 'to build the cost of something into one's financial plan' and dates from the 1880s. In recent times the word has also become an adjective meaning 'inexpensive, within the financial reach of most people', so that *budget car-hire*, *budget holidays* and *budget ranges* of various goods are now on offer.

☛ When a political opponent derisively calls the Chancellor's budget *bilge*, he is being more accurate than he perhaps realises. Surprising though it may seem, the Chancellor's *budget* and the *bilge* of a ship are etymologically linked. The swollen shape of a leather bag or bottle suggested the curve of a ship's hull and so, in the seventeenth century, *bulge* (from Middle English *bulge*, from Old French *bouge*, 'leather bag', from Latin *bulga*) was used for this part of the vessel before finally being superseded by the variant *bilge*. The foul water that collects in this part of the ship is also called *bilge*, hence the word's use as a slang term for 'rubbish, nonsense' in the early twentieth century. Of course, *bulge* still means 'a protuberance, a hump' in contemporary English. Thus *budget*, *bilge* and *bulge* all owe their origin to the one source.

bugbear
a cause of irritation; an object of irrational dread

One common complaint by many learners is the fear of not being able to remember everything. Unfortunately, this has been a major bugbear for many learners because we have still not moved away from rote learning type of exams, which is a poor assessment of one's intelligence or creative abilities.
(CAPE TIMES, SOUTH AFRICA, 29 OCTOBER 2008)

'Security is a bit of a bugbear for me – I've had my scooter stolen three times.'
(WESTMINSTER TOWN CRIER PETER MOORE IN THE WESTMINSTER REPORTER, SPRING 2009)

The *bugbear* was a Tudor invention, a terrifying ghost, presumably in the shape of a great bear, invoked to terrify the young into good behaviour. In his Italian and English dictionary A WORLDE OF WORDES (1598), John Florio teams this creature with two more endearing spectres common to Tudor children: *Imagined spirits that nurces fraie their babes withall to make them leave crying, as we say bug-beare, or else rawe head and bloodie bone.*

The sixteenth-century adult used *bugbear* as an evocative description of an 'irrational dread or fear' which casts its shadow over life. Alexander Pope, writing in the eighteenth century, employs the term to satirical effect:

To the world no bugbear is so great As want of figure and a small estate.
(IMITATIONS OF HORACE, EPISTLES, 1733)

By the mid-nineteenth century, however, the sense was weakening to mean nothing more than 'a persistent annoyance, an irritation'. In a letter of 14 September 1880, the novelist George Eliot writes: *Our only bugbear – it is a very little one – is the having to make preliminary arrangements towards settling ourselves in the new house.*

Bug comes from Middle English *bugge*, meaning 'scarecrow' and then 'hobgoblin', and was current in that sense until the early eighteenth century: Hamlet (c. 1601) speaks of *bugs and goblins* in his life. Its origins may be Welsh, from *bwg*, meaning 'ghost'. Or it may be related to a Norwegian dialect word *bugge*, 'important man'. There are possible links with *bugaboo* and the nineteenth-century *bogy* or *bogey*, ancestor of the present-day *bogeyman*.

The use of *bug* for 'an insect', especially 'a beetle', which arose in the seventeenth century, may be a transference of the same word, though it is not clear why a term meaning 'scary thing' should be applied to insects. Skeat is amongst those who suggest that the terrifying *bug* may have influenced an Old English word *budd*, meaning 'beetle', and given it an overtone of unpleasantness that *budd* alone did not have. Certainly, the *bedbugs* to which the word was often applied were distasteful enough but hardly terrifying. However, there is no real proof of the theory.

The use of *bug* for 'a germ' and also for 'a device for secretly listening in on people' developed from the sense 'insect' in the twentieth century.

bunkum
an inaccurate or nonsensical statement, opinion or report; claptrap

A lot of bunkum is spoken about coal mining. Usually by ill-informed folk at surface level. The truth is that working in the dark, crawling through low-level

*tunnels and risking your health is both
dirty and dangerous.*
(LIVERPOOL ECHO, 11 JANUARY 2007)

*They've given us some great laughs, but
YouTube and other video-sharing venues
have also smothered cyberspace with
homemade bosh and **bunkum**.*
(WASHINGTON POST,
11 NOVEMBER 2007)

On 25 February 1820 Felix Walker,
the representative for Buncombe
County, North Carolina, addressed
the US Congress in a debate on the
Missouri Question. His speech was
both long-winded and largely irrelevant. Although several of his fellow
members urged him to draw his dia-
tribe to a close, he doggedly persisted.
It had been his intention, he said, *to
make a speech for Buncombe*. In other
words, the primary purpose of his
contribution had not been to add to
the debate but to impress his elec-
torate. Before long *buncombe* and its
variant *bunkum* were being used for
'political rhetoric that is all hot air
and no substance', and then more
generally for 'claptrap, twaddle'. In
the former sense the word had made
its way across the Atlantic by the
middle of the nineteenth century.

The shortened form *bunk* dates from
around the beginning of the twentieth
century in American English. It was
famously used by Henry Ford, founder
of the Ford motor company, who said:

*'History is more or less bunk. It's
tradition. We don't want tradition.
We want to live in the present, and
the only history that is worth a tinker's
damn is the history that we make today'.*
(CHICAGO TRIBUNE, 1916)

bureau
a desk; an office

*MEN WANTED. Free passage on cattle
boats to Liverpool feeding cattle. Low fee.
Easy work. Fast boats. Apply International
and Atlantic Employment **Bureau** –
Greenwich Street.*
(SINCLAIR LEWIS, OUR MR WRENN,
THE ROMANTIC ADVENTURES OF A
GENTLE MAN, 1914)

*Hannah picked her way around the room's
rim...She made a pretence of digging
around in the writing **bureau** as Harry
collapsed on the sofa.*
(KATE MORTON,
THE HOUSE AT RIVERTON, 2006)

Burel was a type of rough-textured
brown woollen cloth, sometimes used
for coarse clothing. The word, which
was borrowed from Old French, is a
diminutive of *bure*, 'dark or russet
brown', which ultimately goes back to
Latin *burrus*, and Greek *purros*, 'flame
red'. This Greek adjective, in turn, is a
derivative of *pur*, 'fire'.

Written references to *burel* in English
date back to around the beginning of
the fourteenth century. Chaucer speaks
of men roughly clad in *borel* (a variant of
burel). An adjective *borel*, which meant
'unlearned, rough-mannered', derived
from this particular use:

> *How he I am but rude and borrel'
> Yet nearer ways I know.*
> (SPENSER, SHEPHEARDS
> CALENDER, 1579)

In France from the thirteenth century
onwards, however, there are records of
burel being spread over writing tables in
courts and offices to provide a firm
surface that yielded under the pressure
of the soft quill nib. Gradually, from this
particular use, French *burel* was transformed into *bureau* and was eventually,
according to Randle Cotgrave, variously
applied to the cloth, the desk beneath it

and even, on occasion, to the office where the desk was situated (DICTIONARIE OF THE FRENCH AND ENGLISH TONGUES, 1611). Thus when *bureau* was borrowed into English in the eighteenth century, it denoted both 'a chest of drawers with a writing flap' and 'an office for public administration'.

Nowadays a *bureau* can be an antique desk (with a substantial price tag to match), a *ticket bureau* or *Citizens Advice Bureau*, or a government department (the *employment bureau*). This last sense is particularly common in America. As *bureaux* (usually British English) or *bureaus* (usually American) have proliferated, so have the *bureaucrats* (mid-19th cent) that staff them and the *bureaucracy* (early 19th cent) associated with them. It's a long way from a piece of common, rough cloth on the back of a medieval Frenchman.

butterfly
an insect with a long body and large, usually brightly coloured wings

*Now he wasn't hungry any more – and he wasn't a little caterpillar any more. He was a big, fat caterpillar. He built a small house, called a cocoon, around himself He stayed inside for more than two weeks. Then he nibbled a hole in the cocoon, pushed his way out and...he was a beautiful **butterfly**!'*
(ERIC CARLE, THE VERY HUNGRY CATERPILLAR, 1970)

*I had caught her studying me curiously, as if she was watching a **butterfly** emerge from its chrysalis. She was pleased with me, I felt.*
(JULIAN CLARY, MURDER MOST FAB, 2007)

Anyone watching these graceful creatures flit around the garden buddleia or nettle bed would be convinced by the theory that the insect was not originally called a *butterfly* but a *flutterby* – an understandable confusion since fluttering is what butterflies do best, while the insect in them certainly suggests some species of fly. Sadly this can be nothing more than a charming folk etymology; the word goes back a thousand years and no evidence of *flutterby* has ever been recorded. Old English had the compound *buttorflēoge*, which became *butterflie* in Middle English, so what can the connection with *butter* be?

One theory promotes an old-wives' tale that butterflies stole milk and cream; Skeat cites German *molken-dieb*, 'milk-thief', as an alternative to *butterfliege*, 'butterfly', though this really only serves to confirm that the belief was once prevalent. An even less appealing suggestion rests on the Dutch synonym *boterschijte*, literally 'buttershit', and points out that the butterfly's excrement is both creamy and yellow, like butter. This last offering is probably the more likely of the two.

See CATERPILLAR.

buttonhole
to seize someone physically or metaphorically in order to speak to him

*The Los Angeles Area Chamber of Commerce sent 50 folks to Capitol Hill this week to **buttonhole** members of Congress to return California's 'fair share' of the revenue it sends to Washington.*

George Kieffer, chairman of the chamber, said that California gets about 84 cents out of every dollar it sends to Washington and that it should get more to help deal with illegal immigration, crowded port issues and other needs.
(WASHINGTON POST, 20 MAY 2004)

In the eighteenth century, when a gentleman wished to detain someone in conversation, it was common practice for him to seize a button of his jacket and hold on to it, thereby forcibly keeping his undivided attention. In Oliver Goldsmith's play THE GOOD-NATURED MAN (1768), for example, the line *I take my friend by the button* meant 'I detain him in conversation'. The habit was so common that, by the early nineteenth century, the term *buttonholder* had been coined, to be followed some thirty years later by the verb *to buttonhold*.

The custom was something of a nuisance, for *to buttonhold* implied that the person was being kept very much against his will. Sometimes drastic action was called for; the American periodical HOME JOURNAL (21 January 1880) reported that *Charles Lamb, being button-held one day by Coleridge...cut off the button*. Nor was this annoying habit uniquely British, for the French had an equivalent phrase, *serrer le bouton à quelqu'un*.

Folk etymology has it that in the 1860s, when jackets that buttoned to the neck were finally abandoned in the interests of fashion, tailors still made a top buttonhole in the lapel which was just large enough to hook a finger through, so that the verb *buttonhold* gradually changed to *buttonhole*. It is more likely, however, to be a simple matter of confusion between two very similar words, *buttonhole* being the more common as well as possibly easier to pronounce.

buxom
well-rounded, full-bosomed

*There were two women seated on the other side of the table: one was old and armed with a Catherine Cookson novel, the other, leafing indifferently through a celebrity magazine, was a fortyish blonde, **buxom***
as an overstuffed turkey. She was wearing siren-red lipstick and a top to match that was half a size too tight.
(KATE ATKINSON, WHEN WILL THERE BE GOOD NEWS?, 2008)

*Travelling with Rose is Victoria (Tor), her **buxom** best buddy, who hopes a sojourn in India will furnish a well-connected expatriate hubby.*
(MSLEXIA, APRIL/MAY/JUNE 2009)

This adjective has undergone startling changes in meaning over the centuries. The word goes back to an Old English verb *būgan*, 'to bend'. From this, early Middle English (perhaps via an unattested Old English form) derived the adjective *būhsom* with the sense of 'pliant' and hence 'yielding, humble, obedient'. By the fourteenth century the forms *boxam* and *buxam* had evolved, still meaning 'compliant'.

By the late sixteenth century, however, *buxom* had come to mean 'lively, spirited'. Shakespeare uses the word in this way in HENRY V (1599), where Pistol says:

Bardolph a soldier, firm and sound of heart,
Of buxom valour.

Liveliness suggests physical well-being, and so the next shift of meaning was towards 'healthy, vigorous'. To be *in buxom health* was a blessing in an age of primitive medical care, and men and women alike were described as *buxom*. It was only in the nineteenth century that the word was restricted to women, with the emphasis on general plumpness (considered a sign of good health), and then on having full breasts.

☛ Old English *būgan*, 'bend', is also the source of *bow*.

For other words that have undergone a complete change in meaning, see NICE and SILLY.

C

cad

a man who acts dishonourably, one who does not take the feelings of others into account

'You won't go back to your wife?' I said at last.
'Never.'
'She's willing to forget everything that's happened and start afresh. She'll never make you a single reproach.'
'She can go to hell.'
'You don't care if people think you an utter blackguard? You don't care if she and your children have to beg their bread?'
'Not a damn.'
I was silent for a moment in order to give greater force to my next remark. I spoke as deliberately as I could. 'You are a most unmitigated **cad**.*'*
'Now that you've got that of your chest, let's go and have dinner.'
(W SOMERSET MAUGHAM, THE MOON AND SIXPENCE, 1919)

Cads are bottom-pinchers. They steal your drink, flirt with your mother and smell of stewed smoke and hair wax. And they pull very, very well. Something about that heady combination of arrogance and lust draws women close, nightly.
(THE OBSERVER, 21 JULY 2002)

Sarkozy's behaviour towards Her Majesty was that of a **cad***, a buffoon, a jerk, a pathetic human being with no manners – a bad European, and a worse Frenchman.*
(THE TELEGRAPH, 5 JUNE 2009)

The origins of this word lie in CADET and *caddie*. In the seventeenth century *caddie*, a Scottish term derived from *cadet*, denoted a porter, 'someone who made a living by doing odd jobs'. By the 1830s the word had been taken up and shortened to *cad* by the English upper classes. At public schools such as Eton and in particular at Oxford University, a *cad* was a rough, low-class townsman who hung about the college precincts waiting to be hired to fetch and carry for the students, and then more generally 'a coarse-mannered fellow'. A verse from Arthur Hughes Clough's satirical poem DIPSYCHUS (1850) captures the superior, dismissive tone:

I drive through the streets, and I care not
a damn;
The people they stare, and they ask who
I am;
And if I should chance to run over a cad,
I can pay for the damage if ever so bad.
So pleasant it is to have money, heigh ho!
So pleasant it is to have money.

Cad has survived into the twenty-first century as a term for 'a man who shows scant regard for the feelings of others', but now has a dated ring.

For other words for 'scroundrel', see BLACKGUARD and VILLAIN.

caddy (tea-caddy)

a container (for storing tea)

On the walls hung boathooks and field tools, posters advertising tea and

*illustrations demonstrating the processes of picking and blending and packing. Glass cabinets displayed the pages of yellowed manuals, antique spoons, silver tongs, **caddies** and decorated ceramics.*
(PHIL HOGAN,
ALL THIS WILL BE YOURS, 2005)

*It took her a couple of seconds of panic before she realised it was an urn, and that inside the urn was what was left of her mother. For some reason she had expected something tasteful and classical...not something made from a kind of plastic material that looked for all the world like a tea **caddy**.*
(KATE ATKINSON,
ONE GOOD TURN, 2006)

Rather disappointingly this cosy little word associated with everything that is warm and comforting about a nice cup of tea is nothing more than a measurement of weight commonly used in China and Southeast Asia. The *katî*, a word of Malay origin, was roughly equivalent to 1⅓lb (625 grammes). The term was taken into English for commercial purposes as *catty* in the sixteenth century. *Caddy*, found from the end of the eighteenth century, is a corruption of this and referred either to 'a small box containing one caddy of tea', or simply to 'a box for storing tea'.

Such storage boxes, however, were decorative and lined with lead foil and, since good quality tea was very expensive, could be locked with a key. Walsh quotes *an affecting advertisement from a London newspaper copied by Horace Smith in 'Tin Trumpet'*:

If this should meet the eye of Emma D–, who absented herself last Wednesday from her father's house, she is implored to return, when she will be received with undiminished affection by her almost heart-broken parents. If nothing can persuade her to listen to their joint appeal, – should she be determined to bring their grey hairs with sorrow to the

grave, – should she never mean to revisit a home where she had passed so many happy years, – it is at least expected, if she be not totally lost to all sense of propriety, that she will, without a moment's further delay, send back the key of the tea-caddy.

In recent years *caddy* has been applied to any storage container for small items: a box that protects DVDs, for instance, or a *kitchen caddy* for collecting compostable kitchen waste.

For a different meaning of *caddy*, see CADET. See also TEA. And for other words from Malay, see WORDS FROM THE MALAY ARCHIPELAGO (page 65).

cadet
a younger son; a young recruit in the armed services, police, etc.

*The boy-waiter came back, tentative as a fox cub, and made to take the tray, a carroty lock falling limply forward from his brow. With that colouring he could be yet another of the Duignan clan, **cadet** branch.*
(JOHN BANVILLE, THE SEA, 2005)

*The Ogre appears at the door and the dart-throwing stops. Boys stand to attention, like army **cadets**.*
(ROSE TREMAIN, PEERLESS, 2005)

*Space **cadets** will love this reconstruction of the American space shuttle at the Euro Space Center in Belgium.*
(THE TIMES, 9 MAY 2009)

In the fifteenth century, the younger son of a noble Gascon family was known as the *capdet*, 'little chief', (from Late Latin *capitellum*, 'little head', a diminutive of Latin *caput*, 'head'). Many of these younger sons were sent to court with others of their kind from all over France to enter the army. Here their dialect word *capdet*, which became French *cadet*, was understood to mean 'younger son' and then more specifi-

WORDS FROM THE MALAY ARCHIPELAGO

From the early sixteenth century the Portuguese, the Dutch and the English vied for trading rights in the Malay Archipelago. A number of Malay words in English reflect this exploration and commerce. Among them are:

bamboo (16th cent): from a Malay word introduced into Europe as *mambu* by the Portuguese. Its use in English was eventually supplanted by *bambos*, from *bamboes*, an unexplained Dutch variant (the initial *b* and final *s* are a mystery). In English this was misunderstood to be a plural, so in the eighteenth century the *s* was dropped to give *bamboo*.

batik (19th cent): this method of producing a pattern in fabric by waxing the areas not to be penetrated by the dye was originally a Javanese term meaning 'painted'. It came into English through Malay.

cockatoo (17th cent): from Malay *kakatua* through Dutch *kaketoe*. Several authorities assume the word is imitative of the bird's cry. The English spelling is undoubtedly influenced by *cock*.

compound (17th cent): from Malay *kampong*, 'enclosure, village, cluster of buildings'. Borrowed into English by way of either Dutch *kampoeng* or Portuguese *campon*. The term was used for European factory sites or residential enclosures, first in the Malay Archipelago and then in India, China, etc.

gecko (18th cent): from Malay *ge'kok*, representing the noise the lizard utters.

gong (17th cent): from Malay *gōng*, representing the sound of the instrument.

kapok (18th cent): Malay *kāpok*, the name of the fibre surrounding the seeds inside the fruit of the silk cotton tree.

orangutan (late 17th cent): Malay *ōrang ūtan* means 'man of the forest', and hence 'wild man'. In the seventeenth century, this was not the Malay term for the animal but was probably used by some of the population to refer to the uncivilised tribesmen who inhabited the dense forests. It was the Europeans who mistakenly understood it to refer to the apes.

sago (16th cent): from Malay *sāgū*. English originally had *sagu* from Portuguese. The form *sago* is from Dutch and gradually gained acceptance in the seventeenth and eighteenth centuries.

See also CADDY and FROM ALL POINTS OF THE COMPASS (page 16).

---

cally 'a younger son of noble birth who was embarking upon a military career as an officer'. This was a common practice for young gentlemen up to the French Revolution. The hero of Edmond Rostand's play CYRANO DE BERGERAC (written in 1897 but set in the seventeenth century) was the leader of a company of Gascon cadets. The word *cadet* in both French senses was borrowed into English in the early seventeenth century; nowadays it refers mainly to 'a young trainee in the armed forces or police force'.

Cadet met with a different fate across the border in Scotland, where the variant English forms *cadee* and *caddie* were used. Initially they were synonymous with the French term, but by the mid-eighteenth century *caddie* had come also to refer to a man or boy who waited about in the street to be hired for porterage, errands and other odd jobs. In one of his LETTERS FROM THE NORTH OF SCOTLAND (c. 1754) Edward Burt describes to a friend in London the customs and manners of Inverness, remarking how the caddies organised themselves into bands, rather like an army:

The Cawdys, a very useful Black-Guard, who attend...publick Places to go of Errands; and though they are Wretches, that in Rags lye upon the Stairs, and in the Streets at Night, yet are they often considerably trusted... This Corps has a kind of Captain.., presiding over them, whom they call the Constable of the Cawdys.

This use eventually gave rise to a slang term for 'a scoundrel' (see CAD), and by the mid-nineteenth century *caddie* (variant *caddy*) also referred to the lad who carried a golfer's clubs around the links in the Scottish sport of golf.

☛ Latin *caput*, 'head', is found in many English words, among which are:

biceps (17th cent): a muscle with two 'heads' or tendons, from Latin *biceps*, a compound of *bi-*, 'two', and *ceps* from *caput*, 'head'.

capital (13th cent): from Old French (12th cent), from Latin *capitālis*, 'of the head', and hence 'principal', 'chief'.

captain (14th cent): Middle English *capitain*, from Old French, from Late Latin *capāneus*, 'chief, head man', from Latin *caput*, 'head'.

chief (13th cent): Middle English *chef, chief*, from Old French, from unattested Vulgar Latin *capum*, from Latin *caput*, 'head'. The use of *chef* for 'a head cook' was taken into English from the French phrase *chef de cuisine*, literally 'head of the kitchen', in the first half of the nineteenth century.

cadge
to beg, to scrounge

*Time to **cadge** some rhubarb roots from friends or neighbours, February is the calm before the storm, says our gardening guru Caroline Foley.*
(THE OBSERVER, 1 FEBRUARY 2008)

*They are the ex-smokers of devolved power, boring the room to death with accounts of how much better they feel, and how they've started noticing the stale smell on those yet to see the light, but they're secretly gagging for a drag. The minute the missus leaves the room, they'll **cadge** a crafty puff, and before you know it they'll be back on 30 a day.*
(THE INDEPENDENT, 28 MAY 2009)

In the fifteenth century, a *cadger* was a travelling dealer who would buy dairy produce in the country to sell in the town, and manufactured merchandise in the town to take back to the country. It is thought that the word comes from an unattested Middle English *caggen* 'to carry produce'. It seems that over time the cadger turned from an honest dealer into a rogue who made extra money for himself wherever possible by coaxing and begging from his customers, for in the first half of the nineteenth century the meaning of the word shifted from 'hawker' to 'one who makes a livelihood from begging'. The HOLDERNESS GLOSSARY (1877) defines *cadger* as *a loose character who goes from door to door soliciting assistance.*

The noun *cadger*, meaning 'a scrounger', is still found in modern English, but less so than the verb *to cadge*, a back-formation which remains common – the desire to get something for nothing seems not to have changed down the centuries.

calculate
to work out, to reckon

The typical Londoner drives 3,650 miles a year, drinks 78 pints of alcohol but just 12 litres of mineral water, eats 7lbs of sweets and throws away nearly half a ton of waste.

*The fascinating insight into daily life comes in a report aimed to **calculate** the impact London has on the environment.*
(EVENING STANDARD,
24 SEPTEMBER 2002)

'How old are you?' he asked.

*Shmuel thought about it and looked down at his fingers and they wiggled in the air, as if he was trying to **calculate**. 'I'm nine,' he said. 'My birthday is April the fifteenth nineteen thirty-four.'*
(JOHN BOYNE, THE BOY IN THE
STRIPED PYJAMAS, 2006)

In Latin a *calculus* was 'a small pebble', the word being a diminutive form of *calx* (stem *calc-*), 'limestone'. It was also the term for 'a counter on an abacus' since small pebbles were used for this purpose. The derived Latin verb *calculāre*, therefore, meant 'to reckon, to compute'. *Calculate*, which comes from *calculāt-*, the past participle stem of *calculāre*, was taken into English in the sixteenth century.

The sense 'to plan for a purpose, to design' dates from the first half of the seventeenth century.

☛ The stem of *calx* (which ultimately derives from Greek *khalix*, 'pebble') is *calc-*, from which the New Latin word *calcium* was derived by the British chemist Sir Humphry Davy in 1808 as a name for the reactive metalic element he had just isolated.

In the seventeenth century Latin *calculus* was also borrowed directly into English in two very different contexts. As it meant 'small stone' in Latin, it

was not surprising that it should be applied in medicine to the 'stones' or hard masses which form in organs such as the kidneys or gall bladder. Given the connection with *calculate*, developing strands of mathematics, such as *integral* and *differential calculus*, were appropriately so called.

calendar
a table of the months, weeks and days in a year

*Ampliatus had never cared much for Vulcanalia. The festival marked that point in the **calendar** when nights fell noticeably earlier and mornings had to start by candlelight: the end of the promise of summer and the start of the long, melancholy decline into winter.*
(ROBERT HARRIS, POMPEII, 2003)

*If he stretched out his own hand now and touched the wall, he could feel where the plaster had been scratched away by men who'd lain here years before.... One man had scored a **calendar**, but he had given every month thirty days, so the calendar was next to useless.*
(SARAH WATERS,
THE NIGHT WATCH, 2006)

Each moneylender in ancient Rome kept a *calendārium*, an account-book which detailed the interest he would collect on the *calendae*, that is 'the Calends', the first day of the month. *Calendārium* progressed into Middle English in the thirteenth century by way of Anglo-French *calender* and Old French *calendier*. The word can be traced back still further. Latin *calendae* goes back to the root *kal-*, 'to shout', since on the Calends of each month the pontifex minor would publicly proclaim the days upon which the Nones and Ides (normally the 5th and 13th, sometimes the 7th and 15th) would fall, together with any festivals.

The *calendula*, the orange- or gold-coloured pot marigold, obviously takes its name from the *calends*, though authorities differ in their suggestions as to why. Some say that the flower came into bloom on the first of the month, but this seems rather vague: a more satisfying explanation is that the medicinal qualities of the plant, which are still recognised today, were helpful during menstruation.

canard
a fabricated report or news item, an unfounded story or view

*All nations have national narratives which are, at best, partial and, at worst, hallucinatory. They are always clichés. The old **canard** that the Brits were 'tolerant, fair-minded, self-sacrificing and incorruptible' has simply been replaced by a new one to which Leith vigorously and unquestioningly subscribes. British Teeth colludes in the fundamental simplification that we have become vicious dullards and crap at everything to boot.*
(EVENING STANDARD,
13 AUGUST 2001)

*It [the Lan Club] is also ridiculous because the massive space is so ostentatiously and extravagantly decked out that it jars in communist China. And lest any Kissingeresque character should repeat his **canard** that China is no longer communist, they should try standing at Tiananmen Square and just mumbling something derogatory about the Chinese leadership, or loving about the Falun Gong gang. Then they will see if China is still communist or not.*
(THE SPECTATOR, 7 NOVEMBER 2007)

Canard is the French word for 'duck'. It comes from Old French *canart*, a derivative of *caner*, a verb that is imitative of a duck's quack. But *canard* has also come to mean 'an unfounded piece of news, a tall story' in both French and English.

Indeed, there is a satirical newspaper in France called LE CANARD ENCHAÎNÉ, literally 'The Chained-Up Duck', a reference to the muzzled press:

'News stops at the bedroom door.' This is the enshrined view of the French media expressed this week by the satirical weekly Le Canard Enchaîné *in response to speculation about the unborn child of France's minister for justice, Rachida Dati. It is also, one suspects, French for 'we don't know who the father is'.*
(THE INDEPENDENT,
6 SEPTEMBER 2008)

In this particular sense *canard* has been current in English since around the middle of the nineteenth century. In his DICTIONNAIRE DE LA LANGUE FRANÇAISE (1877) the French lexicographer Littré traces it to an old French idiom: *vendre le canard a moitié* literally means, 'to half-sell a duck'. Anyone trying to do this, of course, has no intention of selling and is merely trying to make a fool of a gullible customer. *Vendeur de canards a moitié* to denote a seller thus engaged also appears in Randle Cotgrave's DICTIONARIE OF THE FRENCH AND ENGLISH TONGUES (1611). This meaning of *canard*, therefore, seems to have originated in a humorous story that has been lost in the mists of time.

Some authorities, evidently ignorant of Cotgrave's dictionary entry, have attributed the term to Norbert Cornelissen, a Frenchman who is said to have carried out a hoax on the French press. As the story he told was about ducks and was widely believed by his readers, *canard* came to mean 'tall story'. Cornelissen claimed that he had twenty ducks. He killed one of them and threw it to the other nineteen, who snapped it up. He then killed a second duck and threw that to its remaining fellows. Similarly he killed a third and a fourth and so on until only one was left. The last duck had thus feasted upon all its companions. And if you believe that, you have just been sold half a duck.

canary
a songbird of the finch family, kept domestically in a cage

Little Clotilda,
Well and hearty,
Thought she'd like to give a party.
But as her friends were shy and wary,
Nobody came
But her own **canary**.
(ANON)

Mary had a pretty bird,
Feathers bright and yellow,
Slender legs – upon my word
He was a pretty fellow.

The sweetest notes he'd always sing,
Which much delighted Mary;
And near the cage she'd ever sit
To hear her own **canary**.
(ANON)

Miners always used to carry a **canary** *in a cage when they went underground. If there was any escaping gas the bird would croak, allowing the miners to get the hell out of there in time.*
(BOB GELDOF,
GELDOF IN AFRICA, 2005)

'You are looking well, Oscar,' I said, shaking him warmly by the hand. He was wearing **canary**-*yellow kid gloves and sporting the green coat with the astrakhan collar that I had seen him wearing in the cab in the Strand two days before.*
(GYLES BRANDRETH,
OSCAR WILDE AND THE
CANDLELIGHT MURDERS, 2007)

This small yellow songbird is native to the *Canary Islands*. It did not lend its name to the islands, however, but took its name from them. Curiously these volcanic islands, situated off the north-western coast of Africa, were named after a different creature altogether.

Early in the first century, Juba II (c. 50 BC–AD 24), king of the North African states of Numidia and Mauretania, sent a company of men on a voyage of exploration to the islands. The men returned with tales of a breed of great dog which lived on the largest of them. The island therefore came to be known to the Romans as *Canāria insula*, 'Dog Island', from Latin *canārius*, 'pertaining to dogs', from *canis*, 'dog'. Although King Juba's account of the voyage is long lost, some the facts contained in it are available through the writings of Pliny the Elder (AD 23–79).

At the end of the fifteenth century, the Canaries became part of the Kingdom of Castile, and the islands lent their name to various European imports: the popular, sweet canary wine much loved by Shakespeare's Falstaff; a spirited sixteenth-century court dance mentioned by Nash, Shakespeare and others; and, of course, the little songbirds, initially known as *canary birds*, which arrived in England in the sixteenth century. The colour of the captive cagebirds' plumage is now the *canary yellow* of the paintbox, a result of interbreeding over the centuries.

☞ Other words from Latin *canis*, 'dog', are:

kennel (15th cent): from unattested Old Northern French *kenil*, from Old French *chenil*, from unattested Vulgar Latin *canil*, from Latin *canis*, 'dog'.

chenille (18th cent): the French word means 'caterpillar', from Latin *canicula*, 'little dog' from its hairy appearance, from *canis*, 'dog'. The velvety cord was therefore named because its appearance and texture was like that of a hairy caterpillar.

A word that has no connection with *canis*, though many have made the link, is CANNIBAL. See also GORILLA.

cancel
to withdraw, to nullify

*The lamb curry was prepared. She had made it last night with tomatoes and new potatoes. There was chicken saved in the freezer from the last time Dr Azad had been invited but had **cancelled** at the last minute.*
(MONICA ALI, BRICK LANE, 2003)

*Just as every plate of soba noodles I eat today **cancels** out a Lord Toffingham lolly I consumed in my youth, so – I like to think – every enlightened thought I have in my thirties compensates for an unenlightened one I had in my teens.*
(ANDREW COLLINS,
WHERE DID IT ALL GO RIGHT?, 2003)

The verb *to cancel* has the same origin as CHANCELLOR. In Roman times, when a deed, a legal document or a contract was nullified it was done by crossing it through horizontally and vertically, the result being a lattice pattern. This gave the verb *cancelāre*, 'to score out in a lattice form', from *cancelli*, 'lattice-work'. Medieval legal practices followed the Roman pattern and so French had *canceller*, from which English borrowed *cancel* in the first half of the fifteenth century. This original sense of *cancel*, 'to cross out', is still current, though today a simple line serves the purpose. Towards the end of the fifteenth century the verb was also applied more generally to mean 'to annul, to invalidate', with regard to debts, promises, arrangements or appointments.

☛ The east end of a church has been known as the *chancel* since about 1300. This word is also from Latin *cancelli* and came into English by way of Late Latin *cancellus* and then Old French *chancel*. Formerly, this area, which contains the altar and the choir stalls, was separated off from the main body of the building by a latticed screen.

cancer
a malignant tumour, a diseased growth

*A long hard working life in a factory – its structure lined with asbestos – and the accompanying lifestyle of stress and smoking was more than likely to end that way. She was also lonely and bitter, and the past, like the **cancer** itself, gnawed away at her.*
(MAVIS CHEEK,
THE SEX LIFE OF MY AUNT, 2002)

*For a week, I compose a great and poetic speech for my children about how there are little thoughts in your head that can grow until they eat your entire mind. Just tiny little thoughts – they are like a **cancer**, there is no telling what triggers the spread, or who will be struck, and why some get it and others are spared.*
(ANNE ENRIGHT,
THE GATHERING, 2007)

The name of this much-feared disease originates in Greek *karkinos*, meaning 'a crab' and then 'a zodiac constellation' and, finally, 'a tumour'. According to the second-century Greek physician Galen, the malignant tumour was so named because the swollen and distorted veins in the surrounding tissue looked something like the legs of a crab. *Karkinos* was taken into Latin as *cancer*, where it had the same senses as the Greek term. Latin *cancer* was borrowed twice into English.

First of all, it was taken into Old English as *cancre* under the influence of Old Northern French. The term became *canker* and was used for any chronic festering ulcer but more particularly for 'a cancer'. Nowadays, *canker* is applied to 'ulcerous sores' in animals and to 'rotting plant tissue'.

In the fourteenth century the word was borrowed into Middle English, this time as *cancer*, and was used in the astrological sense to denote 'the fourth sign of the zodiac'. And then, in the first half of the sixteenth century, *cancer* started to be used as a medical term, initially to describe any kind of non-healing sore or ulcer and later, in the early seventeenth century, 'a malignant tumour'. *Cancer* had more or less replaced *canker* in this latter sense by around 1700.

candidate
someone who seeks nomination for a job or position

'In the present circumstances, where we have more than two obvious candidates, the most egalitarian method would seem to be to take a vote by way of a ballot. Each person should write the name of their preferred candidate on one of these pieces of paper.'
(CARO FRASER,
A CALCULATING HEART, 2004)

At Oxford in the late fifties some of the teaching I did was for Magdalen… One year I was also drafted in to help mark and interview candidates for the history scholarships. It didn't seem all that long since I had been interviewed myself, and I was nervous lest my marks should differ from those of my more experienced colleagues by whom I was every bit as intimidated as the candidates were.
(ALAN BENNETT,
UNTOLD STORIES, 2005)

In Shakespeare's TITUS ANDRONICUS (1584), Titus is begged to stand for election as emperor of Rome by his brother Marcus, the people's tribune:

Titus Andronicus, the people of Rome,
Whose friend in justice thou hast ever been,
Send thee by me, their Tribune and
their trust,
This palliament of white and spotless hue;
And name thee in election for the empire
With these our late-deceased Emperor's
sons:
Be candidatus then, and put it on,
And help to set a head on headless Rome.

In ancient Rome anyone who put himself forward for election to an office would appear in public in a white toga, a symbolic statement that his character was spotless and that he was therefore upright and trustworthy. Such a man was described as *candidātus*, 'wearing a white robe', a word derived from *candidus*, 'shining white', from *candēre*, 'to shine, to be white'. The word, if not the associated white toga, entered English in the early seventeenth century.

☛ *Candēre* is the source of several other words in English:

candid (17th cent): meaning 'frank, straightforward, honest', comes from French *candide*, from Latin *candidus*, 'gleaming white', and hence 'pure, sincere', from *candēre*.

candle: an Old English ecclesiastical borrowing of Latin *candēla*, 'light, torch', from *candēre*, 'to shine'.

candour (17th cent): from Latin *candor*, 'whiteness, purity, sincerity', from *candēre*.

For another word whose etymology lies in Roman politics, see AMBITION.

cannibal
a person who eats the flesh of other human beings

I knew I had seen eyes like that before and then, all at once, I remembered the cannibals – half a dozen dissolute-looking, furtive-mannered men shackled outside the Vila court

house years ago. My father had said, 'See their eyes? That's how you spot a cannibal, Sandy, and it's worth bearing in mind in case chaps like that ever ask you to lunch.'
(ALEXANDER FRATER,
CHASING THE MONSOON, 1990)

How did you choose the metaphor of the cannibal?

RP: If your son, daughter, husband, or wife was a cannibal, you wouldn't let them sit in the basement and eat body parts and store them in the refrigerator. So if it's not okay to be a cannibal, why is it okay to be an addict?
(INTERVIEW WITH ROBERT
POZNANOVICH AND ANDREW
WAINWRIGHT, AUTHORS OF IT'S NOT
OKAY TO BE A CANNIBAL: HOW TO
KEEP ADDICTION FROM EATING YOUR
FAMILY ALIVE, IN MINNESOTA
MONTHLY, 1 FEBRUARY 2007)

The most northerly regions of South America and the islands of the Lesser Antilles were once occupied by people who called themselves *Galibi*. A related form of this name in one of the local languages was *Caribes*. The name signified 'valiant men' and this was borne out by their legendary ferocity. When Christopher Columbus landed in Cuba in October 1492, he recorded the name as *Canibales*, influenced, no doubt, by the fact that he believed himself to be in Asia, his intended destination, in lands ruled by the Great Khan.

The Spaniards became convinced that the natives in those parts ate human flesh, and so *Canibal* denoted 'a man-eating Carib'. The acceptance of this specific form of the new word was probably reinforced by an early sixteenth-century etymology – popular but false – that attempted to derive the term from Spanish *can* and Latin *canis*, both meaning 'dog'.

The word *cannibal* excited the European imagination with dark tales

of the New World. It was also user-friendly; the alternative was the ponderous classical term *anthropophags*. It was used in English to denote specifically a man-eating Carib from the mid-sixteenth century. Shakespeare mentions cannibals in his plays: Othello speaks of *Canibals that each others eate* (1604), and the name of the character *Caliban*, the semi-human savage in THE TEMPEST (1611), is a variant of *Cariban*. By the eighteenth century, however, *cannibal* had simply come to mean 'a man who eats the flesh of another'.

☛ *Caribbean*, an adjective applied to some of the West Indian islands and the surrounding sea, derives from *Carib*, which is still used in its own right to describe the language and culture of areas once occupied by these people.

carnival
fair or festival

*...it had never occurred to him that Edinburgh was in the middle of 'the Festival' and that there would be **carnival** hordes of people milling around as if the end of the war had just been declared.*
(KATE ATKINSON,
ONE GOOD TURN, 2006)

*The Notting Hill **Carnival** faces cancellation next year amid grave concerns over public safety.*

Council chiefs have threatened to withdraw their support for the annual street party unless organisers dramatically improve their preparations. They claim this year's event was let down by 'profound organisational failure' and it is their duty to avoid the 2009 carnival being marred by similar chaos.
(EVENING STANDARD,
27 NOVEMBER 2008)

Scholars have identified *carnival* as a continuation of pagan springtime feasts in the ancient world which revolved around the concept of death and renewal. More particularly they say that it evolved from the Roman feast of Saturnalia, which celebrated the sowing of the year's harvest and was marked by a period of great revelry. Saturnalia was such a popular festival that it continued to be celebrated in Christian Rome. The church could not approve of its pagan character but was reluctant to deny the people their festivities. It sought, therefore, to lend them a new significance by attaching them to Lent.

The word *carnival* has its origins in Medieval Latin *carnelevāmen*, a compound of *carō* (stem *carn-*), 'flesh' and *levāre*, 'to raise, to remove'. This became *carnelevare* in Old Italian, then *carnevale* in Italian. The basic sense is 'the lifting or putting away of meat' and reflects the fact that the Roman Catholic church required its members to refrain from eating meat during Lent.

This meaning and the ultimate form of the word strengthened a persistent but erroneous supposition that it derived from *carne*, 'flesh' and *vale*, 'farewell' and thus meant 'Farewell, flesh', a statement of self-denial. This folk etymology has had wide circulation since at least the time of John Florio, an influential linguist and translator in the late sixteenth century, and was perpetuated by Byron in these lines from BEPPO (1818):

> *This feast is named the Carnival,*
> *which being*
> *Interpreted, implies 'farewell to flesh' –*
> *So called, because the name and thing*
> *agreeing,*
> *Through Lent they live on fish both salt*
> *and fresh.*

Certainly the carnival season was seen as a last fling, a chance to enjoy and indulge oneself in revelry and feasting before the sombre and reflective season of Lent. As such it received the blessing and even the patronage of the papacy. Pope Paul II (1464–71), for instance, was a vain man who loved spectacle and show. During his papacy masked balls were organised and races of different kinds took place in Rome. Some of the expense fell on the Jews, who were forced to contribute to the merry-making. The carnival season was originally lengthy, stretching from Epiphany (6 January) to Shrove Tuesday in February or early March. As time went on, however, it was confined to the last few days before Lent.

Carnival customs first spread throughout Italy and then through Catholic Europe. From there settlers in Catholic colonies in the New World introduced the festivities to the American continent. Today Carnival is celebrated widely, most spectacularly throughout Brazil, particularly in Rio di Janeiro, and in New Orleans.

The word entered English in the mid-sixteenth century via Italian *carnevale* to describe the pre-Lenten revelries in Catholic Europe. By the end of the century it was being applied loosely to any kind of riotous celebration or festival, not connected with any particular season. In modern English a *carnival* is also 'a procession with floats followed by sideshows'.

For other words on a related theme, see LENT and SHROVETIDE.

carol

a song of joy, particularly on a religious theme at Christmas

In the fore-court, lit by the dim rays of a horn lantern, some eight or ten little field-mice stood in a semi-circle... As the door opened, one of the elder ones that carried the lantern was just saying, 'Now then, one

*two, three!' and forthwith their shrill little voices rose on the air, singing one of the old-time **carols** their forefathers composed in fields that were fallow and held by frost, or when snow-bound in chimney corners, and handed down to be sung in the miry street to lamp-lit windows at Yule-time.*
(KENNETH GRAHAME,
THE WIND IN THE WILLOWS, 1908)

*Out in the larger ward, Jackson could hear children's voices singing Christmas **carols**, quite badly. He noticed for the first time some half-hearted gaudy decorations hanging in his room. He had forgotten all about Christmas.*
(KATE ATKINSON, WHEN WILL THERE BE GOOD NEWS?, 2008)

Although the exact etymology of this word is disputed, authorities agree that it has a classical origin. In medieval Europe a *carol* was 'a ring-dance' in which men and women joined hands to form a circle and then sang and danced to a musical accompaniment. *Carol* was borrowed into Middle English from Old French *carole* around the end of the thirteenth century. However, literary references in Old French are much older and date back to the middle of the twelfth century.

The Swiss Romance and Old Provençal forms (*coraula* and *corola* respectively) are just one indication that the word once began with *co-*. Some authorities consider that it originally meant 'circle' and attempt to link it to Latin *corolla*, 'coronet, garland'. However, most etymologists consider that *carol* evolved from Late Latin *choraula*, 'dance song'. This, in turn, came from Latin *choraulēs*, a name for 'an instrumentalist who piped the accompaniment for a choral dance'. This was a borrowing of the Greek compound *khoraulēs*, formed from *khoros*, 'a chorus, a round dance' and *aulos*, 'a flute, a reed instrument'.

Carols were sung in Latin, English or, frequently, a mixture of the two, as in the BOAR'S HEAD CAROL below. The subject matter was not prescribed, except that carols were songs of joy whose main feature was the repetition of a burden or refrain. Christmas was celebrated with much enthusiasm and songs with similar repetitions were composed in honour of the season. These also became known as *carols*, whether they were ring-dances or not, by virtue of their refrains. This jolly carol was written to accompany the bringing in of the boar's head at the feast:

> *Caput apri defero,*
> *Reddens laudes Domino.*
> *The bore's heed in hande bring I,*
> *With garlands gay and rosemary.*
> *I pray you all synge merelye*
> *Qui estis in convivio.*
>
> *The bore's heed, I understande,*
> *Is the chief service in this lande,*
> *Look wherever it be fande,*
> *Servite cun cantico.*
>
> *Be gladde lordes both more and ladde,*
> *For this hath ordeyned our stewarde,*
> *To cheere you all this Christmasse,*
> *The bore's heed with mustarde.*
> *Caput apri defero,*
> *Reddens laudes Domino.*
> (PUBLISHED BY WYNKYN DE WORDE, 1521)

Others, such as this fifteenth-century carol, celebrated the religious significance of the season:

> *I sing of a maiden*
> *That is makeles;*
> *King of all kings*
> *To her son she ches.*
>
> *He came al so still*
> *There his mother was,*
> *As dew in April*
> *That falleth on the grass.*
> *He came al so still*
> *To his mother's bour,*

As dew in April
That falleth on the flour.

He came al so still
There his mother lay,
As dew in April
That falleth on the spray.

Mother and maiden
Was never none but she;
Well may such a lady
Goddes mother be.

The once popular ring-dances have long since passed away, but over the centuries the celebration of Christmas has gathered up traditions that defy change and are still with us today.

☞ Greek *khoros*, 'band of dancers and singers', is responsible for:

chorus (16th cent): from Latin *chorus*, 'band of singers and dancers', and Greek *khoros*.

choir (13th cent): earlier *quire*, from Middle English *quere*, borrowed from Old French *cuer*, from Medieval Latin *chorus*, 'church singers', from Latin *chorus*, 'company of singers and dancers', from Greek *khoros*.

carouse
to indulge in a drinking bout

*Alcohol, on the other hand, was clearly a problem. Poe wasn't a **carouser** or a barfly; and he didn't drink away whatever money he had. All it took, according to eyewitnesses, was less than a glass of wine.*
(SHELLEY COSTA BLOOMFIELD, THE EVERYTHING GUIDE TO EDGAR ALLAN POE, 2007)

*Elveden Hall has memories for Peter O'Toole. Granted, for an old stomping ground, it doesn't hold the nostalgia of the drinking dens of Soho where he once **caroused**.*
(THE TIMES, 6 DECEMBER 2008)

This word has its origins in medieval German drinking bouts. When drinking someone's health or celebrating a great event or victory, the assembled company would fill their glasses brim full and encourage one another to *garaus trinken*, 'to drink down the contents to the last drop'. The adverb *garaus* is made up of *gar*, 'completely', and *aus*, 'out'. Other countries followed suit; Spanish had *caraos* from German *garaus*, and French had *carous*. English borrowed from the French and so, in the sixteenth century, *to quaff* or *drink carouse* meant 'to drain one's cup', and a *carouse* was 'a toast, a generous measure drunk to the dregs':

Then in his cups you shall not see him shrink,
To the grand devil a carouze to drink.
(MICHAEL DRAYTON [1563–1631], MOONCALF)

By the late seventeenth century a *carouse* had come to mean 'a drinking bout'. *Carousal* was an eighteenth-century variant for the same thing. Today, the verb *to carouse* (which also dates back to the sixteenth century) is more commonly used.

For another word originating in a drinking refrain, see LAMPOON.

cartoon
a preliminary sketch; a humorous or satirical drawing; a film of the animation of drawn figures

*That is what I do when I draw a **cartoon** – I make the design big and paint it as I know the wool will look when woven, with less blending of colours and more bright, even patterns. Cartoons are not so beautiful as paintings, but they are essential for the weaver to follow as he works.*
(TRACY CHEVALIER, THE LADY AND THE UNICORN, 2003)

Isaac noticed a piece of newsprint joining the chin area to the neck: it was a section of the Camp, *Central's own newspaper, some sort of advert or announcement, decorated with flowers and a* **cartoon** *of a couple dancing.*
(DAVID BADDIEL,
THE SECRET PURPOSES, 2004)

...Jalil had let on that an American film was playing at his cinema. It was a special kind of film, what he'd called a **cartoon**. *The entire film was a series of drawings, he said, thousands of them, so that when they were made into a film and projected onto a screen you had the illusion that the drawings were moving.*
(KHALED HOSSEINI, A THOUSAND
SPLENDID SUNS, 2007)

The Italian word *cartone* denoted 'thick paper, pasteboard', being an augmentative of *carta*, 'paper', from Latin *charta*, 'leaf of papyrus, paper'. When preparing their work – a fresco, tapestry or oil painting – artists made preliminary full-size drawings on pasteboard. In time, *cartone* was applied not only to the material used for the drawing but also to the sketch itself, a transference which was complete by the time the word was borrowed into English as *cartoon* in the seventeenth century by way of French *carton*.

This specialised use of the word is still current, but a more familiar modern meaning emerged in the 1840s when satirical papers such as PUNCH published full-page comic sketches which they termed *cartoons*:

Punch has the benevolence to announce, that in an early number of his ensuing Volume he will astonish the Parliamentary Committee by the publication of several exquisite designs, to be called Punch's Cartoons!
(PUNCH, 24 JUNE, 1843)

These were the forerunners of the outline drawings in present-day newspapers and periodicals which make a humorous or satirical statement on daily life or current affairs. Animated cartoons date from around 1915.

☛ Papyrus is an aquatic reedlike plant, indigenous to Egypt. From it was made the material on which the ancients wrote. The Greeks used the word *khartēs* to denote 'a layer of papyrus', and this was borrowed into Latin as *charta*. This, in turn, has produced a number of English words, some of which, like *cartoon*, came through Italian.

card (15th cent): from Old French *carte* and Italian *carta*, 'card'.

cartel (16th cent): from French *cartel*, from early Italian *cartello*, diminutive of *carta*, 'paper'. The early sense of the word was 'a written letter of challenge'. In the late seventeenth century it was used in times of war to denote 'a formal written agreement for the exchange of prisoners'. Only in the early twentieth century, under the influence of German *kartell*, did it acquire its more familiar present-day meaning of 'an agreement between independent businesses to regulate marketing, output and prices'.

carton (19th cent): from French *carton*, a borrowing of Italian *cartone*, 'pasteboard'.

cartridge (16th cent): a corruption of French *cartage*, 'a charge of powder for a pistol'. This was a variant of *cartouche*, a borrowing of Italian *cartoccio*, 'cornet of paper', augmentative of *carta*. The term arose from the practice of wrapping shot in a folded, cornet-shaped piece of paper, ready measured for easy use. From here military science applied the term to the tubular cases of propellent and primer of the cartridge proper.

chart (late 16th cent): 'a map to navigate by', from Old French *charte*, 'paper, map', from Latin *charta*, which later developed the sense 'map' besides that of 'paper'. *Chart* was introduced to replace *carte* and *card*, both of which were used to mean 'map' from the fifteenth to the seventeenth centuries. *Carte* is now obsolete, but may have influenced the development of *cartographer* in the nineteenth century.

charter (13th cent): from Old French *chartre*, from Latin *chartula*, 'a small leaf of paper, a deed', diminutive of *charta*.

cataract
a waterfall; an opacity of the lens of the eye, causing impaired vision

*The photograph was certainly very off-coloured. An unkind critic might easily have misinterpreted that dim surface. It was a dull grey landscape, and as I gradually deciphered the details of it I realized that it represented a long and enormously high line of cliffs exactly like an immense **cataract** seen in the distance, with a sloping, tree-clad plain in the foreground.*
(SIR ARTHUR CONAN DOYLE, THE LOST WORLD, 1912)

*Ma was suffering badly from **cataracts**; although she hated needing a guide round her own kitchen, she was in so much trouble with her vision, she admitted she could use help. Ganna knew nothing of Roman domestic procedure now – but by the time my mother had finished with her, she would.*
(LINDSEY DAVIS, SATURNALIA, 2007)

The Greek word *kataráktēs*, meaning 'hurtling down' (from the compound verb *katarassein*, 'to dash down, to fall headlong', from *kata-*, 'down' and *rassein*, 'to strike hard'), was used to denote 'a plunging thing': this might be a swooping bird, for instance, a waterfall rushing headlong, a storm or even a plummeting portcullis. The word became *cataracta* in Latin, where it meant 'waterfall', 'floodgate',

'portcullis' – senses which Old French retained when it borrowed the term as *cataracte*.

The word's use in Middle English was restricted to 'floodgate', as in the expression *cataracts of heaven*, (from the French *cataractes du ciel*), which supposedly controlled the rainfall. Late sixteenth-century English then used the word to denote 'a mighty waterfall tumbling over a sheer drop', a sense that had been common in Latin and Old French.

In French and then in English from the mid-sixteenth century onwards, the ancient application to a 'portcullis' became an important medical term when *cataract* was figuratively applied to the 'opacity of the eye lens' which impairs vision. The apparent reasoning was that the cataract obscures vision in the same way that a portcullis obstructs a gateway. In this sense, *cataract* gradually replaced *web in the eye*, an earlier term for the condition dating back to the fourteenth century. A fifteenth-century manuscript prescribed *succle* [honeysuckle], *a good medycyne for ye web in ye eye* – later equally efficacious against cataracts.

caterpillar
the larva of a butterfly or moth

*Ah, 'what's a butterfly? At best
He's but a **caterpillar** drest.*
(JOHN GAY, FABLES, 1727)

*In the light of the moon a little egg lay on a leaf. One Sunday morning the warm sun came up and – pop! – out of the egg came a tiny and very hungry **caterpillar**.*
(ERIC CARLE, THE VERY HUNGRY CATERPILLAR, 1970)

*Blackberries scrambled over brass bedsteads, and a sunken tank of sootwater provided the wherewithal to discourage greenfly, **caterpillars** and anything else*

that might want to eat his cabbages and cauliflowers, all of which seemed to be covered in a thin black film of soot.
(ALAN TITCHMARSH,
TROWEL AND ERROR, 2002)

A vivid visual imagination is required to appreciate the origin of this odd word. To the medieval French eye, the hairy varieties of caterpillar resembled she-cats, giving rise to the Old French *chatepelose* and its northern dialect variant *catepelose*, 'hairy she-cat' (from *cate*, 'female cat', from Late Latin *catta* and *pelose*, the feminine form of the adjective *pelous*, 'hairy', from Latin *pilōsus*, from *pilus*, 'hair'). Strange though it may seem, this was a not uncommon association – the Lombards referred to a *caterpillar* as a 'cat' or 'kitten' and the Swiss as a 'devil's cat'. Stranger still is the Scottish term *hairy woubit*, literally 'woolly bear'.

Middle English borrowed the French word as *catyrpel* in the fifteenth century. The later addition of the suffix -*er*, to give *caterpiller*, was probably influenced by *piller*, 'a pillager, a plunderer', because caterpillars are destructive to crops. Indeed, in the sixteenth and seventeenth centuries, *caterpiller* itself (as it was then regularly spelt) was used synonymously with *piller* to figuratively denote 'a greedy, predatory person'.

The modern spelling with a final -*ar* was occasionally found in the seventeenth century but was established by Dr Johnson in his DICTIONARY OF THE ENGLISH LANGUAGE (1755).

Incidentally, the humble caterpillar provides still more evidence of vivid imagination in the French. See the note under CANARY.

See also BUTTERFLY.

cemetery
a burial ground

*When he reached the **cemetery**, he couldn't remember where Elvira's grave was. There were so many hundreds of people buried here and he hadn't visited the place in five years.*
(ROSE TREMAIN, THE BEAUTY OF THE DAWN SHIFT, 2005)

*Just outside Florence's city walls, marooned in the middle of a huge great ring road, lies a foreign field that is for ever England. Well, it's really for ever Switzerland. The English **Cemetery** of Florence is owned by the Swiss Reformed Evangelical Church and is officially called the Protestant Cemetery of Florence. But, because the English presence looms so large in Florence, the Florentines call it the Cimitero degli Inglesi.*
(THE SPECTATOR, 28 NOVEMBER 2007)

Here lapped in hallowed slumber Saon lies, Asleep, not dead; a good man never dies (Callimachus, c. 260–240 BC). Many common words and expressions connected with death are euphemisms. This epitaph tells us that Saon of Acanthus 'fell asleep'. Had he been a Christian he would have been 'laid to rest' in a 'dormitory'. *Cemetery* comes from the Greek word *koimētērion*, which literally meant 'a sleeping-room, a dormitory' but was used by early Christian writers to denote a 'burial ground'. It was derived from the verb *koiman*, 'to put to sleep'. The Late Latin borrowing *coemētērium* referred to the Roman catacombs, and it is in this particular sense that the word first came into Middle English as *cimitery* in the fourteenth century. Later, in the fifteenth century, it was applied to a churchyard and first denoted a 'burial-ground' in general in the early seventeenth century.

The inevitability of the grave and the cemetery is proverbial:

A piece of the Church-yard fits everybody.
(GEORGE HERBERT, JACULA
PRUDENTUM, 1640)

Six feet of earth make all men equal.
(JAMES HOWELL, PROVERBS IN
ENGLISH, ITALIAN, FRENCH AND
SPANISH, 1659)

The grave is the general Meeting-Place.
(THOMAS FULLER, GNOMOLOGIA,
1732)

*He who seeks equality should go to a
cemetery.*
(GERMAN PROVERB)

and has given rise to grave humour:

*The fence around a cemetery is foolish, for
those inside can't get out and those outside
don't want to get in.*
(ARTHUR BRISBANE, THE BOOK OF
TODAY, 1923)

*Due to industrial action, the cemetery will
be run by a skeleton staff.*
(PETER GAMMONS, ALL PREACHERS
GREAT AND SMALL, 1989)

The word *catacomb* comes from the name
of a particular cemetery known throughout the Middle Ages as the *Coemētērium
ad Catacumbas*. It was notable because,
for a while, the bodies of both St Peter
and St Paul were deposited there. The
origin of the name *Catacumbas* is,
however, a mystery. The general application of *catacomb* to the subterranean
burial chambers around Rome dates
from the seventeenth century.

For more words on a funereal theme,
see COFFIN, HEARSE and
SARCOPHAGUS.

cesspool, cesspit
a drainage pit for effluent

*The veneer of my 'respectable', semi-
detached home in Winsford Way did not
mask a* **cesspit** *of secrets and lies. Behind
that metaphorical picket fence – actually*
*we had an unlovely, standard-issue wire
mesh fence – lurked a family of five who
largely ate together, played together and
stayed together.*
(ANDREW COLLINS, WHERE DID IT
ALL GO RIGHT?, 2003)

*Kamfers Dam, near Kimberley, is the only
nesting site in the country – and one of only
six breeding areas in the world. It has
hosted more than 50,000 flamingos, and
this year 9,000 chicks hatched on the
dam's artificial flamingo island.*
   *But conservationists believe that pollution
from a sewage plant is causing deformities
and could force the birds to desert the site.
The dam is being used to dump raw sewage
from a malfunctioning treatment plant
owned by the Sol Plaatje Municipality.*
   *'Without urgent action, the dam will
become a polluted* **cesspool** *devoid of
birdlife,' said Duncan Pritchard, of
BirdLife South Africa.*
(THE INDEPENDENT, 11 JULY 2008)

Since the *pool* element is self-evident, it
must follow that *cess* is an old term for
'muck and mire, nightsoil and sewage'.
This is the line a number of commenta-
tors on this word have taken. As a result
the origins of *cess* have been sought from
sources as varied as the English word
cess, 'bog', the Italian *cesso*, 'latrine' (from
Latin *secessus*, 'privy, drain') or dialect
words such as *suss*, 'hogwash' or *soss*
'sloppy mess' (proposed from the form
suspool). Sadly all of these ingenious
suggestions are inconclusive. More probable is a theory which treats *cesspool* as a
whole rather than as a compound and
makes no etymological connection with
pool at all.
   THE ANNALLS OF IPSWICHE
(1583) contain a reference to the form
cesperalle, used to denote 'a cesspool'. It
appears to be a variant of *suspiral*, which
in the fifteenth century denoted 'a
water-pipe' or 'air-vent' but which, by
the sixteenth century, was also sometimes applied to 'a tank for the collec-

tion of water or liquid waste'. *Suspiral* was a borrowing of Old French *souspirail* which ultimately derived from Latin *suspīrāre*, 'to breathe' or 'to sigh' (a verb applicable as much to deep breathing as to the sighs of a lovesick maiden, and source of the now practically defunct poetical verb *suspire*).

If this is the correct origin, then the *pool* element of the modern word is merely a folk etymology inspired by visions of collected waste and effluent, and *cesspit*, which dates from the nineteenth century, would be a logical variant.

chancellor
a high-ranking officer

*A lot of people aren't sure of the difference between the **Chancellor** and the President in Austria, but it's quite simple. The Chancellor decides national policy and runs the country, while the President rounds up the Jews.*
(BILL BRYSON,
NEITHER HERE NOR THERE, 1991)

*My, but it's been another busy week for the **chancellor**. Not as busy as it has been for retailers desperately repricing goods to take account of the 2.5% reduction in VAT he announced as part of his recession-busting box of carrots, sticks and tricks, but pretty lively nevertheless.*
(THE GUARDIAN, 29 NOVEMBER 2008)

The Lord Chancellor may not be flattered to know that the office in which he takes such pride began with a humble lattice grating. In the Roman Empire a *chancellor* was a low-ranking officer, an usher who stood at the lattice screen separating the judges in a law court from the crowd. He took the title of his job *cancellārius* from the screen (*cancelli*, 'lattice-work', from *cancellus* 'a grating'). Later, in the Eastern Empire, the chancellor discharged the duties of a secretary. In time, he was given certain additional judicial responsibilities and, eventually, the duties of overseer. Gradually, therefore, the role became more prestigious.

Edward the Confessor (1042–66) was probably responsible for creating the office of Chancellor in England. Under the Norman kings who succeeded him, the title was given to the king's secretary, who was accountable for all documents of state and keeper of the king's seal. The office developed an increasingly important judicial role because of the large number of appeals submitted to the king's justice. In early times the chancellor was usually a churchman who was also the king's confessor, the 'keeper of the king's conscience', and so he must, even today, be a member of the Church of England. The chancellor's power gradually increased until it was second only to that of the sovereign and princes of the blood. The present-day Lord Chancellor is not only head of the judiciary but also the Speaker of the House of Lords and, usually, a senior cabinet minister.

The title chancellor is also held by the Chancellor of the Exchequer, an appointment that originated in the reign of Henry III (1216–72), and the Chancellor of the Duchy of Lancaster. It is an ancient administrative title in the church and also the name given to the head of a university. Some countries – Germany, for instance – have chosen the title for their chief minister of state.

See also CANCEL and EXCHEQUER.

chapel

a private place for prayer and worship; a non-conformist meeting house

*The **chapel** is carved from the grotto where the half-legendary St Marina lived – a virgin clothed as a monk, who saved a dying child with her miraculous milk; and women whose milk has run dry come to her altar and tend her candles.*
(COLIN THUBRON,
THE HILLS OF ADONIS, 1968)

*According to the estate agent who negotiated the sale, the house was once a Methodist manse, a conclusion that was reached by virtue of its being attached to a non-conformist **chapel**. But when we asked at what point the chapel ceased being a place of worship and when exactly it was converted into a home, there were blank faces all round.*
(DAILY MAIL, 20 FEBRUARY 2009)

The whole history of this word is contained in a holy relic; the cape of St Martin of Tours. Martin's father was an officer in the Roman army and Martin, too, began a military career. One day in about the year AD 337, he came across a shivering beggar. Moved with compassion, Martin tore his cloak in two so that the beggar could share it. That night, in a dream, he saw Christ wrapped in the piece of cloak that he had given away. Martin became a Christian and, because he would no longer fight, left the army.

After years of preaching and conflict with church authorities, followed by a period as a recluse, Martin became a follower of St Hilary, then Bishop of Poitiers, and eventually, in 372, was made Bishop of Tours. During his twenty-five-year episcopate, Martin was zealous in his efforts to reach the heathen. Upon his death his following spread rapidly and his shrine at Tours became one of the foremost objects of pilgrimage in France.

Artistic representations show Martin sharing his cloak with the beggar.

This cloak was treasured by the Frankish kings, who used to carry it into battle. It was kept in a sanctuary called the *cappella*, a Late Latin word meaning 'little cloak', a diminutive of Latin *cappa*, 'cloak'. Later the same word was applied to other sanctuaries containing holy relics, and later still extended to buildings designated for Christian worship. *Chapele* was borrowed into Middle English directly from Old French in the thirteenth century.

Ironically, in England during the second half of the seventeenth century, *chapel*, despite its Catholic origins, was often applied to the places of worship used by the growing numbers of non-conformist groups. The term conveniently set these simple meeting places and their congregations apart from those of the established Church of England.

This same idea of the separation of a group of like-minded individuals is probably the inspiration for a *chapel* of Trades' Union members, or the local branch of a club or association. Both are contexts in which the word is found today.

☞ English *chaplain* comes from Medieval Latin *cappellanus*, which originally denoted 'one who had the charge of St Martin's cloak'. This same term was then applied to guardians of other sanctuaries. It became *chapelain* in Old French and was borrowed into Middle English as *chapeleyn* in the fourteenth century.

chauvinism

extreme, insensitive promotion of a cause or country

*...schoolteachers are all at fault for what goes on in class; they are the ones who have a chance to change the youngsters' mentality.... I did what I could; I never had them sing the 'Marseillaise,' the words are so bellicose, so **chauvinistic** that for me it was out of the question to make them learn and recite it.*
(EMILIE CARLES,
TR. AVRIEL H GOLDBERGER,
A WILD HERB SOUP, 1991)

*The authors give clear and intelligent explanations as to why religion thrives in the most advanced, modern society on the planet, and why it seems to be doing so well in societies that seek to emulate the American model. Even Mikhail Gorbachev has discovered his Orthodox roots, while Vladimir Putin also knows the value of clouds of incense in concealing **chauvinism** and thuggery.*
(THE TELEGRAPH, 6 JUNE 2009)

The word derives from the name of Nicolas *Chauvin*, soldier and patriot, of Rochefort in France. During his service in the French army, Chauvin gained a reputation for tireless devotion to Napoleon and to his country. Admiration turned to ridicule, however, when Chauvin's behaviour was deemed fanatical. Wounded many times, he retired only when he was physically incapable of fighting on. His reward was a medal, a ceremonial sabre and a meagre pension of 200 francs a year, but still his patriotism and loyalty to his emperor were undiminished.

Chauvin's reputation came to the notice of the playwrights Charles and Jean Cogniard, who exploited it in a musical comedy, LA COCARDE TRICOLORE (1831), in which the young Chauvin, idolator of Napoleon, sings the refrain *Je suis français, je suis*

Chauvin ('I am French, I am Chauvin'). The character became a favourite with other comedy writers and the word *chauvinisme*, 'excessive and bellicose patriotism', was born. The term, publicised by the plays, was first used in England around 1870. By the mid-twentieth century *chauvinism* was no longer exclusively linked to patriotism but was also applied to 'blind and intolerant belief in the pre-eminence of any cause or set of people', the most obvious example in recent times being that of *male chauvinism*.

See JINGOISM.

cheat

someone who uses deceit to benefit him or herself

*Money did not come in quickly, for Ellen **cheated** him by keeping it back, and dealing improperly with the goods he bought.*
(SAMUEL BUTLER,
THE WAY OF ALL FLESH, 1903)

*Chanu worked hard and the harder he worked the more he suspected he was being **cheated** of his reward.*
(MONICA ALI, BRICK LANE, 2003)

*His disgrace is not the consequence of a momentary aberration. On the contrary, throughout his life he has profited from being a **cheat** and a liar.... The few who attempted to expose Black's dishonesty were suppressed amid a torrent of libel writs. No newspaper ever risked confronting Black in court, preferring to publish apologies.*
(EVENING STANDARD, 13 JULY 2007)

The Middle English word *chete* is a shortening of *eschet*, meaning 'an escheat'. In feudal times this was a forfeiture of a fief to the lord when the holder died without immediate legal heirs. The word is a borrowing of Old French *escheoite*, which literally means 'that which falls to one' and hence 'that which falls as one's due, one's heritage'. The term comes from the verb *escheoir*, 'to befall, to pass to', from unattested Vulgar Latin *excadēre*, 'to fall away', from Latin *ex-*, 'out' and *cadere*, 'to fall'.

The Crown was the main beneficiary of this law. The county officers appointed by the Exchequer to manage these affairs were known as *escheators*, or sometimes as *cheaters*. Shakespeare uses *cheater* in this sense in THE MERRY WIVES OF WINDSOR (1602) when Falstaff says *I will be a cheater to them both, and they shall be exchequers to me.*

No tax-collector is ever a popular figure, but the fact that many *escheators* took advantage of their position to exploit people gave them a reputation for deviousness and dishonesty. From the early seventeenth century, then, *cheater* was used to denote 'one who practises fraud, a swindler'. Although this form persisted well into the nineteenth century and beyond, it has been superseded by the briefer *cheat*, which arose in the second half of the seventeenth century.

As a verb, *cheat* had come to mean 'deceive' by the early seventeenth century. The expression *to cheat on*, meaning 'to be sexually unfaithful', dates from the first half of the twentieth century and is American English in origin: *A woman married a louse that beat her and cheated on her* (JOHN O'HARA, APPOINTMENT IN SAMARRA, 1934).

chess

a game for two people played on a chequered board, each player attempting to capture the other's king piece

*Poe, for instance, really was morbid; not because he was poetical, but because he was specially analytical. Even **chess** was too poetical for him; he disliked chess because it was full of knights and castles, like a poem. He avowedly preferred the black discs of draughts, because they were more like the mere black dots on a diagram.*
(G K CHESTERTON, ORTHODOXY, 1909)

*She watched him coming along the strand, his form at first no more than an indigo stain against the darkening shingle, sometimes appearing motionless, flickering and dissolving at its outlines, and at others suddenly closer, as though moved like a **chess** piece a few squares towards her.*
(IAN MCEWAN, ON CHESIL BEACH, 2007)

As early as AD 500 the ancient game of chess was known in India as *chaturanga*, 'the four angas'; these were the four divisions of an army – horses, elephants, chariots and foot soldiers. The game was adopted and adapted by the Persians and, following the Islamic conquest of Persia, caught the interest of the Arabs, who were in turn responsible for introducing it to Europe through Spain during the Moorish conquest in the tenth century. It was the Europeans who gave the chess pieces the names, reflecting medieval society, that we are familiar with today. The game was brought to England at the time of the Norman conquest, when it was popular at court. A mark of its popularity in the Middle Ages is that the second book published by Caxton, in 1474, was THE GAME AND PLAYE OF CHESSE.

The Spanish and Portuguese words for *chess* are derived from the Arabic, Old Persian and Sanskrit terms: *shatranj*, *chatrang* and *chaturanga* respectively. Other languages, however, took inspiration from the object of the game itself, which is to place the opponent's king in checkmate. The Arabic term *shāh* (from Persian *shāh*, 'king') meant both 'king' and 'check' in chess; in Arabic *shāh māt* meant literally 'the king is dead', hence 'checkmate'. From *shāh* in the eleventh century Old French derived *eschec* to mean 'check' in chess, using the plural *esches* for the game itself. *Esches* was borrowed into Middle English as *ches* in the thirteenth century.

From *eschec* Old French derived the verb *eschequier*, 'to play chess', in the twelfth century. Borrowed into English *to check* developed a range of figurative uses inspired by the game: 'to arrest progress', 'halt', 'restrain', 'hold in check'. These finally gave rise to 'control by examining for accuracy', 'verify'. All of these senses are current today.

Along with the notion of 'verify', in the seventeenth century the noun *check* denoted 'the counterfoil of a bank bill' that could be looked over for forgery. Nowadays, in American English a *check* is 'a written order for money' to a bank. The English spelling *cheque* was probably influenced by EXCHEQUER.

chocolate

a drink or sweet produced from processed cacao seeds

Chocolate. Just the word brings a smile to my face. I'm the one who always orders whatever chocolate is on a dessert menu, ever in search of the perfect molten chocolate cake or the ultimate flourless chocolate cake. I even had a dark chocolate cake with dark chocolate icing for my wedding.
(WASHINGTON POST,
13 FEBRUARY 2003)

For many, the ultimate sin is dark **chocolate.** *It is fantastic for enriching and thickening a red wine sauce. Pair the two with the sumptuous, lean red meat of venison and you have an intriguing combination to wow dinner party guests.*
(THE TIMES, 15 NOVEMBER 2008)

When Cortés entered the Aztec capital Tenochtitlán in 1519, the importance of the cocoa bean in the Aztec economy was immediately obvious since it was used for religious ritual, currency and trade. The rulers and nobility also enjoyed a drink made by roasting cocoa beans and crushing them to a paste which was mixed with water, chilli, vanilla and powdered aromatic flowers. This was known as *xocolatl* in the Nahuatl language, a compound of *xococ*, 'bitter' and *atl*, 'water'. The Spaniard Bernal Diaz reported how the foaming drink was served to the Emperor Moctezuma in a golden cup before he visited his wives.

Naturally, when Cortés returned to Spain in 1528 he took the recipe for *xocolatl* and a supply of cocoa beans with him. *Chocolate*, as the Spaniards called it, immediately became a popular drink at court, although the recipe was modified somewhat: the chilli was omitted in favour of nutmeg, cinnamon and sugar. Chocolate was exported to Spain in paste form. However, since supplies of cocoa beans were limited, the Spaniards kept their discovery a close secret to the extent that, when a Spanish ship laden with chocolate paste was seized by English and Dutch pirates, the cargo was not recognised and was thrown overboard with cries of *cacura de carneros*, 'sheep shit'.

For about a hundred years Spain enjoyed her cocoa monopoly, but gradually the secret leaked out, possibly through the comings and goings of missionary activity and certainly through the marriage of Philip II of Spain's daughter to Louis XIII of France, which took the beverage to the French court. Chocolate was probably introduced into England from France in the 1650s. It was available in coffee houses for a price. Samuel Pepys records a visit *to a Coffee-house, to drink jocolatte* in his diary for 24 November

1664, adding that it was *very good*. Before long chocolate could be had at specialist chocolate houses such as the Cocoa Tree (see SANDWICH) and widespread cultivation of the cocoa bean made it more affordable. The English love-affair with chocolate had begun.

For the etymology of chocolate-drink ingredients, see COCOA and VANILLA. For other beverages new to seventeenth-century tastebuds, see COFFEE and TEA.

cider
an alcoholic drink made from fermented apples

'I think I've got cider in my blood, even when I haven't had a drink,' says Kevin Minchew. The 51-year-old has mastered making the amber liquid after 24 years at the press. He was born on a smallholding in Ashchurch, near Tewkesbury.

'For as far back as I can remember my father had a barrel of cider or perry in the stable with the animal feed,' he says.
(GLOUCESTERSHIRE ECHO, 29 DECEMBER 2007)

Mr Crowden said while cider was consumed everywhere, especially on farms and in rural areas until the Second World War, beer and wine drinking picked up in the following decades, leaving traditional cider sales to plummet.
(REVIEW OF CIDERLAND BY JAMES CROWDEN, IN THE PLYMOUTH WESTERN MORNING NEWS, 24 SEPTEMBER 2008)

Cider is a word of Hebrew origin whose journey into English vocabulary was begun by early translators of the Bible. The Hebrew verb *shīkar* meant 'to be drunk', and the word for 'strong drink' of any kind was the derived noun *shīkār*. *Shīkār* appears several times in the Old Testament: in Judges 13, for

instance, an angel appears to Manoah's barren wife and tells her to refrain from strong drink because she is to give birth to Samson.

When the need was felt for a translation of the Hebrew scriptures into Greek, translators of the Septuagint Old Testament (translated between the third and first centuries BC) rendered *shīkār* as *sīkera*. Later the Latin Vulgate Bible (translated in the early fifth century) had *sīcera*. Old French borrowed this Late Latin term as *sisdre*, becoming *sidre*. (It is unclear how the medial *d* came about in the Romance languages: Italian has *sidro* and Spanish *sidra*.)

Cider-making was well established in Europe by the time of the Norman Conquest, and during the Middle Ages cider was produced in monasteries. The French began to apply the name *sidre* not just to strong drink but, more particularly, to strong cider. Middle English borrowed *sidre* from Old French in the early fourteenth century. John Trevisa's translation of Bartholomaeus Anglicus's work on the properties of things, DE PROPRIETATIBUS RERUM (1398), tells us that *Hony cometh of floures, sidre of frute, and ale of corne.*

Nevertheless John Wycliffe, whose translation of the Bible in the second half of the fourteenth century was based on the Vulgate rather than original texts, continued to use *sidur, sidir* and *cither* to render Latin *sicera* in the original sense of 'strong drink', as did other writers referring to Bible passages throughout the fourteenth and fifteenth centuries.

For the etymology of another alcoholic drink, see ALE.

cigar

tightly rolled tobacco leaves for
smoking

And a woman is only a woman, but a good
cigar is a smoke.
(RUDYARD KIPLING,
THE BETROTHED, 1885)

'It's not fair for you to come here,' I tell
Depression. 'I paid you off already. I served
my time back in New York.'
    But he just gives me that dark smile,
settles into my favourite chair, puts his feet
on my table and lights a cigar, filling the
place with his awful smoke.
(ELIZABETH GILBERT,
EAT PRAY LOVE, 2006)

There was a picture of Marshall Tito
shaking hands with Roza's father, and a
picture of Winston Churchill waving a
cigar. There was one of Stalin, and one of
Fidel Castro with his own huge Havana
and prophetic beard.
(LOUIS DE BERNIÈRES,
THE PARTISAN'S DAUGHTER, 2008)

It was the Spaniards who first brought
tobacco to Europe from the Americas
and recorded the native custom of twisting the leaves and wrapping them in
maize husks or palm leaves to smoke
them. It might be supposed, then, that
Spanish *cigarro*, which English borrowed
as *cigar* in the eighteenth century, is
derived from a local language. This is
not necessarily the case, however.

There are a number of theories to
account for the word. One is that it
comes from a Mayan word *sicar*,
meaning 'smoke'. Other etymologists
have remarked upon its similarity to
Spanish *cigarra*, meaning 'cicada'; they
see a resemblance between that creature's cylindrical body and tapering apex
and the shape of a cigar. Others look to
the word *cigarral* for an explanation.
Cigarrales were Spanish country houses
built for recreation and surrounded by
orchards and gardens in which tobacco
could be grown. All these suggestions are
unproven speculations.

When tobacco was gradually introduced into Europe throughout the sixteenth century, it was smoked in pipes.
Cigars as we would recognise them
today were first made in Spain with
Cuban tobacco in the early eighteenth
century. An unlikely story claims that
Catherine the Great was addicted to
cigars and insisted on having them
wrapped to avoid staining her fingers –
hence the cigar band.

☛ The word *cigarette*, a diminutive of
cigar, is French. In her PILGRIMAGE
TO AUVERGNE (1842) Louisa
Costello remarks that *the habit of*
smoking cigarettes…is quite la grande mode
of late with certain French ladies.

See also TOBACCO.

cliché

an overused idea or expression that
has lost its impact

He turned to Isabel and smiled. 'Your city
is very beautiful,' he said. 'We Italians
think of Scotland as being so romantic and
here it is, just as we imagined it!'
    'And we have our own ideas about Italy,'
said Isabel.
    He inclined his head slightly. 'Which
are?'
    'So romantic,' said Isabel.
    Tomasso's eyes widened with mirth.
'Well,' he said. 'We are in the realm of
cliché, are we not?'
(ALEXANDER MCCALL SMITH,
FRIENDS, LOVERS, CHOCOLATE, 2005)

Hard put for conversation, she found herself
falling back on some of her stock stand-bys.
It wasn't quite 'How far did you have to
come?' but the literary equivalent. 'How do
you think of your characters? Do you work
regular hours? Do you use a word-
processor?' – questions which she knew were

clichés and were embarrassing to inflict
had the awkward silence not been worse.
(ALAN BENNETT,
THE UNCOMMON READER, 2007)

Cliché was a term used by French printers to denote a 'stereotype'. It was a
time-consuming business to assemble a
text from individual letters, and so if
one particular phrase appeared over
and over again a mould would be made
of it and a metal printing plate cast to
speed things up. *Cliché* is the past participle of the verb *clicher*, a variant of
cliquer, 'to click', and the word imitates
the sound that was made when the
mould was dropped into molten lead
that was just on the point of cooling.

Cliché was borrowed into English in
the first half of the nineteenth century,
also to denote 'a stereotype'. By the
late nineteenth century it was being
applied figuratively in French, and then
in English, to a phrase which, like the
stereotype, had been used *ad nauseam*.

coach

a horse-drawn vehicle, usually for
carrying passengers, a carriage; a bus,
comfortably equipped for longer
journeys; a tutor, trainer

Charlie chased her out of the house and
down the street, bellowing, 'Bitch!' all
the way, and would have caught her but
*for a **coach** rumbling along Bastille Row*
that she darted in front of and that he
was forced to stop for.
(TRACY CHEVALIER,
BURNING BRIGHT, 2007)

Summer holidays had always been spent in
the UK for two reasons: my mother's fear
of flying and my father's obsession with
Pembrokeshire. But after braving the icy
Welsh waters one time too many, a decision
was taken: the family was going abroad.
Planes were naturally out of the question,
so it was left to mother to decide on the
mode of transport. And so, one July

morning, she, my dad, my sister and I
found ourselves standing at Cardiff bus
*station waiting for a **coach** to take us all*
the way to Italy.
(THE OBSERVER, 25 FEBRUARY 2007)

Although Keothavong has been helped by
***coaches** Claire Curran and Nigel Sears,*
the head coach for women's tennis at the
Lawn Tennis Association, she likes to spend
as much time as possible on her own; she
knows her own mind, knows her own game,
and likes her independence.
(THE TELEGRAPH, 15 JUNE 2009)

The *coach* takes its name from the
Hungarian village of *Kocs* (pronounced
'kotch'). Here, in the second half of the
fifteenth century, a large horse-drawn
carriage known as the *kocsi szeker*, literally 'cart from Kocs', was produced.
The vehicle was well-designed, with
steel-sprung suspension, and during
the first half of the sixteenth century
demand for it spread throughout
Europe. Many European languages,
therefore, have a word derived from the
adjective *kocsi*, 'of Kocs'. Spanish and
Portuguese have *coche* (in Spain it
remains the modern word for 'car') and
German *Kutsche*. English borrowed
coche directly from French. The spelling
coach was introduced in the seventeenth century and has been used for a
vehicle or carriage in horse-drawn, rail
(19th cent) and motorised (20th cent)
transport ever since.

In the nineteenth century, there was
a less obvious extension of the term.
Coach became a piece of university slang
for 'a private tutor', the idea being that
the tutor carried trainees through their
examinations to success on the back of
his experience and expertise:

Besides the regular college tutor, I secured the assistance of what, in the slang of the day, we irreverently termed 'a coach'.
(FRANK SMEDLEY, FRANK FAIRLEGH, OR SCENES FROM THE LIFE OF A PRIVATE PUPIL, 1850)

The transfer to *sports coach* dates from the end of the nineteenth century and was particularly applied to a trainer for a boat race.

cocoa

a powder made from roasted and ground cocoa beans; a milky drink made from this powder

Christened Theobroma, *which means 'food of the gods',* **cocoa** *is indisputably one of the most desired and valuable substances in the world. Purists would say that it is at its best used in a bar of chocolate, unadulterated by any other taste. But we think it can be just as exciting when transformed into a dessert or cake, or more unexpectedly, into a hearty stew or spicy sausage.*
(CAROLINE JEREMY, GREEN & BLACK'S CHOCOLATE RECIPES, 2003)

For years after, the smell of Stubbins & Co. beeswax, the crackle of tyres on gravel, a certain type of bell and I'd be fourteen again, tired after a long day's work, sipping **cocoa** *by the servants' hall fire while Mr Hamilton orated select passages from* The Times.
(KATE MORTON, THE HOUSE AT RIVERTON, 2006)

The cacao tree is native to the tropics of the Americas and may have come from the Amazon or Orinoco river basins. The Mayans were among the tribes who discovered the properties of the beans. When they migrated north, they began to cultivate the cacao tree in the humid tropics of the Yucatán Peninsula. Cacao beans were highly prized: they often featured in religious ceremonies; roasted, ground and mixed with various spices and flavourings, they were made into a bitter CHOCOLATE drink. They were also used for currency and were a trading commodity. One of the peoples who traded for beans was the Aztecs, who learnt to value them as much as the Mayans. The Aztecs lived in an arid area unsuitable for the cultivation of cacao trees and so they depended on the Mayans for their supplies. As they became more powerful, the Aztecs demanded beans as a tribute from their conquered neighbours.

The delights of the cacao bean were revealed to Europeans in the sixteenth century, following the Spanish explorer Cortés's expedition to Mexico in 1517. In Nahuatl, the Aztec language, the bean was known as *cacahuatl* and the first part of this word was taken into Spanish as *cacao*. This was borrowed directly into English in the sixteenth century but the eighteenth century saw the appearance of the corrupted form *cocoa*, which gradually won out. Originally the two words were pronounced with three syllables: *ca-ca-o* and *co-co-a*. However, considerable confusion arose over the spelling of *coconut*, sometimes written as *cocoanut*, and this led to a corruption in the pronunciation of *cocoa*, which was reduced to two syllables.

The word *cacao* is still current in English to denote both the tree and its bean. *Cocoa* is reserved for the powder obtained from grinding the beans, and for the drink made from it.

See also COCONUT. For further information on the history of cocoa, see CHOCOLATE.

coconut

the seed of a type of palm, with a hard shell, and white flesh and milky fluid inside

We chatted about the rains. When I mentioned Trivandrum's great fiery prayer meeting the physician smiled. 'Yes, yes, but there is really no need to go to all that trouble. If you break tender young coconuts on a statue of Shiva as the priest chants certain mantras you will get rain. Within twenty-four hours. Absolutely guaranteed.'
(ALEXANDER FRATER,
CHASING THE MONSOON, 1990)

A waiter came to their table and Aruna ordered tea. Shastry ordered idlis, steamed lentil and rice cakes, with no sambhar but with extra coconut chutney.
(FARAHAD ZAMA, THE MARRIAGE BUREAU FOR RICH PEOPLE, 2008)

When Portuguese explorers in India came across the *coconut* palm and then saw its fruit, they were struck by the three dark indentations at its base which suggested a horribly grinning face. They called the fruit *coco*, meaning 'grimace, goblin', and this word was borrowed into English around the middle of the sixteenth century. In the early seventeenth century it was made into a compound with the addition of *nut*, so that *coconut* gradually replaced *coco* altogether.

The publication of Dr Johnson's DICTIONARY OF THE ENGLISH LANGUAGE (1755) brought long-lasting confusion to the spelling of the word. Johnson himself used the standard spelling *coco* in his writings, but in the dictionary records *cocoa*:

CO'COA. n.s. [coca, or coco, Span. and Port.] A species of palm-tree, cultivated in the East and West Indies.

The result was that even careful writers were misled and misspelt the word.

The poet William Cowper was one of these, and Mrs Beeton in her BOOK OF HOUSEHOLD MANAGEMENT (1861) instructs her readers *Whisk the eggs until they are very light; add the sugar gradually; then stir in the cocoa-nut.*

The confusion continues to this day, so that some modern dictionaries record *cocoanut* as an alternative spelling.

For more information on the confusion between *coconut* and *cocoa*, see COCOA.

coffee

a mildly stimulating drink made from coffee berries

English coffee tastes like water that has been squeezed out of a wet sleeve.
(FRED ALLEN,
TREADMILL TO OBLIVION, 1954)

We prefer our coffee as strong as love, as black as sin, and as hot as Hades.
(THOMAS HALE BOGGS,
HOUSE OF REPRESENTATIVES,
US CONGRESS, 1960)

'Are you all right?' he asked.
'No. I need someone to unscrew my percolator. May be reduced to many things, but not to instant coffee.'
(DEBORAH MOGGACH,
THESE FOOLISH THINGS, 2004)

As I pull up outside the house, I notice a police panda car parked there. I walk into the kitchen to find Valentina and the village policeman sharing a joke over a cup of coffee.
(MARINA LEWYCKA, A SHORT HISTORY OF TRACTORS IN UKRAINIAN, 2005)

There was once an astute Ethiopian goatherd who observed that his flock became skittish when allowed to browse upon a certain bush. Curious, he sampled a few of the berries himself and found them invigorating. This, at any rate, is the legend and indeed it is thought that coffee was originally made into a paste and eaten for its stimulating qualities. It was in Arabia that a drink was first made out of the beans. Some say it was intended as a substitute for the wine the Muslims were forbidden to touch, and indeed the stimulant was censured by strict Muslims. Nevertheless, by the fifteenth century, coffee had spread to North Africa, Persia and Turkey. It came to Europe by way of Italy through Venetian trade with North Africa and the Middle East.

Coffee derives from the Arabic word *qahwah*. The significance of the term remains a mystery, however. Some Arab authorities say it originally referred to a kind of wine, others hazard the theory that it derives in some way from *Kaffa*, the region of Abyssinia (now Ethiopia) where the bush is indigenous. The Arabic word was borrowed as *kahve* by the Turks and from there passed into all the European languages around 1600. Throughout the first half of the seventeenth century English writers attempted anglicised spellings, *cahve, caffa, capha* and *cauphe* amongst them. *Coffee* became more frequent, probably under the influence of Italian *caffè* in the second half of that century.

The beverage became popular in England when enterprising businessmen began to open coffee houses in the cities. These soon became the haunts of the professional classes, who met to discuss business and exchange news. Some say the first such establishment was opened in Oxford in 1649, others that it was in London in 1652, but whatever the truth may be, by the mid-1660s London alone boasted over eighty of them. Nor did they serve only coffee. TEA and CHOCOLATE, also novelties in the seventeenth century, were often on offer as well.

☛ A number of words we associate with light refreshment derive from terms for *coffee* in other languages:

café is a French word for both 'coffee' and 'coffee house' and in the latter sense was borrowed into English in the early nineteenth century.

cafeteria originated in American English and is from American-Spanish *cafeteria*, 'coffee shop', from *cafetero*, 'coffee seller or maker', from *café*, 'coffee'. It was borrowed into British English in the first half of the nineteenth century.

caffeine, the stimulant chemical in coffee which gives the brew its kick, is a nineteenth-century borrowing of French *caféine*, from French *café*, 'coffee'.

coffin
a box to contain a body for disposal

*So the clergy and choir came to meet us at the door, then turned and moved up the Cathedral nave chanting in solemn procession, 'I am the Resurrection and the Life saith the Lord'. But meanwhile there was a dreadful struggle at the steps leading up from the Cloisters to the door. The bearers were quite unequal to the task and the **coffin** seemed crushingly heavy. There was a stamping and a scuffling, a mass of struggling men swaying to and fro, pushing and writhing and wrestling while the coffin sank and rose and sank again. Once or twice I thought the whole mass of men must have been down together with the coffin atop of them and some one killed or maimed at least.*
(FRANCIS KILVERT, DIARIES, FRIDAY, 2 DECEMBER 1870)

*As the men carried the **coffin** out of the door and placed it in the cart, the gathered crowd in the street bowed their heads and the men removed their hats.*
(TRACY CHEVALIER, BURNING BRIGHT, 2007)

Today the word *coffin* has a melancholy, funereal ring to it, so much so that a study of some of the uses to which it was applied in past centuries makes strange reading. From the fifteenth to the eighteenth centuries a *coffin* was 'a raised piecrust', made of an inedible paste as a container for the tasty filling. The title character in Shakespeare's TITUS ANDRONICUS (1594) seeks this gory revenge:

> *Hark, villains! I will grind your bones to dust,*
> *And with your blood and it I'll make a paste;*
> *And of the paste a coffin I will rear,*
> *And make two pasties of your shameful heads;*

In the late sixteenth and the seventeenth centuries, *coffin* also denoted the pie dish itself. In THE TAMING OF THE SHREW (1594) Petruchio teases Katharina over the purchase of a cap with these words:

> *Why, thou say'st true; it is a paltry cap,*
> *A custard-coffin, a bauble, a silken pie...*

And in Ben Jonson's THE STAPLE OF NEWS (1625) we read:

> *Therefore if you spend*
> *The red-deer pies i' your house, or sell them forth, sir,*
> *Cast so that I may have their coffins all*
> *Return'd here, and pil'd up.*

From the sixteenth to the nineteenth centuries, a *coffin* was 'a conical screw of paper' into which a grocer might weigh out goods such as spices. Around the mid-seventeenth century the term was applied to both 'the carriage of a printing machine' and 'a container in which objects were fired in a furnace'. And in the first half of the nineteenth century *coffin* or *coffin-ship* was a colloquial term given to 'an unseaworthy vessel', likely to be the burial container of all on board. This last lugubrious sense obviously evolved from the present meaning of the word, 'a box to contain a corpse for burial', which has been current since the first quarter of the sixteenth century.

These very varied applications share a common characteristic: they are all containers of one sort or another. In the fourteenth century a *coffin* was first and foremost a general term for 'a basket, box or chest'. It was a direct borrowing of *cofin*, an Old French word of the same meaning. This, in turn, came from Latin *cophinus* and Greek *kophinus*, 'a basket'.

Modern society is rather squeamish about death and cloaks the inevitable, unthinkable truth in euphemism. In the mid-nineteenth century American English abandoned the stark *coffin* for the more comforting *casket*, much to Nathaniel Hawthorne's scorn: *'Caskets'! a vile modern phrase, which compels a person...to shrink...from the idea of being buried at all* (OUR OLD HOME, 1863). But when it comes down to it, since *casket* comes from the Old French *cassette*, a diminutive form of *casse*, meaning 'box', there really is very little to choose between them.

☛ Also from *cophinus* comes Old French *coffre*, meaning 'a strong box, a chest'. This was borrowed into Middle English at the turn of the fourteenth century, eventually becoming *coffer*.

Other funereal words discussed in this book are CEMETERY, HEARSE and SARCOPHAGUS.

comb
a toothed instrument for tidying the hair

'...if you look scruffy and you haven't bothered to iron your shirt, what does that say about your attitude to business? It's the same when you're looking for a job. If

*you're scruffy and haven't made the effort
to **comb** your hair or shave properly it just
gives completely the wrong impression.'*
(THE SUNDAY TIMES, 25 JANUARY 2009)

See UNKEMPT.

comfort

to console; something that brings
about a sense of ease and relaxation

*'Poppy,' said Aunt Fish, 'don't just stand
there. Be a **comfort** to you mother.' And so
while she plagued the Irish for a facecloth
soaked in vinegar, and more pillows, and a
jug of hot chocolate, I stood by my mother's
side and wondered what kind of comforting
to do.*
(LAURIE GRAHAM,
THE UNFORTUNATES, 2002)

*When I had first arrived I had been taken
from the plane and placed under house
arrest. A polite letter was handed to me
stressing that this was for both my **comfort**
and protection. However, I was under no
circumstances to leave the building…*
(BOB GELDOF,
GELDOF IN AFRICA, 2005)

The Bayeux tapestry, which dates from
the eleventh or early twelfth century,
shows scenes depicting the Norman
Conquest of England in 1066. In one
of these scenes Bishop Odo, the
brother of William the Conqueror, is
seated on horseback behind his squires,
brandishing a stout staff. The Latin
inscription reads *Hic Odo Episcopus
baculum tenens confortat pueros*, 'Here
Bishop Odo with a staff in his hand
comforts his troops'. What kind of
comfort is this?

Comfort was originally a much more
robust word than it is today. Its source
is *confortāre*, the Late Latin verb that
appears in the Bayeux caption. This
was a compound composed of the
Latin intensive prefix *con-* and *fortis*,
'strong', and it meant 'to strengthen,

to encourage, to hearten' someone's
spirit or resolve. Its journey into
Middle English in the thirteenth
century was by way of Old French *con-
forter*. Before long, however, the sense
of 'strengthening' someone's spirit
began to slide into that of 'soothing'
their distress, and the current meaning
of the word emerged.

As a noun *comfort* passed from
'support' and 'encouragement', to
'solace' and 'consolation', the word
coming to denote the 'creature comforts' that bring contentment and a
sense of well-being in the seventeenth
century.

companion

someone who accompanies another,
and is of like mind

*My new friends at the Red Cross took me
for younger than twenty, especially as I
didn't have a beau as yet. As I explained
to them, I hadn't even had my debut, what
with Pa's passing and my being needed
as a **companion** and helpmeet to Ma.*
(LAURIE GRAHAM,
THE UNFORTUNATES, 2002)

*Walking out of a Mel Ramos exhibition the
other day, my **companion** remarked on
how benignly amusing his paintings now
seemed. Back in the 1970s, when she was
a younger, more fiery feminist, his works
infuriated her.*
(NEW YORK TIMES,
25 JANUARY 2009)

The notion behind this word is that of
sharing a meal with someone. Scholars
say that by the fourth century the population of the Roman Empire included
several million people of Germanic
extraction. Commerce between the
Empire and Germanic tribes beyond its
northern border was also thriving, so
that a certain amount of linguistic
exchange between Germanic languages
and Vulgar Latin was inevitable.

Companion may be a result of Germanic influence on Latin.

Some of the northern tribes referred to those with whom they rubbed shoulders on a daily basis as 'sharers of bread'. Gothic, for instance, had the word *gahlaiba*, and Old High German the similar compound *galeipo* 'one who eats bread with another', (from *ga*, 'with' and *laib*, 'bread'). It is possible that Vulgar Latin borrowed this concept and made a direct translation of it, forming the word *compāniō* (stem: *compāniōn-*) from *com*, meaning 'with', and *pānis*, 'bread'. From this Old French derived *compaignon,* which Middle English then borrowed as *compainoun* in the late thirteenth century.

☛ English *company* (13th cent) comes from Old French *compagnie*, which also derived from Latin *compāniō*.

Latin *pānis*, 'bread', is also responsible for:

pannier (14th cent): from Old French *panier*, from Latin *panārium*, 'bread basket'.

pantry (14th cent): Middle English *pantrie*, from Old French *paneterie*, 'room for storing bread', from *panetier* (13th cent), 'panter', that is 'one in charge of the bread and food supplies', from *pan*, 'bread', from Latin *pānis*.

consider

to be of the opinion; to deliberate, give careful thought to

*'Rats! Hang it all! I wish I was dead. I don't know what I do want to do,' he groaned, and cast himself upon his bed. He was sure of nothing but the fact that he was unhappy. He **considered** suicide in a dignified manner, but not for long enough to get much frightened about it.* (SINCLAIR LEWIS, OUR MR WRENN, THE ROMANTIC ADVENTURES OF A GENTLE MAN, 1914)

*Virginia was just too late for the sixties revolution. She had worked at a bank – which was **considered** an excellent job until the sixties burst all that wide open – instead of at an art gallery, and she had married a plumber instead of a lawyer.* (MAVIS CHEEK, THE SEX LIFE OF MY AUNT, 2002)

The Romans believed that the relative position of the planets influenced earthly events. The endeavours of the astrologers and augurs as they scrutinised the night sky are encapsulated in the Latin verb *consīderāre*. It meant 'to study the stars with great care', being a combination of the intensive prefix *con-* and *sīus*, 'constellation, star'. It soon came to be used more generally with the sense 'to observe carefully, to examine', before developing the figurative use 'to reflect upon'. In these senses it was borrowed into Old French, and from there into Middle English in the fourteenth century.

☛ The verb *desire*, which came into English in the thirteenth century via Old French *desirer*, is also derived from *sīdus*. It comes from Latin *dēsīderāre* which meant 'to regret, to miss' and hence 'to long for'. The original sense of *dēsīderāre* and its connection with 'star' is obscure, but Skeat suggests 'to note the absence of stars' and hence the regret that the auguries were hidden.

Also from *sīus* comes English *sidereal*, 'concerning the stars', which was borrowed from Latin *sīdereus* in the seventeenth century.

For other words connected with augurs, see AUSPICIOUS and TEMPLE. See also DISASTER and INFLUENCE.

EARLY LATIN INFLUENCES

It would be not unreasonable to imagine that a significant number of Latin words became established in Old English through the Roman conquest of Britain in AD 43, especially since the island was under Roman rule for around 400 years after that. Surprisingly, there are very few. Although Latin was the official language, and that of the ruling elite, its use could not have been sufficiently widespread among the ordinary population to ensure its survival. It is likely that Latin fell into disuse not long after the withdrawal of the Roman troops around 410, and was certainly incapable of surviving the turmoil of the Germanic invasions which began some 40 years later. When the Angles, Saxons and Jutes arrived in Britain, they completely submerged the Celtic culture that existed there at that time. Thus, from the store of over 600 words that the Celts had taken from Latin, very few were passed on:

port, 'harbour', 'gate', from Latin *portus*
torr, 'tower', 'rock', from Latin *turris*
munt, 'mountain', from Latin *mons*
wīc, 'village', from Latin *vīcus*
ceaster, 'camp', from Latin *castra* (evident in place names such as Chester, Lancaster, Gloucester, Manchester, etc.)

The stock of Celtic words that came into Old English is equally meagre. That is not to say, however, that there was no more Latin influence on English until French arrived with William the Conqueror in 1066 and until the revival of classical scholarship and influence in later centuries. A second source came from

contemplate
to meditate upon, think about

*They are not going quietly into their rocking chairs. They are as self-reflective – some say self-absorbed – as ever, and they are changing the way Americans **contemplate** their so-called golden years.*

Sixty, as they say, is the new 40. There were 76 million babies born between the years 1946 and 1964, and their choices and life challenges changed the way Americans lived in the 20th century.
(PORTLAND PRESS HERALD,
9 APRIL 2006)

See TEMPLE.

crazy
mad, insane

*Author's note: The word '**crazy**' will be used many times in this story. Synonyms include: wild, passionate, fanatical, and extreme, among others. From a literary perspective, a writer should strive to use as many variations and slants on a particular word to keep a story moving. Somehow...in this particular instance...without apology... 'crazy' seems to be the only appropriate term to use.*
(HERALD NEWS, JOLIET, ILLINOIS,
24 JUNE 2006)

*He had tried to spend that first night on the sofa, but it was uncomfortable and Jean was of the opinion that **crazy** behaviour* the invading Germanic tribes themselves. On the Continent they had had considerable trading links with the Roman Empire, resulting in a mutual exchange of words (see, for example, the entries COMPANION and MINT). When the Anglo-Saxon invasion of Britain took place, therefore, the language of the conquerors already contained a stock of Latin words.

From trade came words such as: *cēap*, 'trade', 'bargain', 'cheap' (L *caupō*, 'tradesman'); *mangere*, 'monger' (L *mangō*, 'dealer'); *mynet*, 'coin' (L *monēta*, 'mint', 'money'); *pund*, 'pound' (L *pondō*, 'pound weight'); *wīn*, 'wine', (L *vīnum*).

From everyday life: *cytel*, 'kettle' (L *catillus*); *pyle*, 'pillow' (L *pulvīnus*); *cycene*, 'kitchen' (L *coquīna*); *cuppe*, 'cup' (L *cuppa*); *disc*, 'dish' (L *discus*); *mortere*, 'mortar' (L *mortarium*); *line*, 'line', 'rope' (L *linea*); *cīese*, 'cheese' (L *cāseus*).

From communications: *stroet*, 'street', 'road' (L *strāta*); *mīl*, 'mile' (L *mīlia*).

The third, and greatest, influence of Latin on Old English came via the church. From the earliest mission in 597 to the end of the Old English period over 500 years later, a large number of borrowings took place. These were initially to do with church organisation, since Old English did not have equivalents of its own to draw upon: examples include *abbot, altar, angel, chalice, deacon, hymn, mass, nun, pope, provost, psalm* and many more. Also borrowed was a further stock of words relating to monastic life, including education and medicine, which then passed into general domestic use.

For other early influences on Old English, see VIKING CONQUESTS (page 303).

---

encouraged crazy ideas. So he relocated upstairs.
(MARK HADDON,
A SPOT OF BOTHER 2007)

In the fourteenth century, the verb *to craze* meant 'to break into pieces'. Its source is thought to be unattested Old Norse *krasa*, 'to shatter'. The adjective *crazy*, derived from this in the sixteenth century, first meant 'full of cracks, damaged'. In his COMMENTARIE UPON THE EPISTLE OF ST PAUL TO TITUS (1612), Thomas Taylor writes *of a crazie pitcher which is vnfit to hold water.* From here the word came to be used figuratively to describe a person whose physical health was frail and then, during the seventeenth century, one whose mental health was failing. Soon,

however, this latter sense began to be applied to someone who appeared mad through being in the grip of an excessive enthusiasm or eagerness. The phrase *to go crazy* dates from the eighteenth century and *to be crazy about someone*, meaning 'to be madly in love with', dates from the nineteenth century:

Daisy Daisy,
Give me your answer do!
I'm half crazy,
All for the love of you!
It won't be a stylish marriage,
I can't afford a carriage,
But you'll look sweet on the seat
Of a bicycle built for two!
(HARRY DACRE, DAISY BELL, 1892)

☛ *Crazy paving* is an early twentieth-century term suggested by *crazy quilt*, which nineteenth-century American woman used to describe a patchwork quilt of random design.

criss-cross

to move about in intersecting directions, backwards and forwards

*Standing at the camp perimeter, his feet slowly sinking into snowprints, Isaac looked out toward England, his vista **criss-crossed** by the barbed wire. The sea looked calm, virtually crystalline in the cold.*
(DAVID BADDIEL,
THE SECRET PURPOSES, 2004)

*Muriel's family's trade was now, far from discreetly, **criss-crossing** Britain in brand new thick black lines. Muriel's grandfather, Thomas Brassey, had employed eighty-five thousand men, more than the British Army, and had built one in every three miles of the railways laid on Earth in his lifetime.*
(FRANCES OSBORNE,
THE BOLTER, 2008)

The horn-book was an early primer. It consisted of a thin wooden board on which the alphabet, the numbers and the Lord's Prayer (and sometimes a formula for exorcism) were written. This surface was protected by a thin sheet of horn *to save from finger wet the letter fair* (William Shenstone, THE SCHOOL-MISTRESS, 1742). The board had a handle and was hung from the child's belt. Shakespeare, in a longer passage full of plays on words from LOVE'S LABOUR'S LOST, (1595), gives this exchange:

Armado: [to Holofernes] *Monsieur, are you not lettered?*
Moth: *Yes, yes; he teaches boys the horn-book. What is a, b, spelt backward with the horn on his head?*
Holofernes: *Ba, pueritia, with a horn added.*
Moth: *Ba, most silly sheep with a horn. You hear his learning.*
Holofernes: *Quis, quis, thou consonant?*
Moth: *The third of the five vowels, if You repeat them; or the fifth if I.*
Holofernes: *I will repeat them: a, e, i…*
Moth: *The sheep; the other two concludes it: o, u.*

As Armado goes on to comment on this exchange, *it is indeed true wit!*

In the sixteenth century and perhaps earlier, the alphabet itself was known as *Christ-cross-row*. This was because *Christ-cross*, a character resembling a Maltese cross, preceded it in the horn-book. Before a child repeated the alphabet he would recite the formula *Christ's cross me speed*. In A PLAINE AND EASIE INTRO-DUCTION TO PRACTICALL MUSICKE (1597), Thomas Morely gives an example of such a recitation: *Christes crosse be my speede, in all vertue to proceede, A, b, c, d, e, f, g, h, i, j, k, l, m, n, o, p, q, r, s, & t, double u, v, x with y, ezod, & per se tittle tittle est Amen. When you haue done begin againe, begin againe.*

When an illiterate person was required to sign his name he would print the Christ-cross as his mark. A character in Smollett's translation of DON QUIXOTE (1755) remarks, *I am even ignorant of the a, b, c; but provided I remember my christcross, I shall be sufficiently qualified.*

Rapid repetition of *Christ-cross* led to its being pronounced *criss-cross*, so that eventually the sense of the original was forgotten and the term was simply regarded as a repetitive coupling similar to *mish-mash*, *zig-zag*, etc. As such, in the early nineteenth century, *criss-cross* made an appearance as a verb with the sense 'to mark with a crossing pattern'.

For further recitations from the horn-book, see AMPERSAND.

crocodile

a large reptile; a file of schoolchildren walking two by two

*In dry watercourses I saw **crocodiles**,*
squatting on ridiculous bowed legs, that
yawned like antique colonels in the sun.
(DOM MORAES,
MY SON'S FATHER, 1968)

On Thursday evening she and Jacob laid
out the Brio train set on the living-room
carpet. The bridge, the tunnel, the freight
crane, the chunky track with its interlocking
*jigsaw ends. Jacob arranged a **crocodile** of*
trucks behind Thomas, then crashed them
into a landslide of Lego.
(MARK HADDON,
A SPOT OF BOTHER, 2006)

Alan and Joan Root devised all sorts of
ways to film wildlife under water, from a
glass-fronted punt to a thinly disguised
underwater hide. It was the first time
*that hippos and **crocodiles** had been*
seen below the surface.
(MICHAEL BRIGHT, 100 YEARS OF
WILDLIFE, 2007)

Alligators and crocodiles are closely related but there are nevertheless several differences between the two: the head of the alligator, for instance, is flattish and almost rectangular, while the crocodile's is triangular. There is, in fact, a third member of the Crocodilia order: the gavial, found in India and south-west Asia. It has a longer, narrower and weaker jaw.

Although crocodiles are widespread, the name was first applied to the reptiles of the Nile in particular. In the fifth century BC, the Greek historian Herodotus wrote: *The name of crocodiles was given them by the Ionians, who remarked their resemblance to the lizards, which in Ionia live in the walls, and are called crocodiles.*

The original Greek term would have been the unattested *krokodrīlos*, meaning 'worm of the pebbles' (from *krokē*, 'pebbles' and *drilos*, 'worm'), reflecting the reptile's habit of basking. However, the word Herodotus uses is *krokodīlos* (minus the second *r*), which Latin borrowed as *crocodīlus*. Medieval Latin corrupted the classical Latin word by relocating the *r* to give *cocodrillus*, and this was taken into Old French as *cocodrille* and from there into Middle English as *cocodrille* and *cokadrill* around the beginning of the fourteenth century. From the late sixteenth century onwards, however, the word was standardised after Latin *crocodīlus*.

The story that the crocodile attracted its prey by pitiful moaning before devouring it with hypocritical tears of remorse is very old. In 1356 we find Sir John Maundeville describing *in a certain countree...cokdrilles*, adding that *theise Serpentes slen men, and thei eten hem wepynge* (VOIAGE AND TRAVAILE). Later, Shakespeare has Othello accuse his wife of shedding *crocodile tears*.

For another word whose spelling was standardised after the Latin in the sixteenth century, see AMETHYST.
For the etymology of other creatures, see ALLIGATOR, ANTELOPE, ELEPHANT and LIZARD.

curfew

a period when citizens are ordered to be off the streets

*'There is no time,' she said. 'For one thing, none of the nearby pharmacies have it. So you'd have to fight through traffic from one place to the next, maybe all the way across town, with little likelihood that you'd ever find it. It's almost eight-thirty now, so you'll probably get arrested for breaking **curfew**.'*

(KHALED HOSSEINI,
A THOUSAND SPLENDID SUNS, 2007)

*Navigating the patchwork of **curfew** rules across the Southland can be the parental equivalent of learning advanced algebra. Each municipality has its own time when kids need to be off the streets, with most having one curfew for weekdays and another for weekends.*

(SOUTHTOWN STAR, CHICAGO,
13 JULY 2008)

In medieval times, ordinary dwellings were of timber construction and built close together. Their wooden frames and thatched roofs made them a great fire risk. Towns had no high-pressure water supply for fire-fighting; water for this purpose had to be fetched from wells and streams. Demolishing houses or ripping off thatched roofs to make a fire-break was more effective and tools for this purpose were kept by the town authorities.

In the houses of this period, a domestic fire did not burn in a chimney against a wall but on a hearth in the centre of the room, the smoke drifting out through a hole in the roof. If precautions were not taken to tend it well, then a slipping log falling onto the straw or rushes that covered the floor might reduce that house and its neighbours to ashes. A law, in force throughout Europe, guarded against this. The regulation was known in Old French as *cuevrefeu*, literally 'cover the fire' (from *couvrir*, 'cover' and *feu*, 'fire'), which gave *coeverfu* in Anglo-French and *curfeu* in Middle English. Each evening, usually at eight o'clock, a bell would be rung as a signal either to extinguish the fire or to cover the embers until morning. In time, *curfeu* was applied to the bell as well as to the regulation. Indeed, in the earliest written references, which date from the thirteenth century, the word is obviously applied to the signal alone, or to the hour of its ringing.

Using the curfew as a means of controlling the people first arose in the reigns of Edward I and Edward III, when anyone carrying arms was forbidden to walk the streets after the bell had rung. Christopher Hibbert (THE ENGLISH, 1987) notes that servants in Norwich risked imprisonment if they were not safely back under their masters' roofs by eight o'clock, and the same fate awaited inhabitants of Beverley abroad after nine, or visitors to the town out after eight o'clock without both a light and a good reason. From this use comes the present-day meaning of curfew, 'an order, often in times of unrest or danger, obliging people to clear streets and public places and return home by a certain hour'.

The curfew bell was still sounded long after the need for the fire regulation had passed, when it functioned as a general signal for everything to settle down for the night:

The Curfew tolls the knell of parting day,
The lowing herd wind slowly o'er the lea,
The ploughman homeward plods his
weary way,
And leaves the world to darkness and
to me.

(THOMAS GRAY, ELEGY IN A COUNTRY
CHURCHYARD, 1750)

In countless villages farmers locked up their livestock when it rang while, according to Walsh, in Durham it was the signal for the college gates to be closed and in Newcastle for the shops to shut. The curfew bell was gradually petering out by the end of the nineteenth century but is still traditionally sounded in some towns and villages, such as Morpeth in Northumberland and Sandwich in Kent.

For another word whose etymology includes the French *couvre*, see HANDKERCHIEF.

custard

a sweet dessert sauce made of milk, eggs and sugar

Custard has all the attributes of the best comfort food – plenty of carbohydrate, sweetness and a sloppy texture. But proper comfort custard is very different from the thinner, lighter crème anglais. At the back of every comfort food devotee's mind is the thick and unyielding yellow stuff that came from Mr Bird's blue and yellow drums.
(EVENING STANDARD, 26 JANUARY 2007)

In March environmental protester Leila Deen, of Plane Stupid, attacked Peter Mandelson, the Business Secretary, throwing green custard in his face.
(THE TELEGRAPH, 16 JUNE 2009)

When the word *custard* first appeared in Middle English in the fifteenth century it did not refer to a sweet sauce but to a kind of tart. The tart could contain fruit, meat or a mixture of the two but the filling was always covered with a thick, sweet sauce made of milk thickened with eggs and flavoured with spices. THE BOKE OF KOKERY (c. 1440) contains a recipe for *custard lumbarde*. The custard is filled with beef marrow, dates and prunes and the sauce is made of cream and eggs sea-soned with sugar, salt and parsley. The recipe recommends using almond milk and omitting the eggs and the marrow in Lent, when dairy and meat produce was forbidden.

The word *custard* is a corruption of the earlier *crustade*, 'pie': THE FORM OF CURY (c. 1390), a cookery book from the court of Richard II, has recipes for *Crustardes of Flessh and Crustardes of Fysshe*, and the fourteenth-century BABEES BOOK has one for a *crustade ryal*. This was a borrowing of the unattested Anglo-French word *crustade*, a term derived from Old French *crouste*, 'crust'.

By the early seventeenth century the word custard was being transferred from 'pie' to denote a cooked and sweetened egg and milk mixture served either in a pastry case or baked on its own.

☞ The English word *crust* (14th cent) is a borrowing of Old French *crouste*. This, in turn, comes from Latin *crusta* which denotes 'shell, rind, crust' or any other hard surface.

cynic

someone who sees base motives behind virtuous acts, and expects the worst; a scornful mocker

Until now I had not even mentioned Justinus' letters to Helena. She and her mother instantly colluded and swore never to tell Claudia... From what I knew of the daft relationship between Claudia and Justinus, he would probably confess to his wife himself. They had never had secrets. A cynic would say that explained their problems.
(LINDSEY DAVIS, SATURNALIA, 2007)

All Messiahs have feet of clay. This one will be no different. But let's allow ourselves a moment of good faith and pride that politics can, just sometimes, defy the **cynics** *and see the best rise.*
(EVENING STANDARD, 21 JANUARY 2009)

According to the Greek philosopher Antisthenes (c. 445–c. 360 BC), virtue is the highest good. It can be achieved through exercising self-sufficiency and self-control, which bring freedom from needs and desires. Such a philosophy naurally demands a very basic life-style. Antisthenes and his disciples practised what they preached: Diogenes (411–322 BC) even went so far as to live in a tub, although his self-control did not stop him from showing open disdain for the pleasures enjoyed by society at large. Milton in COMUS (1634) declared:

> O *foolishness of men! that...*
> *fetch their precepts from the Cynic tub,*
> *Praising the lean and sallow Abstinence!*

The gymnasium where Antisthenes taught was called *Kunosarge*, and the term *kunicos*, 'cynic', was probably derived from this. However, *kunicos* also meant 'dog-like', so that the word was popularly supposed to be a comment on the critical, carping attitude of the philosopher and his followers. Indeed *kuōn*, 'dog', became a nickname for 'a cynic', a fact alluded to by Heywood in IRON AGE (1632): *Peace Cinicke, barke not dogge.*

Cynic came into English by way of Latin *cynicus* in the sixteenth century. At first it properly referred to one who adhered to Antisthenes' philosophy. Almost immediately, however, it became a term for 'a fault-finder, a critic'. Since the nineteenth century modern usage has extended the meaning further so that it now denotes 'one who disbelieves any purity of intent in the actions of others and responds with disdain and sarcasm':

What is a cynic? – A person who knows the price of everything and the value of nothing.
(OSCAR WILDE, LADY WINDERMERE'S FAN, 1892)

D

deadline

the cut-off point for newspaper copy, payment, the completion of a task, etc.

And that is the story of how Tigger on the Couch *came to be. As in any fairy-tale quest, it was not without its villains – nasty* **deadlines** *crept up from dark corners and had to be fought – but, eventually, good won over evil and the book was written.*
(LAURA JAMES,
TIGGER ON THE COUCH, 2007)

…in order to get a presentation done well, and for it not to dominate the days just before delivery, it's best to think about a series of key dates, rather than one final **deadline**. *In other words, construct a critical path for yourself, marking in the dates you want to hit.*
(JAMES CAPLIN,
I HATE PRESENTATIONS, 2008)

This word originates from the prison camps of the American Civil War (1861–5). The *dead line* was a line marked out about 5 metres (17 feet) from the inner fence. Any prisoner who dared pass over it would be shot down to prevent his escape. Later, in the early twentieth century, *deadline* was applied to the guideline on the bed of a cylinder printing press over which the prepared type surface should not pass. The word was used figuratively by the American press in the first quarter of the twentieth century to denote 'a time by which all material had to be handed in ready for publication'. It is now more widely applied to the time or date by which any task has to be completed or payment made.

decimate

to reduce a group by a large proportion; to inflict great damage on something so that it is almost destroyed

Nightclubs were the new venue for dancing. The sons of the families living in the private palaces lining London's parks had been **decimated** *in France and these houses were being sold and demolished, their ballrooms and vast drawing rooms with them.*
(FRANCES OSBORNE,
THE BOLTER, 2008)

The environment is another concern for any modern president… Jimmy Carter famously put solar panels on the roof, a symbolic gesture meant to encourage Americans to think about their energy consumption. The solar panels were removed by the Reagans when they came into power, **decimating** *the solar energy industry at a stroke.*
(SUNDAY TELEGRAPH,
18 JANUARY 2009)

The Latin verb *decimāre* was derived from *decimus*, 'a tenth', and *decem*, 'ten', and meant 'to take one tenth'. It had a twofold application in ancient times.

The first of these was military and referred to a strategy which Roman generals sometimes employed to keep their men in order. Whenever a general got wind of mutinous rumblings among his troops he would have one in ten of their number picked out by lot for execution to bring the remainder into line. The practice was not confined to Roman times: in 1599 Elizabeth I appointed Robert Devereux, second Earl of Essex, Lord Lieutenant of Ireland with orders to quell the rebellion there. The stiff resistance of the Irish, however, dismayed the English troops. During a skirmish at Wicklow on 29 May, Sir Henry Harington's company showed cowardice under fire and ran away. In Dublin on 11 July, Essex disciplined the company, imprisoning Harington and executing one soldier in every ten. The earliest recorded use in English of *decimate* with the sense 'to destroy one in ten' refers to this episode.

Initially the verb was confined to this meaning and to historical and military contexts. By the second half of the seventeenth century, however, it was being applied more widely and with the looser sense 'to destroy or remove a large proportion of', as though up to nine out of ten had been destroyed and one tenth saved, rather than the other way around. Even today some writers still reject this second sense, insisting on 'one in ten'.

The second application of *decimāre* was a fiscal one and meant 'to levy a tax of one tenth'. Its use in English was largely restricted to the exacting of a one-tenth tax imposed by Cromwell on the Royalists in 1655. In his comedy THE WILD GALLANT (1663), for instance, Dryden writes of being *as poor as a decimated Cavalier*. *Decimate* in this sense did not survive the eighteenth century and never replaced the old familiar term *tithe* which derived from Old English *tēotha*, 'tenth', in the twelfth century.

☛ Latin *decem*, 'ten' is also responsible for:

December, which was originally the tenth month. See MONTHS OF THE YEAR (page 176)

decimal (17th cent): from Medieval Latin *decimālis*, 'of tithes', from *decimus*, 'a tenth', and *decem*, 'ten'. Applied initially to Arabic notation and later to decimal fractions.

dime (14th cent): in Middle English 'a tenth part, a tithe', from Old French *dime*, from Latin *decima*, 'tithe, tenth part', feminine of *decimus*, 'a tenth', from *decem*, 'ten'. Chosen as the name for a ten-cent coin in the United States in 1786 and still current in this sense.

derrick

a large crane, hoisting equipment

There, in a glass box the size of a large aquarium, a sort of oil **derrick** *made of brightly coloured rods and sockets and toothed wheels pivoted up and down, allowing a series of blue marbles to roll the length of its spine and land in a metal saucer.*
(ANNE TYLER, BACK WHEN WE WERE GROWNUPS, 2001)

Mr [Red] Adair was born in Texas in 1915 and after school worked as a labourer, first on the railways and then in the oil fields. While he was working on an oil **derrick** *a valve blew, and instead of running for cover he stayed and repaired the damage.*
(THE GUARDIAN, 9 AUGUST, 2004)

The principal place of execution in London from 1388 to 1793 was at Tyburn, close to the present-day Marble Arch. Generally large crowds gathered and there was something of a carnival atmosphere, for hanging days were designated public holidays. The grizzly spectacle was intended to serve as a deterrent to the citizens who went to watch.

In 1571 a huge triangular gallows was erected at Tyburn where up to twenty-one victims could be hanged at the same time. The prisoners would arrive on a cart which came to a stop under the gallows. Once the rope had been secured around the victim's neck the horse was urged forward and the victim left dangling. Accounts speak of girls offering the condemned prisoners flowers and of crowds pushing forward to touch the corpses once they had been cut down, in some macabre belief that they were imbued with healing powers. Given the immense public interest in executions, the executioner himself must have been a well-known figure.

The hangman at Tyburn at the turn of the seventeenth century bore the surname Derick. Over the years, he was responsible for dispatching more than 3,000 prisoners, among them a man said once to have shown him mercy. The story goes that as a soldier Derick had served at the sacking of Cádiz (1595) under the second Earl of Essex (see DECIMATE). Here he was charged with rape, found guilty and would have hanged had not the Earl pardoned him on condition that he became hangman at Tyburn. A few years later Essex, who had lost favour with Queen Elizabeth, tried to provoke an uprising in London, and was accordingly charged with high treason and condemned to death in the Tower. The man engaged to behead him (the nobility were beheaded rather than hanged – see GUILLOTINE) was none other than Derick, who took three blows to sever the Earl's head. Essex had been a popular figure and it is said that Derick himself narrowly escaped death at the hands of the mob on the day of the execution. Two street ballads remain to testify to the depth of popular feeling. One of them, entitled UPON THE EARLE OF ESSEX HIS DEATH, runs:

Derick, thou know'st at Cales I sav'd
Thy life lost for a rape there done,
Where thou thyself canst testifie
Thine own hand three and twenty hung.

Such was Derick's notoriety that his name was soon applied to gallows and to hangmen in general. In THE SEVEN DEADLY SINNES OF LONDON (1606), Thomas Dekker has *I would there were a Derick to hang vp him too*, and in GLOSSOGRAPHIA (1656), a dictionary of hard words, Thomas Blount defines *derrick* as a term *abusively used for a Hang-man; because one of that name was not long since a famed executioner at Tiburn.*

References to *derricks* as gallows were superseded in the following century when the term was applied to 'hoisting equipment'. This happened first of all in a naval context – some have suggested that sailors' 'gallows humour' made them see the connection between a device for hanging and one for lifting tackle on the mizzen mast. The nineteenth century saw *derrick* applied to a 'crane' and by extension, originally in America, to the 'framework constructed over an oil-well to support the drilling equipment and to hoist and lower lengths of pipe'.

The etymology of *derrick*, however, can be taken back far beyond London's boundaries, for the name is of Dutch origin; *Diederik, Dierryk* and *Dirk* are all variants. This, in turn, is the same as German *Dietrich*, which comes from *Theoderic* (454–526 AD), the great king of the Ostrogoths, an Eastern Germanic tribe of political significance during the late Roman Empire.

desultory
aimless, haphazard, unmethodical

If Walter Smith is feeling the heat after a
***desultory** start to the season and the loss*
of his best player, he showed no signs of it
on the eve of his side's home game against a
resurgent Hearts. He charmed, he laughed,
he wisecracked. It was hard to reconcile the
avuncular figure in front of us with the
supposedly besieged manager who had just
had his latest transfer target...swiped from
under his nose by the folk at Parkhead.
(SCOTLAND ON SUNDAY,
17 AUGUST 2008)

Furriballs are tailor-made fake fur covers –
from baby pink to sleek black – that turn
the fitball into a talking point and make
it hard to resist. My son comes home from
*school and lolls on it, doing **desultory***
***push-ups** while watching* The Simpsons.
My husband does a few crunches when he
thinks nobody is looking.
(TELEGRAPH.CO.UK, 27 JANUARY 2009)

The Roman circus, a huge oval building enclosed by banks of seats, was the
scene of a variety of spectacles, including horse and chariot races. A *dēsultor*,
literally 'one who leaps down' (from
dēsultus, past participle of *dēsilīre*, 'to
leap down'), was an equestrian acrobat
who entertained the crowd by leaping
from one swiftly moving horse to
another. Generally only two horses
were ridden at the same time,
although there are records of up to
four horses abreast at full gallop. The
derived Latin adjective *dēsultōrius*,
which literally meant 'belonging to a
leaper', and by extension 'superficial,
casual', was borrowed into English as
desultory in the sixteenth century with
the same figurative sense of 'random,
flitting from one thing to another,
unmethodical'.

☞ Latin *dēsilīre* is derived from *dē-*,
'down' and *salīre*, 'to jump'. *Salīre* is
present in a number of other common
English words:

assail and *assault* (13th cent): both
words ultimately derive from Latin
assilīre, 'to leap at', from *ad-*, 'at', and
salīre, 'to jump'.

result (15th cent): from Medieval
Latin *resultāre*, from Latin *resultāre*, 'to
leap back', from *re-*, 'back', and *saltāre*,
from *salīre*, 'to jump'.

salacious (17th cent): from Latin
salāx, applied to male animals jumping
up to mate, from *salīre*.

salient (16th cent): from *saliēns*, the
present participle of *salīre*. In English,
originally used as a heraldic term for
'jumping'.

See also INSULT.

dirge
an anthem sung at a service for the
dead; any sad, mournful music

REQUIEM, n. A mass for the dead
which the minor poets assure us the winds
sing o'er the graves of their favorites.
Sometimes, by way of providing a varied
*entertainment, they sing a **dirge**.*
(AMBROSE BIERCE,
THE DEVIL'S DICTIONARY, 1911)

The Commonwealth Games also gives the
Brits a chance to win a bucketful of medals
and from Melbourne you have probably
already witnessed a fair few tears shed on
the podium to the accompaniment of BBC
hysterics as the band strikes up 'Pomp and
Circumstance', 'Land of My Fathers'....
Mostly over these 10 days, however, the
*uncomplicated lightweight **dirge** 'Advance,*
Australia Fair' will be the runaway top of
the pops. Four years ago in Manchester, the
Aussies won 48 medals in the swimming
pool alone.
(THE SPECTATOR, 18 MARCH 2006)

In the Latin rite for the Office of the Dead, the anthem *Dirige, Domine, Deus meus, in conspectu tuo viam meam* is prescribed for Matins. The line comes from Psalm 5:8 and translates into English as 'Direct, O Lord, my God, my way in thy sight'. From the earliest records in the thirteeth century, the entire service was referred to by the first word of the anthem, *dirige* (the singular imperative of Latin *dīrigere*, 'direct, guide').

Of course, these offices had to be paid for. Selden's TABLE-TALK (published 1689, thirty-five years after his death) includes this piece of ready reckoning: *The Priest said Diriges, and twenty Diriges at fourpence a piece comes to a Noble.* Fortunately one of the benefits offered by medieval guilds was the provision of funeral masses for the souls of its members: *When any Broder or Suster of this Gilde is decessed oute off this worlde...ye Steward of this Gilde shall doo Rynge for hym, and do to say a Placebo and dirige, wt a masse on ye morowe of Requiem* (1494). And medieval wills sometimes left a sum of money to pay for the funeral feast or *dirge-ale* (see ALE): *Brede & Ale to Spende atte my dyryge* (1408).

By the sixteenth century the word, sometimes contracted to *dirge*, was also applied to any funereal music or song of lament. Shakespeare uses it of a swansong in THE RAPE OF LUCRECE (1594):

And now this pale swan in her watery nest
Begins the sad dirge of her certain ending.

Thereafter, *dirge* was much used by other writers in doleful mood. Gray's ELEGY WRITTEN IN A COUNTRY CHURCH-YARD (1750) describes the funeral of the youth that *Melancholy marked for her own*, borne slowly through the churchway path with *dirges due in sad array*. Nowadays the word is often used to describe any mournful-sounding music.

For a word with a similar origin, see PLACEBO.

disaster

a serious misfortune, a calamity

*My mother was no fool, though, As I trotted through the door at the end of my long day she would ask, 'So where did you go today?' and I would tell her. Academically I was a **disaster,** but by the time I left school I knew an awful lot about small blue birds.*
(CHARLIE HAMILTON JAMES, KINGFISHER: TALES FROM THE HALCYON RIVER, 2009)

*...Sir David Walker – a stalwart of Morgan Stanley – has proposed his own 39 steps to better bank governance in the hope of averting future **disasters** on the scale of the collapse of the Royal Bank of Scotland. But has he pulled it off?*
(THE WEEK, 25 JULY 2009)

In past centuries it was believed that the stars influenced both the characters and the affairs of men. *Disaster* is a product of this belief. Its source is an Old Italian adjective, *disastrato,* which meant 'ill-starred'. This was formed by adding the pejorative prefix *dis-* to *astro*, 'star' (from Latin *astrum*, from Greek *astron*, 'star'). From *disastrato* came the Italian back-formation *disastro*, a noun meaning 'bad luck, disaster', the implication being that the misfortune was the result of inauspicious planetary activity.

Disaster made a late appearance in English at the end of the sixteenth century, probably by way of French *désastre*. Shakespeare linked the new word to its heavenly origins in HAMLET (1601), where Horatio speaks of *disasters in the sun*. In KING LEAR (1605), Gloucester's bastard son Edmund mocks his father's conviction that his own problems and those of the world are no fault of man but are dictated by the planets:

This is the excellent foppery of the world,
that, when we are sick in fortune, – often
the surfeits of our own behaviour, – we
make guilty of our disasters the sun, the
moon, and stars; as if we were villains on
necessity; fools by heavenly compulsion;
knaves, thieves and treachers, by spherical
predominance; drunkards, liars, and
adulterers, by an enforc'd obedience of
planetary influence; and all that we are evil
in, by a divine thrusting on: an admirable
evasion of whoremaster man, to lay his
goatish disposition on the charge of a star!

☛ Greek *astron* has the stem *astro-*,
'star, in the shape of a star'. This was
used in Greek compounds such as
astronomos, literally 'star-arranger'
(from *astro-*and *-nomos*, from *nemein*,
'to arrange'), the source of English
astronomy (13th cent) and *astronomer*
(14th cent).

Astro- is now widely used to form
modern compounds relating to the
shape of a star (*asteroid*, *astrocyte*) or
the science of stars and space (*astro-
chemistry*, *astronautics*, *astrophysics*, etc.).

For other astrological terms see
CONSIDER, INFLUENCE and
INFLUENZA.

dismal
gloomy, dreary, woeful

'And Eliza is just the same old snobbish
Eliza – smoke-screens to disguise life's
reality, everything is for the best and in
the best of possible taste. And she lives
*in such a little flat in such a **dismal***
part of town now. It's a far cry from
the gabled semi with garage.'
(MAVIS CHEEK, THE SEX LIFE OF
MY AUNT, 2002)

I tried so hard to fight the endless sobbing.
I remember asking myself one night... 'Is
there anything about this scene you can
change, Liz?' And all I could think to do
was stand up, while still sobbing, and try

to balance on one foot in the middle of my
living room. Just to prove that – while
I couldn't stop the tears or change my
***dismal** interior dialogue – I was not yet*
totally out of control: at least I could cry
hysterically while balanced on one foot.
Hey, it was a start.
(ELIZABETH GILBERT,
EAT PRAY LOVE, 2006)

Besides saints' days, holy days and festivals, medieval calendars also marked
twenty-four 'Egyptian days', said to be
the result of ancient studies by
Egyptian astrologers. These were
inauspicious, evil days, the medieval
equivalents of 'Friday the thirteenth',
and there were two of them each
month. Medieval Latin called them *diēs
malī*, 'evil days', and from this Anglo-
Norman had *dis mal*. This subsequently
appeared as the compound noun
dismal, often in the expression *in the
dismal*, meaning 'in the evil days'.

Some medieval writers, Chaucer
included, misunderstood the origin of
dismal, believing it to derive from Old
French *dis mal* and to mean 'ten evils', a
reference to the ten plagues of Egypt
mentioned in the Bible (Exodus 6–12).
Skeat quotes Chaucer's BOKE OF THE
DUCHESSE (c. 1369). Here the knight,
describing the emotional turmoil he
was in as he told his tale of love to his
lady, says:

I not wel how that I began,
Ful euel rehersen hit I can;
And eek, as helpe me God withal,
I trowe hit was in the dismal,
That was the ten woundes of Egipte.

From the early fifteenth century *dismal*
began to be used as an adjective, curiously to describe the word *day*, the
result being a tautological coupling:
Her disemale daies and her fatal houres
(JOHN LYDGATE, THE STORY OF
THEBES, C. 1420).

By the last quarter of the sixteenth century *dismal*, with its overtones of foreboding and disaster, was being widely used to qualify any noun where the sense 'sinister, disastrous or wretched' was intended. The modern sense of 'dark and dreary, depressing' developed in the first half of the seventeenth century.

dollar

a unit of currency, particularly in the United States but also widely in other countries

*...the shirt-sleeved street traders hawking up phlegm the size of a Hong Kong **dollar**...*
(TONY PARSONS,
ONE FOR MY BABY, 2001)

*Travel agents at the event were in less buoyant mood and full of stories about a 14-day Caribbean cruise in a suite next month selling for only £1,000 including flights, and of American lines offering vouchers for hundreds of **dollars** to spend on board.*
(THE TIMES, 29 NOVEMBER 2008)

Jachymov is a spa-town situated in the Erzgebirge Mountains in the Czech Republic. In the sixteenth century it was known as Sankt Joachimsthal, and was in Bohemia. Around 1519 coins were minted there under the direction of the Count of Schlick, using silver from a nearby mine which had opened a few years earlier. The coins bore the image of St Joachim, St Joseph in English, the man to whom the Virgin Mary was betrothed. A single coin was known as a *Joachimstaler*, 'from the valley of Joachim'. This was soon shortened to *thaler* in High German, becoming *daler* in Low German and Dutch. English borrowed this Low German term around the mid-sixteenth century; the spelling *dollar* dates from the early seventeenth.

Initially the *daler* circulated in the German states, but was then used for similar coins minted by other countries. In the sixteenth century the *Spanish dollar* was widely used in the Spanish New World territories. Thriving commerce meant that, by the eighteenth century, these coins were circulating widely in Britain's North American colonies. By the time Thomas Jefferson was considering a monetary unit for the United States, he was forced to acknowledge that *The unit or [Spanish] dollar is a known coin and the most familiar of all to the mind of the people. It is already adopted from south to north* (NOTES ON A MONEY UNIT FOR U.S., 1782). And so, on 6 July 1785, the Continental Congress resolved *that the money unit of the United States of America be one dollar.*

One can, of course, never have too many dollars, as this moving anonymous verse makes clear:

Almighty dollar, thy shining face
Bespeaks thy wondrous power,
In my pockets make thy nesting-place,
I need thee every hour.
(THE WORLD'S PRAYER, c. 1891)

And in COLLECTIONS AND RECOLLECTIONS (1898) the Irish nationalist, poet and critic George William Erskine Russell published this witticism about the fanciful tradition that President George Washington once threw a silver dollar across the mile-wide Potomac river:

Mr Evarts, formerly Secretary of State, showed an English friend the place where Washington was said to have thrown a dollar across the Potomac. The English friend expressed surprise; 'but,' said Mr. Evarts, 'you must remember that a dollar went farther in those days.' A Senator met Mr Evarts next day, and said that he had been amused by his jest. 'But,' said Mr Evarts, 'I met a mere journalist just afterwards who said, "Oh, Mr. Evarts, you should have said it was a small matter to throw a dollar across the Potomac for a man who had chucked a Sovereign across the Atlantic."'

For notes on another currency, see STERLING.

draconian
severe, very harsh

Andy Murray has launched an outspoken attack on anti-doping rules which require athletes to inform testers of their location every day, describing the regulations as 'draconian'.
(THE GUARDIAN, 6 FEBRUARY 2009)

Aipac's [American Israel Public Affairs Committee] 6,000 delegates are being urged to bombard Capitol Hill with demands that Congress support ever more draconian sanctions against Iran, whose Government has threatened to wipe Israel off the face of the map.
(THE TIMES, 5 MAY 2009)

The adjective derives from the name of *Draco*, who was chief magistrate at Athens. In around 621 BC he compiled the first written legal code for the city. Justice was no longer to be left up to the individual interpretation of the magistrates: there was now a penalty for every crime. The punishments, however, were so harsh, the death penalty figuring largely for even trivial offences, that in 594 BC much of the code was repealed by Solon, who retained the death penalty only for homicide. The adjective *draconian* was coined in the nineteenth century (supplanting largely the earlier *draconic*), to denote any measures demanding uncalled-for severity or brutality.

dunce
a person of poor academic ability

'I'm a poor man, your Majesty,' the Hatter began, in a trembling voice, '– and I hadn't begun my tea – not above a week or so – and what with the bread-and-butter getting so thin – and the twinkling of the tea–'
'The twinkling of the what?' said the King.
'It began with the tea,' the Hatter replied.
'Of course twinkling begins with a T!' said the King sharply. 'Do you take me for a dunce? Go on!'
(LEWIS CARROLL, ALICE'S ADVENTURES IN WONDERLAND, 1865)

The last we heard of Jim Knight, the Cambridge-educated minister for school standards, he was wearing a dunce's cap after his political blog proved to be riddled with spelling errors.
(THE TELEGRAPH, 22 FEBRUARY, 2009)

It is ironic that a word denoting someone who is incapable of learning should derive from the name of a gifted scholar. John Duns Scotus (c. 1265–1308) was a Scottish-born Franciscan monk of great intellectual ability who, on the strength of his writing and teaching on philosophy and theology, gained a great following in universities at home and abroad. He lectured at the universities of Oxford, Paris and Cologne. Those who subscribed to his school of thought were known as Scotists.

Duns Scotus was particularly known for his insistence on the doctrine of the Immaculate Conception and that of free will, which he described as a horse under the control of its rider, grace, who could at any moment be unseated. His teaching that human reasoning could prove neither the existence of God nor that of the after-life brought him and the Scotists into conflict with the followers of

Thomas Aquinas, who upheld that faith and reason were in harmony, faith building upon reason to a revelation of the one true God.

The Scotists were esteemed until the sixteenth century when, due to their opposition to the revival of classical study that characterised the Renaissance, they met fierce opposition from the humanists and the religious reformers who accused them of quibbling and hair-splitting: *A Duns man would make xx. distinctions,* wrote William Tyndale (THE PARABLE OF THE WICKED MAMMON, 1528).

In their tirades the humanists nicknamed the Scotists *Dunsmen* or *Dunses* so that, by the late sixteenth century, the term *dunce* had become synonymous with 'an obfuscator, a nitpicker', and then 'one who is incapable of any learning'. From the first quarter of the seventeenth century some inns of court even had *dunce-tables* for the less able students preparing for the bar. The *dunce's cap*, a Victorian invention supposed to goad a child into learning through fear of being humiliated, was a conical hat to be worn by the child who could not recite his lessons.

· E ·

earwig

an insect with a long, slender, shiny body and pincers at the rear of its abdomen

*Consider the persistence of the **earwig**! Each afternoon, it feasts on the dahlia blooms. First sight. Each morning, we empty the flower pots and drown the earwig.... But still they come! Nature's remorseless. If we did this for one million years all over the world, could we make some small dent in the pattern of evolution? Would we produce an earwig that could swim?*
(JOHN MORTIMER, A VOYAGE ROUND MY FATHER, 1982)

*Television often throws up unpleasant images to surprise you, like finding an **earwig** in the sugar.*
(THE SPECTATOR, 1 APRIL 2009)

An article in a 1983 edition of NEW SCIENTIST quotes Professor Sharp of the Memorial University of Newfoundland saying that *earwig* is *a case of a dropped 'e'. The original word was earsewig. Drop the first letter and you get an insect that wiggles its arse, which seems plain enough.*

The explanation is plain, even entertaining, but untrue. Written references to this insect in English date back a thousand years. The word is from Old English *ēarwicga*, a compound of *ēare*, 'ear', and *wicga*, 'insect'. As its name suggests, this lithe little creature was thought to make a habit of scurrying into people's ears as they slept and, from there, penetrating their heads. The French, Germans and Dutch were all tormented by the same fear: French has *perce-oreille*, 'ear piercer', German *ohrwurm* and Dutch *oorworm*, both meaning 'earworm'. Happily there was a remedy; centuries earlier, in his HISTORIA NATURALIS, Pliny (AD 23–79) had suggested spitting into the ear to flush the offender out – not as easy as it sounds.

easel

a frame to support an artist's canvas, a blackboard, etc.

*…you can certainly see why Taos has always attracted artists and writers – or at least you can until you get to Taos itself. I had expected it to be a sweet little artists' colony. Full of people with smocks and **easels**, and it was just a tourist trap, with slow-moving traffic and stores selling ugly Indian pottery and big silver belt buckles and postcards.*
(BILL BRYSON, THE LOST CONTINENT, 1989)

*It's a lovely morning and the sharp blue light in the sky creates patterns on the beach, which is about half a mile long. A few painters are out with their **easels**, and Victoria and I aren't the only people running.*
(SARAH TUCKER, THE CONTROL FREAK CHRONICLES, 2009)

PORTMANTEAU WORDS

The Victorian author Lewis Carroll was fond of the nonsensical and enjoyed coining what he called 'portmanteau words' (a *portmanteau* was a large travelling bag). Carroll explains himself through Humpty Dumpty in THROUGH THE LOOKING GLASS (1872): *Well, 'slithy' means 'lithe and slimy'…. You see it's like a portmanteau – there are two meanings packed up into one word. Slithy* is familiar through the popularity of the nonsense poem JABBERWOCKY; other 'portmanteau words', however, have entered into current use.

Mimsy, according to Humpty Dumpty, is a blend of 'flimsy' and 'miserable'. The OED says that *mimsy* – a dialect word meaning 'clumsy, flimsy' – already existed in Carroll's time. It does, however, accept that the word may well have been separately invented by him, adding that in any case his use of the word has influenced the meaning.

The verb *galumph* is probably a combination of 'gallop' and 'triumphant', since it originally described the gait of the boy who slew the Jabberwock, severed its head and *went galumphing back*. In modern usage it means 'to stomp, to gallop about clumsily or heavily'.

Chortle merges 'chuckle' and 'snort'. The result is a very onomatopoeic term for a rich, throaty gurgle of laughter.

Over the last century a good number of other words invented on similar principles have been accepted into the language, several originating in American English:

aquacise	aqua + exercise	*guesstimate*	guess + estimate
bit	binary + digit	*identikit*	identity + kit
bo(a) tel	boat + hotel	*mingy*	mangy + stingy
brunch	breakfast + lunch	*motel*	motor + hotel
camcorder	camera + recorder	*sitcom*	situation + comedy
Chunnel	Channel + tunnel	*smog*	smoke + fog
cyborg	cybernetic + organism	*stagflation*	stagnation + inflation
dormobile	dormitory + automobile	*televangelist*	television + evangelist
franglais	français + anglais	*transistor*	transfer + resistor

It is a pity that others, created for humorous effect, have not made the grade:

ambisextrous, for a bisexual
beerage, for either ennobled leaders of the drinks trade, or heavy-drinking peers
hoolivan, for the vehicle used by police to monitor unruly crowds
red-tapeworm, for parasitic bureaucracy

Carroll's use of the term 'portmanteau word' also lives on in combinations such as *portmanteau quotation, portmanteau term* and *portmanteau form*. The jargon of linguistics even has *portmanteau morph,* where a single morph represents two morphemes (as the French *du* stands for *de* + *le*).

Easel was borrowed into English in the seventeenth century from Dutch *ezel*, whose literal sense is 'ass'. It comes from Middle Dutch *esel*, a word which goes back to Latin *asinus*, 'ass'. The allusion is to a beast of burden carrying a load.

Other languages derive their words for *easel* in a similar way. In the Romance languages, a diminutive of 'horse' is used: French, Italian and Spanish have *chevalet*, *cavalletto* and *caballete* respectively.

English, of course, also uses *horse* figuratively for various frames, particularly those with legs, that support or carry loads; tanning, whaling and clock-making are just some of the trades where such apparatus was once used. A carpenter still uses a trestle-like support known as *horse* or *sawhorse* to hold the wood while he saws it and in a domestic setting the *clothes horse*, 'a wooden frame on which washing is spread to dry', has been in use since the sixteenth century:

My mother's life became a grim litany of tiresome and repetitive cooking, washing by hand, pegging out, draping things over clothes horses, and washing again. Drip, drip. Drip, drip. Not just the washing, but her life was dripping away. Year after year.
(ANNE FINE IN THE TELEGRAPH, 12 JUNE 2009)

eavesdrop
to listen in secretly, to snoop

'I meant to write, Gracie,' he said quickly. Small branches cracked underfoot, the trees seemed to eavesdrop.
(KATE MORTON,
THE HOUSE AT RIVERTON, 2006)

He and Pinky Madam would sit in the back of the car, chatting about life, about India, about America – mixing Hindi and English together – and by eavesdropping

on them I learned a lot about life, India and America – and a bit of English too.
(ARAVIND ADIGA,
THE WHITE TIGER, 2008)

The eaves – *efes* or *yfes* in Old English – are those edges of a roof or thatch which overhang the side of the building so that water is directed away from the walls. Indeed, *efes* ultimately appears to come from the same Germanic root which produced *over*. In Saxon times, before gutters were commonly used, an ancient law forbade the construction of any building less than 2 feet [60 cm] from a boundary in order to protect the adjoining property from water cascading from the eaves. This water was referred to as *yfesdrype*, literally 'eavesdrip', in Old English, but the word was remodelled as *evesdrop* in Middle English. The regulation strip of land around the eaves was also referred to as the *evesdrop*. The word *eavesdropper* was formed in the fifteenth century to denote 'a nosey person who lurked within the eavesdrop', *vnder mennes walles or wyndowes…to here tales.* (MODUS TENENDI LUR BARON VON VISU FRANCI PLEGII, c. 1515). From Anglo-Saxon times this activity has been an offence under common law punishable by a fine and a requirement of good behaviour. The verb *to eavesdrop* is a back-formation coined in the seventeenth century.

elephant
a huge animal with large ivory tusks and a long trunk

The only elephant that was still in the camp's vicinity was Shwe Doke, the dead man's mount. The hsin-ouq had taken charge of his nephew's riderless elephant after the accident. She was restless, he said, and nervous, frequently flapping her ears and clawing the air with the tip of her

trunk. This was neither uncommon nor unexpected, for the elephant is, above all, a creature of habit and routine. So pronounced an upheaval as the absence of a long-familiar handler can put even the gentlest of elephants out of temper, often dangerously so.
(AMITAV GHOSH,
THE GLASS PALACE, 2000)

There were more palm trees out there, tousled and spindly, their grey bark looking thick and tough as **elephant** *hide.*
(JOHN BANVILLE, THE SEA, 2005)

This word is traceable back as far as Greek *elephās*, which first meant 'ivory' and then later 'elephant', showing the importance of the animal's tusks as an expensive material for artistic embellishment. It was taken into Latin as *elephantus*, 'elephant', which became corrupted to the unattested *olifantus* in Vulgar Latin. This term then passed into Old English as *olfend*, 'camel' (an easy error for people who rarely came across either animal) and into Old French as *olifant*, 'elephant'.

Middle English had another stab at adopting the word, this time borrowing it from Old French as *olifaunt* around the beginning of the fourteenth century. At last English had managed to separate elephants from camels:

Olifauns, and camelis,
Weoren y-charged with vitailes.
(KING ALISAUNDER, c. 1300)

In the late fourteenth and early fifteenth centuries some attempts were made to refashion the word after Latin *elephantus*, but the spelling did not really begin to settle down until the second half of the sixteenth century. Richard Eden shows the uncertainty in THE DECADES OF THE NEW WORLDE OR WEST INDIA (tr. 1555): *The elephante (which sum caule an oliphant) is the biggest of all foure footed beastes.*

In his HISTORIE OF FOURE-FOOTED BEASTES (1607) Edward Topsell says this of the elephant:

There is no creature among al the Beasts of the world which hath so great and ample demonstration of the power and wisdome of almighty God as the Elephant: both for proportion of body and disposition of spirit; and it is admirable to behold, the industry of our auncient forefathers, and noble desire to benefit us their posterity, by serching into the qualities of every Beast, to discover what benefits or harmes may come by them to mankind: having never beene afraid either of the Wildest, but they tamed them; the fiercest, but they ruled them; and the greatest, but they also set upon them. Witnesse for this part the Elephant, being like a living Mountain in quantity & outward appearance, yet by them so handled, as no little dog became more serviceable and tractable.

He then goes on to say that elephants worship the sun and the moon, that touching an elephant's trunk cures a headache and that the *blood of an elephant and the ashes of a Weasil, cure... Leprosie.*

engine
a mechanical device for converting energy into motion

But as I grew up, in those far-off days, I saw myself as a child of the future. I was enamoured – little thinking that the object of my passion was doomed, too, soon to become an anachronism – of that roaring, hurtling, up-to-the-minute thing, the steam **engine**.
(GRAHAM SWIFT, EVER AFTER, 1992)

She was trying to imagine the encounter between Faith Botumile and Mr J L B Maketoni. Had the interview taken place in the garage, while his head was buried in some car's **engine** *compartment? Or had he taken her into the office and interviewed*

her from the desk, wiping his hands free
of grease as she told her story?
(ALEXANDER MCCALL SMITH,
THE GOOD HUSBAND OF
ZEBRA DRIVE, 2007)

To the contemporary mind the word *engine* might conjure up the mysteries under the car bonnet or perhaps, to those who hanker after a bygone age, a mental picture of a steam train. The term does not originate in mechanics of any kind, however: it derives from the Latin *ingenium*, meaning 'an inborn skill' and source of the word *ingenious*. From this Old French had *engin* or *engien*. This word had several meanings, all of which were borrowed into Middle English.

Initially *engin* retained its Latin sense of 'innate ability'. The twelfth-century French writer Wace used it in this sense and, in his CANTERBURY TALES (1387), Chaucer states that *A man hath sapiences thre, Memorie, engin, and intellect also*. From this primary sense emerged the related meaning of 'ingenuity', often with the implication of 'cunning' (Old French had a phrase *mal engien* which meant 'trickery').

Engin was next extended to the 'product of ingenuity', in other words 'a plot, a deception'. In the thirteenth-century Provençal courtly poem AUCASSIN ET NICOLETTE, for instance, the heroine, imprisoned in a tower, wonders by what means or *engien* she might rejoin her forbidden love, Aucassin. This sense is reflected in English literature from the fourteenth century.

The next step was the application of *engin* to a 'tool or mechanical device' that was the product of such innate ability. At the turn of the fourteenth century the word referred to machines of war (a *siege engine*, for instance), but was swiftly extended to all kinds of appliances. This use of *engine* to mean

'implement' sometimes has a comical ring to modern ears. In his poem THE RAPE OF THE LOCK (1714), for example, Pope describes the climactic moment when the lock of fair Belinda's hair is severed thus:

Just then, Clarissa drew with tempting grace
A two-edg'd weapon from her shining case;
He takes the gift with rev'rence, and extends
The little engine on his fingers' ends;
This just behind Belinda's neck he spread,
As o'er the fragrant steam she bends
her head.

The *engine* here is, of course, a pair of scissors. It would be another sixty years or so before the gathering momentum of the industrial revolution knew the power of the *steam engine*, which gradually pushed all these other senses into obscurity.

☛ Latin *ingenium*, 'talent' gave the Medieval Latin verb *ingeniāre*, 'to contrive', and the derivative *ingeniātor*, 'contriver'. This became *engigneor* in Old French and *enginer* in Middle English. *Engineer* followed the same pattern as *engine*: an 'author, designer or plotter'; 'one who designs and builds military fortifications and machines'; 'one who makes engines' (depending here on the particular sense of engine); 'one who designs bridges, roads, etc.' (*civil engineer* from the eighteenth century).

etiquette
a code of prescribed social behaviour

There was something unsettling in this
communication too. Mike seemed to have
dispensed with the normal rudiments of
style, with capital letters for example.
And then the tone, while not actually
disrespectful, was uncharacteristically
familiar – that circle and cross by the
signature, presumably betokening kisses and
so forth. Presumably such endearments were

*a part of e-mail **etiquette**. In which case, was he expected to do likewise?*
(SALLY VICKERS,
  MR GOLIGHTLY'S HOLIDAY, 2005)

*After a mumbled 'Thank you', Bill lay in silence beside her, his mind full of the automatic masculine post-coital question. How soon can I leave? Books of **etiquette** are sadly inadequate in defining the recommended time-lapse between an act of intercourse and the first 'Oh, well, I'd better be on my way.'*
(SIMON BRETT, THE PENULTIMATE
CHANCE SALOON, 2006)

Etiquette is, of course, a French word that has been borrowed directly into English. From the Old French verb *estiquier*, 'to attach, to fix' (from Middle Dutch *steken*, 'to stick, to fix' – source of the English verb *to stick*), came *estiquette* to denote 'a written order that assigned a soldier to his billet'. This became *étiquette* in modern French with the sense 'a note or notice posted up'. In this sense it was adopted into English in the sixteenth century as *ticket*, the short unstressed vowel at the beginning of the French word having been dropped.

During the reign of Louis XIV, however, the French word was promoted to royal circles when visitors to the French court were issued with an *étiquette*, a card bearing instructions which outlined correct dress and procedure. By the time it was borrowed into English in the mid-eighteenth century, this time as *etiquette*, the application of the term had been transferred from the card itself to the code of behaviour written on it.

Stories abound of the difficulties royal personages have been forced to endure in the name of etiquette. In many European courts, touching royalty was forbidden except to a very few. A story is told of the second wife of Charles II of Spain who was once riding a very spirited horse when the animal tried to throw her. The queen fell to the ground but with one foot caught fast in the stirrup. Irritated, the horse bucked and kicked but no one dared come to the queen's assistance, for no one qualified to touch her was present. Eventually two courageous cavaliers ran to her aid. The saving deed done, both men prepared to flee for their lives until they were informed by a messenger that the queen had interceded with the king on their behalf and they had been freely pardoned. The modern British monarchy, though much more relaxed, still has its etiquette and those who break its rules are heavily censured, if only by the popular press. This happened in the early 1990s when the Prime Minister of Australia slipped an over-familiar, matey arm around the Queen's waist, a faux pas duplicated by the American First Lady Michelle Obama on a visit to Britain in 2009.

From the strictures of court ceremonial, *etiquette* was later applied to behaviour in legal, professional and diplomatic circles, and finally to the behaviour expected of any well-bred person in society. In the Victorian era the market for books of etiquette boomed among the rising and prosperous middle classes, eager to learn the behaviour of the social elite. Readers were told how to dress and behave on particular occasions, how to order and leave visiting cards, how to greet people of different social classes, and how to speak. A keen memory was required to remember one's table manners alone. MANNERS AND RULES OF GOOD SOCIETY (1888) has these niceties on eating cheese:

When eating cheese, small morsels of cheese should be placed with a knife on small morsels of bread, and the two conveyed to the mouth with the thumb and finger, the piece of bread being the morsel to hold as the cheese should not be taken up in the fingers, and should not be eaten off the point of the knife. As a matter of course, young ladies do not eat cheese at dinner parties.

It is easy to imagine that society in the late twentieth century had become so relaxed that etiquette was an out-of-date concept. No so. New acts of courtesy were demanded to suit the changing age:

At one time a man always walked on the right to keep his sword arm free; later he walked nearest the road to protect her from splashes and passing robbers. Today, in cities like New York, men are beginning to walk on the inside to ward off muggers in doorways.
(MOYRA BREMNER, MODERN ETIQUETTE AND SUCCESSFUL BEHAVIOUR, 1989)

And the computer world also has its proper ways of behaving:

FACEBOOK ETIQUETTE: 10 RULES FOR BETTER SOCIALISING
There's no shortage of ways to irritate friends on Facebook. We'll help you avoid the biggest etiquette pitfalls with these expert tips (computerworld.com.au, August 2009).

For another word signifying a 'code of behaviour', see PROTOCOL.

exchequer
treasury, financial reserves

*The Queen's 'income tax', in the form of profits from the Crown Estate paid to the **Exchequer** today, has gone up by more than 10 per cent on last year to £163.3 million. The amount is more than 4.5 times the total cost of the royal family, which stands at £35.3 million.*
(EVENING STANDARD, 9 JULY 2002)

*It is to be hoped that the economy recovers as quickly as the Chancellor of the **Exchequer**. Less than a fortnight ago, Alistair Darling's time at the Treasury looked over. There can rarely have been such a rapid improvement*

in political fate and, just to add to Mr Darling's sunny disposition, it looks like the British economy could be improving too.
(THE TIMES, 13 JUNE 2009)

In the days of the Norman and Plantagenet kings the huge treasury counting table was covered by a cloth that was divided up into squares upon which coloured counters were used to calculate revenue. In Anglo-Norman this was known as the *escheker*, from Old French *eschequier*, 'chessboard'. This in turn derived from Medieval Latin *scaccārium*, 'chessboard', from Vulgar Latin *scaccus*, 'check', and *scacchi*, 'chess'; DIALOGUS DE SCACCARIO (c. 1170), 'The Dialogue of the Exchequer', was a treatise written in Latin by Richard FitzNigel, Henry II's treasurer, detailing Exchequer procedure. The term *exchequer* was transferred from the checkered counting table to the department of state itself by the fourteenth century.

See also CHANCELLOR and CHESS.

excruciate
to inflict extreme pain, physical or mental, to torture

*...he [Pope] suffered **excruciating** torments every time he travelled along the bumpy roads of eighteenth-century England.*
(PAT ROGERS, INTRODUCTION TO POPE'S COMPLETE POETICAL WORKS, 1978)

*It was past 11.00 and she was alone on the floor. She suddenly felt **excruciatingly** bored. After a while she got up and walked to the end of the hall.*
(STIEG LARSSON, THE GIRL WITH THE DRAGON TATTOO, 2008)

*The **excruciatingly** painful end of this fascinating biography – Assia Wevill would gas herself and Shura, her daughter by Ted Hughes, to death – overshadows everything we can learn about this*

unfortunate woman, even as we fantasize, as with all suicides, that we can still save her somehow before the last page and rewrite her story.
(THE INDEPENDENT, 10 AUGUST 2008)

Crucifixion was a horrific form of execution used among the Phoenicians, the Persians and the Carthaginians. Under the Romans, methods of crucifixion varied in different parts of the Empire, but each subjected the victim to long, racking torture. Death was sometimes hastened by Roman guards, who had to remain at the site until the condemned prisoners were all dead. This would be done by piercing the victims with a spear or breaking their legs.

The Latin verb *excruciāre*, 'to torture', derives from this brutal punishment. It is composed of the intensive prefix *ex-*, 'thoroughly', and *cruciāre*, 'to torment', a derivative of *crux* (stem *cruc-*), 'cross, stake'. The verb *to excruciate* was taken into English from Latin in the sixteenth century with the literal meaning 'to subject to torture' and the related meaning 'to inflict extreme pain'. Figuratively it was also used with the sense 'to cause intense mental agony'. In his play TAMBURLAINE (1586), Christopher Marlowe writes of

*...a matter that doth excruciate
The very substance of my vexed soul.*

Like many etymologically powerful words, *excruciating* lends itself to hyperbole. Instances of this date from the early nineteenth century but are still common today:

Come back, Sharon Osbourne – all is forgiven. Well, maybe not all. Certainly not your creepy flirting with male contestants younger than your son. Or your excruciating, hamster-on-helium voice (THE TELEGRAPH, 12 DECEMBER, 2008).

☞ Other words which have come into English from Latin *crux* (stem *cruc-*) are:

cross (10th cent): Old English *cros*, from Old Irish *cross*, probably by way of Scandinavian languages, from Latin *crux*.

crucial (18th cent): from French *crucial*, a medical term for the crossing ligaments at the knee. The sense 'critical' (19th cent) comes from Bacon's phrase *instantia crucis*, 'crucial instance' (NOVUM ORGANUM, 1620). This was a metaphor from a finger-post (*crux*) at a crossroads which Bacon used to indicate a point of critical decision.

crucible (15th cent): from Medieval Latin *crucibulum*, originally 'a nightlamp', perhaps one lit before a crucifix, later 'a melting-pot'.

crucifix (15th cent): from Old French *crucefix*, from Latin *crucifixus*, 'fixed to a cross'.

crusade (16th cent): in the 1500s the French form *croisade* was used (from Old French *croisée*, from the past participle of *croiser*, 'to receive the mark of the cross', from *crois*, 'cross', from *crux*). English *crusade* is an eighteenth-century blend of this and *crusado* (from the similarly derived Spanish word *cruzada*). Before this, Middle English had *croiserie*, a borrowing of the Old French word which was current at the time. The figurative use of *crusade* to mean 'vigorous opposition to a perceived evil' or 'an enthusiastic movement in support of a cause', dates from the eighteenth century.

For a word with a related sense, see AGONY.

explode
to go off, blow up; to refute, reject

*It is not generally known that President Reagan was shot with an **exploding** bullet in the assassination attempt on him in 1981, but that it failed to explode. Surgeons had to take special precautions when operating, since even the use of ultrasound or microwave diagnostic techniques could have set it off.*
(JOHN MAY,
THE BOOK OF CURIOUS FACTS, 1993)

*There was, apparently, a nuclear reactor at a place called Indian Point, just thirty miles away in Westchester County. If anything bad happened there, we were constantly being informed, the 'radioactive debris', whatever this might be, was liable to rain down on us... Then there was the question of dirty bombs. Apparently any fool could build a dirty bomb and **explode** it in Manhattan. How likely was this? Nobody knew.*
(JOSEPH O'NEILL, NETHERLAND, 2008)

Why they did not hiss and explode him off the stage... wrote Abraham Cowley (VERSES AND ESSAYS, 1663). Cowley was not, of course, suggesting that dynamite should be used to remove the ham actor from the stage, but that he should be clapped off. *Explode* is a borrowing of Latin *explōdere* (from *ex-*, 'out' and *plaudere*, 'to clap'). Theatre audiences in ancient times did not tolerate actors whose performances were not up to scratch. Instead they would make their dissatisfaction obvious by hissing and clapping, so that the players could no longer continue and were forced to leave the stage. Figuratively applied, *explōdere* meant 'to reject scornfully', and it was in this sense of 'to cry down, to discredit' that it was taken into English in the sixteenth century. David Hume's AN ENQUIRY CONCERNING HUMAN UNDERSTANDING (1748) talks of *exploding* forgery and superstition: *How many stories of this nature have, in all ages, been detected and exploded in their infancy? How many more have been celebrated for a time, and have afterwards sunk into neglect and oblivion?* Modern English still speaks of *exploding* a myth, hypothesis, theory, fallacy, lie, etc.

The original theatrical meaning was not adopted into English until the first quarter of the seventeenth century. The learned cleric Robert Burton found use for it in his ANATOMIE OF MELANCHOLY (1621), when he wrote: *Virtue and Wisdom...were hissed out, and exploded by the common people*. In the second half of the seventeenth century, however, a new sense began to emerge when the verb was applied to a bullet being expelled from a gun with a sudden report, or to coals being spat from a fire with a sharp crack. By the late eighteenth century the word had evolved still further to mean 'to burst apart with great force, to detonate', the familiar modern meaning.

For another word with the same Latin sense, see PLAUDIT.

· F ·

family

parents and their children; parents, children and other relatives

*All happy **families** resemble one another, every unhappy family is unhappy in its own fashion.*
(LEO TOLSTOY,
ANNA KARENINA,1873-77)

*Pre-industrial societies have little notion of a person as a separate entity. A Nigerian psychiatrist told me that, when a psychiatric clinic was first set up in a rural district of Nigeria to treat the mentally ill, the **family** invariably accompanied the sufferer and insisted upon being present at the patient's interview with the psychiatrist. The idea that the patient might exist as an individual apart from the family, or that he might have personal problems which he did not want to share with them, did not occur to Nigerians who were still living a traditional village life.*
(ANTHONY STORR, SOLITUDE, 1988)

*In this sprightly, resolutely unglum, indeed death-defying memoir, the **family** ricochets from one disaster and misunderstanding to another but always with a nonchalant smile and a dead-pan acceptance that theirs is the way of the world.*
(TIM HEALD IN SLIGHTLY FOXED,
AUTUMN 2008)

In Latin a *famulus* was a 'domestic servant'; *familia* was a collective noun that denoted 'all the servants in a Roman household'. When the word was borrowed into Middle English as *familie* around the beginning of the fifteenth century, it was with this original meaning: *I was a single man, 'tis true, but I had a family of servants whom I kept at my business*, writes H F, the protagonist of Daniel Defoe's A JOURNAL OF THE PLAGUE YEAR (1722). This sense persisted until the nineteenth century and during that time was variously used to include the retinue of a nobleman, the servants on a plantation or the staff of a high-ranking military officer.

During the sixteenth century the term was also applied to 'an entire household', that is, everyone who lived under the same roof: the master, his wife and children, and their domestic servants. Not until the mid-seventeenth century did the modern sense of *family* gradually begin to emerge: father, mother and children, whether or not they were living together, the connection being that they were all of the same blood.

Nowadays, the term is also used by businesses and institutions to indicate that their branches all share the same basic values:

Newfrontiers is a worldwide family of churches together on a mission, with over 600 churches in over 40 nations around the world.
(NEWFRONTIERS WEBSITE,
OCTOBER 2008)

Welcome to the David Lloyd Family.
Next Generation and David Lloyd Clubs are merging.
This unique and historic merger will automatically make you a member of one of the largest racquet, health and fitness groups in Europe.
(BROCHURE, OCTOBER 2008)

fan, fanatic
an overzealous devotee

'And does God feel the same?' I asked.
'Probably. I feel sorry for him actually...
He's a very easy target. And who does he
get left with? **Fanatics** *and maniacs of*
every faith and every persuasion, who want
to kill the heretics and blow themselves to
pieces in his name.'
(JAMES ROBERTSON, THE TESTAMENT
OF GIDEON MACK, 2006)

Meanwhile, there is another time-travelling
television project on his mind. As a father
of four children, he has become a big **fan** *of*
Dr Who since it was revitalised four years
ago by the Welsh writer Russell T Davies.
(NEW ZEALAND HERALD,
15 JUNE 2009)

Fanatic is from the Latin adjective
fānāticus, which in turn comes from
fānum, 'temple'. *Fānāticus* had two
meanings: 'belonging to a temple' and,
by extension, 'inspired or possessed by
a divinity'. In sixteenth-century English
fanatic described either 'irrational,
frantic behaviour or speech indicating
demon possession' or a person acting in
such a way.

By the second half of the seventeenth century the word, with all its
implied criticism, was being used as a
noun to denote a 'person prompted by
excessive enthusiasm', particularly with
regard to religion and, towards the end
of that century, more specifically 'a
member of a Nonconformist congregation', one who would argue against the
established church, claim to be directed
by the Holy Spirit and be motivated by
a fervent missionary zeal. Thus *fanatic*
became synonymous with 'religious
maniac'.

The noun was given a new lease of
life in late nineteenth-century America,
where it was applied to zealous baseball
supporters who gave every indication
of being demon-possessed when they
watched a game. From baseball its
scope was widened to include other
sports and then still further to apply to
non-sporting hobbies and interests.
The term, which was almost immediately shortened to *fan*, hit Britain in
the second decade of the twentieth
century.

These days there are fans of anything from pop groups to home-made
jam; those who want to set a better
tone refer to themselves, with a term
borrowed from Spanish, as *aficionados*.

For other words concerning temples,
see ANATHEMA, MINT and TEMPLE.

farce
an exaggerated comedy for humorous
effect; something vain and utterly
pointless

In the book the story was told as a lovable
where-are-my-trousers **farce**, *but the*
revelation caused a sensation at Aunty
Janet's branch of the Women's Institute...
(TONY PARSONS,
ONE FOR MY BABY, 2001)

The doorbell sounded again.
Christ, thought Leo, if the situation
wasn't so serious, it would be verging
on the **farcical**.
(CARO FRASER, BREATH OF
CORRUPTION, 2007)

It's obvious that a silly misjudgement was
made, but to claim that Damian Green's
arrest is an earth-shattering event that will
'transcend everything else' is ridiculous.
This is 'histrionics, not history; high **farce**,
not tragedy; and cock-up, not conspiracy'.
(THE WEEK, 6 DECEMBER, 2008)

French culinary terms seem to crop up
in the strangest contexts, in this case
ecclesiastical. The basic meaning of the
Latin verb *farcīre* was 'to stuff'. This
passed into Old French as *farcir*, 'to
stuff', and the derived *farce*, 'stuffing'.
The Middle English borrowing *farse* is

accordingly found in cookery books dating back to the fourteenth century. THE FORM OF CURY (c. 1390), a collection of recipes prepared by the master-cooks of King Richard II, instructs the reader to *Make a Coffyn an ynche depe & do (th)e fars (th)erin.*

From these beginnings, the word took a surprising metaphorical turn in the Middle Ages. In France and in England from the thirteenth century it became common to expand the set text of the Latin liturgies with laudatory statements or to introduce expository passages in the native language into the Latin chanting of the epistle. *Farse* was used to describe such insertions which were 'stuffed' into the plain text.

In a similar way, Old French *farce* was then used to describe the off-the-cuff jokes and comic interludes that actors in religious plays inserted into their set lines so that, in France during the thirteenth century and then in England during the first half of the sixteenth, *farce* came to denote 'a short play intended to make people laugh'.

An article in the London EVENING STANDARD (4 January 2007) demonstrates a further application of the word dating back to the seventeenth century, where something that is 'a sham' or 'ridiculously pointless' is compared to a theatrical farce:

The British Airways lost luggage farce deepened last night when it emerged that the airline is sending thousands of bags out of Heathrow to be sorted through in Milan, only for them then to be sent back to England.

For another word derived from a French culinary term, see HOTCH-POTCH.

fiasco

a total disaster, a debacle

*I took the job. Laeta then told me the background. It was worse than I thought. Missions from the Palace always were. Not many were as bad as this, but as soon as I had heard Veleda's name I had known this particular **fiasco** would be special.*
(LINDSEY DAVIS, SATURNALIA, 2007)

*Seventy-three miles of [Hadrian's] wall stretch from Carlisle to Newcastle and once included 30 forts, 80 mile-castles, 160 turrets, with a ditch to the north and the great defensive Vallum earthwork to the south. Incredibly, it only took three legions just six years to build and if you compare that to the recent Wembley stadium **fiasco**, it really does beggar belief.*
(YORKSHIRE LIVING, APRIL 2009)

Fiasco is an Italian word for 'a bottle' or 'a flask', derived from Late Latin *flascō*, 'bottle'. Its use to denote an 'embarrassing failure' arose from an Italian idiomatic expression *fare fiasco* (literally 'to make a bottle'), which meant 'to break down, to fail in a performance'. It was apparently traditional in Italian opera houses for the audience to cry *Ola, Ola, fiasco!* when a singer sang out of tune or generally failed to please. Walsh quotes from an issue of the SATURDAY REVIEW, which carried a piece about an Italian critic who used this custom in an ingenious visual way to assess each performance:

An Italian contemporary, in reviewing the past musical season, adopted recently a system of symbols which we may commend to the notice of English journalists. Appended to the notice of each new opera was the picture of a wine-flask, which varied in size with the degree of failure achieved by the particular work. Every one who remembers that the word fiasco – popularised as a synonym with failure – is really the Italian for a flask, will perceive the convenient possibilities opened up by this method. At present the critic is often condemned to write whole columns of which the gist might be comprised in two words. How much better it would be if we adopted the delightfully terse symbolism thus suggested! One column would be reserved every week, the names of the pieces set down, and opposite we should put a finely-graded series of wine-flasks, showing the precise degree of good and ill success attained.

Etymologists have pondered long and hard over exactly how *fiasco* came to be synonymous with 'failure'. Some have suggested that an empty wine bottle fails to please. Others have turned to the skilful Venetian glassmakers for inspiration. They advance the theory that whenever a flaw was discovered in the bulb of a beautiful piece of glassware the blower would simply turn it into an ordinary flask, a *fiasco* and, therefore, 'a failure'. Yet another inspired guess, this one from an Italian dictionary, is that *fare il fiasco* once meant 'to play a game where the loser has to buy the bottle of wine', hence 'an expensive error'.

Fiasco was borrowed into English in the mid-nineteenth century via French and was used both theatrically and generally to mean 'a shameful failure'.

☛ Other words from Late Latin *flascō* (variant *flasca*), 'vessel, bottle', include:

flagon (15th cent): from Old French *flacon*, from Late Latin *flascōn-*, the stem of *flascō*, 'bottle'.

flask (14th cent): from Old French *flasque*, from Late Latin *flasca*, 'bottle'.

filibuster
to obstruct legislation by delaying tactics, usually very long speeches

*Winning 60 seats or more would be a major boon to the Democrats because it would make it nearly impossible for the opposition Republicans to use a **filibuster** to kill legislation. A filibuster, a procedural way to extend debate indefinitely and keep a proposal from coming to a vote, can be cut off in the Senate with a supermajority of 60 votes.*
(EVENING STANDARD,
4 NOVEMBER 2008)

*Senator Strom Thurmond, of South Carolina, spoke for 24 hours and 18 minutes in 1957 in an unsuccessful attempt to **filibuster** the Civil Rights Act. He ate a sirloin steak and took a steam bath in preparation, but failed: the Bill was passed 65–15.*
(FROM THE TIMES ARCHIVES IN THE TIMES ONLINE, 30 MAY 2009)

The history of this word and its repeated borrowings into English is complex, but the term originated as a Dutch compound noun *vrijbuiter*, from *vrij*, 'free', and *buiter*, 'a pillager', which English borrowed as *freebooter*, 'a pirate, one who lives by plunder'. There is also a single sixteenth-century record in English of *flibutor*, 'a freebooter', which is obviously from the same Dutch word.

The trading history of the New World records how, in the seventeenth century, bands of pirates raided the Spanish colonies in the Americas and the Caribbean. French borrowed the Dutch term as *flibustier* to refer to these pirates, and this word then moved on into Spanish as *filibustero*. In the eighteenth century, English borrowed the word again, this time from French as *flibustier*, and used it to refer back to these seventeenth-century pirates.

And then, in the mid-nineteenth century, a third borrowing took place when English adopted the word from Spanish as *filibuster* to describe a military adventurer from the United States who targeted countries in Central America and the Spanish West Indies with a view to inciting revolution. In 1850–51, for instance, Narciso Lopez brought forces against the Cuban government and between 1855 and 1858

William Walker led expeditions to the State of Sonora, in Mexico, and to Nicaragua. Both men were eventually captured and executed.

The verb *to filibuster* dates from the mid-nineteenth century and soon developed a political life of its own in American English when it was used with the sense 'to obstruct legislative action'. This sense gained momentum in the latter part of that century when the powers that had been given to the presiding officer in the American Senate to curtail lengthy or irrelevant speeches were revoked. This move opened the door to that favourite weapon of legislative assemblies, delaying tactics. Senators employing them were accused of subverting and destabilising normal process, just as the adventurers had been doing in Central America. In short they were *filibustering*. Since then the verb has crossed the Atlantic and is freely used in Britain to describe the same practice of obstruction and delay. One who uses these methods is known as a *filibusterer* and the 'delaying tactic' itself is *a filibuster*.

For another word arising from questionable political practice, see GERRYMANDER. For other piratical words, see PIRATE and BUCCANEER.

flabbergast
to amaze totally, render speechless, gobsmack

*Ready to take a risk? OK, even in Venice fast food outlets are springing up all over the place, but I'd like to suggest three dishes in particular. Perhaps to be tried on different occasions, because they have demanding flavours. You could **flabbergast** your taste-buds and startle your paramours: the high onion content is a foolproof anti-kiss device.*
(THE GUARDIAN, 8 FEBRUARY, 2008)

When Danielle Smith and her family posed for their Christmas card photo last year, they knew they'd share it with family and friends. But the Missouri family wasn't expecting it to show up in the Czech Republic, splashed across a huge storefront advertisement.

*About 10 days ago, a college friend was driving through Prague when he spotted their huge smiling faces in the window of a store specialising in European food. He snapped a few pictures and sent them to a **flabbergasted** Smith.*
(THE INDEPENDENT, 11 JUNE 2009)

Flabbergast was a slang term that was either an invention or a dialectal borrowing of fashionable society in the eighteenth century. It was first recorded as a new word in 1772. The inspiration behind the coinage is not known for certain, but a humorous combination of *flabby* and *aghast* has been reasonably suggested. The result is a word that speaks of a loose, gaping mouth and eyes opened wide in amazement.

The verb *agasten* meant 'to terrify' (from the intensive *a-* and *'gasten*, 'to frighten'). It is found from the early thirteenth century onwards and goes back to Old English *gæstan*, 'to torment'. Modern English *aghast* is a later spelling of the past participle *agast*; the *h* was inserted in the early fifteenth century in Scotland, probably influenced by words like *ghost*, and became the standard spelling by the eighteenth century.

Flabby was a late seventeenth-century adaptation of *flappy*, itself a derivative of the verb *to flap*. *Flap* is an onomatopoeic word which, in the fourteenth century, meant 'to give a blow with a broad instrument or weapon' and also 'to applaud'. The sense 'to sway about limply', often implying that the movement is made with a slapping noise, developed from this in the first half of the sixteenth century. In the

1590s, therefore, someone described as *flappy* had swinging folds of spare flesh: *...to grow flappy, withered, or wrimpled* (John Florio, A WORLDE OF WORDES, 1598). To the seventeenth-century mind, however, the sharp-sounding *flappy* was not sufficiently evocative of round rolls of flaccid flesh and so the word was modified to *flabby*, to give a heavier ring. Three hundred years on, *fighting the flab* became a national pastime, the derived noun emerging with this particular sense in the 1950s.

☞ *Gasten*, 'to frighten', is also the source of *ghastly*. In the fourteenth century this described something that evoked intense horror, but by the nineteenth it was used as a hyperbole to describe something unpleasant, or just plain bad. The original spelling was *gastly*. The Elizabethan poet Edmund Spenser was the first to use the spelling *ghastly*, the introduction of the *h* apparently influenced by *ghost*.

See PORTMANTEAU WORDS (page 111) for other examples of words made up from two separate words.

flour
milled grain

Flour, water, yeast. For centuries we have used just three ingredients to make bread. Examine a supermarket loaf, though, and you will find some other, odd substances.
(THE INDEPENDENT, 13 JUNE 2009)

See FLOUR.

flower
a bloom, blossom

*She made a great effort to think of more pleasant things, of Alan arriving and smiling at her, of his basically kind if naturally rather severe face, as he stood there looking concerned and holding out a bunch of pink lilies. Alan loved lilies and he would choose pink for a girl; he wasn't brilliant at **flowers** and he would go for the obvious.*
(DAVID NOBBS, SEX AND OTHER CHANGES, 2004)

*The downstairs dining-room window that overlooks the garden is open and my father is sitting there with his glasses on and a book on his knees. There's a tablecloth on the table instead of newspaper, and some plastic **flowers** in a vase.*
(MARINA LEWYCKA, A SHORT HISTORY OF TRACTORS IN UKRAINIAN, 2005)

The unattested proto-Indo-European base *bhlō-*, meaning 'to flourish', influenced both Latin and the Germanic languages so that 'floral' words which appear very different are, in fact, related. *Bhlō-* was responsible for Old English *blōstm*, a general word for 'flower' which has become 'blossom' in modern English. It is also the source of Middle English *blom* or *blome*, meaning 'bloom', so that, eventually, a finer distinction was drawn between 'blossom', which heralded fruit, and 'bloom', which was considered the ultimate glory of the plant.

Latin *flōs*, 'flower', also has its origins in *bhlō-*. *Flōs* had the stem *flōr-*, from which the Romance languages derived their words for 'flower'. Old French had *flor* or *flour*, both of which were borrowed into Middle English.

In the thirteenth century the word began to denote the 'flower' or the 'finest meal', from whatever grain, that could be separated off by sifting, and eventually became a general term for 'ground grain'. When the variant spelling *flower* arose in the first half of the sixteenth century, the forms *flour* and *flower* were used interchangeably in both senses of the word. By the end of the sixteenth century *flower* was being

HOW DOES YOUR GARDEN GROW?

The common names of plants make a fascinating study. Some flowers are named for their appearance – *snowdrop*, *bluebell* and *sunflower* for instance. Others are more fanciful:

Carnation. Originally in the sixteenth century the plant was called the *coronation*, a reference either to its jagged flower which resembled a little crown or to its use in floral garlands. Towards the close of the century, however, the name was confused with *carnation*, a colour term meaning 'flesh colour' (from French *carnation*, from Italian *carnagione* 'the colour of one's complexion', from Latin *carbātiōnem*, 'fleshiness', from *carō*, stem *carn-*, 'flesh'), doubtless because the flowers were sometimes of this colour.

Coltsfoot. The shape of the leaves suggests the hoof of a colt. Other animals also occasionally lent their names to this plant: *fole foote*, *horse houe* or *bull foote*. Should the allusion seem too tenuous, French has *pas-d'âne*, 'ass's foot'.

Cranesbill. This name, which is now applied to various species of geranium, though originally only to the *Geranium dissectum*, is a translation by sixteenth-century herbalists from German and Dutch terms. It alludes to the long, pointed 'beak' of the fruit.

Dandelion. Middle English had *dent-de-lion*, from an Old French translation of Medieval Latin *dens leonis*, 'lion's tooth', an allusion to the jagged leaves. Vulgarly the plant was called *pissabed*, in French *pissenlit*, because of its diuretic properties.

Foxglove. The Old English name for this plant was *foxes glōfa*, 'fox's glove', because the individual flowers look like finger-stalls. The connection with foxes is obscure; it may refer to the pattern inside the flower, which looks something like paw marks. Norwegian has *revhjelde*, 'fox bell'. The modern Latin name for the plant is *Digitalis*, from Latin *digitalis*, 'of the fingers', and was bestowed by the German herbalist Fuchs in 1542 after the German name *Fingerhut*, 'thimble'.

Garlic. The Old English compound is *gārlēac* where *lēac* means 'leek' and *gār* 'spear', descriptive of the shape of the leaves.

Orchid. The Greeks named this plant *orkhis*, 'testicle', because of the shape of the tubers. The English word is formed from the Latin borrowing *orchis*. Seventeenth-century botanists erroneously believed the Latin stem to be *orchid-*, thus introducing the final *d*.

Pansy. This viola was popularly called *pensée*, 'thought', by the French, possibly because its markings resemble a face with a thoughtful look. English borrowed the word at the turn of the sixteenth century, but the modern spelling did not evolve until the eighteenth.

Snapdragon. To the classical and sixteenth-century imaginations the two-lipped flowers of the *antirrhinum* (from New Latin, from Greek *antirrhion*, 'plant with snout-like flowers') were fashioned like a dragon's mouth.

continued overleaf

HOW DOES YOUR GARDEN GROW? *continued*

Tulip. Originally named for its resemblance to a turban. Sixteenth-century English from New Latin *tulipa*, from the vulgar Turkish term *tülibend*, a borrowing of unattested Persian *dulband*, 'turban'.

Other plants were named for the place in which they grew. Sixteenth-century botanists list the *wallflower* and *cornflower*, for instance, but other names are less obvious:

Cowslip. In Old English the plant was *cūslyppe* or *cūsloppe*, where *cū* meant 'cow' and *slyppe* 'a slimy dropping'. Thus the plant was named for its proliferation in fields abundantly fertilised by grazing cattle.

Houseleek. In Old English this was probably *hūslēac* (from *hūs*, 'house', and *lēac*, 'leek'), giving *howsleke* in Middle English. The plant was so named because it was often grown on roofs, perpetuating the belief held by the Romans that it offered the household protection against lightning and evil. For this reason it was also known as *Jove's beard*, Jove (or Jupiter) being the god of the elements.

Oxlip. The name was formed like cowslip from Old English *oxan*, 'of an ox', and *slyppe*, 'dung', giving *oxanslyppe*.

Rosemary. This is a native of southern Europe and was known in Latin as *rōsmarīus*, 'sea dew' (from *rōs*, 'dew', and *marīnus*, 'of the sea', from *mare*, 'sea'), supposedly because the plant grew profusely on the coast. The word came into Middle English as *rosmarine* via Old French *rosmarin* and Late Latin *rosmarinum*, but its form was soon altered because of the elements' similarity to *rose* and *Mary*, the name of the Virgin.

Other plants were named for the uses to which they were put. The euonymus, for instance, was commonly known as the *spindle-tree* as its wood was excellent for making spindles (see SPINSTER):

Thyme. The Greeks evidently used this herb as a burnt offering. Its name ultimately derives from Greek *thuos*, 'sacrificial incense', and *thuein*, 'to offer a burnt sacrifice to the gods'. Thus the Greeks called the herb *thumon* because of its sweet fragrance when burning. From it Latin derived *thymum* and from this Old French *thym*, which was borrowed into Middle English as *tyme*.

Many of the uses to which plants were put were of course medicinal, and this is reflected in their common names: *feverfew, fleabane* and *sneezewort*, for instance:

regularly used to denote 'bloom', although either form continued to be used for 'milled grain'. In his dictionary (1755), however, Dr Johnson refused even to recognise the spelling *flour*, let alone make a distinction in meaning between the two forms; indeed, as late as 1806, a travel book about France advised that *in a long voyage flower will not keep.*

☛ Other words deriving from Latin *flōs*, 'flower', and its stem *flōr-* include:

flora (16th cent): from Roman mythology, *Flora*, goddess of flowers.

floral (17th cent): initially from Latin *flōrālis*, 'pertaining to Flora', then a new term derived from *flōr-*.

florist (17th cent).

flourish (14th cent): from Old French

Sage. *Sauge* in Middle English, a borrowing from Old French *sauge*, from Latin *salvia*, which means 'the healing plant' (from *salvus*, 'healthy').

According to medieval belief, plants with particular medicinal properties bore a *signature*, that is a mark, feature or colouring, which indicated their usefulness. Thus the *lungwort*, which has white-spotted leaves reminiscent of a diseased lung, was thought to heal pulmonary disorders. The *viper's bugloss* was deemed efficacious against the viper's bite because its seed looked like a viper's head, while its stem resembled snake skin. Wounds from agricultural implements were treated with *self-heal*, a herb whose flower bears a petal shaped like a billhook.

Plants might also be named after a particular characteristic they displayed:

Daisy. The Middle English forms *daisie* and *dayeseye* derived from the Old English *dægesēage*, literally 'day's eye' (from *dæg*, 'day' and *ēage*, 'eye'), an allusion to the fact that the petals open in the day to reveal the flower's yellow 'eye' and close again in the evening.

Honeysuckle. Old English had *hunigsūce* (from *hunig*, 'honey' and *sūcan*, 'to suck') which gave *honysouke(l)* in Middle English. Originally the word was used of any flower, especially the clover, which readily yielded nectar for honey and then, in the sixteenth century, was applied specifically to the climbing woodland shrub familiar to modern gardens.

Lupin. The plant was originally grown for animal fodder and for its seed, which was used as a vegetable. The Romans called it *lupīnum*, derived from *lupīnus*, meaning 'wolf-like' (from *lupus*, 'wolf'). Ancient belief held that, just as the wolf was a greedy, ravenous creature, so the lupin destroyed the soil, sucking out all the goodness.

Nasturtium. This is a kind of cress with edible leaves. According to Pliny, their pungent taste gave rise to the plant's Latin name, *nāsturtium* (from unattested *nāsitortium*, from *nāsus*, 'nose' and *tortus*, from *torquēre*, 'to twist'). The allusion is to the burning felt at the back of the nose when the plant is eaten. French has *nasitort* from the same source.

Soapwort. *The stalkes of Sope-woort are slipperie*, declared John Gerard in his HERBALL (1597). The plant is named because a lather forms when its stems are rubbed. Dutch and German have similar names and the English term is perhaps fashioned after these.

---

florir, 'to flower', from unattested Vulgar Latin *flōrīre*.

florid (17th cent): from French *floride*, from Latin *flōridus*, related to *flōrēre*, 'to bloom').

For the origins of some individual flower names, see HOW DOES YOUR GARDEN GROW? (page 125).

fornication
consensual sexual intercourse outside marriage

For a rape trial to go ahead in Pakistan, four adult Muslim men, 'all of a pious and trustworthy nature', must have witnessed the attack and be willing to testify. Evidence from female and non-Muslim witnesses is considered worthless. A woman

*who can't produce those witnesses can be prosecuted for **fornication** and alleging a false crime, the penalties for which are stoning, lashings or prison.*
(THE OBSERVER, 17 SEPTEMBER 2006)

This word derives from Latin *fornix* (stem *fornic-*), 'arch, vault'. By extension, it also signified a 'vaulted underground chamber'. The basements of buildings were often inhabited by down-and-outs and prostitutes, so that early Christian writers in particular used the term to denote 'a brothel', giving rise to the Late Latin verb *fornicārī*, 'to have sexual intercourse outside marriage' and the derived noun *fornicatiō*, 'fornication'. The word *fornication* came into English at the end of the thirteenth century with the Christian sense of 'illicit sex', that is adultery or sex outside marriage: *'Fornycacyoun' [ys],whan two vnweddyde haue mysdoun* (Robert Mannyng of Brunne, HANDLYNG SYNNE, 1303).

freelance
a self-employed professional

*The Devil, according to the Muslims, was once God's sidekick, until he fought with Him and went **freelance**, and ever since, there has been a war of brains between God and the Devil.*
(ARAVIND ADIGA,
THE WHITE TIGER, 2008)

*I've started writing books rather than doing journalism and she has started working as a research fellow rather than **freelancing** in dangerous war zones.*
(GOOD HOUSEKEEPING, APRIL 2009)

In the fourteenth to the sixteenth centuries mercenaries operated throughout Europe, knights who, being free of any particular allegiance, would take their lances into battle for whichever prince or state had paid most for their services. Nineteenth-century authors writing about the period coined the term *freelance* when referring to them. In IVANHOE (1819), for example, Sir Walter Scott refers to such knights as *lances*:

I can form no guess – unless he be one of the good lances who accompanied King Richard to Palestine.

They form a company:

He is a monarch by whom Fitzurse and De Bracy hope to rise and thrive; and therefore you aid him with your policy, and I with the lances of my Free Companions.

Finally they demonstrate one of the earliest uses of the term that we know today:

'Ay,' said Fitzurse, 'such is indeed the fashion of Richard – a true knight-errant he, and will wander in wild adventure, trusting the prowess of his single arm – What dost thou propose to do, De Bracy?'
'I? – I offered Richard the service of my Free Lances, and he refused them – I will lead them to Hull, seize on shipping, and embark for Flanders; thanks to the bustling times, a man of action will always find employment.'

During the second half of the century the word was figuratively applied to 'a rogue politician' who, being independent of party loyalty, was free to side as inclination took him. The modern application to 'one who works for himself' arose in the last quarter of the nineteenth century. The verb *freelance*, 'to earn one's living as a freelance', dates from the early years of the twentieth century and may have originated in American English.

· G ·

gargantuan

huge, colossal, of vast proportion

It's easy to forget that for all his **gargantuan** *symphonic structures, Mahler's orchestration is often of chamber-like refinement and subtlety.*
(EVENING STANDARD,
14 AUGUST 2007)

They were standing at the edge of a lake, and there were three fountains rising up from the horizon, over the Baltic Sea in the distance, each of the sprays a throbbing column of gold that flickered like a **gargantuan** *candle.*
(CHRIS BOHJALIAN,
SKELETONS AT THE FEAST, 2008)

Gargantua was the name of a giant celebrated in medieval French folklore. In 1534 François Rabelais further popularised the character when he wrote LA VIE INESTIMABLE DU GRANT GARGANTUA, PERE DE PANTAGRUEL, based on a chapbook of legends about him. The story was a peg upon which to hang a bawdy and irreverent satire on the systems and society of sixteenth-century France; the church, the law, politics, education and social conventions were all ridiculed by Rabelais, who promoted the humanistic thinking and learning that was emerging in Europe at that time.

Gargantua's name was probably derived from Spanish *garganta*, 'throat'. It was particularly apt since he was portrayed as having an enormous, insatiable appetite: on one occasion he accidentally swallowed five pilgrims along with the rest of his dinner. Shakespeare made reference to a throat that could gulp down such a meal with ease in AS YOU LIKE IT (1599):

Rosalind: *Answer me in one word.*
Celia: *You must borrow me Gargantua's mouth first before I can utter so long a word: 'tis a word too great for any mouth of this age's size.*

Indeed, the giant Gargantua was so colossal in stature that his horse sported the stolen bells of Notre Dame about its neck and flattened a forest with a swish of its tail. Small wonder, then, that his larger-than-life exploits captured popular imagination and gave rise to the French adjective *gargantuesque* and our own *gargantuan*, to describe anything of vast proportion – *this Gargantuan bag-pudding*, for instance (Thomas Nashe, HAVE WITH YOU TO SAFFRON-WALDEN, 1596).

gerrymander

to change electoral boundaries for political advantage

Gov. Arnold Schwarzenegger's unveiling Tuesday of his redistricting reform proposal was a welcome affirmation of his commitment to changing a broken system. Because of a meticulous **gerrymander** *by the Legislature following the 2000 census, all but two or three of the 153 congressional and state legislative seats up for election in even-numbered years are so tilted to one party that there is no chance they will change hands.*
(DAILY BREEZE, 7 DECEMBER 2006)

This word was coined in part from the name of Elbridge Gerry who, in 1811, was re-elected Governor of Massachusetts as a Democrat. In order to give their party increased representation in the State Senate, Governor Gerry and his colleagues on the Democratic legislature rearranged the state district boundaries so that the Federalist minority would be unable to achieve representative power. The act authorising these changes was duly signed by Governor Gerry on 11 February 1812.

The story goes that in his Boston office Benjamin Russell, editor of the Federalist newspaper the COLUMBIAN CENTINEL, was pondering over a map of the nonsensical divisions proposed for Essex County which hung on his wall. Suddenly the painter Gilbert Stuart, who was in the office at the time, seized his pencil and rapidly transformed the outline of the new county boundaries into a creature by adding a head, wings and claws. 'That will do for a salamander,' he said. 'Gerrymander,' retorted Russell.

Whether or not these are the exact circumstances under which gerry-mander was coined, the caricature was appropriated for the Federalist cause. Soon the term gerrymander was transferred from the creature to the tactics and, within a few months, had also become a verb meaning 'to tamper with election district boundaries in order to achieve unfair political advantage'.

The redistribution of Essex County gave the desired result; the Federalists polled a greater total vote but won only 11 seats to the Democrats' 29. It was, perhaps, a crumb of comfort to the Federalist party that Gerry was a casualty of the election and that the bill of 1812 was repealed in the following year.

For another term denoting a questionable political practice, see FILIBUSTER.

gingerly
delicately, tentatively

*He closed the curtains, turned the knob to hot, shut his eyes, removed his clothing, manoeuvred himself into the jet of water, massaged some shampoo **gingerly** into his scalp, then turned slowly like a kebab to rinse himself.*
(MARK HADDON,
A SPOT OF BOTHER, 2006)

*His reedy crooning suggests there may be more than one Bryan Ferry album in his collection, but as he sheds his inhibitions and **gingerly** dances, he turns into something closer to a blaring Bono.*
(THE GUARDIAN, 12 JUNE 2009)

This word has nothing at all to do with *ginger,* the pungent spice: its origins lie in good breeding. The Latin verb *gignere* meant 'to beget'; its past participle was *genitus*, 'born', which had evolved the sense 'of noble birth' by the time it had made its way into Old French as *gent* in the eleventh century. Those who were well born had graceful manners, so the word also came to mean 'delicate, gentle'.

The comparative *gensor* was also used with the sense 'delicate' and first appeared in English as an adverb, with the addition of the suffix -*ly*, in the early sixteenth century. It meant 'elegantly, daintily', and often referred to dance steps. This sense soon lost its positive connotations, however, and was used instead as a sneer at those considered effeminate. In THE ANATOMIE OF ABUSES (1583) Philip Stubbes mocks *dansing minions, that minse it ful gingerlie...tripping like gotes, that an egge would not brek vnder their feet.*

By the early seventeenth century the word was applied not just to walking or dancing but to any action performed with great care so as to avoid hurting oneself, harming something or causing alarm. Political evasiveness is nothing new, as Samuel Pepys shows. In his diary entry for 3 July 1667, he records how Sir William Penn made a formal speech in answer to the king, who had asked whether sunken ships left in the river would spoil it. *But, Lord! how gingerly he answered it*, Pepys then exclaims in frustration.

☞ Latin *gignere*, 'to beget', is also the source of:

genital (14th cent), *genitive* (14th cent), *progenitor* (14th cent).

indigenous (17th cent): from Late Latin *indigenus*, 'born in a country', from Latin *indigena*, 'native' (literally 'in-born person'), from *indi-*, 'in', and *gignere*.

ingenuous (16th cent): from Latin *ingenuus*, 'native, free-born' and hence possessing the qualities of a free person: noble, honest.

giraffe
a large African cud-chewing animal, with long neck and legs, and a spotted skin

*Anarchism adjures us to be bold creative artists, and care for no laws or limits. But it is impossible to be an artist and not care for laws and limits. Art is limitation; the essence of every picture is the frame. If you draw a **giraffe**, you must draw him with a long neck. If, in your bold creative way, you hold yourself free to draw a giraffe with a short neck, you will really find that you are not free to draw a giraffe. The moment you step into the world of facts, you step into a world of limits.*
(G K CHESTERTON, ORTHODOXY, 1909)

*It made Rebecca see, at long last, that this really was Will Allenby – a lanky, big-eared **giraffe** of a boy who never had quite learned how to manage his own limbs.*
(ANNE TYLER, BACK WHEN WE WERE GROWNUPS, 2001)

The Greeks called the giraffe *kamēlopardalis*. This was a compound of *kamēlos*, 'camel' and *pardalis* (variant of *pardos*), 'leopard' and was descriptive of the creature which has a head like a camel's and the patterned skin of the leopard. Latin borrowed this as *camēlopardalis*, which became *camēlopardus* in Medieval Latin. The word came into English as *cameleopard* in the late fourteenth century, the spelling erroneously influenced by that of *leopard*. It was regularised as *camelopard* in the seventeenth century, and remains a heraldic term.

In the late sixteenth century, however, *camelopard* was put under pressure by a new term which eventually won out. Italian had *giraffa* and French *giraffe*, words derived from Arabic *zirāfah*, which may ultimately be of African origin. English texts of the sixteenth and seventeenth centuries show evidence of borrowing from both Italian and French sources, although by the eighteenth century the French spelling was settled upon. Ironically, French spelling has since changed; Modern French has *girafe*.

For another term describing an exotic creature, see ELEPHANT.

gorilla

a very large, strong African ape

*He'd met them lots of times before, and they were called Mr and Mrs McEwan. They'd taken him to the London Zoo, to see Guy the **gorilla**, and to a teashop called Lyons Corner House, where he had a big ice cream called a Knickerbocker Glory.*
(MARY CAVANAGH,
A MAN LIKE ANY OTHER, 2007)

*As for **gorillas**, their weight is a handicap to arboreal travel and they feel more at ease on the ground.*
(CYRIL RUOSO & EMMANUELLE
GRUNDMANN, THE GREAT APES, 2007)

Evidence for this word, like that for CANARY, rests on a surviving translation of a lost original. In this case the PERIPLUS or 'Circumnavigation', an account of a voyage written in the Punic or Carthaginian language, has come down to us in Greek. When Hanno, the Carthaginian navigator, sailed the west coast of Africa in the fifth century BC he returned with tales of a tribe made up mostly of exceptionally hairy women known as *Gorillas*:

Leaving this place, we sailed along the burning coast for three days and came to the gulf named the Horn of the South. At the end of it was an island like the first one, with a lake in which was another island full of savages. The greater parts of these were women. They had hairy bodies and the interpreters called them Gorillas. We pursued some of the males but we could not catch a single one because they were good climbers and they defended themselves fiercely. However, we managed to take three women. They bit and scratched their captors, whom they did not want to follow. We killed them and removed the skins to take back to Carthage. We sailed no further, being short of supplies.

Many centuries later, in 1847, Dr Thomas Staughton Savage, an American missionary and naturalist working in Liberia, acquired a number of bones and the skull of an unknown species of great ape which he named *Trogolodytes gorilla* after Hanno's find. It is just possible, of course, that the wild hirsute tribeswomen Hanno came across may have been gorillas all along, in which case Dr Savage's observation was a mere rediscovery.

gossip

a person, usually a woman, who talks about others behind their backs; idle rumour; a chat, a natter

*The men of the new regiment watched and listened eagerly, while their tongues ran on in **gossip** of the battle. They mouthed rumors that had flown like birds out of the unknown.*
(STEVEN CRANE, THE RED BADGE OF
COURAGE, 1895)

*'I always speaks fair of folks when I can,' continued Mrs Pringle self-righteously, putting down her dustpan and settling herself on the front desk for a good **gossip**.*
(MISS READ, OVER THE GATE, 1964)

*'That's why he's moving to the area… He's somehow heard about your new job and the fact that TV cameras are coming to town, and perhaps he thinks you're going to make it big, and then he'll become known as your ex-husband. He won't be able to control **gossip** about him, which he'll hate.'*
(SARAH TUCKER, THE CONTROL FREAK
CHRONICLES, 2009)

Gossip derives from Old English *godsibb*, a compound noun made up of *god* and *sibb*. While *god* is readily understood in modern English, *sibb* meant 'kinsman, relative' and is apparent today in the word *sibling*. *Godsibb* denoted a 'godparent', someone who agreed to assist the spiritual nurturing of a child. Richard Verstegan, an antiquary and zealous Catholic writing at the beginning of the seventeenth century, expressed the relationship thus:

Our Christian ancestors understanding a spiritual affinity to grow between the parents, and such as undertooke for the child at baptisme, called each other by the name of Godsib, that is, of kin together through God: and the child in like manner called such his godfathers and godmothers.

Since friends of the parents were invited to enter into this special relationship it is not surprising that, by the fourteenth century, *godsib* had come to mean a 'familiar friend':

Truely Johan Johan we made a pye
I and my gossyp Margery.
(JOHN HEYWOOD, JOHAN JOHAN, THE HUSBANDE, TYB HIS WYFE, AND SYR JHAN THE PREEST,1533)

Friends generally enjoy a good chat in each other's company and so, by the second half of the sixteenth century, a *gossip* also denoted 'someone who indulges in tittle-tattle'.

Gossips were usually women – possibly because a woman's particular chums were usually invited to attend her in childbirth (the term *gossip* was used in this context also), but more likely through an already centuries-old reputation women had for talkativeness – and the word carries this gender bias to the present day. Surprisingly, *gossip* as a term for 'idle chit-chat' or 'a juicy rumour' has been current only since the early nineteenth century.

grape
a small round fruit, growing in clusters on a vine, often used to make wine

THE FOX AND THE **GRAPES**
One hot summer's day a Fox was strolling through an orchard till he came to a bunch of grapes just ripening on a vine which had been trained over a lofty branch. 'Just the thing to quench my thirst,' quoth he. Drawing back a few paces, he took a run and a jump, and just missed the bunch. Turning round again with a One, Two, Three, he jumped up, but with no greater success. Again and again he tried after the tempting morsel, but at last had to give it up, and walked away with his nose in the air, saying: 'I am sure they are sour.'
It is easy to despise what you cannot get.
(AESOP'S FABLES, 6TH CENTURY BC)

I studied the tapestries. These were of **grape** *harvesters, men cutting the vines while women stamped on the grapes, skirts tucked high to reveal their spattered calves.*
(TRACY CHEVALIER, THE LADY AND THE UNICORN, 2003)

It isn't only strawberries; we're eating less unprocessed or melanged fruit altogether. Orange sales have plummeted. I expect plum sales are plummeting. We drink cartons of boiled fruit juice, but we can't be bothered to peel one. When was the last time you ate a **grape** *with a pip in it?*
(THE TIMES, 14 JUNE 2009)

Grapes have been cultivated since late prehistoric times, not so much for their fruit as for the production of wine. The Old English word *winberige*, literally 'wineberry', reflects this. The thirteenth-century borrowing *grape* which replaced it takes its name from a tool used in viticulture. Unattested proto-Germanic *krappon-*, 'hook' was ultimately responsible for the Old French noun *grape*, 'hook', and the derived verb *graper*, which meant 'to gather clusters with a vine-hook'. From this

Old French had *grape* to denote 'a bunch of grapes' (the modern French term is *grappe*) and this was the sense in which the term was first borrowed into Middle English. The new word, however, was mostly used in contexts which demanded a plural so that, when searching for a singular in English, *grape* erroneously came to refer to a single berry.

grapefruit
a large, round citrus fruit with an acid pulp

*Eating **grapefruit** can increase the risk of breast cancer by almost a third, a study suggests. It is thought the fruit boosts blood levels of oestrogen, the hormone associated with the risk of the disease. According to the research, eating as little as a quarter of a grapefruit a day raises the danger by 30 per cent among older women.*
(DAILY MAIL, 13 SEPTEMBER, 2007)

*But there are other diversions, too: visit Moorea's pineapple and **grapefruit** plantations, or a pearl shop to find out about the South Pacific's famous export.*
(THE INDEPENDENT, 22 MARCH 2009)

In her book IN THE TRADES (1884) the celebrated Victorian traveller Lady Annie Brassey muses upon the grapefruit. *It looks and tastes much like a shaddock*, she writes, then adds *it does not bear the slightest resemblance to a grape*.

Lady Brassey is right in suggesting that the word is a perplexing one. She is also correct in describing the grapefruit's taste and appearance as being like that of the *shaddock*, for it is a hybrid of the orange and that fruit (formally known as the *pampelmoes*, but renamed in the seventeenth century for Captain Shaddock of the East India Company who first took its seed to Barbados).

The word *grapefruit* had been introduced into English by John Lunan in HORTUS JAMAICENSIS (1814), a book about the botany of Jamaica. Lunan may have seen a grapefruit but he had certainly never tasted one. He assumes it is named *on account of its resemblance in flavour to the grape.*

So, if the grapefruit is named neither for its appearance nor its taste, what is the secret of its etymology? The answer is that it grows in clusters on the tree which, when the fruits are small and green, look a bit like bunches of grapes.

See GRAPE.

great
large, big; important, prominent

*And for an hour I have walked and prayed Because of the **great** gloom that is in my mind.*
(W B YEATS, A PRAYER FOR MY DAUGHTER, 1919)

*'I remember when the **Great** War began,' said Grandfather proudly, staring into the fire and shaking his head. 'I remember you coming home to tell us how you had joined up and I was sure that you would come to harm.'*
(JOHN BOYNE, THE BOY IN THE STRIPED PYJAMAS, 2006)

*Fuentes is an elegant writer, the best news to come out of Spanish crime fiction since the **great** Manuel Vázquez Monalbán.*
(THE TIMES, 29 NOVEMBER 2008)

In the ninth century the opposing adjectives *great* and *small* had the meanings 'stout' and 'slender' respectively. The concept 'large in size' was denoted by *mickle*, an adjective that is now rarely heard.

Great, a derivative of West Germanic *grautaz*, gradually acquired the general sense 'large' around the beginning of the fourteenth century, its importance as an adjective of size and stature increasing steadily to supersede *mickle*. In the same period the word was also applied figuratively to people or events to give the meaning 'distinguished', 'eminent', 'prominent'.

Towards the end of the thirteenth century a new and powerful little word, possibly of Norse origin, started to appear in the works of writers in the north-eastern counties. *Big* originally meant 'strong, powerful, mighty'. Strong men or cities are usually of substantial proportion, however, and so by the sixteenth century *big* had developed the sense 'of large size'. In modern English *big* has largely usurped *great* just as *great*, in earlier centuries, ousted *mickle*.

Great still reigns, however, as an adjective of pre-eminence and status; there is a world of difference between a *great* man or woman and a *big* one.

grocer
a shopkeeper who sells food and household items

He put in a solitary lemon, a precious possession he'd been lucky enough to find in his local grocery store...
(ROSE TREMAIN, THE BEAUTY OF THE DAWN SHIFT, 2005)

Wincanton, the trucking firm which delivers Heinz baked beans to your local grocer, admitted today that savage job cuts last month will not prevent it from failing to hit most City analysts' profit targets.
(DAILY MAIL, 4 FEBRUARY 2009)

In medieval France a dealer in spices was known by the derived term *espicier* (*épicier*, 'grocer', in modern French). Middle English had the equivalent *spicer*, but the word became obsolete in the early seventeenth century. Instead English developed the word *grocer* (Middle English *grosser*) which, in the

early fourteenth century, denoted 'a wholesale dealer in a particular commodity', such as wine or fish. It was especially applied to merchants who traded in spices and imported foodstuffs. The term came from Old French *grossier* and Medieval Latin *grossārius*, 'wholesale dealer', the latter being a derivative of Latin *grossus*, 'thick, large'. By the second half of the fifteenth century, however, *grocer* was beginning to lose its exclusive 'wholesale' application and was being applied to retailers in spices, dried fruit, sugar and the like, eventually supplanting *spicer*.

☞ Latin *grossus* is also responsible for *engross*. One of the particular meanings of the verb at the turn of the fifteenth century was 'to buy up the entire stock for sale at a premium' (Middle English *engrossen*, from Anglo-French *engrosser*, from Old French *en gros* 'wholesale'). From this developed the senses 'to need the entire use of something' and, at the beginning of the eighteenth century, 'to absorb one's attention totally'.

See SPICE.

guerrilla
a member of an independent group engaged in irregular warfare

The native people of Britain had a reputation as ferocious warriors. They would paint themselves with woad and hurl themselves without fear into the conflict. They were used to the terrain and could disappear into the hills, popping out like guerrillas to attack the Romans when they were least expected.
(PHILIP WILKINSON, WHAT THE ROMANS DID FOR US, 2000)

...at Vaser Rosa, a village close by the Latvian border, is a network of tunnels and dug-outs that were built by the Forest

Brothers, a resistance network that kept up a **guerrilla** campaign against the Soviet army for almost twenty years after the Second World War ended.
(MICHAEL PALIN, NEW EUROPE, 2007)

Guerrilla is a Spanish word. It literally means 'a little war' and hence 'a skirmish', being a diminutive of *guerra*, meaning 'war'. It was borrowed into English during the Peninsula War (1808-14) in which Britain, together with Spain and Portugal, fought against the Napoleonic invasion of Iberia. Initially the word referred to the independent tactics of the resistance movement. In one of his despatches early in the war (1809), however, the future Duke of Wellington applied the term to individuals thus engaged rather than to the warfare itself. This is generally how it has come to be used in English, where a *guerrilla* is one who is involved in *guerrilla warfare*.

Spanish *guerra* ultimately comes from the unattested proto-Germanic base *werr-*, 'confusion, strife', source of English *war* via Old Northern French *werre* and Old French *guerre*.

guillotine
a device for beheading criminals, political opponents, etc.

We are like prison chaplains in here, dealing with the remnant human person after the civic powers have had their say. We are trying to ready, to steady the person for what? The axe, the **guillotine** of sanity?
(SEBASTIAN BARRY,
THE SECRET SCRIPTURE, 2008)

For a while he and Lucie took refuge in their family home near Bordeaux. But the arrival of the **guillotine** in the city in October 1793 drove them into hiding – Lucie, with her small son and newborn baby in cramped rooms near the centre from which she could hear the daily thud of the executions, her husband in a series of

---

WHO WAS WHO?

An eponym is a word that goes back to a name. In this book are the stories of BLOOMERS, GUILLOTINE, SANDWICH, TANTALISE, WELLINGTON and others.

There are several categories of eponyms: most go back to individuals, but some refer to places (see GIPSY) and others to trade names (see JEEP and TABLOID). Tests of their acceptance into the general vocabulary are various. For example:

• the initial capital is no longer used (*aspirin*, not *Aspirin*).
• the word is employed even for a competitor's product. How many people realise the contradiction when they *xerox* a document with a machine that does not come from the Xerox Corporation? And in an edition of THE ENGINEER (11 November, 1971) a journalist asked *How many housewives Hoover the carpet with an Electrolux?*.
• one is surprised to discover that the word once referred principally to a proprietary product (*biro, diesel, plimsolls*).

---

perilous hiding places outside.
(REVIEW OF 'DANCING TO THE PRECIPICE' BY CAROLINE MOOREHEAD, IN THE SPECTATOR, 25 FEBRUARY 2009)

Just before her execution in 1536 Anne Boleyn is said to have remarked with thankfulness that she had a little neck: she knew that decapitation with an axe or sword seldom rushed the victim into oblivion. Two hundred and fifty years later this suffering stirred a politician to action, and gave the world a new word.

In common with other European countries, France had a two-tier system of execution. Beheading was the prerogative of the nobility; the common people suffered the gallows. This inequality, together with concern for the agonies endured by victims, troubled a certain Joseph Ignace Guillotin, a physician and a Deputy of the Constituent Assembly. On 10 October 1789, he voiced his concern during an assembly debate on reforms in criminal jurisprudence. He proposed that *in all cases where the law shall pass sentence of death upon a convicted person, the punishment shall be the same, whatever the nature of the offence of which he shall be found guilty. Such punishment shall be decapitation, and the execution shall be carried out by a simple machine.*

Guillotin probably already had a *simple machine* in mind, for contraptions similar to the guillotine had been used in Scotland during the sixteenth and seventeenth centuries, and in Italy in the thirteenth and fourteenth. When, in 1792, his reform was finally adopted, Guillotin consulted with a surgeon, Dr Antoine Louis, who came up with the *louison* or *louisette*, a machine originally named after its inventor, but which soon became known as the *guillotine* after its champion. The miscreant who had the honour of trying out the efficiency of the contraption was a highwayman named Pelletier, who knelt beneath the gleaming blade on 25 April 1792. What he thought of it has not been recorded.

The word *guillotine* entered English in 1793. This is not surprising, since the year was marked by two deeply shocking events. First, it saw the beginning of the Reign of Terror in France, when the guillotine was used for the systematic execution of thousands who were charged with opposing the revolution. Second, it brought the execution of King Louis XVI and his queen, Marie Antoinette.

It is rumoured that after the French Revolution, the original guillotine was sold by the public executioner to a man named Curtius, who then sold it at a profit to his niece, a certain Madame Tussaud. That good lady recouped the price and more by displaying it in her Chamber of Horrors. Dr Guillotin is supposed to have tried to disassociate his name from the machine after the horrific use to which it was put, but to no avail. On his death in 1814 his children did the next best thing and sought legal permission to change their name.

Since the mid-nineteenth century *guillotine* has been used in a wide variety of industries to refer to any number of devices which cut with a slicing movement. Also since that century the word has been used in political contexts: in the United States to refer to the dismissal of government staff when a new President is sworn in, and in England to describe a means of limiting the debate on a bill by naming a day when the committee stage must close:

There were no fewer than 35 groups of amendments, which once the guillotine motion passed would leave 12 minutes to debate each. (Since a vote takes a full quarter-hour, that would leave minus three minutes for each topic – a period of discussion that the government probably regards as ideal.)
(THE GUARDIAN, 6 JUNE 2000)

For another word connected with execution, see DERRICK.

gymnasium

a room containing equipment for physical exercise

*We walked past temple after temple, praying to god after god, and then went in a single file between a red temple devoted to Hanuman and an open **gymnasium** where three body builders heaved rusted weights over their heads.*
(ARAVIND ADIGA,
THE WHITE TIGER, 2008)

*The Club boasts 28 outdoor lawn tennis courts, ten indoor lawn tennis courts, two real tennis courts, two rackets courts, three squash courts and a **gymnasium**.*
(THE TIMES, 2 MAY 2009)

In ancient Greece, athletic competitions, held to celebrate the gods or in honour of a hero, were important religious and social events. So much so that special schools equipped for the physical training of male athletes were founded. The Greeks developed a belief that exercise, health and education were linked and so these institutions began to offer instruction in morals and ethics as well as exercise programmes.

Greek athletes trained and performed naked, a custom said to have begun in Sparta in recognition of the beauty of the toned male form. This fact is reflected in the etymology of *gymnasium*, which goes back to the adjective *gumnos*, 'naked'. The derived verb *gumnazein* literally meant 'to train naked', and hence 'to train, to exercise'. From this the noun *gumnasion* was formed to denote 'a school offering athletic training'. Latin borrowed the word as *gymnasium*, 'a gymnastic college, school', and English took the word from Latin in the late sixteenth century, using it initially in texts about the classical world.

In English *gymnasium* has almost always denoted 'a place for athletic exercise', and the term is now often shortened to *gym* or replaced altogether by *health club* or *fitness centre*. The word has rarely been used to denote 'school', although in the second half of the seventeenth century a certain Mark Lewis ran a private school he called a *gymnasium* at Tottenham High Cross, where pupils were *perfected in the tongues by constant conversation*. In Germany and some other countries, however, a *gymnasium* is a 'high school'.

The noun *gymnast*, first recorded in English at the end of the sixteenth century, was a borrowing of the Greek word *gumnastēs*, a derivative of *gumnazein*, 'to train'. Although English has always used the word to mean 'one who practises gymnastics', in ancient Greece a *gumnastēs* was 'a trainer', a person responsible for teaching and assessing the youths in their care.

For another word from ancient Greek athletics, see AGONY. For details of a philosopher who taught in a gymnasium, see CYNIC.

gypsy, gipsy

an itinerant trader of the Romany people; a rootless wanderer

*Then, in high summer, more **gipsies** come, bearing gaudy flowers made of wood-shavings and dyed all the colours of the rainbow.*
(MISS READ, OVER THE GATE, 1964)

*Politicians beg for votes, advertisers beg for sales and many stars of television beg shamelessly for attention. And yet when **gypsy** mothers, shunned in their native countries, appear begging in Underground stations, the public recoils in horror as though stretching out your hand for a few coins were a mortal sin.*
(JOHN MORTIMER,
SUMMER OF A DORMOUSE, 2000)

He abhorred those who were born into wealth, and rather enjoyed doing things the 'sophisticated people' would never do.

One of those things was visiting seaside resorts. He loved the attractions, the salty food, the **gypsies** *and fortune-tellers and weight guessers and diving girls. And we both loved the sea.*

(MITCH ALBOM, THE FIVE PEOPLE YOU MEET IN HEAVEN, 2003)

When gypsies first appeared in England, people looking at their dark skin and black hair and listening to their foreign chatter assumed that they were from Egypt and referred to them as *Egyptians*. In speech, however, the soft, unstressed initial vowel was often lost, reducing the word to *Gypcyans*. In a letter dating from 1537, Lord Cromwell wrote that *The Kings Maiestie, about a twelfmoneth past, gave a pardonne to a company of lewde personnes within this realme calling themselves Gipcyans, for a most shamfull and detestable murder.*

The modern spellings evolved during the seventeenth century and were generally accepted, although as late as the mid-eighteenth century *Egyptian* was still insisted upon by sticklers for correctness:

A company of Egyptians, or as they are vulgarly called, gipsies.

(HENRY FIELDING, TOM JONES, 1749)

This was ironic, because the gypsies had not, in fact, come from Egypt at all. They were a wandering people of low-caste Indian origin who migrated first to Persia and then to continental Europe during the fourteenth and fifteenth centuries.

Traditionally gypsies have earned their way by tinkering, fortune-telling, handicrafts and horse-dealing. The latter persists to this day; there is still a gypsy horse fair at Stow-on-the-Wold in the Cotswolds every spring.

· H ·

haggard
tired and drawn, through anxiety,
hunger or ageing

*He could plainly see how old all the rest of
his family and acquaintance were growing.
Anne **haggard**, Mary coarse, every face in
the neighbourhood worsting, and the rapid
increase of the crow's foot about Lady
Russell's temples had long been a distress
to him.*
(JANE AUSTEN, PERSUASION, 1818)

*Dr Moran later described his patient as
haggard and dirty, noting that over the
next three days Poe was alternately
delirious and lucid, hot and cold.*
(SHELLEY COSTA BLOOMFIELD,
THE EVERYTHING GUIDE TO EDGAR
ALLAN POE, 2007)

Hawking, or falconry, is the ancient
practice of hunting with a trained bird
of prey. The hawks were not originally
bred in captivity but were taken as
nestlings or captured as adults. In the
sixteenth century, birds caught after
they had gained their adult plumage
were known as *haggards*, from Middle
French *hagard*. The source of this word
is unknown but, since the haggard had
the freedom of the hedgerows before its
capture, it has sometimes been connected with a French dialect word
deriving from *haie*, 'hedge'.
    Initially the newly captured wild
birds resisted confinement and training
with all their might, so that *haggard*
made an evocative metaphor when
applied to 'a person of difficult and
wayward disposition'. Thus, when

Petruchio compared his mastery of
Katharina to the manning of a falcon
in Shakespeare's THE TAMING OF
THE SHREW (1596), he was making a
very topical comparison:

> *My foulcon now is sharp, and passing
> empty,*
> *And 'till she stoop she must not be
> full-gorg'd,*
> *For then she never looks upon her lure.*
> *Another way I have to man my haggard,*
> *To make her come, and know her keeper's
> call;*
> *That is, to watch her, as we watch those kites*
> *That bate, and beat, and will not be obedient.*
> *She eat no meat today, nor more shall eat;*
> *Last night she slept not, and to-night she
> shall not.*

The terror of a wild creature newly captured and anxious for its freedom
prompted a further application of the
adjective in the seventeenth century
when it was used to describe 'a face
marked by the ravages of fatigue or
fear', the current sense. In the nineteenth century the word evolved
further and also came to mean 'gaunt
and sagging through ageing', an application that was apparently influenced
by the similar sounding *hag*, 'witch,
hideous old woman'. In his HISTORY
OF FRIEDRICH II, CALLED THE
GREAT (1858), Thomas Carlyle wrote
of one poor woman who was *getting
haggard beyond the power of rouge*.

For another word from falconry, see
MEWS.

halibut

an edible flatfish

There is a slight bias towards fish dishes, including pan-fried garlic king prawns with saffron rice and crisp salad, and pan-fried **halibut** *steak resting on asparagus spears with pepper coulis and buttered new potatoes, both of which were faultless.*
(YORKSHIRE LIVING, APRIL 2009)

See HOLY.

ham

the upper thigh of a pig or other animal, prepared for food

'I shall take a mere mouthful of **ham** *and a glass of ale,' he said, reassuringly. 'As a man with public business, I take a snack when I can. I will back this ham,' he added, after swallowing some morsels with alarming haste, 'against any ham in the three kingdoms. In my opinion it is better than the hams at Freshitt Hall – and I think l am a tolerable judge.'*
'Some don't like so much sugar in their hams,' said Mrs. Waule. 'But my poor brother would always have sugar.'

'If any person demands better, he is at liberty to do so; but, God bless me, what an aroma! I should be glad to buy in that quality, I know. There is some gratification to a gentleman' – here Mr Trumbull's voice conveyed an emotional remonstrance – *'in having this kind of ham set on his table.'*
(GEORGE ELIOT, MIDDLEMARCH, 1872)

The guests had departed, and Lucas's father and mother had gone to bed. It was only Lucas and Catherine in the parlor, with what had been left behind. Empty plates, the rind of a **ham**. *The ham had been meant for Catherine and Simon's wedding, It was lucky, then, to have it for the wake instead.*
(MICHAEL CUNNINGHAM, SPECIMEN DAYS, 2005)

Ham was not always a sandwich filling. The word goes back to an assumed Germanic *kham-*, 'to be crooked'. Old English *hamm* originally denoted 'the hollow at the back of the knee', a sense which lingers in the compound *hamstring*, the name for either of the tendons which run through this part of the leg. In the mid-sixteenth century

---

FROM SWINE TO PORK

When the victorious Normans communicated with the conquered Saxons it was presumably with much arm waving and broken attempts at each other's language. For a long time French was the language of the social élite, while English was confined to the uneducated masses. A farmyard-to-table study bears witness to this. The animals that the peasants reared and tended have retained their Old English names: the meat that was served to the Norman masters is known by French equivalents:

Old English	French
swine (Old English *swin*)	
pig (Old English *picga*)	*pork* (Old French *porc*, 'pig')
ox (Old English *oxa*)	*beef* (Old French *boef*, 'ox')
sheep (Old English *sce-ap*)	*mutton* (Old French *moton*, 'sheep')
calf (Old English *cealf*)	*veal* (Old French *veel*, later *veau*, 'calf')

the term was extended to refer to 'the back of the thigh', and then to 'the back of the thigh, including the buttock'. The seventeeth century saw the word applied to the 'thigh of a slaughtered animal', more especially to that of a pig which had been cured, and from there to the meat itself.

The word *hamburger* has nothing to do with *ham* but is short for *Hamburg steak*, a delicacy made of seasoned minced beef that originated in the German city of Hamburg. German immigrants introduced it into the United States in the mid-nineteenth century, where it proved extremely popular. By the late 1880s it was known as a *Hamburger steak* and twenty years later was often just referred to as a *hamburger*. Since the end of the Second World War, both American and British English have been even more economical, clipping the word to a mere *burger*.

It must be a great comfort to the travelling American that he can now enjoy what has become his national dish at fast-food outlets worldwide. Indeed, even the quaintest of British high streets boasts at least one brash burger bar. Congratulations, therefore, to the TIMES journalist who, in an article dated 30 January 1960, timorously predicted that *the mounting number of hamburger bars suggests that it is here to stay*.

handicap
a hindrance to performance or success; a disability, physical or mental

He had been airlifted to the military hospital, and eventually, because of his handicap, was discharged and flown home to America. He had heard, months later, that the Captain had not made it.
(MITCH ALBOM, THE FIVE PEOPLE YOU MEET IN HEAVEN, 2003)

FALSE DIVISION

Mostly it is very clear how to divide a word up into its different elements. *Impossible*, for instance, is *im- + possible*, and *hamstring* is *ham + string* (see HAM) In some places a false division can hint at some very misleading – but diverting – origins. Quite a number of wits have capitalised on this for humorous effect.

allegro	chorus line
antimony	inheritance from aunt
bedrug	bed covering
counterspy	shop detective
firecracker	burnt biscuit
incommode	engaged, occupied
largesse	capital S
lawsuit	judge's attire
locomotion	faint noise
mandate	male partner
maritime	wedding day
nitrate	overnight tariff
shamrock	counterfeit diamond
stalemate	boring partner
stowaway	sailor with large appetite
tenet	group of 10 singers

'Which tees would you play off?'
'The men's.'
'You aren't muscular enough.'
'I'm becoming more muscular by the day, and, in any case, who will I be handicapping but myself?'
'I'm glad you mentioned handicaps,' smirked the PP. 'The whole handicap system is based on gender. I cannot just transfer your handicap willy-nilly from woman to man. That would be the road to anarchy.'
(DAVID NOBBS, SEX AND OTHER CHANGES, 2004)

Handicap is a contraction of the phrase *hand in the cap* or *hand i' cap*. This was a game of chance based on bartering. One person would challenge another for a particular possession and offer something of his own in exchange. If the challenge was accepted an umpire would be appointed and all three would place forfeit money into a hat, keeping their hands in the cap. The umpire would then consider the value of the proposed articles and decide what extra payment should be offered by the owner of the inferior item to make the exchange fair. The two players then withdrew their hands; holding on to one's money indicated that the deal was off, an empty hand signalled acceptance. If both players were in agreement, the exchange was made or cancelled accordingly and the umpire took all the forfeit money. On the other hand, if the players disagreed, no exchange was made but the one who had indicated a willingness to trade took all the forfeit.

The game was an old one. It is described in the Middle English poem PIERS PLOWMAN where a hood is offered for a cloak, the *noumpere* (umpire) judging that the owner of the hood should also give a cup of ale. In the fourteenth century, however, the game was known as *Newe Faire*. The name *hand in the cap* is of later date and is not found in written records until the seventeenth century. In his diary entry for 18 September, 1660, Samuel Pepys calls the game *handicap*, adding that he has never heard of it before but that he enjoyed playing it immensely.

In the 1680s the rules of *handicap* were applied to certain horse races, although they were not referred to as *handicap races* until the mid-eighteenth century. In these races the appointed umpire decided upon the extra weight that should be carried by the stronger horse and the system of forfeits operated as before. In the following century *handicap* was extended to any kind of race or competition where superior competitors were penalised in some way to create an evenly matched contest.

By the second half of the nineteenth century, besides its use in sporting contexts, the verb *to handicap* had the more general sense of 'to place someone at a disadvantage'. In the early twentieth century the past participle, *handicapped*, became an adjective to describe anyone 'physically or mentally disabled'.

For other words originating in games, see HAZARD and RIGMAROLE. For more about umpires, see that entry.

handkerchief

a square of cloth, carried in the pocket, for wiping the nose, etc.

HANDKERCHIEF, *a small square of silk or linen used at funerals to conceal one's lack of tears.*
(AMBROSE BIERCE,
THE DEVIL'S DICTIONARY, 1911)

She read the notice warning people that the llamas spat.
'Nannie won't let me spit. She says it's common to spit. She didn't say about llamas.'
*'She's quite wrong to tell you never to spit. You must never swallow phlegm. If you've forgotten your **handkerchief**, always spit it out. Wouldn't you like to spit at the llamas?'*
(DANE CHANDOS, ABBIE, 1947)

*'I must go,' she says in a little voice that only just manages to escape from her throat. She pulls a **handkerchief** out of her sleeves, and dabs it to her eyes. 'I'll just tidy myself up a little first, perhaps.'*
(MICHAEL FRAYN, SPIES, 2002)

In the Middle Ages women covered their heads with a cloth known as a *coverchief*. This compound noun was borrowed from Old French *couvrechief* or *cuevrechief* (from *couvrir*, 'to cover' and *chief*, 'head', from Latin *caput*). In the Middle English of about 1300 the word was often contracted to *curchef* or *kerchef*. Sometimes kerchiefs were also worn about the neck or to cover the breast. In the sixteenth century *kerchief* became part of a new compound, *handkerchief*, to denote a 'square of fabric carried in the hand to mop the face or nose'.

The *handkerchief* today does not have all the associations it had in the past. In the sixteenth and seventeenth centuries it was elaborate and decorative – something of a fashion item. When, in Shakespeare's OTHELLO (1604), Othello is tricked into believing that his wife Desdemona has passed on to Cassio a *Handkerchiefe Spotted with Strawberries* that he has given her as a token of his love, it is enough to incite the jealous rage in which he smothers her. And in his diary (1666) Samuel Pepys takes his wife to task for buying a laced handkerchief without his permission.

Sometimes *handkerchief* and *kerchief* were used interchangeably. In this passage from Henry Fielding's JOSEPH ANDREWS (1742), Joseph has been wounded while rescuing Fanny from an attacker. Her *handkerchief* has been torn from her shoulders:

This modest creature, whom no warmth in summer could ever induce to expose her charms to the wanton sun, a modesty to which perhaps they owed their inconceivable whiteness, had stood for many minutes barenecked in the presence of Joseph...at last, when the cause of her concern had vanished, an admiration at his silence, together with observing the fixed position of his eyes, produced an idea in the lovely maid, which brought more blood into her face than had flowed from Joseph's nostrils. The snowy hue of her bosom was likewise changed to vermilion at the instant when she clapped her handkerchief round her neck.

The pronunciation of *handkerchief* was for centuries reflected in the common alternative spelling *handkercher*. Voltaire (1694–1778) apparently commented to his countrymen on the discrepancy between spelling and pronunciation in this word. Eventually, the versions that are standard today asserted themselves. The abbreviation *hanky*, at first very properly spelt *handky*, dates from the late nineteenth century.

For another word whose etymology includes the French *couvre*, see CURFEW.

harbinger
a forerunner, one who announces something shortly to happen

*The gates of mercy had clanged shut against her, and here had come the **harbingers**, carrying in their bills the key to her release.*
(SALLY VICKERS,
MR GOLIGHTLY'S HOLIDAY, 2003)

*A good Easter weekend invariably fires the starting gun on a successful year for the horticultural sector while a wet one, the chances of which increase the earlier the event falls, is usually the **harbinger** of a rotten year.*
(THE TIMES, 10 APRIL 2009)

Today *harbinger* is often a rather literary word found in phrases like *the harbinger of doom*. It is hard to believe that for a part of its history it was a military term. Its source is a Germanic compound *heriberga*, meaning 'an army encampment' (from *heri*, 'army' and *berga*, 'protection, shelter'). This term had already gained the extended sense of 'lodging, hostelry' when Old French borrowed it in the eleventh century, together with both its senses, as *herberge* (modern French has *auberge* for 'inn'). The derivative *herbergere* therefore meant 'a person who provides lodgings, an innkeeper, a host', and this was borrowed directly into Middle English in the twelfth century.

From the late medieval period a *her-berger* was someone who was sent on ahead of an army or a royal progress to find a suitable camping ground or to procure accommodation for the entire party. The task of a royal harbinger was not an easy one since the scale of such operations was often enormous: as many as 30 coaches, 300 carts and 1000 pack-animals might be needed to move the Elizabethan court from place to place, for instance. The royal harbinger had to inspect the places to be visited along the route. Would some of the party need to be lodged in tents or was there sufficient accommodation available in nearby towns? Were there enough provisions available locally to feed such a vast company for the length of their intended stay? Was the neighbourhood free of disease? People needed time to prepare and advice on how to welcome the queen with due state.

The role of harbinger was still in force in the reign of Charles II. In LIFE OF BISHOP THOMAS KEN (1837), William Hawkins records this incident over the seventeenth-century cleric's refusal to play host to the king's mistress Nell Gwyn:

On the removal of the court to pass the summer at Winchester, bishop Ken's house which he held in the right of his prebend, was marked by the harbinger for the use of Mrs Eleanor Gwyn; but he refused to grant her admittance and she was forced to seek for lodgings in another place.

Around the second half of the sixteenth century, this notion of going on ahead to procure lodging gave rise to a figurative use of the word, that of 'forerunner, one who anticipates a future event', and this is the only sense with which we are now familiar. In A MIDSUMMER NIGHT'S DREAM, (c. 1595), Shakespeare has Puck describe the coming of the dawn in these terms:

*For night's swift dragons cut the clouds
full fast,
And yonder shines Aurora's harbinger;
At whose approach, ghosts, wandering here
and there,
Troop home to churchyards*

while Milton compares Dalila to a stately galleon in SAMSON AGONISTES (possibly 1647):

*With all her bravery on, each tackle trim,
Sails fill'd, and streamers waving,
Courted by all the winds that hold them
play,
An amber scent of odorous perfume
Her harbinger.*

As for spelling, the term underwent a change in the fifteenth century with the introduction of the letter *n* to give *herbengar*: a similar alteration took place with *messenger*, SCAVENGER and *passenger*. A new spelling of the first syllable, *har-*, began to take hold in the following century, though the emergence of *harbinger* was not complete until the seventeenth century.

☛ **Harbour** is a related word. In late Old English *herebeorg* meant 'a place of shelter', and the derived verb meant 'to provide lodging' or 'to quarter soldiers' (today we speak of *harbouring* terrorists). *Harbour* in the sense of 'port' or 'haven' was used by extension in the late Middle Ages.

hazard
risk, chance, peril

Winter's icy grip loosened on much of Britain today as weathermen warned of a new hazard – floods.
(EVENING STANDARD,
30 JANUARY 2004)

Another peril can be added to the hazards of the innocent-looking computer keyboard. Not content with encouraging repetitive strain injury, the type-pads sometimes harbour more filth than the average loo seat and house millions of bacteria which can cause diarrhoea and vomiting, a study has shown.
(THE GUARDIAN, 1 MAY 2008)

In the twelfth century an army of crusaders, engaged in the siege of a Palestinian fortress called *Hasart* or *Asart*, invented a game of chance played with dice to while away their moments of inactivity, naming it for the castle. This, at any rate, is the account offered by William of Tyre. Unfortunately, *Ain Zarba* is thought to have been the actual name of the castle, which rather spoils the story. Instead, the name of the game is believed to have derived ultimately from an Arabic word *al-zahr*, meaning 'luck, chance'. (See WORDS FROM ARABIC, page 20, for a discussion of *al-*.) This passed into Spanish as *azar*, 'a throw of the dice, chance', and from there into Old French as *hasard* in the twelfth century. Middle English adopted the game at the beginning of the fourteenth century.

Over the years the game increased in popularity, as did the size of the stakes. By the eighteenth century vast fortunes could be won or lost in London's fashionable clubs. In one of his letters (1770) Horace Walpole tells how, *At the Cocoa-tree Lord Stavordale, not one-and-twenty, lost eleven thousand last Tuesday, but recovered it by one great hand at hazard.*

Such associations with chance had made *hazard* an obvious candidate for figurative use, so that by the mid-sixteenth century, in French and then in English, it had also come to mean 'peril or risk'.

☛ *Haphazard* (16th cent), is a tautological compound of *hap*, 'chance, luck' (from Old Norse *happ*, 'chance') and *hazard*.

For other words originating in games, see HANDICAP and RIGMAROLE.

hearse
a vehicle for carrying a coffin

'Are you tired?' I asked.
 'Just a little.'
 'Perhaps we should talk. What is the best thing about being a hearse driver?'
 'Widows,' said Dalip. 'Yaarraghaa!' he went, yawning again.
(ALEXANDER FRATER,
CHASING THE MONSOON, 1990)

 The old Grey Hearse goes rolling by,
 You don't know whether to laugh or cry;
 For you know some day it'll get you too,
 And the hearse's next load may consist
 of you.
 (ANON)

Dusk had already fallen over the towering fells and dark waters of the Lake District when the hearse pulled up at the discreet rear entrance of Keswick Memorial Hospital. The doors swung open to reveal a black body bag on a hospital trolley, a porter at one end.
(VAL MCDERMID,
THE GRAVE TATTOO, 2006)

Surprisingly *hearse* began as *hirpus*, an Oscan term for 'wolf'. (The Oscans were an ancient people who lived on the Italian peninsula.) The route from 'wolf' to 'vehicle for carrying a coffin' is tortuous and contains a couple of imaginative twists.

The first of these occurred when the fanciful Romans borrowed the Oscan word as *hirpex* and applied it to the large rake or harrow they used for breaking up the soil – an allusion, it would seem, to a wolf's jagged teeth. The term came into Old French as *herce* or *herse*, retaining its agricultural meaning (the modern French is *herse*). In medieval times, however, it was customary to erect a triangular frame with spikes to hold candles and decorations over the bier of an important person. And here we have the second twist: since the shape and teeth of the harrow bore a resemblance to this spiked framework, Old French used *herse* to refer to it. It was in this sense of 'taper hearse' that the word was first borrowed into English in the fourteenth century. Edward Hall's THE UNION OF THE TWO NOBLE AND ILLUSTRATE FAMELIES OF LANCASTRE AND YORKE (1548), illustrates how richly these hearses were often decorated: *The body was taken out, and carred into the Quire, and set under a goodly Herce of waxe, garnished with Banners, Pencelles, and Cusshions.*

Hearses of one sort or another, fixed and temporary, were commonly used well into the second half of the seventeenth century, but that century also saw a change in the application of the word. During the first fifty years or so it was sometimes used rather generally to denote a 'coffin' or 'tomb', but the second half of the century saw *hearse* applied in the modern sense to a 'vehicle constructed for carrying a coffin'.

For another word from the same source, see REHEARSE. For words on a similarly funereal theme see CEMETERY, COFFIN, DIRGE and SARCOPHAGUS. For words based on imagined likenesses see LIZARD, LOBSTER, MUSCLE and VANILLA.

hibernation
the state of dormancy some animals and plants assume during winter

Four hundred tortoises have come out of **hibernation** *earlier than usual because of Britain's milder weather. Staff at Tortoise Garden in St Austell, Cornwall, were expecting the animals to wake up as usual in March after bedding down in December. But a warm winter has seen over 400 come out of hibernation in the last few days – well short of their normal 12-week kip.*
(DAILY MAIL, 4 FEBRUARY 2008)

Mother bears nursing young cubs put lots of energy into milk production and, after living on a subsistence diet of plants, they are badly in need of the salmon when they arrive. Also, the young cubs have to eat lots of fish if they are to put on enough weight to survive their first winter's **hibernation**.
(JEFF TURNER,
NATURE'S GREAT EVENTS, 2009)

Unattested proto-Indo-European *gheim-*, 'snow, winter', is the ultimate source of Latin *hiems*, 'winter'. From this word Latin derived an adjective *hībernus*, 'wintry', and from this a noun *hīberna*, meaning 'winter quarters'. Further derivatives were the verb *hībernāre*, 'to spend the winter', and *hibernātiō*, (stem *hibernātiōn-*), 'the action of over-wintering'.

The noun *hibernation* (from *hibernātiō*) was borrowed into English in the seventeenth century to denote 'the passing of the winter in suitable quarters or conditions'. This applied equally to plants in the greenhouse or vizirs searching for a congenial place to spend the season. However, it was the British naturalist Erasmus Darwin, grandfather of Charles Darwin, who brought the term into prominence at the beginning of the nineteenth century when he used it in a scientific sense to describe 'the torpor in which many animals and plants spend the winter'. At the same time Darwin was responsible for the introduction of the verb *hibernate* (from *hībernāre*) into English.

The ability of animals to remain dormant over very long periods of time has been a matter of fascination and investigation for many years. The toad was an early subject of research. In 1777 a Frenchman called Hérissant encased three live toads in plaster. When he looked at them again eighteen months later in the archives of the French Academy of Sciences, two were still alive. This experiment did not work forty years later when a Dr Edwards took the additional step of putting the plaster blocks into water. The key lies in access to at least minimal oxygen. In 1825 the English geologist Buckland placed twelve toads in dense sandstone, twelve in porous limestone. Over a year later, all the first were dead, all the second still alive.

☞ *Gheim-* is responsible for Sanskrit *hima*, 'snow'. This word, in combination with *alaya*, 'abode', gives *himalayah*, 'Himalaya', literally 'abode of snow'.

hobnob

to be on familiar terms with, to socialise

*She didn't often wear the big diamond, just occasionally if they were going out somewhere. He made her go out places, theatre, restaurants, opera, concerts, dinner parties – even, God help her, to charity fund-raisers where the rich and richer **hobnobbed** at two thousand a table.*
(KATE ATKINSON, WHEN WILL THERE BE GOOD NEWS?, 2008)

*The ideal party spot, Sturehof has several guises. As you enter, it's a **hobnobbing**, place-to-be-seen brasserie, though the posh quota reduces the further you continue up the three floors.*
(THE TIMES, 28 FEBRUARY 2009)

This informal modern verb appears as a phrase in Shakespeare who uses it in the sense 'give or take':

Hob, nob, is his word: giu't or take't.
(TWELFTH NIGHT, 1601)

It seems to be a variant of the earlier phrases *hab nab* and *hab or nab*. These meant 'hit or miss, win or lose, whatever might happen' and are recorded from the mid-sixteenth century. The expressions, however, must be much older than this, since they clearly derive from *habbe* and *nabbe*, subjunctive forms of the Middle English verbs *habben*, 'to have' and *nabben*, 'not to have'. However, since these were already obsolete by the mid-sixteenth century it must be assumed that *habbe nabbe* and *habbe or nabbe* (meaning literally 'have he [I, we, etc.] or have he [I, we, etc.] not') were Middle English expressions which survived in spoken language.

In the eighteenth century a social application of the variant phrase began to emerge. *To hobnob* meant 'to drink to each other, to toast one another by clinking glasses', and the phrase *hob and nob* was used by two people drinking in this way. In GREAT EXPECTATIONS (1861) Dickens describes one such exchange between Mr Pumblechook and a sergeant:

'Have another glass!'
'With you. Hob and nob,' returned the sergeant. 'The top of mine to the foot of yours – the foot of yours to the top of mine – Ring once, ring twice – the best tune on the Musical Glasses! Your health.'

In the nineteenth century such scenes of conviviality gave rise to a more general sense of *hobnob*, when it came to mean 'to be on familiar terms with somebody socially', the sense that the verb has retained in modern English.

holiday

time set aside for rest and relaxation

*Then along came a man called Sir John Lubbock... Sir John was a cricket fan and believed that bank employees should be allowed to watch. Thus, as is the nature with privilege, the **holiday** dates were fixed according to the cricket schedule... Imagine if he had been Danish like me. Instead of a run of holidays in May, we might have had a succession of days off in the herring season!*
(GOOD HOUSEKEEPING, MAY 2009)

See HOLY.

hollyhock

a tall plant from the mallow family

*This is the month when the road ahead shimmers in the afternoon heat, panting dogs slurp greedily at their water-bowls, and **hollyhocks** in the cottage gardens begin to fold over in the midday sun.*
(THE INDEPENDENT, 24 AUGUST 2008)

See HOLY.

holocaust

a terrible period of widespread destruction and loss of life, specifically that of the Jews during the Second World War

*Down in the camps whole nations lay huddled, wasted and ill. What everyone in those meetings was talking about was nothing less than the African **holocaust**. What they were describing was the death and hunger, the humiliation and hurt of millions upon millions of people who need not suffer it. What the figures meant was the sum total of our disregard for each other.*
(BOB GELDOF,
GELDOF IN AFRICA, 2005)

*In the interview Bishop Williamson strayed into very controversial territory. He said that no Jews were gassed during the Second World War and that 300,000 – not six million – had died in the **Holocaust**.*
(SUNDAY TELEGRAPH, 1 MARCH 2009)

The word comes, via Old French *holocaust* and Late Latin *holocaustum*, from Greek *holokauston,* and literally means a 'total burning' (from *holos*, 'whole, total', and *kaustos*, 'burnt'). It denoted a sacrificial offering to a god that was completely consumed by fire, 'a whole burnt offering'.

Within the Christian tradition, *holocaust* appears in a mid-thirteenth-century English text with reference to Abraham's offering to God of his son, Isaac. And in his translation of Mark's Gospel (1526) William Tyndale renders Mark 12: 33, which speaks of loving God with all one's might, as being *a greater thynge then all holocaustes and sacrifises*.

It was in the second half of the seventeenth century, however, that the term came to be used more generally, to denote 'a total consumption by fire'. Milton was the first to use it in this way. It subsequently broadened out still further to describe 'complete destruction' by any means; an article in the SUNDAY TELEGRAPH for 23 November 1987 carried the headline *Aids: the new holocaust*.

During the Second World War (1939–45) Nazi Germany attempted systematically to annihilate the European Jewish population, whom they accused of infesting their territories. Six million Jews were subjected to intense cruelty before meeting a hideous death in extermination camps. Throughout the war *holocaust* was a word chosen to describe these atrocities by those aware of them, because of their enormous scale. When it ended historians referred to this savage treatment of the Jews as *the Holocaust* (usually written with a capital letter) and it is by this specific term that this particular mass extermination is known today.

☛ The two elements that make up *holocaust* have both provided other words in English:

catholic (14th cent), 'entire, universal', is ultimately made up of Greek *kata-*, 'according to, in respect of' and *holou*, from *holos* 'whole', to give *katholicon*, 'in general', and *katholicos* 'universal'.

caustic (16th cent) comes from *kaustikos*, 'capable of burning'. *Caustic soda* literally burns, while *caustic comments* sear the heart.

For other words concerning temple or sacrifices, see ANATHEMA, SCAPEGOAT and FANATIC. See also MINT and THYME in HOW DOES YOUR GARDEN GROW? (page 125).

holy
sacred, set apart

*Grace was said in Italian, by one of the novices, and then we all tucked in. No rule of silence here. No reading aloud of dreary **holy** books as at convent school. Supper was enlivened by conversation, joking and laughter.*
(MICHÈLE ROBERTS, READER, I MARRIED HIM, 2004)

*An Italian mobile phone company has caused uproar among Catholic Church leaders, by offering downloads of images of saints. Barbara Labate came up with the idea with her business partner as a replacement for the **holy** cards that millions of Italian carry around in their wallets.*
(DAILY MAIL, 5 DECEMBER 2007)

Middle English had *holy, holi, hali* from Old English *hālig*. This was from unattested proto-Germanic *khailagaz* 'free

from injury', source of English *whole*. *Holy*, therefore, in all its religious applications, carried the general notion of being whole, free from the contamination of sin, 'unblemished' and hence 'set apart'.

Holy is the first element in several common compounds:

Holidays were originally *holy days*, days of Christian significance set aside by the church either for prayer and fasting or for church attendance and celebration. *Holy days*, therefore, were a welcome interruption to the daily routine and – at a time when the right to a fortnight off with pay was unheard of – became associated with rest and recreation. For over five hundred years the terms *holiday* and *holy day* were interchangeable but, during the sixteenth century, when a day off was no longer restricted to church festivals, the need was felt to make a distinction. Thus a *holy day* had religious significance while a *holiday* merely denoted a day of leisure.

It was customary in the church to abstain from meat on holy days and to eat fish instead. Middle English had the word *butte*, a general term for 'flatfish'. This, combined with *haly*, 'holy', in the fifteenth century, gave *halybutte*, then *halibut*, the word for the largest of the flatfish and an excellent holiday dish. Other languages have similarly constructed words for the fish: Swedish, for instance, has *helgeflundra* from *helg*, 'holy' and *flundra*, 'flounder'.

Similarly, the name *hollyhock* is a compound of *holi*, 'holy' and *hoc*, 'mallow', giving *holihoc* in Middle English. Some authorities have erroneously suggested that the plant came originally from the Holy Land and was brought to England during the Crusades. However, in both Welsh and Medieval Latin it was known as the 'blessed mallow', and yet another name for it was *St Cuthbert's cole* ('cabbage') after a seventh-century monk who lived on Holy Island. It is likely, therefore, that the hollyhock was cultivated in monastic gardens and used in the worship of saints.

hoodlum
a young thug

*Francine Lucas tried to keep her father's identity a secret. After all, who would want to admit to being the daughter of a Harlem **hoodlum** who used to smuggle heroin from Vietnam stashed in the coffins of dead American soldiers?*
(THE INDEPENDENT, 30 NOVEMBER 2007)

*For the first time in Swedish financial reporting, the terms 'organised crime', 'Mafia' and 'gangster empire' were used. Wennerström and his young stockbrokers, partners and Armani-clad lawyers emerged like a band of **hoodlums**.*
(STIEG LARSSON, THE GIRL WITH THE DRAGON TATTOO, 2008)

In the early 1870s the streets of San Francisco were haunted by bands of young thugs intent on crime. The BOSTON JOURNAL (1877) had this to say about them:

You at the East have but little idea of the hoodlums of this city [San Francisco]. They compose a class of criminals of both sexes…travel in gangs; and are ready at any moment for the perpetration of any crime.

These young toughs had been referred to locally as *hoodlums* since about 1869. When their notoriety spread to other parts of America, interest was shown in the term but, by then, its origin was lost. This spurred correspondents with various newspapers into offering suggestions to account for it. Here are some of them:

A newspaper man in San Francisco, in attempting to coin a word to designate a gang of young street Arabs under the beck of one named 'Muldoon', hit upon the idea of dubbing them 'noodlum,' that is, simply reversing the leader's name. In writing the word the strokes of the n did not correspond in height, and the compositor, taking the n for an h, printed it 'hoodlums'.
(THE CONGREGATIONALIST, 26 SEPTEMBER 1877)

Before the late war there appeared in San Francisco a man whose dress was very peculiar. The boys took a fancy to it, and, organizing themselves into a military company, adopted in part the dress of this man. The head-dress resembled the fez, from which was suspended a long tail. The gamins called it a 'hood,' and the company became known as the 'hoods.' The rowdy element in the city adopted much of the dress of the company referred to, who were soon designated as 'hoodlums'.
(SAN FRANCISCO MORNING CALL, 27 OCTOBER 1877)

A gang of bad boys from fourteen to nineteen years of age was associated for the purpose of stealing. These boys had a place of rendezvous, and when danger threatened them their words of warning were, 'Huddle 'em! Huddle 'em!' An article headed 'Huddle'em,' describing the gang and their plan of operations, was published in the San Francisco Times. The name applied to them was soon contracted into hoodlum.
(LOS ANGELES EXPRESS, 25 AUGUST 1877)

hotchpotch, hodgepodge
a mixture of ill-assorted ingredients,
a mess

It Just Occurred to Me...*is accurately
described by its author as 'a **hotchpotch** of
thoughts and memories' ranging back and
forth over his long life and taking in such
important matters as the way to make
perfect scrambled eggs and the best defence
against six of the best at Eton (slices of ham
down the back of the trousers, apparently).*
(REVIEW OF 'IT JUST OCCURRED TO
ME' BY HUMPHREY LYTTELTON, IN
THE SPECTATOR, 12 APRIL 2007)

*If we speak of Chinese as a language, we
mean the set of characters that knit together
several, perhaps many, spoken languages –
the written symbols, not the spoken words,
are what united China. The changes
brought about by time and spelling reforms
have led to a linguistic **hodgepodge** in
which any given character can be written in
several styles, be pronounced in several
ways, and mean a multitude of things.*
(MARK ABLEY,
THE PRODIGAL TONGUE, 2008)

Hotchpotch is a rhyming alteration of
hotchpot. Middle English had *hochepot*, a
direct borrowing of an Old French word
made up of *hocher*, 'to shake' and *pot*,
'pot'. This was a culinary term for a
ragout or stew, in which a variety of
ingredients was stirred and shaken
together in one big cooking pot. In
Anglo-Norman, however, *hochepot* is first
recorded as a legal term in the late thirteenth century, when it applied to the
collecting together of various properties
in order to distribute them fairly. Not
until the late fourteenth century does
hochepot appear in an English recipe.

Both *hotchpot* and its variant *hotchpotch* were put to figurative use early in
the fifteenth century to denote 'a
jumble of unrelated things, a mish-
mash'. In a sermon preached to Edward
VI and his court, the Protestant clergyman Hugh Latimer spoke against people
who *made a myngle mangle and a hotchpotch of [God's word]...partely poperye,
partelye true religion mingeled together*.

Over the years a variety of other
forms have appeared, including *hodge-
podge* in the sixteenth century. This corruption was based on the name *Hodge*,
an altered form of *Roger*, which was used
to denote a typical rustic. In England
hodgepodge is an alternative term, but in
Scottish and American usage it is the
preferred form. Walsh, an American,
gives this Scottish example:

*During the earlier visits of the royal family
to Balmoral, Prince Albert, dressed in a
very simple manner, was crossing one of
the Scotch lakes in a steamer, and was
curious to note everything relating to the
management of the vessel, and, among other
things, cooking. Approaching the 'galley,'
where a brawny Highlander was attending
to the culinary matters, he was attracted
by the savory odors of a compound known
by Scotchmen as 'hodge-podge,' which the
Highlander was preparing.*
*'What's that?' asked the prince, who was
not known to the cook.*
'Hodge-podge, sir,' was the reply.
'How is it made?' was the next question.
*'Why, there's mutton intil't, and turnips
intil't, and cairots intil't, and–'*
*'Yes, yes,' said the prince, who had not
learned that 'intil't' meant 'into it,' 'but
what is intil't?'*
*'Why, there's mutton intil't, and turnips
intil't, and cairots intil't, and–'*
'Yes, I see; but what is intil't?'
*The man looked at him, and, seeing that
the prince was serious, replied,*
*'There's mutton intil't, and turnips
intil't, and–'*
*'Yes, certainly, I know,' urged the
inquirer; 'but what is intil't – intil't?'*
*'Ye daft gowk!' yelled the Highlander,
brandishing his big spoon, 'am I no telling ye
what's intil't? There's mutton intil't, and–'*
Here the interview was brought to a

close by one of the prince's suite, who was fortunately passing, and stepped in to save his royal highness from being rapped over the head with the big spoon.

☛ There is no connection between *hotchpotch* and *hotpot*. The latter came into use at the very end of the seventeenth century as a slang term for hot beer with spirits or spices added. Its common meaning today of 'a stew of mutton or beef cooked in an earthenware pot' is found only from around the middle of the nineteenth century onwards.

husband
the man to whom a woman is married

*The bandages were part of my preparation for the great **husband** hunt. I was only fifteen years old, but my mother recognized a difficult case when she saw one. She had taken up the challenge the day after my twelfth birthday and had never spared herself since.*
(LAURIE GRAHAM,
THE UNFORTUNATES, 2002)

*Her picture of Louise was of a bored and rather hard woman, living with a **husband** who was probably unfaithful to her but staying with him because he provided material security.*
(ALEXANDER MCCALL SMITH,
FRIENDS, LOVERS,
CHOCOLATE, 2005)

This word originally denoted 'the head of a household' and was a late Old English borrowing of Old Norse *husbondi*, a contracted form of the earlier *husbuandi*, 'the master of a house'. This was a compound noun made up of *hus*, 'house', and *buandi*, a word which denoted 'a peasant who owned his own house and land' (hence the English word *husbandry*, 'farming'). *Buandi* in turn was derived from *bua*, 'to dwell'.

Not until the late thirteenth century did *husband* begin to denote 'the man to whom a woman is married'. It was a logical application, however; the head of the household naturally ruled over his wife too. Until then, the word for 'husband' was *wer*, which also denoted 'a man'.

☛ *Wer* became redundant during the thirteenth century. It was no longer required for 'husband' and, when the Old English coinage *WOMAN* became established, the word *man*, which was originally applied to a person of either sex, was left to denote 'an adult male person'. *Wer* is still evident, however, in the compound noun *werewolf*, which belongs to the late Old English period and describes a man who, according to popular belief, was able to turn himself into a wolf.

hypocrite
one who speaks or acts apparently virtuously, but at variance with his true, baser motives

*The Dean was observed to be extraordinarily moved, and said his prayer of thanksgiving in a voice that was not at all steady. Frank Ashworth, halfway down the nave, remarked this to himself with a kind of disgust; to him, the Dean's **hypocrisy** knew no bounds.*
(JOANNA TROLLOPE,
THE CHOIR, 1988)

*Arthur despises those fellows who are good liars, who organize their emotional lives – their marriages even – on the basis of what they can get away with, who tell a half-truth here, a full lie there. Arthur has always thundered the importance of truth-telling at his children; now he must play the fullest **hypocrite**.*
(JULIAN BARNES,
ARTHUR AND GEORGE, 2005)

In the theatre of ancient Greece an *hupocritēs* was 'an actor', someone skilled in playing a part, in feigning emotion. The term derived from the verb *hupokrinein*, which meant 'to separate gradually', being a compound of *hupo*, 'under' and *krinein*, 'to separate'. A series of new senses then evolved beginning with 'to answer', later 'to have dialogue with one's fellow actor', and finally 'to play a part'. Not surprisingly, the noun *hupocritēs* was figuratively used for 'a dissembler' and with this meaning it passed into Late Latin as *hypocrita* to denote 'one who gives an outward display of piety that belies his true character or way of life'. In this sense the word was taken into Old French as *ypocrite* and into Middle English as *ipocrite* or *ypocrite*.

Its earliest appearances were in religious texts. THE ANCRENE RIWLE, the thirteenth-century devotional manual that was used by those called to a solitary religious life, calls the false recluse an *ipocrite*, and in his translation of Matthew 23:13–15 (1382) Wycliffe uses *ypocritis* in Jesus's three-fold denunciation of the scribes and Pharisees. Soon, however, the contexts in which the word was found became more varied and applied to any situation where virtuous behaviour was a screen for base motives.

In the mid-sixteenth century attempts were made to regularise the spelling and, in both French and English, the word was pulled back into line with its classical roots and spelt with an initial *h*.

I

idiot

a fool, a person of poor judgement; a person of very limited intelligence

*June continued to look interested, but she wasn't listening. She was wondering how she could have been such an **idiot** as to expect Rutter – clearly a man with officialdom in his veins, clearly a man who didn't go to the bathroom without written authorisation – to wave her freely on into the camps without all the necessary correspondence in place.*
(DAVID BADDIEL,
THE SECRET PURPOSES, 2004)

*'I suppose I'm just trying to justify my instincts. Even though I know for a fact how many people have drowned in the Loe Pool – strong swimmers as well as **idiots** – I was surprised when I heard about Harry's accident.'*
(NICOLA UPSON,
ANGEL WITH TWO FACES, 2009)

According to the devout Augustinian friar John Capgrave, St Augustine once described the twelve apostles as *twelue ydiotes*. The saint's intention was neither to shock nor to offend. He was using the word in one of its early senses and simply meant that *thei not lerned were* (LIFE OF ST CATHERINE, c. 1440).

In ancient Greece an *idiōtēs* (from *idios*, 'private') denoted a 'private person' in the sense that he was uneducated and held no profession or official position that would bring him public attention. From here, quite logically, the term came to denote a 'man

in the street', a 'plebeian' and eventually an 'uneducated, ill-informed person'. It was in this final sense that Latin borrowed the word as *idiōta*. From there it was absorbed into the Romance languages, coming into English at the end of the thirteenth century by way of Old French *idiot*. Written records of the period show three kinds of *idiot*: the 'unlearned person', the 'mentally deficient' and the 'fool'. Of these the first sense is now obsolete.

During the sixteenth century *idiot* was sometimes written *nidiot*, the *n* being transferred from the indefinite article: *an idiot – a nidiot* (see UMPIRE). *Nidiot* itself was sometimes corrupted to *nidget*, so that Thomas Heywood writes of *a company of fooles and Nigits* (THE WISE WOMAN OF HOGSDON, 1638). This variant became obsolete around the middle of the nineteenth century.

imp

a demon, an evil spirit; a mischievous child or person

*'Feel free to bring a date,' Mrs Kowalski had told Michael – in his mother's presence, no less. (Oh, Mrs Kowalski was widely known to be a bit of an **imp**.)*
(ANNE TYLER, THE AMATEUR
MARRIAGE, 2004)

But while weighing all this, and sweeping and dusting, and now in the kitchen making scones, another part of me seems to have been considering it quietly, like a little

OTHERWORLDLY INFLUENCES

The stars and planets were once held to be influential in forming people's characters (see INFLUENCE). In his MAG-ASTROMANCER, OR THE MAGICALL-ASTROLOGICALL-DIVINER POSED, AND PUZZLED (1652), John Gaule, the puritan minister of Great Staughton in Huntingdonshire, denounced the *physiognomists, metoposcopists and chiromantists,* who believed that people are shaped by their stars and were intent upon *first judging and pronouncing the man, or the member, to be saturnine, jovial, martial, solar, venereal, mercurial, lunar.*

These adjectives may no longer hold astrological significance in modern English, but their present-day meanings reflect these ancient beliefs.

Jovial (late 16th cent) from French *jovial,* from Italian *gioviale,* 'born under the planet Jove', from Latin *jovialis,* 'pertaining to Jove', from *Jovis,* 'Jove'. The Roman deity Jove, also known as Jupiter (a classical Latin contraction of *Jovis Pater,* 'Jove the Father'), was the majestic lord of heaven and the well-spring of happiness. The largest known planet was named in his honour and those born under its influence rejoiced in a cheerful, convivial disposition.

Martial (14th cent) from Old French martial, from Latin *mārtiālis,* 'pertaining to Mars', from Latin *Mārs,* (stem *Mārt-*) 'Mars'. Mars had a savage, passionate nature. In Rome, where he was worshipped as the god of war, he was second only to Jupiter, and his name was given to the blood-red planet. When the adjective *martial* was first borrowed into English it meant 'fit for war, belonging to warfare'. A person described as *martial* had the valiant character of a warrior. Today the adjective is widely used of anything war-like.

Mercurial (14th cent) from French *mercuriel,* from Latin *mercuriālis,* 'belonging to Mercury', from *Mercurius,* 'Mercury'. The name of this Roman god derives from *merx,* 'merchandise', since, amongst his other responsibilities, Mercury was responsible for commerce. He was also something of a thief and those who were *mercurial,* that is to say 'born under the planet Mercury', were eloquent and vivacious with a shrewd head for business and a tendency to

---

imp in a basement room working by candlelight while the rest of the house sleeps. And, to my astonishment, this imp comes up with a judgement quite different from my own.
(JILL DAWSON,
THE GREAT LOVER, 2009)

When Chaucer in the prologue to 'The Monk's Tale' (CANTERBURY TALES, c. 1387) wrote that *Of fieble trees ther comen wrecched ympes,* he was referring not to some sort of woodland sprite but to a 'shoot', for the word was originally a horticultural one. Old English had

impa to denote 'young shoot of a plant, sapling', from the verb *impian* 'to graft on'. This was probably from an unattested Romance verb *impotare,* a derivative of early Medieval Latin *impotus,* 'graft', itself from the Greek adjective *emphutos,* 'implanted', and *emphuein,* 'to implant'.

References to *imp* as a horticultural term date from the writings of King Alfred in the ninth century to the early eighteenth century:

devious practice. In seventeenth-century English, however, *mercurial* started to develop the sense 'having a volatile or changeable nature'. Although this new sense initially arose out of the older one, it is commonly perceived as being influenced by the characteristics of the metal *mercury*, the planetary name given to quicksilver in medieval times.

Saturnine (15th cent) from unattested medieval Latin *Sāturnīnus*, 'of Saturn', from Latin *Sāturnus*, 'Saturn'. The establishment of civilisation (springing from agriculture, of which he was god) was attributed to this deity. In spite of the riotous revelry which took place at his festival Saturnalia (see CARNIVAL), Saturn had a dour and taciturn nature, which he generously passed on to all born under the influence of his planet. A *saturnine* person is a gloomy person.

Solar (15th cent) from Latin *sōlāris*, 'pertaining to the sun', from *sōl*, 'sun'. According to astrology, the *solar* man was impressive and did everything on a grand scale. He was dignified, magnificent, proud and generous. Sadly we no longer describe distinguished, energetic people as *solar*; the adjective is confined to things pertaining to or coming from the sun: *solar eclipse, solar heating.*

Venereal (15th cent) Middle English *venerealle*, from Latin *venereus*, from *Venus* (stem *Vener-*), 'love, Venus'. Beautiful Venus was the Roman goddess of sexual love. The Latin adjective *venereus* meant 'concerning sexual desire or pleasure'. This was borrowed into Middle English as *venerealle* with the same meaning. It is still occasionally found today in this sense. Those born under the influence of Venus were said to be 'lecherous and lustful', but *venereal* was rarely applied in this way and this sense has been obsolete since the eighteenth century. Today the word is most commonly found in the coupling *venereal disease*, which has been current since at least the second half of the seventeenth century. This term, however, though still current, is gradually being supplanted by the more explicit *sexually transmitted disease*, which dates from the 1960s, the era of sexual liberation.

> *...a barren tree,*
> *Which, when the gardner on it pains*
> *bestows*
> *To graffe an impe thereon, in time it growes*
> *To such perfection, that it yeerly brings*
> *As goodly fruit as any tree that springs.*
> (WILLIAM BROWNE, BRITANNIA'S PASTORALS, 1613)

> *[Ivy] is a sneaking insinuating Imp.*
> (ANDREW MARVEL, THE REHERSAL TRANSPOS'D, 1672)

In the late fourteenth century, however, the word began to be figuratively applied to 'a child', the offshoot of the parent stock, and in the early fifteenth century to 'the child of a noble house'. In his chronicle of THE UNION OF THE TWO NOBLE AND ILLUSTRATE FAMELIES OF LANCASTRE AND YORKE (1548), Edward Hall describes Prince Edward as *that goodly ympe*, while the epitaph to Lord Denbigh in the Beauchamp Chapel, Warwick (1584) reads *Heere resteth the body of the noble Impe Robert of Dvdley...sonne of Robert Erle of Leycester.*

Imp gained a sinister new dimension in the sixteenth century when it denoted 'a child of the devil, a child of evil'. During the seventeenth century this particular sense was then used to denote 'a mischievous child, a scamp', which is how the word is most commonly used today.

inaugurate

to initiate something ceremoniously; to open a new building, or appoint someone to office with a formal ceremony

*The Queen yesterday presented her son the Prince of Wales with the the Royal Horticultural Society's prestigious Victoria Medal of Honour for services to gardening at the Chelsea Flower Show ahead of its opening to the public... Only 63 horticulturists can hold the award, **inaugurated** to commemorate the years of Queen Victoria's reign, at any one time.*
(THE TELEGRAPH, 18 MAY 2009)

See AUSPICIOUS.

influence

an indirect power to affect, an ability to bring about change in a person, state of affairs, etc.

*As with Latin and Arabic, political and economic might gave (and continues to give) Chinese some serious cultural cachet, and Japanese and Korean have been considerably **influenced** by the Chinese language. As a result, each language features two separate number systems, one native and one Chinese.*
(ELIZABETH LITTLE,
BITING THE WAX TADPOLE, 2007)

*An intense misfit, brilliantly clever but startlingly plain, she [George Eliot] graduated from teenage religious fanaticism to proud and rebellious rejection of conventional Christianity, under the **influence** of a freethinking – and sexually bohemian – Midlands couple, the Brays.*
(SUNDAY TIMES, 14 JUNE 2009)

Influence was originally an astrological term for a supernatural fluid that was thought to flow from the stars and sway the destiny and character of mankind:

What euill starre
On you hath frownd, and pourd his influ-
ence bad?
(SPENSER, THE FAERIE QUEENE, 1590)

The word derived from Medieval Latin *influentia*, 'a flowing in' (from Latin *influēns*, present participle of the verb *influere*, 'to flow in', a compound of *in-* and *fluere*, 'to flow'), and came into Middle English in the fourteenth century via Old French. Not until the end of the sixteenth century did the modern sense of *influence*, 'a person or thing exercising an intangible or imperceptible power over another', begin to emerge.

☛ The following words are also derived from Latin fluere, 'to flow':

fluent (16th cent): from Latin *fluēns*, from *fluere*, 'to flow'.
influx (17th cent): from Late Latin *influxus*, 'a flowing in', from Latin *influere*, 'to flow in'.
effluent (18th cent): from Latin *effluēns*, from *effluere*, 'to flow out', from *ex-*, 'out', and *fluere*, 'to flow'.

For another word deriving from this source, see INFLUENZA. For other words with astrological origins, see CONSIDER, DISASTER and ZODIAC.

influenza

a common infectious viral disease

Just before the end of term Petrova had **influenza**. *She had the worst kind, that is gastric, and makes you sick all day. She felt so miserable for a week that she did not care about anything.*
(NOEL STREATFEILD,
BALLET SHOES, 1936)

The doctor said there was nothing he could do for her now and if we valued our lives we were to keep away. For it was no ordinary head cold that had her in its grip, but a particularly virulent **influenza**, *said to have come all the way from Spain.*
(KATE MORTON,
THE HOUSE AT RIVERTON, 2006)

The Medieval Latin word *influentia*, 'a flowing in, an influence', originally referred to celestial power attributed to the stars and in this astrological sense it was taken into the various Romance languages, coming into English as *influence* through Old French (see INFLUENCE). In Italian it became *influenza* where, in addition to the various meanings it shared with other languages, it had gained, by the early sixteenth century, the further sense of an 'outpouring of a disease, an epidemic', such outbreaks being seen as ordained by the stars.

The word first appeared in English in 1743 when an epidemic of a cold-like fever gripped Italy and then swept through the rest of Europe. An issue of the LONDON MAGAZINE for that year reports *news from Rome of a contagious Distemper raging there, call'd the Influenza*, and a letter dated 12 February 1743 from the diplomat Horace Mann to his friend Horace Walpole informs that *Everybody [in Rome] is ill of the influenza, and many die.*

Today many people diagnose themselves as having *influenza* when they are really afflicted by nothing more terrible than a bad cold. Our forebears were no different in their bid for sympathy and recognition: in a letter of 1762 Mrs Montagu, the queen of the bluestockings, wrote that her husband *had been much pulled down by the fashionable cold called l'influenza*, while a century and a quarter later the authors of a nineteenth-century medical work identified *The practice, so common among the higher classes in this country, of designating as influenza any catarrhal attack that happens to be painful and distressing* (Fagge & Pye-Smith, THE PRINCIPLES AND PRACTICE OF MEDICINE, 1886).

In modern English *influenza* is rarely used in everyday communication. *Flu* is a much easier term to croak for anyone with a sore throat, aching limbs and a raging temperature. The word was shortened in the first half of the nineteenth century, some careful writers apologising for trimming it down by inserting an apostrophe, *'flu*. Today *flu* is so familiar and overused that this convention has generally been dropped.

For another illness with an Italian name, see MALARIA.

insult

to say or do something insensitive or offensive, to abuse someone verbally; an insulting remark or act

Whoopi Goldberg has been fired from her lucrative advertising job with the diet food firm Slim-Fast after **insulting** *George W Bush.*
(DAILY MAIL, 15 JULY 2004)

Insult *is a wonderful thing, and we need more of it before we turn into a nation of Ikes, constantly running to matron because Smythe in Lower Four called us 'Speccy' or 'Podge'. Insult braces. It startles and exhilarates, because as the root word suggests, it jumps into the conversation*

unexpectedly and with vigour. Then the trading of insults begins, and as soon as trade is involved, you know something has a secure place in the culture.
(THE OBSERVER, 24 FEBRUARY 2008)

The Latin verb *insultāre* meant 'to leap upon, to attack', being a compound of the prefix *in-*, 'on, upon', and *saltāre*, 'to jump' (from *salīre*, 'to jump'). However, Latin also used the word figuratively with the sense 'to attack verbally, to scoff, to mock'. When the word was taken into French as *insulter*, it meant 'to behave arrogantly, to glory over', and it was borrowed into English with the same sense in the second half of the sixteenth century. This notion of bragging and triumphing over someone endured, just, into the nineteenth century. The modern sense of bringing someone down with offensive words or actions had been on the rise since the first half of the seventeenth century.

For more words from Latin *salīre*, see DESULTORY.

interloper
an interfering outsider

'It seems to me,' began the Scarecrow, when all were again assembled in the throne room, 'that the girl Jinjur is quite right in claiming to be Queen. And if she is right, then I am wrong, and we have no business to be occupying her palace.'
*'But you were the King until she came,' said the Woggle-Bug, strutting up and down with his hands in his pockets; 'so it appears to me that she is the **interloper** instead of you.'*
(L FRANK BAUM, THE MARVELOUS LAND OF OZ, 1904)

The tendency, when espying one of the squirrels that inhabits Britain's parks, is to think along the lines of 'Awww.' This reaction, according to some, is tragically mistaken – the mathematical likelihood is

*that you are gurgling at a grey squirrel, a plentiful North American **interloper** that threatens to obliterate our native red squirrel.*
(THE GUARDIAN, 31 JANUARY 2009)

This mongrel word of sixteenth-century English coinage is made up of the Latin prefix *inter*, 'between', and Dutch *loper*, 'running', a derivative of Dutch *loopen*, 'to run'. Thus *interloper* meant 'one who runs between'. The word initially referred to 'a trader or ship illegally trespassing on another's trading rights'. The first known use, which is found in a navigational account dated around 1590, relates to foreign infringements upon the trading rights of the Moscovy Company, an English chartered company, formed in 1555, which had been granted a monopoly on commerce with Russia. The East India Company, chartered in 1600, also had to repel interlopers who tried to seize some of their trade.

The meaning was extended in the first half of the seventeenth century to refer to 'a person who interferes in the affairs of others, usually for his own benefit'.

intoxicate
to inebriate, produce the effects of alcohol or drugs

*The Mole never heard a word he was saying. Absorbed in the new life he was entering upon, **intoxicated** with the sparkle, the ripple, the scents and the sounds and the sunlight, he trailed a paw in the water and dreamed long waking dreams.*
(KENNETH GRAHAME, THE WIND IN THE WILLOWS, 1908)

Solitary drinking is a strange and dangerous thing. You can drink all night and not feel the remotest sense of **intoxication,** *but when you rise you discover that while your head feels clear enough, your legs have suddenly decided to go in for a little moonwalking or some other involuntary embarrassment.*
(BILL BRYSON,
NEITHER HERE NOR THERE, 1991)

The origin of this word lies with warfare in the classical world where arrows were commonly smeared with poison before being loosed. The Greek expression for this substance was *toxikon pharmakon*. *Pharmakon* means 'drug' or 'poison', and *toxikon* is the neuter of *toxikos*, an adjective meaning 'of or belonging to a bow/archery' (from *toxon*, 'bow'). When the Greeks inevitably economised on effort by clipping the expression to *toxicon*, the word was inbued with the sense 'poison' that had properly belonged to *pharmakon*. Thus *toxicon* became a noun meaning 'poison to put on arrows'. The word was borrowed into Latin as *toxicum* with the same meaning, though later it became a general term for 'poison'. Medieval Latin derived the adjective *toxicus*, 'poisoned', from this, which English borrowed as *toxic* in the seventeenth century.

Medieval Latin also coined the verb *intoxicare*, 'to poison', from Latin *toxicum* and the prefix *in-*, 'into'. This was borrowed into English as *intoxicate* in the sixteenth century, but by the 1590s the word was already being used in its modern sense to describe 'the effect produced by a drug or, more especially, alcohol'. Some of our forebears must have had a rough time of it judging from some of the potions they unwittingly swallowed in search of good strong ale:

Under the Cathedral-church at Hereford is the greatest Charnel-house for bones, that ever I saw in England. In AD 1650 there lived amongst those bones a poor old woman that, to help out her fire, did use to mix the deadmen's bones: this was thrift and poverty: but cunning alewives putt the Ashes of these bones in their Ale to make it intoxicateing.
(JOHN AUBREY 1626–97, BRIEF LIVES)

But even this is preferable to a poisoned arrow.

☞ From the early Greek connection to archery, the sixteenth-century educationist Roger Ascham coined the word *toxophilus* and used it as the title of his book on archery (literally 'lover of the bow'). His fame as an archer even led to the cabinet for archery equipment being called an *ascham*. His repute certainly reached into the nineteenth century when *toxophilite* ('archer') and *toxophily* ('the practice of archery') were born from the title of his book. These somewhat fancy words are still alive today:

Robert Hardy has had a lifelong interest in the longbow. He belongs to the Royal Toxophilite Society, the British Longbow Society and the Men of Arden, an archery association founded in the 18th century.
(WEEKEND TELEGRAPH,
25 FEBRUARY 1995)

intransigent
unreasonably stubborn, uncompromising (especially in politics)

Truancy remains one of the most **intransigent** *problems in the education system. Schools can put in place any number of initiatives to improve attainment, but if children are bunking off lessons, they won't make a jot of difference.*
(BIRMINGHAM POST,
14 NOVEMBER 2005)

*The **intransigent** nature of political parties and social/religious groups in the United States offers little hope for establishing a just and peaceful nation and world.*

If our leaders would only do what's right based on fairness and equality and not on political expediency and special interests we could make progress toward this goal. But the two-faced nature of the current power groups makes doubtful the possibility of such a change.

(ALBANY TIMES UNION,
12 NOVEMBER 2006)

In Spain the term *los intransigentes* was given to parties who held extremist political views in the Spanish Cortes, the legislative assembly. In the eight-eenth century it was applied to the party of the Extreme Left, in the nineteenth to the radical Republicans who, when the Spanish monarchy was overthrown in 1873 and a republic declared, organised insurgencies because they were excluded from the commission charged with drawing up a new constitution.

Los intransigentes means 'the uncom-promising'. The word is a compound of Latin *in-*, 'not', and *transigente*, the present participle of *transigir*, 'to com-promise'. This, in turn, is a derivative of *trānsigere* (a compound of *trans*, 'through', and *agere*, 'to drive') which means 'to drive through' and hence, 'to reach an agreement'. French fashioned the adjective *intransigeant* from the Spanish coinage, and this was intro-duced into English in the early 1880s by journalists who found it a useful word for critical political comment.

J

jargon
the specialised or technical language of a particular set of people

*Blowen, noun, a prostitute; a courtesan. This is a cant word – an example of the specialized **jargon** used by thieves to prevent others from understanding their conversation.*
(CHRISTOPHER FOYLE,
FOYLE'S PHILAVERY, 2007)

*It is important for you to realise now, at this initial stage, that – as I mentioned earlier – most activities worth pursuing come with their own **jargon**, their private language and technical vocabulary.*
(STEPHEN FRY,
THE ODE LESS TRAVELLED, 2005)

Middle English borrowed *iargon* from Old French *jargoun* in the fourteenth century. Medieval *jargon* was the sound of birds. It described not so much a songster's melodious warbling as the twittering, tweeting and chattering of sparrows and starlings. This original sense was easily transferred to human utterance of the same order. According to Chaucer, the old knight January was as garrulous as a magpie as he made love to his pretty young wife, May:

> *He was al coltissh ful of ragerye*
> *And ful of Iargon as a flekked pye.*
> (THE MERCHANT'S TALE, CANTERBURY
>   TALES, C.1387)

Figuratively, then, *jargon* soon came to mean 'mindless prattle', and by the mid-fifteenth century the word was no longer used of chirping birds but was confined to chattering people. From the end of the sixteenth century onwards *jargon* became a convenient term to describe 'any symbols, ciphers, languages or dialects which were meaningless to an outsider'. In the seventeenth century the term was then further stretched to include particular terminology, such as that used by scientists, philosophers, cloistered academics, and even the cant of trades, sects and social classes.

jeep
a small, tough, all-terrain vehicle, originally in military use

*Kabul was largely at peace. Back in Kabul, if not for the occasional bursts of gunfire, if not for the Soviet soldiers smoking on the sidewalks and the Soviet **jeeps** always bumping through the streets, war might as well have been a rumor.*
(KHALED HOSSEINI,
A THOUSAND SPLENDID SUNS, 2007)

*A few cruises, such as Ocean Village, offer exclusively teenage excursions. It operates seven-night cruises in the Mediterranean, where, under the supervision of the ship's specialist staff, the young can hike up Mount Vesuvius, travel off-road across the Cyprus countryside in a **Jeep** or even jog down the players' tunnel at Barcelona's legendary Camp Nou football stadium.*
(THE TIMES, 29 NOVEMBER 2008)

In 1937 the American motor industry was busy with plans for a four-wheel-drive, multipurpose army vehicle. When it was finally unveiled the vehi-

ACRONYMS

The word *acronym* was coined in the United States around the 1940s. Some of the older acronyms – words made up of the initial letters or syllables of other words – are so much a part of modern speech that their origins are largely forgotten. *Radar*, for instance, stands for '*ra*dio *d*etection *a*nd *r*anging', and *sonar* for '*so*und *n*avigation *a*nd *r*anging'. Similarly *laser* is short for '*l*ight *a*mplification by the *s*imulated *e*mission of *r*adiation'.

More modern is the medical term *AIDS*, '*A*cquired *I*mmune *D*eficiency *S*yndrome'. Dating from the early 1980s, it is now accepted as a normal word and is no longer necessarily written in upper-case letters.

The world of computing has contributed the programming language *BASIC*, '*B*eginners' *A*ll-purpose *S*ymbolic *I*nstruction *C*ode' to the steadily increasing bank of acronyms. Computer users work in the land of *LANs*, '*L*ocal *A*rea *N*etworks' and *WANs*, '*W*ide *A*rea *N*etworks', as they struggle with *wysiwyg*, '*w*hat *y*ou *s*ee *i*s *w*hat *y*ou *g*et', on their screens.

Organisations, political or otherwise, are often more comfortably known by their acronyms than by their cumbersome full titles. One of the earliest examples is *Gestapo*, which stands for '*Ge*heime *Sta*ats-*Po*lizei', the Secret State Police. The Gestapo was organised by Hermann Goering in Prussia in 1933 and covered all Germany by the following year.

A great deal of time and breath has been saved since 1949 by shortening the *N*orth *A*tlantic *T*reaty *O*rganisation to the compact *NATO*, and when the *C*onciliation and *A*rbritration *S*ervice, set up in 1974, had its tongue-twister of a title prefixed by the word *Advisory* the following year, *ACAS* saved many news-

cle was coded GP, signifying 'general purpose', and these letters slurred together gave the word *jeep*. The word and its spelling were probably influenced by the name of a cartoon star. In March the previous year Elzie Crisler Segar had introduced readers of the popular newspaper cartoon strip THIMBLE THEATRE to a little animal called Eugene the Jeep, the pet of Popeye's girlfriend, Olive Oyl. True to his name, this amiable and resourceful creature communicated by calling *jeep*. He was also capable of crossing into the fourth dimension and so, like the vehicle, was able to go everywhere.

jingoism
excessive, belligerent patriotism

Here we go again: pop tunes, nonsense lyrics and the chance for a spot of jingoism. Yes (or, if you prefer, si, oui or ja), it's Eurovision time once again.
(EVENING STANDARD, 14 MAY 2004)

When anyone claims cricket is 'just a game', I always point back to that bright Karachi day and try to explain the euphoria that raced through those stands, the sense of history pausing in its tired, war-mongering steps and considering another route. Observers, both national and international, correctly analysed that the cheers for the Indians revealed the deep desire of 'the average Pakistani' (a term synonymous with 'cricket fan') for the paper column inches. The same can surely be said of the *quango*, which grew to fit its acronym. In 1967 it was known simply as a '*qua*si *n*on-*g*overnment(al) organisation'; by 1976 this had swollen to '*qua*si *a*utonomous *n*on-*g*overnmental *o*rganisation'. Curiously, although the original title and the organisations themselves were of American inspiration, credit for the acronym is claimed by a lecturer at the University of Essex in the late 1960s.

Some organisations begin with a punchy acronym and then work out an appropriate title to fit. *ASH*, for instance, stands for the '*A*ction on *S*moking and *H*ealth'. A tear is a potent symbol of the compassion and social concern of the church, so in its very early days the *EAR* fund changed to The *E*vangelical *A*lliance *R*elief Fund and made its mark as *Tear*fund.

The full form of *VIP*, like those of *radar* and *laser*, is almost never heard, the acronym being so well assimilated into the language. *VIP* dates back to the 1930s and is American in origin. It stands for '*v*ery *i*mportant *p*erson' and may have begun as military slang for a high-ranking guest. It has been in use as an adjective (as in *VIP lounge*) since the mid-1940s. Also from America comes *UFO*, '*u*nidentified *f*lying *o*bject', in use since the 1950s.

When present-day society is not probing for life on other planets, its interest focuses on market forces and spending power. Since the boom years of the 1980s this has spawned a whole clutch of economic acronyms such as *yuppie*, '*y*oung *u*rban (or *u*pwardly mobile) *p*rofessional', and *dinkie*, '*d*ouble *i*ncome, *n*o *k*ids'. Recession has given rise to the *orchids*, '*o*ne *r*ecent *ch*ild, *h*eavily *i*n *d*ebt', and the *sitcoms*, '*s*ingle *i*ncome, *t*wo *c*hildren, *o*ppressive *m*ortgage', while the spending power lies with the *glammies*, '*g*reying, *l*eisured, *a*ffluent, *m*arried'.

---

*governments of both nations to put aside their **jingoism** and bellicose posturing.*
(THE GUARDIAN, 4 MARCH 2009)

In the second half of the seventeenth century *Hey Jingo!* or *High Jingo*, along with *Hey presto*, *Abracadabra!* and *Hocus Pocus!*, was a piece of conjuring jargon with supposedly supernatural connotations. The fact that Motteux chose *by jingo* to translate *par Dieu* ('by God') in his rendition of Rabelais (1694) has led to the conjecture that the term may have been a euphemism for 'by Jesus!'. An alternative view is that it was a borrowing of the Basque *Jinko* or *Jainko* ('God'), picked up from sailors. According to the OED, this origin is not impossible, but cannot be supported by evidence.

From conjuror's cant to popular parlance, by the eighteenth century *by jingo* (or often *by the living jingo*) was generally used as an exclamation: *All of a sudden the lightning let go a perfect sluice of white glare, and somebody sings out:*
'By the living jingo, here's the bag of gold on his breast!' (MARK TWAIN, THE ADVENTURES OF HUCKLEBERRY FINN, 1884).

In 1878 Russia and Turkey were at war and Russian troops were advancing on Constantinople. The British Prime Minister Benjamin Disraeli was strongly advocating intervention on behalf of the Turks. His bully-boy tirades against the Russians were echoed in sentiment in a popular music-hall song, the refrain of which was:

> We don't want to fight, but, by Jingo,
> if we do,
> We've got the ships, we've got the men,
> We've got the money too.

Walsh quotes a contemporary parody of the song which appeared in the PALL MALL GAZETTE:

> We don't want to fight, but by Jingo,
> if we do,
> We've Protestant and Catholic, Turk,
> infidel, and Jew;
> We've 'God' and 'Mammon,' 'Allah,'
> 'Buddha,' 'Brahma,' and 'Vishnu':
> We've collared all the deities, so what can
> Russia do?

Jingo (plural *jingoes*) was soon plucked from these refrains and used by the opposition Liberal party as a sarcastic epithet for those who supported Disraeli's policies. The meaning was subsequently extended to cover any blustering patriot advocating war.

The term *jingoism* was coined in the same year and remains to describe the spirit of 'a warmongering politician' or 'an indiscriminate patriot'. *Jingoistic* was in use by the middle of the next decade.

For another word for unthinking patriotism, see CHAUVINISM.

juggernaut
a very heavy lorry; an irresistible force

*From the tangled forest came the sound of cracking limbs and crashing trunks – Tantor was coming down upon them, a huge **Juggernaut** of the jungle. The priests were becoming uneasy. They cast apprehensive glances in the direction of the approaching elephant and then back at La. 'Fly!' she commanded them and then she stooped and cut the bonds securing her prisoners' feet and hands.*
(EDGAR RICE BURROUGHS, TARZAN AND THE JEWELS OF OPAR, 1916)

In his speech in Cairo, Barack Obama added pointedly that transparent government and the rule of law are associated with stable and successful governments. But, as regards China, that is manifestly untrue: the ruling party that brutally squashed the Tiananmen opposition has gone on to build an economic **juggernaut**. China's state and society have no independent judiciary or press, and are riven with corruption; yet the Chinese today seem far less interested in democracy than in economic wellbeing.
(THE TELEGRAPH, 4 JUNE 2009)

Juggernaut has been in English since the 1630s, when it was used in purely cultural contexts to describe the Juggernaut festival. Its spelling reflects an attempt to transcribe the Hindi word *Jagannath*, a title given to Krishna, one of the avatars or incarnations of the deity Vishnu. The word is of Sanskrit origin, from *Jagannātha*, which means 'Lord of the Universe' (from *jagat*, 'world' and *nāthas*, 'lord').

The Indian town of Pun in the north-eastern state of Orissa is the site of a magnificent temple where Jagannath is worshipped. Each year the journey Krishna took from Gokul to Mathura is commemorated when the images of Jagannath and his two siblings are removed from the main temple and mounted on colossal, ornate cars. It takes 4,000 men to drag the unwieldy cars the kilometre or so to the Gundicha Mandir temple, where the images reside for seven days before being hauled back again.

Europeans were first alerted to this magnificent procession by Friar Odoric, whose account of his travels in the east was published around 1321. The friar's narrative included stories of devotees who fanatically sacrificed themselves to the god by throwing themselves beneath the wheels of the car. These and subsequent accounts are now thought to have been exaggerated, although Jules Verne kept the tradition alive in AROUND THE WORLD IN EIGHTY DAYS (1873):

A group of old fakirs were capering and making a wild ado round the statue; these were striped with ochre, and covered with cuts whence their blood issued drop by drop – stupid fanatics, who, in the great Indian ceremonies, still throw themselves under the wheels of Juggernaut.

In the mid-nineteenth century such accounts were instrumental in lending a figurative dimension to *juggernaut*, so that it came to mean 'any belief or institution which attracts unquestioning, sacrificial devotion', 'an overwhelming, irresistible force'.

In modern British English the word also commonly denotes a 'large, heavy vehicle'. This use arose in the nineteenth century when Thackeray, in the SECOND FUNERAL OF NAPOLEON (1841), wrote: *Fancy, then...the body landed at day-break, and transferred to the car, and fancy the car, a huge Juggernaut of a machine.* But it was the increasing menace of huge articulated lorries on the roads in the 1960s that brought the word to prominence in this context.

K

kidnap

to seize someone in order to exact payment for his or her safe return

*Mustafa, the cowman, had become possessed. This little man, with his matchstick arms and legs, a walking splinter, had **kidnapped** a girl from a neighbouring village and taken her into the jungle for three days and nights.*
(MONICA ALI, BRICK LANE, 2003)

*Here was a man, he felt, who approached his professional life with a complete lack of emotion. What he was doing now, opening an investigation into the **kidnap** of a beautiful young woman adored by her husband, was just an assignment like any other.*
(BARBARA NADEL, HAREM, 2003)

Kidnap is a compound noun. The first element, *kid*, has been a slang term for a child since at least the turn of the seventeenth century and has been frequently used in familiar speech since the nineteenth. It is, of course, a figurative use of *kid*, meaning 'young goat', which derives from an Old Norse word *kidh* with the same meaning. The second element, *nap*, is another piece of seventeenth-century slang, meaning 'to seize, to lay hold of'. It is related to the more familiar *nab* and to other words in Scandinavian languages meaning 'to snatch'. The two elements were combined in the second half of the seventeenth century, probably as a cant term, to describe the crime of abducting young children and carrying them off or selling them to work as servants or labourers in the American colonies.

By the time Dr Johnson had compiled his DICTIONARY OF THE ENGLISH LANGUAGE in 1755 the term had been extended to cover the abduction of a person of any age, such as men who were dragged away to serve as sailors when there were insufficient recruits.

Escaped negro slaves in America were also prime targets for kidnapping, to return them to their southern masters from the abolitionist north. Frederick Douglass was one such; he escaped from the southern states and took up residence in New Bedford, Massachusetts. In 1841 he addressed an anti-slavery convention in Nantucket, and in 1845 published NARRATIVE OF THE LIFE OF FREDERICK DOUGLASS, AN AMERICAN SLAVE WRITTEN BY HIMSELF. These were his feelings on arriving in the north:

I felt like one who had escaped a den of hungry lions. This state of mind, however, very soon subsided; and I was again seized with a feeling of great insecurity and loneliness. I was yet liable to be taken back, and subjected to all the tortures of slavery... I was afraid to speak to any one for fear of speaking to the wrong one, and thereby falling into the hands of money-loving kidnappers, whose business it was to lie in wait for the panting fugitive, as the ferocious beasts of the forest lie in wait for their prey.

kiosk

a small structure from which newspapers or refreshments are sold; a small pavilion

The next thing I remember is whisking through the doors of the police station 50 yards back, and pressing the button by the window that summoned the officer on duty. He obviously didn't quite believe me, even face to face. I suspect that my form of words was, 'I think I've found an abandoned baby in the telephone kiosk by Abinger Place' – or, 'I think there's an abandoned baby...' He took my name, address and telephone number and to what I suppose was my shocked and expectant face said, 'We'll investigate.'
(THE GUARDIAN, 21 DECEMBER 2002)

Fabio Supernova sits on a green wooden bench at 'L'Avamposto', a Caribbean-style kiosk built every summer from bamboo and thatch, on a rocky promontory next to a ruined watch-tower.
(DAILY MAIL, 10 SEPTEMBER 2008)

In the sixteenth and seventeenth centuries, travel writing was used not only to interest the reader in the ways of other cultures, but to inspire merchants to invest in overseas trade, expansion and settlement. The most famous travel writer was Richard Haklyut, who researched the experiences and writings of sailors, travellers and explorers, collated and translated them, and used them to promote investment in the New World. Haklyut is widely credited with encouraging the settlement of North America in the reign of James I (1603–25). Samuel Purchas was a less esteemed travel writer who, upon Haklyut's death, acquired some of his manuscripts and used them in his own later work, HAKLYUTUS POSTUMUS OR PILGRIMES (1625–6). The earliest known record of *kiosk* appears in this.

According to Purchas, a *kiosk* was an open Turkish banqueting house or pavilion with beautiful views. Such light summerhouses became popular in Western Europe and were constructed in parks and gardens. The word *kiosk* came into English via French *kiosque*, a borrowing of

Turkish *köshk*, 'pavilion', (where the *k* is pronounced as *ki*). This, in turn, came from Persian *kūshk*, 'palace'.

In the nineteenth century, the French found another use for the word when it was applied to a small structure, slightly ornate after the style of a Turkish pavilion, from which newspapers were sold or which was used as a bandstand. This usage passed into English, the DAILY TELEGRAPH for 5 December 1865 educating its readers by defining *kiosk* as *a place for the sale of newspapers*.

kowtow
to curry favour with, to show excessive deference

Police chiefs being elected by the general public mean the power of patronage shifts to a new, harder to please selectorate. It means you can only get on if the people you police feel happy. You have to kowtow to the people whose burglaries you refuse to investigate. Imagine!
(THE SPECTATOR, 22 DECEMBER 2008)

When the opera season restarted, Handel had an insurance policy, taking up pensioned court appointments as the Composer to the Chapel Royal and music master to the royal princesses. 'That was enormously canny,' says Edward Blakeman, Handel biographer and the editor of the Radio 3 Handel celebrations next week, 'because it placed him within royal circles without forcing him to kowtow to royalty.'
(THE TIMES, 10 APRIL 2009)

Kow-tow is an anglicised attempt at Mandarin Chinese *ke tóu*, an act of obeisance showing submission or deep respect, such as a subject might have towards his emperor. *Ke* means 'knock' and *tóu* 'head', and the reverence is performed by prostrating oneself and touching the ground with one's forehead. The term entered

WORDS FROM CHINESE

Besides KOWTOW and TEA, which have entries of their own in this book, English has taken a number of Chinese words into its vocabulary.

Japan (16th cent): Chinese *Jih-pun* (from *jih*, 'sun' and *pun*, 'origin') is a translation of Japanese *Ni-pon*, 'sunrise'. This was borrowed into Malay as *Japang* and from there was taken into the European languages.

kaolin (18th cent): a specific type of clay (China clay), used for the manufacture of porcelain, which originally came from a mountain in Jiangxi Province called *gaō-lǐng* (from *gaō*, 'high' and *lǐng*, 'mountain'). It came into English as *kaolin* by way of French.

ketchup (17th cent): this originally referred to the 'brine of pickled fish', known in the Amoy Chinese dialect as *kôechiap* (from *kôe*, a kind of fish, and *chiap*, 'juice'). This was borrowed into Malay as *kichap* and into English as *catchup*, then *ketchup*.

silk (9th cent): probably from Chinese *sī*, 'silk'. Its exact route into English is not known. Part of its history, at least, involves Greek *Seres*, 'the oriental people from whom silk was obtained', and *sērikos*, 'silken'. The Latin derivatives are *Sēres* and *sēricum*.

soy (17th cent): Chinese *shi-yu* was a sauce made from soya beans (from *shi*, 'salted beans' and *yu*, 'oil'). This was borrowed as *shō-yu* in Japanese, which formed the contracted colloquial form *soy*. The Japanese form was also the source of Dutch *soya*, which was borrowed into English in the eighteenth century.

typhoon (16th cent): this is from the Cantonese dialect *daai feng*, 'big wind', (corresponding to Mandarin *dàfēng*), though the spelling was influenced by Greek *Tūphōn*, the mythical hundred-headed monster who begot the winds. Early English forms are *touffon*, *tuffon* and *tuffan*.

yen (19th cent): from Cantonese Chinese *yin-yān*, 'craving for opium'(from *yin*, 'opium' and *yān*, 'craving'). Chinese immigrants took the term to America in the mid-nineteenth century where it entered the slang vocabulary as *yen-yen*, later shortened to *yen*. By the early twentieth century it was generally used to mean a craving of any sort.

English as a noun in the early nineteenth century with reference to the bow. The English statesman Sir John Barrow, who served on the first British embassy to China at the end of the eighteenth century, wrote that *The Chinese were determined they should be kept in the constant practice of the koo-too, or ceremony of genuflection and prostration* (TRAVELS IN CHINA, 1804).

In the 1820s the term's figurative potential was exploited when it was used as a verb, with the sense 'to behave in an ingratiating manner': *The Marquess kotooed like a first-rate Mandarin, and vowed 'that her will was his conduct'* (Benjamin Disraeli, VIVIAN GREY, 1826).

· L ·

lackadaisical
uncommitted, unenthusiastic, languid

She was in the second year of her degree, studying history but in a lackadaisical manner that ignored the political (the Declaration of Arbroath and Tennis-Court oaths) in favour of the romantic (Rob Roy, Marie-Antoinette) and didn't endear her to the teaching staff.
(KATE ATKINSON,
ONE GOOD TURN, 2006)

It was difficult to work out how he managed to beat me on most occasions – although he did explain to me that he didn't really beat me, rather he let me beat myself. Well, that can't have been quite true, because in order to beat myself I had to get the ball to come back at me, which I couldn't have done without some skilful play by the seemingly lackadaisical figure on the other side of the net.
(SIMON GRAY,
THE LAST CIGARETTE, 2008)

She's dead, deceas'd, she's dead; alack the day, wails Nurse when Juliet cannot be roused (Shakespeare, ROMEO AND JULIET, 1597). *Alack the day* or *alackaday* was a common sixteenth-century exclamation of sorrow or reproach which meant 'Woe to the day!' or 'Shame to the day!'. By the eighteenth century the form *lack-a-day* (and its extended form *lackadaisy*) was more common, the expression having lost its initial unstressed vowel. *Lackadaisical* emerged as an adjective in the second half of the eighteenth century, becoming increasingly popular in the nineteenth.

It denoted the limp, languid speech and bearing of one who, overwhelmed by life's little problems and challenges, was given to sighing *Lackaday!*

laconic
brief and sparing in expression, usually in speech

'Pack!' was his laconic greeting to Zarinska as he passed her lodge and hurried to harness his dogs. A few minutes later he swept into the council at the head of the team, the woman by his side.
(JACK LONDON,
SON OF THE WOLF, 1900)

Calmness in the face of adversity, a laconic sense of humour, a sense of decency and fair play, and mastery of understatement are all fundamental facets of the British character – at least, as seen by the British themselves.
(DAVID ELSE, THE LONELY PLANET
GUIDE TO GREAT BRITAIN, 2009)

Laconia was a region in ancient Greece whose capital was Sparta. Its people had a reputation for rigorous austerity. This was evident even in their speech and writing, which were brief and to the point. A well-known story illustrates their succinct style. It tells of Philip of Macedon, whose threat, *If I enter Laconia, I will raze Sparta to the ground*, met with the terse reply, *If*.

The adjective *Laconic* (from Latin *Laconicus* and Greek *Lakōnikos*, 'like the Laconicans') was borrowed into English in the sixteenth century to refer to all things pertaining to that region. Soon it was also written with a lower-case letter to denote 'concisely expressed', whether spoken or written. An early instance of this (1589) is recorded in a hurriedly composed letter by James VI of Scotland. He apologises for its sparse style thus: *excuis me for this my laconike writting*, adding as his excuse, *l ame in suche haist*.

The people of Sparta itself were considered especially frugal and well-disciplined. The adjective *Spartan*, borrowed from Latin *Spartanus* in the fifteenth century, follows a similar pattern to *laconic*. Initially it referred only to the city or its people, but in the seventeenth century its use was extended to allude to their austere, frugal characteristics. Thus Milton speaks of mollifying a *Spartan surlinesse* (AREOPAGITICA, 1644) and Cowper of a *Spartan soul* (EXPOSTULATION, 1781). Today, *spartan furnishings*, a *spartan meal* or a *spartan lifestyle* are all evocative of the simple, spare life led by the inhabitants of the Laconian capital.

lady
an adult female person (used politely); a woman with refined manners; a feminine title of nobility or of rank

Boisterous school playground games have been given the all-clear today by senior judges who threw out a claim by a dinner lady badly injured by a boy playing tag.
(DAILY MAIL, 4 APRIL 2009)

Former prime minister Lady Thatcher will have a 'routine' operation to insert a pin into her broken upper arm following a fall, her spokesman said today.
(THE INDEPENDENT, 18 JUNE 2009)

See LORD.

lampoon
(to perform) a biting satire upon a person or institution

Maybe it was too soon for Saturday night's Archive on 4 to reflect on George W's reign as President of the US of A. After all, there are still three days left of his administration. But Bremner on Bush: A Final Farewell was a missed opportunity. Rory Bremner was presumably hauled in as presenter because of his sharp-witted impersonations of Dubya, a man so easy to lampoon Bremner must sometimes have wondered whether there was any point in making fun of him.
(THE SPECTATOR, 14 JANUARY 2009)

The cartoonist's job, surely, is to caricature and lampoon the great and the good (and the bad), to burst the bubble of their egos, to show their feet of clay.
(THE TIMES, 6 JUNE 2009)

It is a well-known fact that drinking loosens the tongue, bringing private thoughts to public attention. This would seem to be the background of *lampoon. Lampons*, 'Let's drink' (from French slang *lamper*, 'to gulp down, to swig') was a common refrain in French drinking songs of the seventeenth century. The verses themselves must often have been of a biting, personal nature, to account for the coining of *lampoon* from this source. The word, as noun and verb, was first used in English from the middle of the seventeenth century.

The poet Alexander Pope was infamous for invective against those who crossed him. This is part of the portrait of Atticus, otherwise Joseph Addison, with whom he quarrelled:

> *Damn with faint praise, assent with civil leer,*
> *And without sneering, teach the rest to sneer;*
> *Willing to wound, and yet afraid to strike,*
> *Just hint a fault, and hesitate dislike;*

Alike reserv'd to blame, or to commend,
A tim'rous foe, and a suspicious friend...
(EPISTLE TO DR ARBUTHNOT, 1735)

It is easy to see why, in his LIVES OF
THE POETS (1779–81), Dr Johnson
denounces Pope as *a lampooner, who scat-*
tered his ink without fear or decency.

For another word originating in a
drinking refrain, see CAROUSE.

Lent
a forty-day period from Ash
Wednesday to Easter

Everywhere – well, perhaps not everywhere,
not in Bangladesh, for example, but
certainly in an awful lot of places – they
had some kind of carnival before **Lent***, but*
in Britain all you got was pancakes.
(KATE ATKINSON, WHEN WILL THERE
BE GOOD NEWS?, 2008)

The intensity of those events and their
infinite and eternal significance are
celebrated by Christians each year during
Holy Week and Easter. Those celebrations,
if they are to be fitting, will not just
happen. They call for preparation, and
we prepare for them during **Lent***.*
(THE TIMES, 21 MARCH 2009)

Lent is a shortening of Middle English
lenten which comes from Old English
lencten, meaning 'the spring'. This in
turn is from *langgitīnaz*, an unattested
West Germanic compound which literally means 'long day' and hence
'spring', because the days gradually
become longer in that season. There
are cognate forms in many other
Germanic languages, where the sense is
just 'spring'; English alone has given
the word an ecclesiastical significance.

From medieval times onwards, *Lent*
signified a period of forty weekdays
from Ash Wednesday to the eve of
Easter, a figure which reflects the
length of time Jesus Christ fasted in the
wilderness (Matthew 4: 1–11). This

was viewed as a time of abstinence,
penitence and spiritual renewal in
preparation for Easter:

Is this a Fast, to keep
The larder lean
And clean
From fat of veals and sheep?
Is it to quit the dish
Of flesh, yet still
To fill
The platter high with fish?
No; 'tis a Fast to dole
Thy sheaf of wheat
And meat
Unto the hungry soul.
It is to fast from strife
From old debate
And hate
To circumcise thy life.
(ROBERT HERRICK,
NOBLE NUMBERS, 1647)

A season running up to Easter had
been established in the ecclesiastical
calendar throughout Christendom
centuries before the concept of Lent
took hold. From the days of the early
church in the second century, Easter
was a time of baptism for new converts, who were prepared by a series of
classes on the meaning of baptism,
communion, the creeds, the Lord's
Prayer and so on. Justin the Martyr in
Rome and Pantaenus, Clement and
Origen in Alexandria were early teachers of these courses. Records of the
addresses given to these converts still
exist. Over the centuries, this period
of intensive teaching and discipline
for new converts before baptism
became formalised into a forty-day
period of spiritual preparation for
Easter for all believers, a season that
has been called *Lent* or *Lenten* since
about AD 1000.

See CARNIVAL and SHROVETIDE.

MONTHS OF THE YEAR

The final version of the ancient Roman calendar is traditionally credited to Numa Pompilius, the (possibly mythical) second king of Rome, the successor of Romulus. The original Roman year began at the spring equinox and was divided into ten months, each beginning at the full moon. This allowed for 304 days, which left the remaining 61 days mysteriously unaccounted for. Numa Pompilius added the missing two months.

The Roman year followed the agricultural cycle and began in spring. The first month was named *Mārtius*, being dedicated to *Mars*, the protector of agriculture and cattle. Old French had *marz*, from which northern dialects derived *marche*. This was taken into Anglo-French, becoming *March* in Middle English. It is recorded from the early thirteenth century.

April's origins are more obscure. The month was possibly named for *Venus*, the goddess of love – perhaps because of much activity from the birds and the bees at this time of the year. The suggestion is that Latin *Aprīlis* was derived from Etruscan *Apru*. This in turn had been borrowed from Greek *Aphrō*, short for *Aphrodite*, whom the Romans identified with Venus. Middle English had *Averil* from Old French *avrill* in the thirteenth century, but revised the spelling after Latin in the late fourteenth century.

Some ancient writers have connected *Maius* with *Maia*, an Italic goddess of the spring whom the Romans identified as the eldest and most beautiful of the Pleiades. *Maius* was borrowed into Old French as *mai* and Middle English as *May* in the thirteenth century.

Latin *Jūnius* was consecrated to *Juno*, queen of heaven. She was the guardian of womanhood and her month, *June*, was the most auspicious for marriage. Old English borrowed *Junius* from Latin. Middle English also had *Iuyn*, from Old French *juin*.

The remaining months in the ancient Roman calendar were rather unimaginatively numbered:

July, for instance, was originally *Quintilis*, from *quintus*, 'fifth'. However, after Julius Caesar's death in 44 BC it was renamed *Jūlius* in his honour, Quintilis having been his birth month. Middle English had *Julie* from Anglo-French. This rhymed with modern English *duly*, a pronunciation which persisted until

---

lewd
indecent, obscene, licentious

He had, he said, been the greatest of sinners. He had scoffed; he had wantonly associated with the reckless and the **lewd**. But a day of awakening had come...
(THOMAS HARDY, TESS OF THE D'URBERVILLES, 1891)

...four in five British businesses are cutting back and cancelling their office Christmas parties... Obviously, the reason given for party pooperage this year is the recession. In 2005, it was some other excuse, erm, reason. Yes, here it is: 'Employers feared being hit with sexual harassment tribunals resulting from **lewd** behaviour.'
(THE TIMES, 15 NOVEMBER 2008)

as late as the eighteenth century. Skeat suggests the change was to eliminate any possible confusion with *June*.

August was originally *Sextilis*, from *sextus*, 'sixth', but was renamed to honour *Augustus* Caesar, the first Roman emperor (63 BC-AD 14). The adjective *augustus* meant 'venerable, magnificent'. In 27 BC, two years after he was named emperor, Julius Caesar's heir Octavian took it as a title with the sense 'Imperial Majesty'. Old English had *August* directly from Latin.

Latin *September* was derived from *septem*, 'seven'. It was borrowed directly into late Old English.

October was from *octō*, 'eight'. It is recorded in English from the middle of the eleventh century.

November came from *novem*, 'nine'. Middle English borrowed it by way of Old French *novembre* in the early thirteenth century.

December was from *decem*, 'ten'. It appeared in English at the very beginning of the eleventh century and came via Old French *decembre*.

The two months required to complete the year, *January* and *February*, are the ones traditionally credited to Numa Pompilius:

Jānuārius (Middle English *Januarie*) was named after *Janus*, god of gateways and of beginnings, to whom Numa built a temple in Rome.

Februa, a word of Sabine origin, was a festival of purification which fell in mid-February and Latin *februārius* derived from this. It came into Middle English as *Feveryer* through Old French *feverier* and Late Latin *febrārius* in the early thirteenth century, but in the late fourteenth century was remodelled on the original classical Latin.

In 46 BC Julius Caesar had the Roman calendar revised. The new Julian calendar confirmed that a year should have 365 days, but added an extra day every fourth year to compensate for astronomical difference. The beginning of the year was shifted to 1 January, the two-faced god Janus keeping a watchful eye over the departure of the old year and the arrival of the new. However, since the new calendar retained the months in their original order, this step made a nonsense of those names with a numerical derivation.

For characteristics of classical gods, see OTHERWORLDLY INFLUENCES (page 156).

The origin of *lewd* is difficult to determine but its development over the centuries is fascinating. Written history dates back to the ninth century. Old English had the adjective *læwede*, meaning 'of the laity', to distinguish laymen from clergy. This sense remained current until the mid-sixteenth century. However, since the clergy were educated and most of the laity were not, Middle English *lewed* had, by the thirteenth century, picked up the sense of 'unlearned, untutored'.

The ignorant were generally regarded as society's dregs and so, by the fourteenth century, the word had acquired the sense 'common, vulgar' and, by extension, 'base, ill-mannered'.

One of the Paston letters (c. 1481), which chronicle English social life in the fifteenth century, reads: *Plese zow... to forgeve me, and also my wyffe of owr leude offence that we have not don ower dute.*

In a passage discussing the parable of the talents, the puritan Arthur Golding describes the man who wasted his talent by burying it in the ground instead of investing it as *a leaude servant*, meaning 'worthless, good-for-nothing' (HEMINGE'S POSTILL, tr. 1569). And Sir Henry Savile renders a statement from Tacitus's HISTORIES (tr. 1591) as *A state gotten by lewde meanes cannot be retayned.*

The modern sense of 'obscene, lascivious' was a further development of this increasingly negative word in the fourteenth century. Chaucer speaks of *lewed dronken harlotrye* (CANTERBURY TALES, The Miller's Prologue, c. 1387), and young ladies of the period were warned against forward behaviour:

> If thou sit by a right goode manne,
> This lesson look thou think upon.
> Under his thigh thy knee not fit,
> Thou art full lewd, if thou does it.

In the sixteenth century, Shakespeare wrote of *lulling on a lewd Loue-Bed* (RICHARD III, 1594), while a few decades later Samuel Pepys, dipping into L'ESCHOLLER DE FILLES, a pornographic book from France, thought it *the most bawdy, lewd book*, but persevered with it *for information sake* (Christopher Hibbert, THE ENGLISH, 1987).

The playwright Aphra Behn was too outspoken for many. To one critic she was *that lewd Harlot*, while a contemporary, Robert Gould, incensed at her success, derided her play THE CITY HEIRESS (1682) in one of his own THE PLAY HOUSE, A SATYR (1689):

> *...that clean piece of Wit*
> *The City Heiress by chaste Sappho Writ,*
> *Where the Lewd Widow comes with*
> *Brazen Face,*
> *Just seeking from a Stallion's rank*
> *Embrace,*
> *T'acquaint the Audience with her*
> *Filthy Case.*
> *Where can you find a Scene for juster*
> *Praise,*
> *In Shakespear, Johnson, or in*
> *Fletcher's Plays?*

Very little about the word *lewd* has changed since then.

litter

pieces of rubbish thrown carelessly about; the young of an animal born at the same time

*The 30-year-old singer plays his guitar whilst squeezed inside the tiny metal **litter** bin in Cambridge city centre. At 5ft 9 he finds his job cramped and smelly but his singing style is proving a huge hit with passers-by... He said singing in a bin does have its drawbacks.*

'I get people throwing rubbish into the bin not realising I'm inside,' he said.
(THE TELEGRAPH, 6 MAY 2009)

*After Shiner passed on, my son and I both picked two dogs out of the same **litter** in Cunningham, Kan. Dog number two was named Drifter for his tendency to run big; his brother was named Tripper for his tendency to get in the way of everyone's feet.*
(NEVADA DAILY MAIL, 21 JUNE 2009)

When this word first appeared in Middle English as *litere* at the very end of the thirteenth century, it meant 'bed'. It had come into English from Anglo-French and was a variant of Old French *litiere*, also meaning 'bed'. This, in turn, was derived from Medieval Latin *lectāria*, a derivative of Latin *lectus*, 'bed'. *Lectus* itself ultimately goes back to unattested proto-Indo-European *legh-*, 'to lie', source of the English verb *to lie*.

The use of *litter* for 'bed' did not last beyond the late fifteenth century; English already had *bed*, a word of Germanic origin, and stuck to that. However, *litter* was retained in related senses that evolved later.

In the first half of the fourteenth century, the word began to denote 'a stretcher' used to transport the sick or wounded or 'a portable couch' used to convey members of the nobility. In LE MORTE D'ARTHUR (1470–85) Sir Thomas Malory writes of *lyttyers for the wounded knyghtes*, and in 1502 details of the privy purse of Elizabeth of York, wife of Henry VII, include *a covering for a litter of blewe cloth of golde*.

In the second half of the fifteenth century *litter* also began to signify 'all the young of an animal from a single birth', the idea being that they were all born in one bed. The BOKE OF ST ALBANS (1486), a collection of essays on topics such as hawking and hunting, has *A Litter of welpis*.

Also, during the first half of the fifteenth century *litter* also began to denote the straw or rushes that people collected and piled up to sleep on, and the straw spread in an animal's stall. From this notion of scattering straw for bedding the present-day sense of 'bits and pieces strewn about' emerged in the first half of the eighteenth century. In Henry Fielding's novel JOSEPH ANDREWS (1742) Parson Adams's wife, flustered at the unexpected arrival of Lady Booby at the parsonage, exclaims that she is *ashamed to be seen in such a pickle, and that her house was in such a litter; but that if she had expected such an honour from her ladyship she should have found her in a better manner.*

lizard
a reptile

*The place was a small clearing in the centre of a palm grove. In this was one of those boiling mud geysers which I have already described. Around its edge were scattered a number of leathern thongs cut from iguanodon hide, and a large collapsed membrane which proved to be the dried and scraped stomach of one of the great fish **lizards** from the lake.*
(SIR ARTHUR CONAN DOYLE, THE LOST WORLD, 1912)

*A **lizard**, torpid from the cold, struggled wearily up the side of a small rock, searching for the warmth that would enable him to start his day. Just like us, thought Mma Ramotswe.*
(ALEXANDER MCCALL SMITH, THE GOOD HUSBAND OF ZEBRA DRIVE, 2007)

Middle English had *liserd*, *lesard*, a borrowing of Old French *lesard*, which came from the Latin *lacertus* (feminine form *lacerta*). The words *lizard* and ALLIGATOR thus share the same origin. The term is first found in PIERS PLOWMAN by William Langland (c. 1377) and in Wycliffe's translation (1382) of Leviticus 11: 30, which lists a number of creeping creatures that the Israelites were forbidden to eat.

Since the Latin word *lacertus* means both 'the muscular upper part of the arm' and 'a lizard', it has been proposed by some that the reptile was so named because of its resemblance in shape and movement to the forearm. If this is so, it is another instance of people's propensity to associate animals with parts of the body.

See ALLIGATOR and CROCODILE.
See also HEARSE, LOBSTER, MUSCLE and VANILLA for other words based on imagined likenesses.

lobster

an edible marine crustacean with a hard shell

*Tis the voice of the **Lobster**: I heard him
declare
'You have baked me too brown, I must
sugar my hair.'*
(LEWIS CARROLL, ALICE'S
ADVENTURES IN WONDERLAND, 1865)

*...before I could cook my **lobsters**, I needed
to end their watery lives as quickly and
humanely as possible. In the past, I would
always drop them into a pot of boiling
water and clamp the lid on tight. Trevor
Corson had another suggestion. 'The best
way to kill them, according to animal
welfare agencies, is to put them in the
freezer first for 15 minutes,' he said. 'It
slows their metabolism.'*
(NEW YORK TIMES, 9 DECEMBER 2008)

In Latin the word *locusta* meant both
'locust' and 'lobster'. One creature was
obviously named because of its perceived resemblance to the other,
although it is impossible to say with
any certitude which came first. In an
attempt to solve this problem, some
etymologists have suggested a link
between *locusta* and the Greek verb
lēkan, 'to jump', implying that the word
first meant 'locust'.

Locusta in the sense of 'locust' was
borrowed directly into Middle English
in the late thirteenth century, but
Old English has *loppestre, lopystre*,
meaning 'lobster'. These terms show
signs of influence from the Old English
loppe, 'spider', in yet another case of
perceived resemblance. The word *lobster*
had settled down into its modern
spelling with a medial *b* by the late
sixteenth century.

Imagined likenesses and connections
also provide the etymology for
HEARSE, LIZARD, MUSCLE and
VANILLA.

loophole

a narrow slit in a wall for shooting or
looking through; a way of escaping an
obligation

*Captain Smollett made no change in his
arrangements. If the mutineers succeeded
in crossing the stockade, he argued, they
would take possession of any unprotected
loophole and shoot us down like rats in
our own stronghold.*
(ROBERT LOUIS STEVENSON,
TREASURE ISLAND, 1883)

*George W Bush authorised the use of
torture. He did so using the most cowardly
means: the legal **loophole**.*
(THE TIMES, 18 APRIL 2009)

A *loupe* was an 'embrasure', an opening
in a wall made either to look through
or to fire arrows through. In medieval
fortifications they were slits set in the
thick stone walls that gradually
widened out on the inside. When the
castle was under attack they allowed
the defenders within to see the enemy
and to loose their arrows with ease
while offering them protection. *Loupe*
was first recorded in the fourteenth
century and has a probable connection
with the Middle Dutch verb *lupen*, 'to
peer, to spy'. In the late sixteenth
century the same word, now spelt *loope*,
appeared in the compound *loophole*,
with exactly the same meaning.

The figurative use of *loophole* to
mean 'a way out, an escape' dates from
the second half of the seventeenth
century. The word is regularly applied
to a small flaw in the wording of a law,
regulation or contract that makes legal
avoidance possible.

As the actor W C Fields, known for
his heavy drinking and his cynical
views, lay on his death-bed he was
asked why he was reading the Bible. *I'm
looking for a loophole*, came the answer.

lord

a master, a ruler; a male member of the nobility

*...I was immensely grateful when my **lord** and master elected to take charge of the situation. He ordered me to have a little snooze on the pillows I'd plumped up for him, while he cooked me dinner for being such a Good Wife.*
(THE SCOTSMAN, 3 JUNE 2000)

*[Allegra] Huston was 12 when her stepmother Cici sat her down and told her that the film director John Huston was not her father. 'You were a child of love. Your real father is an English **Lord**. I told him he should come and visit you. He's coming tomorrow.'*
(THE TELEGRAPH, 5 APRIL 2009)

Bread of some sort is a staple in many countries. The early nineteenth-century compound *breadwinner*, to denote 'one who supports himself and his dependents', illustrates the importance of this basic food in Britain, but the same dependence upon bread is evident in the much older etymologies of both *lord* and *lady*; the Old English noun *hlāf*, 'loaf', from unattested proto-Germanic *hlaibaz*, is common to both words.

Lord appeared as *hlāfweard* in early Old English. This was a compound of *hlāf*, 'loaf', and *weard*, 'keeper, warden', and thus denoted 'the keeper of the bread' and by extension 'the master of the house', the person responsible for those who ate his bread. *Hlāfweard* was reduced to *hlāford* in later Old English, becoming *loverd* and then *lord* in Middle English.

Lady, on the other hand, was a compound of *hlæf*, 'loaf', and unattested *dīge*, 'kneader', and meant 'kneader of bread', one who makes bread and feeds her dependents, hence 'mistress of the household'. Old English *hlæfdige* became *la(ve)di* in Middle English.

lunch

a light midday meal

*One in five workers in Britain does not eat **lunch**, a new study reveals today. Women were more likely to skip lunch than men, with 21 per cent not eating a midday meal, according to research by NOP and Findus Feeling Great! ready meals.*
(EVENING STANDARD, 27 MAY 2002)

It is often assumed that *lunch* is an abbreviation of *luncheon*, but this was not originally the case. When *lunch* first appeared in the late sixteenth century it denoted 'a thick piece, a hunk' of meat, bread or cheese: *He shall take breade and cut it into little lunches into a pan with cheese* (Richard Surflet, THE COUNTRIE FARM, 1600). This sense has led to the theory that the word is a variant of *lump*, a notion supported by the apparent association between *bump* and *bunch*, and *hump* and *hunch*.

The earliest records of *luncheon* appeared eleven years earlier, with the same meaning. Nevertheless, the term is considered to be an extension of *lunch*. Then from the mid-seventeenth century *luncheon* began to denote 'a light meal, a snack':

Then others more Hungry, their Stomachs to please,
Sit down to their Luncheons of House-hold and Cheese.
(EDWARD WARD, WRITINGS, 1705)

And in the first half of the nineteenth century, the word was reduced to *lunch*, an abbreviation that was originally frowned upon as vulgar.

luxury

something that is expensive and pleasurable but not essential; indulgent comfort

*...the average British household's disposable income has risen 26 percent since 1997. These steady rises have brought a corresponding desire for greater **luxury** and, as a result, companies are scrambling to deliver new luxury fulfillment.*
(INTERNATIONAL HERALD TRIBUNE, 24 NOVEMBER 2006)

*Here is a place to enjoy, entertain or just sit back and relax. The floor plan is simply ideal. With plenty of life's little **luxuries**, from a home theatre room fully decked out with surround sound, to the large projection theatre system, this home is a sheer delight.*
(MORNING BULLETIN, ROCKHAMPTON, AUSTRALIA, 8 NOVEMBER 2008)

Latin *luxus*, the source of *luxury*, was a critical term. It meant 'excess, extravagance', in eating and drinking, for instance, or in debauchery. The word conjures up the stereotypical view of Roman banquets and orgies. Its derivative *luxuria*, a noun which denoted 'riotous living, excess', was borrowed into Old French as *luxurie*, 'debauchery', in the early twelfth century, and from there into Middle English in the first half of the fourteenth. Geoffroy IV de la Tour Landry, a fourteenth-century nobleman from Anjou, wrote a book for his daughters instructing them how to behave at court and warning them about the easy morality of many courtiers. This work had become very popular by the late Middle Ages and was translated from French into English. THE BOOK OF THE KNIGHT OF THE TOWER (c. 1450) warns that *leude touchinge and handelyng...makith... folke falle into orible synne of luxurie*. This sense of lust and lasciviousness lasted into the early nineteenth century, but is now obsolete.

Lust is an excess of sexual desire and, in the first half of the seventeenth century, *luxury* began to be applied to excesses or indulgences of other kinds: food, dress, household trappings, etc. The sense 'something extra to life's necessities' dates from the late eighteenth century: *Necessaries always come before luxuries* (Jeremy Bentham, THE PRINCIPLES OF MORALS AND LEGISLATION, 1780).

M

magazine
a weekly or monthly periodical; a broadcast programme of general interest; an arsenal

[The town] is strongly fortified, but both fortifications and town suffered much in the Brazilian war... The church is a curious ruin; it was used as a powder-magazine, and was struck by lightning in one of the ten thousand thunder-storms of the Rio Plata.
(CHARLES DARWIN,
THE VOYAGE OF THE BEAGLE, 1839)

'What'dya think of this good-lookin' guy?' Noel says. He has a copy of Life **magazine** *open to a photo of a young political candidate. 'How can this guy run for president? He's a kid!'*
(MITCH ALBOM, THE FIVE PEOPLE YOU MEET IN HEAVEN, 2003)

The BBC has come under criticism after it dropped Grange Hill *after 30 years and Radio 4 controller Mark Damazer announced last month that the station's only remaining children's show, the Sunday evening* **magazine** *programme* Go4It, *will finish for good.*
(THE TELEGRAPH, 10 MAY 2009)

When Robinson Crusoe was stranded on his island he made provision for himself by domesticating goats, reasoning that *the keeping up a breed of tame creatures thus at my hand would be a living magazine of flesh, milk, butter, and cheese for me as long as I lived in the place, if it were to be forty years...* (Daniel Defoe, ROBINSON CRUSOE, 1719). Defoe

was using *magazine* in its original sense of 'storehouse'. The term was ultimately an Arabic one, deriving from *khatzana*, 'to store up'. From this Arabic had *makhzan*, 'storehouse', but it is from the plural *makhāzin* that Italian derived its singular noun *magazzino*. This passed into Old French as *magazin*, still meaning 'storehouse', and from there into English in the second half of the sixteenth century. Once in English, *magazine* developed a range of additional senses all based upon the original notion.

Sometimes *magazine* was applied not just to a storehouse but also to its stock, so that it also came to mean 'a store of something'; this might be anything from body fat – which, according to Helkiah Crooke (A DESCRIPTION OF THE BODY OF MAN, 1615) was considered quite desirable by some, being *a Stowage or Magazine of nourishment against a time of dearth* – to the clothing which covered it.

Within a few years of its first appearance in English, *magazine* had been pressed into military service to denote a 'store of arms and ammunition'. In the eighteenth century this was extended to a 'chamber on a gun' which held a supply of bullets. Both of these meanings are still current.

On the literary front, from the 1630s onwards the word was seized upon for the titles of reference books on specific subjects such as THE MARINER'S MAGAZINE (1669) or NEGOTIATOR'S MAGAZINE (1719), these volumes being figurative storehouses of facts or scholarship. The concept of a periodical carrying quality articles of more general interest arose in the first half of the eighteenth century. THE GENTLE-MAN'S MAGAZINE: OR, MONTHLY INTELLIGENCER appeared in 1731, the title and the editor's stated aim being *to promote a Monthly Collection to treasure up, as in a Magazine, the most remarkable Pieces on the Subjects above-mention'd*; in other words, to provide the reader with a 'storehouse' of interest and information. Subsequent general periodicals followed suit and *magazine* gained a new dimension:

Laura, when dressed, was (as I sang before)
A pretty woman as was ever seen,
Fresh as the Angel o'er a new inn door,
Or frontespiece of a new Magazine,
With all the fashions which the last
month wore,
Coloured, and silver paper leaved between
That and the title-page, for fear the Press
Should soil with parts of speech the parts
of dress.
(LORD BYRON, BEPPO, 1818)

The inevitable abbreviation *mag* is surprisingly old, dating from the early nineteenth century. The term *magazine* applied to radio and television programmes that contain miscellaneous items of general interest arose in the 1930s because of their similarity in content to printed periodicals.

magpie
a black and white bird of the crow family; a collector of bits and pieces

*I never see **magpies** myself without repeating the old rhyme: 'One for sorrow, Two for mirth, Three for a death, Four for a birth, Five, you will shortly be In great company.'*
(A C BENSON, ALONG THE ROAD, 1913)

*I wonder if it wasn't the biting cold that moved us to chatter like **magpies**.*
(EMILIE CARIES, TR. AVRIEL H GOLDBERG, A WILD HERB SOUP, 1991)

*I pick at the journal (this **magpie** scholarship), struggle with the Origin, home in on the letters and the Autobiography.*
(GRAHAM SWIFT, EVER AFTER, 1992)

Guillaume Bélibaste, a fourteenth-century peasant from the village of Montaillou, not far from the French town of Albi, was seized with foreboding one day when he noticed a magpie cross his path three times. His companion laughed at him, telling him to *take no notice of signs of birds and other auguries of that kind*, adding that *only old women bother about such things* (Emmanuel Le Roi Ladurie, MONTAILLOU, 1978). Guillaume was not alone in his superstitions. Similar misgivings existed throughout Europe, where the magpie has long been looked upon as a bird of ill omen. In England people would bow, cross their fingers or raise their hats to a magpie. In Staffordshire they would spit three times over their right shoulder and chant *Devil, Devil, I defy thee,* to ward off any evil influence. In folklore the magpie is denounced for not appearing completely in black at the crucifixion and in Scotland it is also charged with treasuring a droplet of the devil's blood under its tongue. But for all its sinister reputation, the bird's name has a surprisingly homely origin.

Magpie is a compound noun. The second element *pie* is a thirteenth-century borrowing of Old French *pie*, from Latin *pīca*, 'magpie', and for several centuries it stood alone as the English term for the bird. *Pie* remains the modern French word for 'magpie'. In sixteenth-century English, however, the bird began to be known as a *madge*, a *maggot-pie* or a *maggoty-pie*. Birds were often called by popular names such as *Robin redbreast*; in this case pet forms of *Margery* and *Margaret* were used, possibly because they were sometimes applied to talkative women and the magpie is known for its noisy chattering. *Magpie* is probably a shortened version of the earlier *maggoty-pie*.

☛ The magpie is responsible for other words arising from its habits or appearance:

It is thought by some that the pastries that have been a mainstay of the English diet since medieval times were called *pies* as a joke, the various ingredients in the filling reminding the diners of the odd bits and pieces a magpie might have collected together.

Alluding to the magpie's plumage, *piebald* usually denotes black and white patched colouring. *Bald* derives from *balled*, 'streaked', which comes from the Welsh *bal* meaning 'with a white streak on the forehead', a term applied to a horse.

It seems that the showy magpie has always been a bird to be noticed.

malaria
a fever transmitted by mosquito

*The clinic was cramped, Amaka said. She had gotten her chloroquine injections there the last time she had **malaria**, and the nurse had boiled water on a smoky kerosene stove.*
(CHIMAMANDA NGOZI ADICHIE, PURPLE HIBISCUS, 2004)

*I am terrified of getting bitten by a mosquito because my mum says I will get **malaria** and die. I cover myself with a thick sheen of insect repellent. I want to bring a mosquito net with me from the hotel but Clare says it will look silly with my hat.*
(STEPHEN MERCHANT IN BALES WORLD MAGAZINE, SUMMER 2009)

The death of Pope Alexander VI (father of the infamous Borgias of Renaissance Italy) was probably brought about by a spot of political intrigue. It was, however, frequently explained away as a case of malaria, a convincing story as the often fatal disease, which was characterised by recurring bouts of fever, struck Rome almost every summer. The Italians called it *mal'aria*, a contraction of *mala aria*, 'bad air', believing it to result from the fetid air rising from the marshes in the surrounding countryside.

The term entered English in the first half of the eighteenth century, initially with reference to the conditions in Rome, since English already had the word *ague*, which had denoted the disease since the fourteenth century. Horace Walpole wrote in 1740 of *A horrid thing called the mal'aria, that comes to Rome every summer and kills one*. Three-quarters of a century later, Joseph Forsyth, describing his travels in Italy, said that *this malaria is an evil more active than the Romans, and continues to increase*.

Only at the beginning of the twentieth century was it finally established that the disease was transmitted by the bite of female mosquitoes hosting the malarial parasite and not by the rank air of marshes and swamps. The name remains unchanged, however, a testimony to earlier medical understanding.

For another illness with an Italian name, see INFLUENZA.

mall
a covered pedestrian area of shops

*Now and again the great, empty landscape is punctured by an isolated shopping **mall**, surrounded by cars.*
(JOHN MORTIMER, SUMMER OF A DORMOUSE, 2000)

...we have come to this 4.2-million-square-foot behemoth – the mother of all **malls**, *a pioneer in the field of destination retailing, and a sprawling, visceral economic indicator – for some talk therapy with shoppers, retailers and management.*
(NEW YORK TIMES,
31 JANUARY 2009)

There can be few towns that do not have a shopping mall at their centre or, increasingly, on the outskirts. These covered, heated precincts are built along American lines but the history of the name originated in Italy and has close associations with London.

Pallamaglio was a popular game in fifteenth-century Italy. As its name implies, it was played with a *palla*, 'hard ball', and a *maglio*, 'mallet', (from Latin *malleus*, 'hammer'). Play took place in a long alley over which a metal hoop was hung. The game became popular in France, where it was known as *pallemaille*, and then in Scotland, where it was played by Mary Queen of Scots, who was connected to the French court through both her mother and her first marriage. An accusatory document in the Calendar of State Papers, Scotland, says that the sporty Mary was playing at Seaton *richt oppinlie at the feildis with the palmall and goif, and on the nycht planelie abusing hir body with Boithwell.* The game was probably introduced to the English court by Mary's son James I of England (and VI of Scotland), who in BASILICON DORON (1599), a guide written to instruct his son Prince Henry on how to be an exemplary monarch, lists *palle maille* among the sports he might enjoy.

During the seventeenth century the game became increasingly popular at court and was known as *pall-mall* or, vulgarly, *pell-mell*. Charles II excelled at it and played it in St James's Park. In his diary for 2 April 1661 Samuel Pepys records seeing *pelemele* played there for the very first time by the Duke of York. So favoured was the royal sport that in that same year the traffic between Charing Cross and St James's Palace was rerouted because dust from the carriage wheels reduced visibility down the new royal alley that had been constructed just inside the park wall. *Pall Mall* and *The Mall*, two wide streets near St James's Park, are sites of former alleys.

The popularity of the game was not enduring, however, and when it waned the tree-lined alley known as The Mall became a fashionable place to promenade. From the early eighteenth century other towns then had their *malls* – shaded walks along which to stroll. The word might have faded into obscurity had it not been given a new lease of life in American English in the mid-twentieth century, when it was dusted down and applied first to a pedestrian area lined with shops and then to a covered shopping precinct.

For other words with their origins in the history of London, see BEDLAM and MEWS.

manure
dung used to fertilise soil

I managed to retain two hundred pounds, which I posted to my mother for her birthday. She was thrilled, and called me up. 'Darling, what a lot of money! I'm going to treat myself to a "Rambling Rector" and some horse **manure***. Thank you, angel-cake, thank you so much!'*
(JULIAN CLARY,
MURDER MOST FAB, 2007)

*He sees the world for what it is,
a mountain of* **manure***,
and aspires to a life beyond it,
to a kingdom pure.*
(ROGER MCGOUGH'S ADAPTATION OF
TARTUFFE BY MOLIÈRE, 2008)

When Oliver Goldsmith in his NATURAL HISTORY (1776) wrote of a man who *is at the trouble neither of manuring his grounds, nor bringing in his harvests*, he did not mean that he had neglected to spread fertiliser but that the ground had not been cultivated. *Manure* was originally a verb meaning 'to till and tend the land by hand'. It originated in the Latin expression *manū operārī*, 'to work by hand' (from *manus*, 'hand' and *operārī*, 'to work'). This verb passed into Middle English around 1400 as *manour*, by way of Medieval Latin *manuoperārī*, Old French *manovrer*, 'to till', and Anglo-French *mainoverer*.

Dung had long been used to feed the soil and various ingenious methods were devised to collect and spread it. A thirteenth-century verse extolling the usefulness of every part of the sheep claims *Of the sheep is cast away nothing*, adding that *To the Lordes great profit goeth his entire dung*. At night the sheep would be gathered together on the fields owned by the lord so that their dung could enrich the soil. Shepherds were also instructed to keep a look-out for sparse places in the pasture and to entice the flock to assemble there by constructing a scratching post (Dorothy Hartley, FOOD IN ENGLAND, 1954).

Dung is an old term of Germanic origin, the earliest written record appearing around the turn of the eleventh century. For centuries this basic, honest word served its down-to-earth purpose until, in the first half of the sixteenth century, it was joined by a new noun, *manure*, derived from the verb *to manure*, so that from the term for 'to cultivate the land' came a new word for the 'dung' that was spread upon it to make that cultivation successful. Exactly why this happened is hard to say. Some suggest euphemism. Whatever the reason, this new noun influenced the old verb from which it sprang, so that, by the end of the six-teenth century, it had the additional sense of 'to spread fertiliser'.

☛ Old French *manovrer* became modern French *manoeuvrer*, which gradually lost its connection with farming, becoming instead a military term, 'to make strategic moves'. It was borrowed into English in this sense as *manoeuvre* in the eighteenth century.

Latin *manus* gave the adjective *manuālis*, 'of the hand', source of English *manual* (15th cent).

English *operate* (17th cent) derives from Latin *operārī*.

marathon

a race of 26 miles 385 yards or 42.195 km; anything of long duration that calls for endurance

*At first doctors thought Lorenzo Amato, 13, had had a stroke, because he couldn't speak or understand what was going on around him. But they later diagnosed severe 'mental detachment' caused by a **marathon** session on his new Playstation.*
(THE WEEK, 29 NOVEMBER 2008)

*But be warned – unless you're about to embark on some serious training for a **marathon**, getting active is not a green light to consume extra protein and huge amounts of carbohydrates.*
(GOOD HOUSEKEEPING, MAY 2009)

Marathon was a village in Attica, Greece, about 42 km (26 miles) from Athens. In 490 BC it was the site of a celebrated victory by the Greeks over the invading Persians. The sturdy mes-senger Pheidippides is reputed to have run from Marathon to Athens to announce the Persian defeat, only to fall down dead when he had done so. When the Olympic Games were revived in Athens in 1896, a long-distance run from *Marathon* to the capital was included in the programme.

Curiously, races covering such taxing distances were never run in ancient Greece. Nor did the modern race remain a purely Olympic event for long. The following year saw the first Boston marathon and, since then, many cities have organised annual international marathons through their streets covering the prescribed distance of 42.195 km (26 miles 385 yards). The nonsensical distance dates back to the 1908 Olympics, which were held in London. A distance of 26 miles plus a lap of the stadium was decided upon, but this was eventually reduced by 201 yards in order to give those in the royal box a better view of the closing moments of the race.

It was not long before use of the word *marathon* widened to embrace other endurance contests. The DAILY CHRONICLE of 5 November 1908 reported on a competition entitled *The Murphy Marathon*, which involved the peeling of a quarter of a hundredweight (about 12.5kg) of potatoes. Besides events such as these, the noun also denotes activities of any kind which are of long duration and require sustained effort.

marmalade
a type of jam, usually made from oranges or other citrus fruits

*This **marmalade** makes a great breakfast treat, spread thickly on buttered country toast or brioche. If, like me, you don't worry too much about the calories, top it with a dollop of crème fraîche. Close your eyes and you could be in Provence.*
(PAUL GAYLER, FLAVOURS OF THE WORLD, 2002)

I worked out that I could copy the familiar Disney characters on to paper and recreate all the colours needed to fill them in using

*...foodstuffs. The brown of Owl could be made using Marmite, the orange of Pooh using **marmalade**, the pale yellow of Rabbit with lemon curd, and so on.*
(ANDREW COLLINS, WHERE DID IT ALL GO RIGHT?, 2003)

The ancient Greeks had a fruit called the *melimēlon*, 'honey-apple', a compound of *meli*, 'honey', and *mēlon*, 'apple'. It was produced by grafting an apple tree onto a quince stock. The fruit might be preserved in a kind of jam, or it might be placed in a jar, covered with willow twigs and topped up with runny honey, the resulting syrup being known as *melomēli* (Don and Patricia Brothwell, FOOD IN ANTIQUITY, 1969). The Romans, too, knew the honey-apple, which they called *melimēlum*, and its delicious honey syrup. Latin *melimēlum* was borrowed into Portuguese as *marmelo*, 'quince'.

The Portuguese made a preserve from the fruit which they called *marmelada*, and this recipe was successful in other parts of the Continent. The French borrowing *marmelade* was taken into English at the beginning of the sixteenth century and then had various spellings until it settled down as *marmalade* in the eighteenth century. The original preserve was a solid jelly that could be cut into squares. In her book FOOD IN ENGLAND (1954), Dorothy Hartley records the following recipe:

QUINCE MARMALADE
A very old and delicious recipe.
Collect your quinces, and pare and chop up at least half of them, including the least ripe, just cover with water, and set to boil to pulp. When soft rub all through a sieve. To this golden red thickness now add the remainder of the quinces, pared, cored, and cut into neat sections. Set the pan back to simmer gently and steadily, till the whole quinces are almost soft, and the pulp pretty thick (stir well, or it will burn). Now add

sugar, 3lb to a quart of the pulp. When the sugar has dissolved, boil fast till it sets when tried. It should be very firm, and a dark bright-red colour. Slices cut from it make good garnishes for plain white 'creams' or it can be melted and used as a sauce over blancmanges.

Marmalade was not just delicious to eat, it was also regarded as an aphrodisiac and, in the seventeenth century, prostitutes were referred to as *marmalade madams*. After a heavy meal *marmalade* could also be a useful stopper to the stomach. John Lyly alludes to this in EUPHUES AND HIS ENGLAND (1580) when he writes: *Therefore you must giue him leaue after euery meale to cloase his stomacke with Loue, as with Marmalade*.

Fynes Moryson recommended the preserve to any queasy traveller eager for foreign parts. In his ITINERARY (1617) he discusses the unpleasantness of seasickness. The reader is cautioned against restraining vomiting altogether, since *that working of the Sea is very healthful*. Instead he is to eat as normal *and after eating, let him seal his stomach with Marmalade*.

By the seventeenth century other English fruit jams were also called *marmalade*, thus severing the unique connection with the quince. In the eighteenth century orange marmalade was produced from bitter Seville oranges, eventually to become the golden preserve of the British breakfast table.

See also TREACLE.

maroon

to put a person ashore on a deserted coast; to abandon a person without means of escape

*Looking up at the sky above St Mark's, he fanned his arms in imitation of a ground-crew technician on the Tarmac signalling to an aeroplane pilot. His motions were so exaggerated that he could just as easily have been taken for a man **marooned** on a desert island desperately trying to catch the attention of a passing plane.*
(JOHN BERENDT,
THE CITY OF FALLING ANGELS, 2005)

*He popped to the kitchen during the ad break and returned with a cup of coffee to find the chap entering his last couple of weeks, **marooned** almost permanently on his sofa and weeping a little in the small hours.*
(MARK HADDON,
A SPOT OF BOTHER, 2006)

Cimarrón was a term the Spanish applied in the sixteenth century to the black slaves in the West Indies and Guyana who, unable to tolerate the harsh conditions of colonialist rule, succeeded in fleeing to remote mountain and forest regions where they lived wild. (The adjective *cimarrón* is still current in Spanish where, applied to animals, it distinguishes the feral from the domesticated.) The term may derive from Spanish *cima*, meaning 'summit, top' (from Latin *cȳma*, 'the sprout of a plant', from Greek *kuma*, 'a swollen thing, a young sprout') and therefore denote 'living on mountain tops'. The French equivalent was *marron*, an abbreviated borrowing of *cimarrón*. This was taken into English in the seventeenth century to refer to fugitive slaves and their descendants. Attitudes towards them can be gauged by John Davies' description in his HISTORY OF THE CARIBBY ISLES (1666):

They will run away and get into the Mountains and Forests, where they live like so many beasts; then they are call'd Marons, that is to say Savages.

In the 1720s the verb *maroon* appeared to describe the practices of pirates who would leave men stranded on deserted islands or stretches of isolated coastline as a punishment, forcing them to scratch a living in the wild like the maroons. Robert Louis Stevenson wrote of it in TREASURE ISLAND (1883):

His voice sounded hoarse and awkward, like a rusty lock. 'I'm poor Ben Gunn, I am; and I haven't spoke with a Christian these three years.'

'Three years!' I cried. 'Were you shipwrecked?'

'Nay, mate,' said he; 'marooned.'

I had heard the word, and I knew it stood for a horrible kind of punishment common enough among the buccaneers, in which the offender is put ashore with a little powder and shot and left behind on some desolate and distant island.

Modern development since the early twentieth century removes the idea of punishment but retains the meaning of being trapped without hope of rescue. One can be marooned by a flood or in rural solitude.

mascot
a charm, animal or person that brings luck

*Woolworths may be disappearing from the high street but it is proving a hit on the internet. There has been keen bidding for staff uniforms and other items of memorabilia on eBay, the online auction site. Wooly, the store's promotional **mascot**, closing down posters and even a mailbag are among the souvenirs on sale.*
(SUNDAY TELEGRAPH, 4 JANUARY 2009)

*The headaches currently faced by telecoms giant BT would have the firm's one-time **mascot**, Buzby, falling off his perch in shock. The yellow bird's catchphrase years ago was 'make someone happy with a phone call' – but there will be few investors in cheerful mood following the group's annual results next month.*
(EVENING STANDARD, 17 APRIL 2009)

Edmond Audran's comic opera LA MASCOTTE had its première on 29 December 1880. French *mascotte* comes from a Provençal word *mascotto*, meaning 'bewitchment, spell', a diminutive of *masco*, 'witch', 'sorcerer', from Late Latin *masca*, 'witch'. The operetta tells the story of Bettina, a charming farm girl who keeps turkeys. Bettina is a *mascotte*; she has the gift of bringing good fortune to those to whom she belongs as long as she remains a virgin, and many seek her out as their good-luck charm.

Such was the success of Audran's operetta in France that Henry Farnie and Robert Reece presented it in English the following year and it became instantly popular among British audiences. The term *mascot* was soon being used to denote 'a person or thing kept to bring good luck'. In his story of active service with the Flying Corps on the Western Front during the First World War, Lt E M Roberts described the superstition of many of the pilots:

Each man had his own little fetish. It was known as the pocket-piece or mascot. In some cases it might be a dice or a playing-card... In other cases it might be a locket, then again a medal, while many of us carried little woollen dolls.
(FLYING FIGHTER: AN AMERICAN ABOVE THE LINES IN FRANCE, 1918)

By the mid-twentieth century the word was also being used to denote 'an emblem':

No mascot shall be carried by a motor vehicle. where it is likely to strike any person with whom the vehicle may collide.
(HALSBURY'S STATUTORY INSTRUMENTS, 1955)

masterpiece

an outstanding example of craftsmanship or artistry

*Within the temple stands the representation of Athena Parthenos herself. The **masterpiece** of Phidias stands resplendent in gold and ivory.*
(PHILIP MATYSAK, ANCIENT ATHENS ON FIVE DRACHMAS A DAY, 2007)

*A voyage of a more quietly intriguing sort is pursued by Eric Karpeles in his quirky but charming compendium Paintings in Proust…a beautifully presented anthology of the images that inspired that most visual of **masterpieces** A la recherche du temps perdu.*
(THE TIMES, 29 NOVEMBER 2008)

Medieval guilds were trade associations formed for the mutual assistance of their members. They were made up of master craftsmen who were recognised for their expertise in a particular field: cobblers, carpenters, bakers, cutlers, dyers, etc. The guilds aimed to regulate the number of craftsmen engaged in their trade and to control the standard of workmanship produced. A young apprentice would serve a master for several years to learn the basics of his chosen trade. He would then become a journeyman or day worker and would be entitled to a salary. He would learn the finer points of his trade and work towards presenting his *masterpiece*, a sample of his work, to his guild. If this was recognised as quality craftsmanship, and if the town could support another business, he would become a 'master' of the guild, enjoying all the benefits of such an association, and would be free to set up in trade himself.

The compound *masterpiece* is a translation of either Dutch *meesterstuk* or German *Meisterstück*. The word *master* comes ultimately from Latin *magister*, 'master'. It was used to describe a 'skilled workman qualified to teach his craft' from the beginning of the fourteenth century. *Piece* came into Middle English in the thirteenth century by way of Anglo-French and Old French *pece*. This was a borrowing of Medieval Latin *pecia*, *petia*, from the unattested Gaulish word *pettia*.

First recorded examples of *masterpiece* date from the very beginning of the seventeenth century, the word denoting a 'product of great skill or outstanding artistic merit', or a 'masterly achievement': *Man is heav'ns Master-peece* (Francis Quarles, EMBLEMES, 1635).

maudlin

intoxicated to the point of tears; mawkishly sentimental

*The Burns Supper, which took place on or about the anniversary of Robert Burns's birth, was of variable quality. In a year when there was a good speaker, the address to the Immortal Memory could be moving. But the occasion could rapidly drift into **maudlin** reflections on the ploughman poet and his carousing in Ayrshire, nothing of which Scotland could be proud, she thought.*
(ALEXANDER MCCALL SMITH, FRIENDS, LOVERS, CHOCOLATE, 2005)

*Fortunately, this heavy message is leavened with lashings of black humour, particularly from the excellent Evets, who never allows his performance to veer into the **maudlin**.*
(THE TIMES, 6 DECEMBER 2008)

Magdala was a town which once stood on the western shore of the Sea of Galilee, probably on the site of the present-day Khirbet Mejdel. Its name derived from Hebrew *migdal*, meaning 'tower'. The town, or its immediate vicinity, was the home of Mary Magdalene, a disciple of Jesus. Greek *Magdalēnā*, 'belonging to Magdala' became *Magdalena* in Late Latin. This was taken into Old French as *Madelaine* and borrowed into Middle English as *Maudeleyn*, becoming *Maudlin* by the early seventeenth century.

According to Luke's Gospel 8: 2, Mary Magdelene became a follower of Jesus after he delivered her from seven demons. The Bible also tells us that she was present in Jerusalem for Christ's crucifixion and was one of the group of women who went to his empty tomb on the morning of the resurrection. The two angels inside ask why she is weeping. Also, in Luke 7, there is a portrait of a woman who, overwhelmed by her sin (said to be that of prostitution), washed Jesus's feet with her tears of repentance, wiped them with her hair and anointed them with costly ointment. The Bible does not disclose this particular woman's identity but the church has traditionally identifed her as Mary Magdalene. Not surprisingly, therefore, she has been shown in Christian art as a weeping figure, shedding tears of grief or repentance. For this reason, since the early seventeenth century, *maudlin* has meant 'weepy, lachrymose'.

Within a few years, however, the tears shed had an over-emotional, senti-mental quality about them. This is particularly evident in the expression *maudlin drunk*, which denoted the tearful stage of intoxication *when a fellow wil weepe for kindnes in the midst of his Ale and kisse you* (Thomas Nashe, THE APOLOGIE OF PIERCE PENNILESSE, 1592). In SCARRONIDES (1667), a poetic burlesque of Virgil's AENEID, Charles Cotton writes:

> *From Dido then a belch did flie...*
> *And tears ran down her fair long Nose,*
> *The Queen was Maudlin I suppose.*

The term is still current in this context:

The whiskey bottle had emptied to the point at which Father Keogh turned maudlin.
(ROY HATTERSLEY, THE MAKER'S MARK, 1990)

There is a fine example of *maudlin* in an essay by Thomas Babington Macaulay published in the EDINBURGH REVIEW in 1828. Macaulay writes of *the salaried Viceroy of France beslobbering his brother and his courtiers in a fit of maudlin affection.*

There are Magdalen colleges at both Oxford and Cambridge universities. In spite of the spelling, the name is pronounced as *maudlin.*

For another word deriving from a corruption of a biblical name, see BEDLAM.

maverick
an independent, strong-willed individual

*With her dyed blonde hair and funky fashion sense, Yumi looks like the **maverick**, but in fact she is far more typical of the Japanese girls at Churchill's than Hiroko.*
(TONY PARSONS,
ONE FOR MY BABY, 2001)

*Don't work with **mavericks** if you are conventional and crave security and predictability. As well as being original thinkers, mavericks challenge bosses and have little regard for hierarchy and cap-doffing.*
(THE OBSERVER, 9 SEPTEMBER 2001)

Samuel Augustus Maverick (1803–70) was a lawyer who lived in Texas. On one occasion he was given a herd of 400 cattle in settlement of a debt. In Texas cattle were usually branded by their owners to prevent theft and then left to roam free. Maverick had little interest in ranching and, when the calves were born, neglected to brand them. It is said that unscrupulous neighbours would watch out for the calves and mark them as their own. These young, unmarked cattle became known among the ranchers thereabouts as *mavericks*, and this term caught on and spread. In 1867 Joseph McCoy, writing about the cattle trade in Texas, Colorado and New Mexico, said that *the term maverick which was formerly applied to unbranded yearlings is now applied to every calf which can be separated from the mother cow.*

By 1880 *maverick* had come to denote to 'a dissenter', 'a wanderer', 'a person of independent mind'. A Texan journalist writing in the GALVESTON DAILY NEWS (1880) vowed to *crush radicals, greenbackers and all other foes of democracy, especially those independent gentlemen, those political mavericks.* The word in this sense was taken into English a decade later.

Nowadays, any person rejecting the standard orthodoxies of society, church or state might be termed a maverick, and mavericks in politics, who refuse to toe the party line, enliven a bland political landscape.

mews
a small street of houses and flats in converted stabling

Our route was certainly a singular one. Holmes's knowledge of the byways of London was extraordinary, and on this occasion he passed rapidly and with an assured step through a network of mews and stables, the very existence of which I had never known.
(SIR ARTHUR CONAN DOYLE, THE RETURN OF SHERLOCK HOLMES, 1905)

Mrs Ada Harris…'does' for clientele in Chelsea and Belgravia, moving from house to flat to mews, letting herself in with latchkeys on relentless, silent scenes of rumpled beds, dirty dishes, scummy baths.
(MAGGIE FERGUSSON IN SLIGHTLY FOXED, WINTER 2008)

Mews addresses are now considered very chic. At one time, however, they were inhabited by hawks. A *mew* was a cage used to confine hawks, especially while they were moulting. The word was borrowed into Middle English in the fourteenth century from Old French *mue*, 'a moulting', a derivative of *muer*, 'to moult', from Latin *mūtāre*, 'to change'.

In 1377 the *King's Mews* were sited at Charing Cross. These burnt down in 1534 and purpose-built stables were erected on the site, although the former name was retained. Things royal invariably set a fashion, and in the seventeenth century the term was applied to other alleys or courtyards containing stabling. When horses no longer had need of them the stables were given over to human habitation. Records of *mews* housing date back to the early nineteenth century.

For another hawking term see HAGGARD, and for another word with its origins in the history of royal London, see MALL.

milliner
a maker of hats for women

'A hat for a lady is always a poor choice,' said Oscar, holding the moment as he stirred his coffee and considered his next thought. *'In ancient Athens there was neither a **milliner** nor a milliner's bill. These things were absolutely unknown, so great was the civilisation.'*
(GYLES BRANDRETH, OSCAR WILDE AND THE CANDLELIGHT MURDERS, 2007)

*As a designer for Philip Somerville, **milliner**-to-the-Queen, Dillon Wallwork has been dressing the heads of some of the UK's most photographed women, including Diana, Princess of Wales, for nearly quarter of a century.*
(THE TIMES, 9 MAY 2009)

Today Milan is one of the fashion capitals of the world. It is not a new reputation, it seems, for the origins of the word *milliner* lie with those decorative Milanese finishes and touches that make an outfit really special.

Originally *Milaner* simply denoted 'an inhabitant of Milan', but, in the sixteenth century, the city became known for its production of ribbons and fancy cloth and for its prettily trimmed capes, gloves and bonnets. Soon a *milaner* (also found in a variety of other spellings, including the one used today) was no longer necessarily Milanese but simply 'a vendor of luxury fripperies made in Milan'. By the nineteenth century the term was being applied to someone who made and decorated women's hats.

A good milliner needed more than nimble fingers, however. He or she also needed an appreciative eye. According to the humorist John Gay in an article for that short-lived periodical THE GUARDIAN (1713), *The milliner must be thoroughly versed in physiognomy; in the choice of ribbons she must have a particular regard to the complexion.*

miniature
a small, detailed picture, often a portrait; tiny, very small

I'd peeped, on my way to the lav, into their bedroom. Twin beds, pink and blue floral counterpanes with frilled valances and matching cushions, twin china shepherdesses topped with pleated lampshades, a shelf of **miniature** *liqueurs, a single kidney-shaped dressing-table.*
(MICHÈLE ROBERTS,
READER, I MARRIED HIM, 2004)

The spiritual and the saucy, the ethereal and the lewd entwine in the intricate **miniatures** *and lavish marginal illustrations that might on the surface be all about piety, but laughter and ribaldry are never far behind.*
(REVIEW OF 'THE MACCLESFIELD PSALTER' BY STELLA PANAYOTOVA, IN THE TIMES, 29 NOVEMBER 2008)

A reasonable supposition might be that *miniature*, with its sense of 'reduced size', belongs to a class of words deriving from Latin *min-*, 'less', along with *minimum*, *minute*, *mini*, *diminish* and *diminutive*. Surprisingly, the origin of the word has nothing to do with smallness at all, but is found in a red pigment that was used to rubricate initial letters or titles in handwritten manuscripts. The pigment, red lead or cinnabar, was known as *minium* in Latin. This gave rise to the Medieval Latin verb *miniāre* meaning 'to colour with red lead' and, by extension, 'to illuminate a manuscript'. Italian borrowed the verb as *miniare*, and the derivative *miniatura* denoted 'an adornment or picture on the illuminated page'.

Miniature was borrowed into English in the sixteenth century. John Evelyn in his diary for 2 September 1680 remarks upon some breviaries that have *a great deal of miniature and monkish painting and gilding*. The diminutive size of these illustrations, together with the similarity to the Latin words mentioned earlier, led to the term's later application to small-scale portraits or to representations which were much reduced in size.

Miniature has been used as an adjective since the early eighteenth century and now denotes anything that is smaller than one might expect, from golf games to railways and from poodles to the bottles of spirits given out on aircraft or standing in the hotel mini-bar.

minion
a subordinate; a slavish follower

*Downstairs, the kitchen was abuzz. Mrs Townsend had the stove fire raging and was barking orders at three village women hired to help. She smoothed her apron over her generous middle and surveyed her **minions** as they basted hundreds of tiny quail.*
(KATE MORTON,
THE HOUSE AT RIVERTON, 2006)

*Where the King went, society tended to follow. If he took mistresses among his friends' wives, then so could and would those of his **minions** with both the time and the inclination.*
(FRANCES OSBORNE, THE BOLTER, 2008)

When the French exclaim over an attractive toddler or a cuddly toy, the adjective *mignon* readily springs to their lips. The English equivalent is 'sweet' or 'darling'. *Mignon* (from Old French *mignot*, through Gaulish, related to Old High German *minna*, 'love') came into English around the turn of the sixteenth century to denote 'a darling, a favourite'. This might be a lady-love, or the favourite of a sovereign. Before the century was out, however, it had become a term of contempt, denoting 'a mistress' or 'a servile follower'. The mistress has slipped into obscurity but the servile follower is alive and well. Today he is the 'dependent underdog', the subordinate who slavishly performs menial or routine tasks.

mint
the place where legal currency is coined; in perfect condition

*An admitted purist, Mr Spowers explains that there are two ways of restoring a classic racer. One is to replace whatever is necessary to bring it back to **mint** condition, what he calls 'chocolate box restoration'. This always sells best.*
(THE TIMES, 6 DECEMBER 2008)

*A few years ago his visits to the **mint**, founded more than 800 years ago, might have seemed eccentric. No longer. From the Russian Georgy Pobedonosets to the American Eagle, gold coin production is being cranked up in mints around the world to satisfy customers believing the assets may be immune to the global financial crisis.*
(THE INDEPENDENT, 5 APRIL 2009)

The Roman goddess Juno Regina, queen of heaven, was the wife of Jupiter and a member of the Capitoline Triad. Her temple on the Capitoline Hill was built by grateful subjects, following her warning of an imminent invasion by the Gauls in 344 BC. This event gave rise to the ancient but probably erroneous supposition that another of her titles, *Juno Monēta*, was derived from the Latin verb *monēre*, 'to warn'. The goddess's temple contained the Roman mint and the epithet *Monēta* was applied both to this and to the coins produced there. *Monēta* made its way into English along two different routes.

Borrowed into West Germanic, probably as *munita*, it reached Old English as *mynet* where, from at least the eighth century, it meant 'a coin'. In the fifteenth century the Middle English form *mynt* (modern English *mint*) began to denote a place where legal currency was coined, the chief officer there being known as the *Maister of the Mynt*. The derived adjective meaning 'perfect' or 'unused', as if freshly minted, dates from the beginning of the twentieth century.

Borrowed into Old French, the Latin *monēta*, 'money', became *moneie* (modern French has *monnaie* for 'loose change') and this was taken into Middle English in the late thirteenth century as *moneye*, 'money'.

For other words concerning temples, see ANATHEMA and FANATIC.

mob
a disorderly crowd (out for trouble)

There was an eddy in the mass of human bodies, and the woman with helmeted head and tawny cheeks rushed out to the very brink of the stream. She put out her hands, shouted something, and all that wild **mob** *took up the shout in a roaring chorus of articulated, rapid, breathless utterance.*
(JOSEPH CONRAD,
HEART OF DARKNESS, 1902)

Giovanni and Dario...are originally from Naples. I cannot picture it. I cannot imagine shy, studious, sympathetic Giovanni as a young boy amongst this – and I don't use the word lightly – **mob.**
(ELIZABETH GILBERT,
EAT PRAY LOVE, 2006)

The Latin term *mŏbile vulgus* (from *movēre*, 'to move') literally means the 'moveable crowd', 'moveable' being understood in the sense of 'fickle, easily influenced, excitable'. It is rendered as *the moeuable poeple* in Chaucer's translation of BOETHIUS (c. 1374). Towards the end of the sixteenth century the Latin term came into vogue to denote 'the common people', 'the rabble', and during the seventeenth century was often abbreviated to *mobile*, pronounced in three syllables as in Latin:

> *Tho' the mobile haul*
> *Like the devil and all,*
> *For religion, property, justice and laws.*
> (NICHOLAS ROWE, SONG OF AN
> ORANGE, STATE POEMS, 1716)

By the late 1680s the term was being further shortened to *mob*. This trend had considerable momentum, as Nares points out. In the preface to DON SEBASTIAN (1690), Dryden uses the word *mobile* but two years later, in the preface to CLEOMENES, he writes:

Yet, to gratfy the barbarous part of my audience, I gave them a short rabble-scene, because the mob (as they call them) are represented by Plutarch and Polybius, with the same character of baseness and cowardice, which are here described.

The brackets indicate Dryden's hesitation over the acceptability of the term. His trepidation was perhaps justifiable, for other men of letters deplored the adoption of abbreviations as new words. The British essayist Sir Richard Steele (1672–1729), writing for his periodical THE TATLER, was among them: *I have done my utmost for some years past to stop the progress of 'mob'...but have been plainly borne down by numbers, and betrayed by those who promised to assist me.* However, he was not let down by his friend Joseph Addison, who wrote in Steele's SPECTATOR (1711): *It is perhaps this Humour of speaking no more than we needs must which has so curtailed some of our Words...as in mob. rep. pos. incog. and the like.*

But the rage for abbreviation continued and was later ridiculed by Swift. In his POLITE CONVERSATION (1738), a satire upon the conversation of fashionable society of the period, he wrote of *Abbreviations exquisitely refined; As Pozz for Positively, Mobb for Mobile.*

Just under two decades later Dr Johnson capitulated by making room for *mob* in his DICTIONARY (1755), along with the longer *mobile*. It would seem that, once the fickle *mŏbile vulgus* has made up its mind, there is nothing the purist with his pen can do to stop it.

money
coins or bills

She borrowed **money***. It was against everything her father had preached – neither a borrower nor a lender be – and he would be furious if he found out.*
(MARGARET FORSTER, KEEPING THE
WORLD AWAY, 2006)

See MINT.

muscle

tissue that stretches and relaxes to bring about movement in the body

The horse was dying to run – she could feel his **muscles** *tensing beneath his satin coat – and Anna had the sense that when they had cleared the marsh she was going to have to let the animal air it out.*
(CHRIS BOHJALIAN,
SKELETONS AT THE FEAST, 2008)

Walking uphill will burn around a third more calories than on the flat and help strengthen bones and **muscles**.
(GOOD HOUSEKEEPING, MAY 2009)

The Romans, doubtless gazing at the firm and finely toned bodies of their athletes, conceived the fanciful notion that when the muscles in the upper arm were flexed, their shape and movement resembled that of a mouse. The Latin word for 'muscle' was therefore *mūsculus*, a diminutive form of *mūs*, 'mouse'. The word was taken into the Romance languages, coming into English in the sixteenth century by way of French *muscle*.

In spite of its different spelling, *mussel* also derives from *mūsculus*. The Romans were very fond of eating shellfish, which they smothered in fancy sauces. They ate mussels fried or boiled with a sauce based on oil, herbs and honey or oil and wine. To the Roman eye the colour and form of this small delicacy also suggested a little mouse, hence *mūsculus*. Alternatively, some say the perceived likeness was to a muscle. Either way, it needed a particularly vivid Roman imagination to see the connection. As for the spelling of the word in English, there is scope for confusion. For several hundred years after its arrival into Old English, our contemporary word *mussel* was spelt *muscle*. From the fifteenth century onwards, there is erratic evidence of the double *s*, apparently influenced by

Middle Low German *mussel*, a word derived from the unattested Vulgar Latin *muscula*, a feminine form of Latin *mūsculus*. The progress of this alternative spelling was slow, however, and it was not finally established until the last quarter of the nineteenth century.

☞ This obsessive likening of things to mice was not unique to the Romans. *Musk*, which was widely used as a perfume base and for medicinal purposes, derives from Sanskrit *muska*. This term was generally used to mean 'testicle', but was also applied to the scrotum-shaped pouch of the musk deer and to the pungent oil secreted by the gland. Originally, however, it meant 'little mouse', being a diminutive of Sanskrit *mūs*, 'mouse'. *Muska* was borrowed into Persian as *mushk*, into Greek as *moskhos* and into Late Latin as *muscus*. It came into Middle English as *muske* in the fourteenth century by way of Old French *musc*.

Imagined likenesses and connections also provide the etymology for HEARSE, LIZARD, LOBSTER and VANILLA.

mussel

an edible mollusc with a grey-black shell

For five miles they stretched along the beaches, a gruesome line of dead starfish. Fishermen and bird-watchers at Pegwell Bay near Sandwich, Kent, discovered a 'carpet' of thousands of the creatures lying on the sand just above the water line... Environment Agency officials are investigating what could have killed the starfish, which had been feeding on **mussel** *beds.*
(DAILY MAIL, 13 MARCH 2008)

See MUSCLE.

· N ·

nasty
unpleasant, offensive

*A month later a seven-year-old boy came in with a worm in his nose... Little Raja listened attentively when I told him how I proposed to get out that **nasty** old worm. 'It won't hurt a bit – just a little tickle in the back of your throat and – poof – we'll be done, and you'll be rid of that naughty worm and on your way home as happy as can be.'*
(THOMAS HALE, ON THE FAR SIDE OF LIGLIG MOUNTAIN, 1989)

*On the rare occasions when he spoke to Bruno, he addressed him as 'little man', which was just plain **nasty** because, as Mother pointed out, he just hadn't had his growth spurt yet.*
(JOHN BOYNE, THE BOY IN THE STRIPED PYJAMAS, 2006)

It's a foul bird that defiles its own nest, runs a European proverb that dates back at least a thousand years. In the Middle Ages such a bird might have been described as *nasty*. The origins of the word are rather obscure, but there is probably a connection with Dutch *nestig* (Middle Dutch *nistich*), which certainly meant 'foul' but may have meant literally 'soiled like the nest of a bird'. There may also be a link between the Middle English form *naxty* and a Swedish dialectal word *naskug*, 'dirty', 'foul'.

When it came into English in the fourteenth century, *nasty* was a forceful adjective to be used with the greatest care. It meant 'exceptionally filthy, offensively dirty'. Abraham Fleming, translating a work of Erasmus's in A

PANOPLIE OF EPISTLES (1576), has *Let vs spring out of our nastie nestes of sluggishnesse*, and in LEVIATHAN (1651) Thomas Hobbes describes the life of man as *solitary, poore, nasty, brutish and short*. In HAMLET (1601) Shakespeare too uses the word in a strong sense:

> *Nay, but to live*
> *In the rank sweat of an enseamed bed,*
> *Stew'd in corruption, honeying and*
> *making love*
> *Over the nasty sty!*

Applied figuratively to people in the fifteenth century, the adjective took on its sense of 'offensive, contemptible'. Applied to things in the sixteenth century it meant 'unpleasant' or 'repellent'. Pity the Lady Margaret then whom Edward Hall describes in his chronicle of the Houses of York and Lancaster (c. 1548) as having a *nasty complexion and euill sauored breathe* – she was obviously no peach.

Around the turn of the seventeenth century *nasty* came to mean 'indecent, obscene' and was applied to conduct, language, lewd jokes and the like. The English are always on the lookout for an adjective to express their feelings about the weather and by the 1630, *nasty* had become a forceful way of complaining about driving rain or thick fog. By the late seventeenth century, however, the word began to lose some of its strength – although even today it is not an adjective to apply lightly to a person or his conduct. By the early eighteenth century it had weakened to 'disagreeable, unpleasant'. The meanings 'spiteful' and 'dangerous' (as in *a nasty temper* or *a nasty bend in the road*) both date from the nineteenth century.

naughty
badly behaved; suggestive, indecent

> *Every night my prayers I say,*
> *And get my dinner every day;*
> *And every day that I've been good,*
> *I get an orange after food.*
> *The child that is not clean and neat,*
> *With lots of toys and things to eat,*
> *He is a **naughty** child, I'm sure*
> *Or else his dear papa is poor.*
> (ROBERT LOUIS STEVENSON, A CHILD'S
> GARDEN OF VERSES, 1885)

(Marie picks up the sandal and slings it at Harry. He ducks and it vanishes in the sand. Harry looks briefly, resumes his strip. Slowly he unbuckles his belt and dangles it suggestively before Marie. She giggles and makes a grab for it.)
Harry: **Naughty!** *You'll be outa the club.*
Marie: *You should be in the clubs.*
(Harry lowers his jeans to his knees, waggles his pelvis. The girls look away, embarrassed, then look back, giggling.)
(E A WHITEHEAD,
THE FOURSOME, 1972)

Signora Clementina sounded happy to hear Montalbano's voice.
*'How long has it been since you last came to see me, you **naughty** man?'*
'Please forgive me, signora, but work, you know...
(ANDREA CAMILLERI,
THE SCENT OF THE NIGHT, 2000)

Naughty but nice whispers an advertising slogan tempting dieters to sink their teeth into a cream-filled eclair. In modern English the adjective *naughty* is largely confined to the censure of petty sins or to the bad behaviour of young children. It was not always so.

The word is from Old English *nāwhit*, 'nothing' (from *nā*, 'no' and

whit, 'living thing', 'thing'). At the time of King Alfred in the ninth century it meant 'nothing', but as a noun could mean 'wickedness, evil'. The word became *nauht* in Middle English. The suffix *-y*, meaning 'having the qualities of', was added to form *nauhty* in the second half of the fourteenth century. Initially this meant 'having naught, poor, needy, worthless', but by the second half of the fifteenth century the old lurking sense of 'wickedness' had been picked up. People described as *naughty* were 'morally bankrupt' and *naughty* behaviour was 'wicked'.

The adjective was first applied in the modern sense to a child's misbehaviour in the seventeenth century. George Herbert records an early use in his collection of proverbs, JACULA PRUDENTUM (1633): *A naughty child is better sick than whole.* The playful or mildly disapproving tone of *naughty* to denote questionable adult behaviour dates from the eighteenth century.

The 1520s saw a further extension of *naughty* in its meaning of 'worthless', when it also came to mean 'inferior, substandard'. The Puritan pamphleteer Philip Stubbes, uncovering dishonest practices in the spinning industry, denounces those who *put in naughty wool, and cause it to be spun and drawne into a very small thred* (ANATOMIE OF MUSES, 1583). Bad food or drink might also be described as *naughty*. In Miles Coverdale's translation of the Bible (1535), as well as the King James Authorised Version of 1611, the bad figs in Jeremiah's vision were described as *naughtie* because they were inedible (Jeremiah 24: 2). Bad health and inclement weather might also fit this use of the adjective. This particular sense is now obsolete but sometimes makes amusing reading in the light of modern usage.

There are many shifts of meaning in the history of words. A common one is the narrowing of a general sense (*naughty* meaning 'morally bankrupt') to a restricted sense (*naughty* meaning 'sexually suggestive, titillating'). This latter meaning began to emerge in the second half of the sixteenth century and persisted. The last decade of the nineteenth century was known as the *naughty nineties* in recognition of the fact that prim Victorian standards were being challenged. And what of the slogan *naughty but nice*? Well, it was first used by Arthur Lloyd in IT'S NAUGHTY BUT IT'S NICE (1873), a song with suggestive lyrics and full of innuendo:

> *You cannot say it's wicked,*
> *For it's not a glaring vice; –*
> *You can only say 'tis naughty, –*
> *Well, 'tis naughty – but 'tis nice.*

nectar

any delicious drink; a sugary fluid produced by plants

*'Holy Virgin!' said Gurth, setting down the cup, 'what **nectar** these unbelieving dogs drink, while true Christians are fain to quaff ale as muddy and thick as the draft we give to hogs!'*
(SIR WALTER SCOTT, IVANHOE, 1819)

*Women in love have the name of their lover tattooed on their tongues. They taste the sweet rain as **nectar**, and smell the brown earth as a sensual musk.*
(MARY CAVANAGH,
A MAN LIKE ANY OTHER, 2007)

In classical mythology where ambrosia was the food of the gods, *nectar* was the heavenly drink. Greek *nektar* came into English in the sixteenth century by way of Latin *nectar*. The word is possibly a Greek compound derived from Greek *nekros*, 'corpse', and *-tar*, 'conquering', signifying its ability to impart immortality. One wonders whether the Australian beer which is described as the *amber nectar* can do the same, or whether it simply pickles those who drink it.

Ambrosia and *nectar* have a lot in common. Both mean 'rendering immortal', both were regularly on the gods' menu, both were first used in English in the sixteenth century, both on occasion could take the meaning of the other (*nectar* was sometimes used for food, *ambrosia* for drink), both have figurative uses.

Since their appearance in English *ambrosia* has been applied to anything delicious to eat, *nectar* to anything particularly pleasant to drink. By extension, since the seventeenth century, *nectar* is the sweet liquid secreted by certain flowering plants which hummingbirds sip and from which bees make honey. The peachy fruit known as the *nectarine* gets its name from the same source. *Nectarine* was an adjective, used from the early seventeenth to the late nineteenth centuries to mean 'as sweet as nectar'. Since the early seventeenth century it has been used as a noun to refer to the fruit, possibly through a shortening of *nectarine peach*.

☛ The Greek origin for nectar given here is disputed; assuming it is right, the term is related to a good number of compounds beginning with *necro-* (from *nekros*, 'corpse'): *necromancy* (15th cent), *necrophilia* (19th cent), *necropolis* (19th cent), *necrobiosis* (19th cent).

See AMBROSIA.

nepotism
favouritism and preferment towards
family and friends

The leadership council was formed
prematurely. It elected Rabbani president.
*The other factions cried **nepotism**.*
Massoud called for peace and patience.
(KHALED HOSSEINI,
A THOUSAND SPLENDID SUNS, 2007)

His tenure was not without controversy,
with some disgruntled local performers
*accusing him of **nepotism** (the conductor's*
second wife, Pamela Helen Stephens, was
a soprano who sometimes sang with the
company).
(OBITUARY OF RICHARD HICKOX IN
THE WEEK, 6 DECEMBER 2008)

From the fourteenth century onwards it
was common for popes to promote their
relatives to the office of cardinal.
Because of their own vows of celibacy
they generally favoured their nephews,
and such appointees were referred to as
cardinal-nephews. Indeed, illegitimate
sons were often passed off as nephews
before they were promoted. Perhaps the
most notorious of all was Cesare Borgia,
one of the illegitimate children of
Pope Alexander VI, who was made
Archbishop of Valencia in 1492 and cardinal the year after at the age of eighteen, although he was always openly
acknowledged as the Pope's son.

The practice was such a scandal that
Italian coined the word *nepotismo* (from
Italian *nepote*, and Latin *nepos*,
'nephew') to describe it. The word
came into English in the 1660s by way
of French *népotisme*. Initially it referred
to the preferment of papal nephews or
to the unfair advancement shown to
relatives of other important ecclesias-
tics. In the nineteenth century the
term broadened out to describe 'the
bestowal of any unmerited advancement or privilege upon a relative'. In
other words *Appointing your grandmother*
to office for the good of the party (Ambrose
Bierce, DEVIL'S DICTIONARY, 1911).

In July 1691 Innocent XII was proclaimed pope and this devout, chari-
table man issued a bull stating that no
pope should freely grant land or offices
to his relatives. A single relative might
be considered for cardinal, but only if
he were particularly suitable.

news
information on noteworthy, topical
events

I have never swum there again. I am not
superstitious, but I don't trust that water.
Not any more. I have swum there twice only,
*but both times I came home to bad **news**.*
(SUSAN FLETCHER, EVE GREEN, 2004)

Brunetti...went over to stand beside
Vianello. 'Anything?' he asked, gesturing
towards the paper.
His eyes on the headlines, which blared
***news** of the latest infighting among the*
various political parties as they attempted
to butt one another aside in their frenzy to
keep their trotters in the trough, Vianello
said, 'You know, I always used to think it
was all right to buy this, so long as I didn't
read it. As though buying it was a venial
sin and reading it a mortal.'
(DONNA LEON,
SUFFER THE LITTLE CHILDREN, 2007)

A popular folk etymology has it that
this word is made up of the initials of
the four points of the compass: N(orth)
E(ast) W(est) S(outh). Apparently
these were used to make up a cross-
shaped figure which was displayed at
the head of some of the early news-
sheets to indicate that the information
had been gleaned from every corner.
However, instances of *news* in its
present-day sense have been found in
texts dating back to before the invention of printing.

The word is based on the adjective
new (Middle English *newe*, Old English

nēowe), which ultimately goes back to the unattested proto-Indo-European term *newos* by way of unattested proto-Germanic *newjaz*. Middle French had the plural noun *nouvelles*, 'news', which had been coined from the singular adjective *nouvelle*, 'new'. A similar thing had happened in Latin when *nova* (neuter plural of *novus*, 'new') was used to mean 'new things' and hence 'news'. In the fourteenth century Middle English translated French *nouvelles* as *news* in the same way.

At first *news* meant 'novelties, new things', a sense which is now obsolete. The term was used to denote 'an account of recent events' from the early fifteenth century. It was, of course, initially treated as a plural noun, and this persisted into the nineteenth century; the poet Shelley writes that *There are bad news from Palermo* in a letter dated 30 July 1820. *News* began to be treated as a singular noun in the reign of Henry VIII. The writings of two Scottish kings show the shift to the singular. In about 1423 James 1 of Scotland used the plural: *Awak...I bring The [thee] newis glad, that blisfull ben.* By 1616 his descendant James VI of Scotland and I of England recognised *news* as singular in the first recorded use of the proverb *No news is good news*:

...if he remaine obstinate, I desyre not that ye shoulde trouble me with an ansoure, for it is to no ende, and no newis is bettir then evil newis.

Shakespeare, too, had *news* as a singular noun:

Oliver: Good Monsieur Charles! What's the new news at the new court?
Charles: There's no news at the court, sir, but the old news; that is, the old Duke is banished by his younger brother the new Duke; and three or four loving lords have put themselves into voluntary exile with him, whose lands and revenues enrich the new Duke; therefore he gives them good leave to wander.
(AS YOU LIKE IT, 1601)

Although *news* is now a singular noun in English, the French term *nouvelles* remains a plural.

nice

pleasant, agreeable; discriminating, refined; precise, exact

I did a little chat to the DVC camera towards the end of the voyage, an inspired idea of David's: ten things we like about France. Number one, of course, was the women – their style, their elegance in dress at whatever age – but number two was the simple fact that everything stops for lunch. Other things were: there are very few signs telling you what to do or not to do, and, surprisingly perhaps, after a month or two there you realize that the French, certainly in the south, are actually **nice**.
(RICK STEIN, FRENCH ODYSSEY, 2005)

Manners at funerals demand **nice** *judgment. When somebody has led a long and happy life, it is acceptable for the congregation to display matter-of-fact cheerfulness. If, however, a natural span has been brutally cut short by accident or disease, mourners exchange no more than strained smiles.*
(THE GUARDIAN, 8 DECEMBER 2008)

This now unexciting little word has undergone a revolution in sense since it was first recorded in the thirteenth century and has passed through so many shades of meaning that only the main threads can be discussed here.

Nice originally meant 'foolish, stupid', being a direct borrowing from Old French where it meant 'silly' or 'simple'. This in turn came from Latin *nescius*, 'ignorant', a derivative of *nescīre*, 'to be ignorant', a verb made up of *ne-*, 'not' and *scīre*, 'to know'. Indeed, in the fourteenth and fifteenth centuries *nice* was occasionally used as a noun to mean 'a foolish person, a simpleton'.

During the fourteenth century *nice* also came to mean 'lascivious', the connection perhaps being that a person so described was foolish and careless of the consequences. This description of wanton Youth, who was simply out for a good time, comes from Chaucer's ROMAUNT DE LA ROSE (c. 1366):

And after daunced, as I gesse,
Youthe, fulfild of lustinesse,
That nas not yit twelve yeer of age,
Wigh herte wilde, and thought volage;
Nyce she was, but she mente
Noone harme ne slight in hir entente,
But oonely lust & jolitee.
For yonge folk, wel witen ye,
Have litel thought but on hir play.

Surprisingly, by the fifteenth century a completely opposite meaning was developing, that of 'shy, coy, overly modest and reluctant'. This remained current until well into the eighteenth century. It was the sense that Dryden intended when he wrote in his heroic play AURENG-ZEBE (1675) that *Virtue is nice to take what's not her own.*

Meanwhile, the fifteenth century also saw the emergence of one of the current meanings of *nice*, that of 'careful, particular, refined', especially with regard to food, taste or manners. In an edition of his periodical THE RAMBLER (1751), Dr Johnson speaks of minds that become *nice and fastidious, and like a vitiated palate.* A related meaning, that of 'demanding special care or precision', developed in the sixteenth century. When the seventeenth-century scientist

Robert Boyle spoke of *nice experiments*, he meant those requiring a high degree of precision. Equally, *nice* came to mean 'painstakingly accurate' and its use as a synonym for 'exact' or 'fine' is related to these senses.

The second half of the eighteenth century saw the downfall of *nice* from its place of precision to its current position as an overused expression of pleasure that comes readily to mind when a more exact adjective would have served better. In modern English *nice* can be used to give a stamp of approval to anything at all from a stunning landscape to a birthday card, so that is often nothing more than a bland, workhorse word – perhaps the inevitable fate of a term with such a long and chequered history. Its status has fallen so low that a careful writer almost has to apologise for using it.

For other words that have undergone a complete change in meaning, see BUXOM and SILLY.

nightmare
a bad dream; a difficult experience

*My feet seemed positively racked with pain, yet I could not move them. They seemed to be numbed. There was an icy feeling at the back of my neck and all down my spine, and my ears, like my feet, were dead yet in torment; but there was in my breast a sense of warmth which was by comparison delicious. It was as a **nightmare** – a physical nightmare, if one may use such an expression; for some heavy weight on my chest made it difficult for me to breathe.*
(BRAM STOKER, DRACULA'S GUEST, 1914)

*I used to have **nightmares** about having petrol poured over me, and being set on fire, and nowadays I have nightmares that I have wooden teeth and that they are continually falling out, as if I had an infinite number of them. It seems that everyone has their own inexplicable fear to have nightmares about.*
(LOUIS DE BERNIÈRES,
THE PARTISAN'S DAUGHTER, 2008)

*The city's rubbish is piled into mountains that smoke and burn like brimstone and turn into treacherous, stinking swamps whenever it rains. Across this towering **nightmare**, tiny figures with plastic sacks pick through the filth, day and night, for anything they can recycle and sell.*
(HABITAT FOR HUMANITY
NEWSLETTER, SPRING 2009)

Among the Germanic peoples of the eighth century and earlier, someone suffering from terrifying dreams and feelings of suffocation in the chest was said to be having a visitation from a spirit or demon which settled upon the breast of a sleeper to torment his rest. According to Walsh, a knife bound in a cloth and swung three times around the body while incantations were repeated would banish the spirit. Mistletoe was also deemed efficacious. The goblin was known as the *mare* or *mære* (from unattested proto-Germanic *maron*, 'goblin') in Old English, and by the compound *nightmare* in the thirteenth century. Not until the sixteenth century was *nightmare* transferred from the spirit to the feelings of suffocation it caused.

According to William Turner (HERBAL, 1562) *the nyght mare* was a strangling sensation, and in his METHOD OF PHISICK (1624), Philip Barrough concurred:

Of the mare. – Ephialtes in Greeke, in Latine incubus and incubo. It is a disease, where as one thinketh himselfe in the night to be oppressed with a great weight, and beleeveth that something cometh upon him, and the patient thinketh himselfe strangled in this disease. It is called in English the mare.

Not until the early nineteenth century did the word came to mean 'frightening dream' in general.

From medieval times the *incubus* (Late Latin, from Latin *incubēre*, 'to lie down upon') and its counterpart the *succubus* (from Late Latin *succuba*, 'prostitute', from Latin *succubēre*, 'to lie under') both denoted evil spirits that induced nightmares and were thus alternatives to the *mare*. The *incubus* was a devil which assumed the form of a man in order to have intercourse with a sleeping woman, while the *succubus* took a female form and lay with men. In the Middle Ages their existence was recognised by the judicial systems of church and state. Italian retains the word *incubo* for nightmare, but Old French borrowed the Germanic term *mare*, which it compounded with the Old French verb *cauchier*, 'to trample upon', so that modern French has the word *cauchemar*, 'nightmare'.

Since the first half of the nineteenth century English has applied the fearful quality of a terrifying dream to any bad experience, even during waking hours. It is now quite possible to talk of having had *a nightmare day at work* without incongruity.

Although *mare*, 'female horse', and *mare* 'demon', look identical and both go back to Old English, they have different origins and are not etymologically connected. *Mare*, 'female horse', ultimately goes back to unattested proto-Germanic *markhaz*, 'horse'. Nevertheless, the apparent similarity has prompted wild speculation that attempts to link horses to bad dreams.

oaf

a clumsy, loutish person

*Plath told a friend that Hughes's infidelity had altered her perception of him at a stroke: he 'now appeared to her as a massive, crude, **oafish** peasant...'*
(EVENING STANDARD,
13 NOVEMBER 2001)

*As I dip my satay sticks into the sauce and wait for them to cook, I see a list of champion eaters stuck to the wall. Leading the ladies' leaderboard is Catherine from St Helens. She managed 81 sticks. Kudos to her. After chomping 30 I leave the restaurant with a cannonball of a belly, a bloated **oaf** stumbling into the tropical dusk.*
(THE INDEPENDENT, 23 MAY 2009)

In past centuries, more credulous than our own, a child who was ugly or slow was said to be an *oaf*, 'a changeling, an elf's child', left in the cradle by the fairies as a substitute for the perfect child that they had stolen.

In his DESCRIPTION OF THE ISLE OF MAN (1731), George Waldron gives an account of the appearance and habits of such a changeling. According to Waldron's witnesses the child never spoke or cried *but if anyone called him a Fairy-Elf he would frown, and fix his eyes earnestly on those who said it, as though he would look them through...* Neighbours often found the child laughing alone and *this made them judge that he was not without Company more pleasing to him than any mortal's could be...* To this was added the further evidence that if he was left dirty he reappeared clean.

Oaf is a variant of the earlier *aufe*, which came from an Old Norse word *alfr,* meaning 'elf or 'goblin'. The word was freely applied to the slow-witted or deformed, with the implication that they were changelings. Over time belief in the fairies waned, but the term lingered to denote any 'clumsy, awkward or stupid person'.

odd

not even (of a numeral); occasional; out of the ordinary, strange, peculiar

HOW TO PLAY MAFIA
*You need an **odd** number of people, ideally nine, 11 or 13. There are three 'mafia' and the rest are 'villagers'. Roles are determined by pulling names out of a hat. No one must reveal their identity unless they are killed during the game.*
(EVENING STANDARD,
20 JANUARY 2003)

*The truth was that she made him a nicer, less awkward, more accessible person but even after sixty years of marriage she still found it **odd** that they got on and that she could cope with his fussing and over-propriety.*
(ALAN BENNETT,
UNTOLD STORIES, 2005)

Odd is a strange word. Its sense 'not even' derives from Old Norse *oddi,* which means 'point, triangle', the concept arising from the image of a triangle which has two base angles with a solitary third thrusting upwards, hence 'two and one left over'. *Oddi* appeared in several Old Norse combinations to this effect:

The expression *standask ī odda*, for instance, meant 'to be at odds, to be in dispute'.

Oddamathr was an 'unpaired' and therefore 'odd man' capable of giving a casting vote. Examples of this usage in English have been recorded since the fourteenth century. William Tyndale wrote of a seventh man as being *the odd man and umpire* (1530).

Odda-tala signified an 'odd number'. Again written records of this sense in English date back to the fourteenth century. A manuscript entitled ART OF NOMBRINGE (c. 1430) instructs the reader to *compt the nombre of the figures, and wete yf it be ode or even*.

Other uses of *odd* emerge from this basic notion of 'unpaired'. The sense 'remainder' (*a hundred and odd*, for example) also dates back to the fourteenth century. It was well established by the time of Aphra Behn:

The King of Coramantien was himself a man of an hundred and odd years old, and had no son, though he had many beautiful black wives: for most certainly there are beauties that can charm of that colour.
(OROONOKO: OR, THE ROYAL SLAVE, 1688)

Lewis Carroll's vision of the world of Alice holds excellent literary examples of *odd* meaning 'strange' or 'different in appearance or behaviour from the rest'. It is a logical development of earlier senses, and it arose in the second half of the sixteenth century. Carroll uses the term extensively:

Tweedledee smiled gently, and began again:

'The sun was shining on the sea,
Shining with all his might:
He did his very best to make
The billows smooth and bright –
And this was odd, because it was
The middle of the night....

But four young oysters hurried up,
All eager for the treat:
Their coats were brushed, their faces washed,
Their shoes were clean and neat –
And this was odd, because, you know,
They hadn't any feet.'
(THROUGH THE LOOKING GLASS, 1871)

The shop was very dark towards the end.
'The egg seems to get further away the more I walk towards it. Let me see, is this a chair? Why, it's got branches, I declare! How very odd to find trees growing here!'
(THROUGH THE LOOKING GLASS, 1871)

omelette
beaten eggs, fried in a round flat pancake shape

*She had been speaking while she prepared the **omelette**. Now it was ready and she slid it on to a plate that had been warming at the side of the stove.*
'Chanterelle mushrooms,' she said. 'They transform an omelette.'
(ALEXANDER MCCALL SMITH, THE SUNDAY PHILOSOPHY CLUB, 2004)

There was a lot of shuffling and jostling and you-go-firsting and then Carole said, 'I'm a vegetarian.'
*Jo thought about the dishes and dishes of non-vegetarian food she had prepared. 'Oh well, would you like me to make you a quick **omelette** or something?'*
(KATIE FFORDE, GOING DUTCH, 2007)

This quick, simple, straightforward dish has a long, complicated and quirky etymology. It begins not in France but in ancient Rome where the Latin word *lāmella* (a diminutive of *lāmina*, 'plate, layer') meant 'a thin metal plate'. When this passed into Old French as *lemelle* it also denoted a 'thin blade' such as that of a knife or sword. So far, so good – but here comes the first quirk. The word and its definite article, *la lemelle*, were often erroneously written as *l'alemelle* which is identical in pronunciation. In this way the noun gained an initial vowel. A slight change in the medial vowel in Middle French then produced *alumelle*, 'thin plate, blade'. Next, this corrupted form was given the diminutive suffix *-ette* to produce *alumette*. By now a mixture of beaten eggs cooked until they resembled a thin flat plate was common fare, its appearance suggesting the name *alumette*. By yet another linguistic quirk the *l* and *m* sounds were reversed so that the word changed from *alumette* to *amelette* during the fifteenth century. Other forms followed as speakers and writers tussled with the initial syllable; *aumelette*, *omelette* and even *oeufmolette* (in an attempt to reconcile the word to *oeuf*, the French for 'egg').

English too struggled with the word, which it borrowed from French in the seventeenth century. During the seventeenth and eighteenth centuries *omelet*, *aumelet*, *amulet* and *aumulet* are all found. The well-known eighteenth-century cookery writer Mrs Hannah Glasse favoured *aumlet*.

During the nineteenth century both *omelet* and *omelette* were current but the twentieth century saw a parting of the ways between American and British English; American English retained the old form *omelet* while the British plumped for the modern French spelling *omelette*.

onion

a very common vegetable with a strong-smelling and tasting bulb

*Lucy-amma was cutting **onions**. Bombay onions. The beards sliced off each onion were heaped on one side. She worked the knife like a stern goddess – a devatara – slicing translucent, perfect semicircles. She was always cutting onions.*
(ROMESH GUNESEKERA, REEF, 1994)

I closed my eyes.
    *When I opened them again, Father Benedict stood above me. He was making the sign of the cross on my feet with oil; the oil smelled like **onions**, and even his light touch hurt.*
(CHIMAMANDA NGOZI ADICHIE, PURPLE HIBISCUS, 2004)

Ancient Greek athletes used to eat large quantities of onions in the belief that they would enhance their performance. When the Roman conquerors came along, onions became a staple of the Roman diet: upper-class citizens enjoyed them as an ingredient in sauces, the lower classes ate them as a vegetable, and gladiators would rub themselves down with onion bulbs to strengthen their muscles.

The source of the word is Latin *ūniō* which, according to Lucius Junius Moderatus Columella, a first-century writer on farming and agriculture, was a rustic dialectal term for a type of onion. *Uniō*, a derivative of *ūnus*, 'one', had two meanings, either of which would satisfactorily explain its metaphorical application to an onion. Firstly, it meant 'unity'; the allusion here would clearly be to the many layers of the vegetable making one whole. Secondly, it meant 'a large, perfect and (according to Pliny) unique pearl'; the comparison being between such a jewel and a perfect translucent pearly onion. *Uniō* made its way from Latin into Middle

English in the fourteenth century as *unyon* (or *oynoun*) by way of Anglo-French and Old French *oignon*.

☛ Latin *ūnus*, 'one', is also ultimately responsible for:

union (15th cent): by way of French *union* and Latin *ūniō*, 'number one, unity'.

  unique (17th cent): through French *unique* and Latin *ūnicus*, 'only, single'.

The prefix *uni-* is derived from *unus* and is combined in a large number of words such as:

unicorn (13th cent): Middle English, from Old French, from Latin *ūnicornis*, literally 'one horn', *from uni-* and *cornū*, 'horn'.

  uniform (16th cent): from Old French *uniforme*, from Latin *ūniformis*, 'of one form', from *uni-* and *fōrma*, 'form'. *Uniform* was first used as a noun to denote 'an outfit worn by every member of a group' in the eighteenth century.

  unison (16th cent): through Old French *unison* and Latin *unisonus*, from *uni-* and *sonus*, 'sound'.

  universe (14th cent): through Old French *univers* and Latin *ūniversum* 'the whole world', from *ūniversus* 'entire, made one' (from *uni-* and *versus*, from *vertere*, 'to turn'). The Latin noun was coined to translate Greek *to holon*, 'the whole'.

Unus itself goes back to the unattested proto-Indo-European form *oinos*. From this came the proto-Germanic form *ainaz*, which is ultimately responsible for English *one*.

opportunity
chance, occasion

*The girl smiled, flattered. A job in the West would be fantastic – if she could just find work for two years or so, she could earn enough to come back and carry on her studies. At the moment she didn't have enough to buy books or pay her fees. All she needed was the right **opportunity** – and Viktor Kroitor seemed to be offering it.*
(CARO FRASER,
BREATH OF CORRUPTION, 2007)

*Sometimes during the breeding season a frenzy of activity erupts involving a number of birds, with the younger ones taking the **opportunity** to practise the complex sequence of moves that determine successful pair formation.*
(JONATHAN & ANGELA SCOTT,
ANTARCTICA, 2007)

In the days of sailing ships few things could have been more dispiriting to a crew than to have their progress towards port impeded by contrary winds or arrested by calms. The Roman sailors coined an adjective *opportūnus*, 'blowing in the direction of the harbour' (from *ob-*, 'to' and *portus*, 'harbour') to describe favourable winds which arose at just the right time. Soon this particular application broadened to give the general sense of 'seasonable, timely, convenient'. From this Old French took *opportun* which passed into English as *opportune* in the early fifteenth century. The derived Latin noun *opportūnitās*, 'favourable circumstances, chance', had already been taken into Middle English as *opportunite* by way of Old French in the fourteenth century.

☛ Latin *portus* was borrowed into Old English as *port*, 'harbour' (see STARBOARD).

For another word based on good sailing weather, see BONANZA.

oscillate

to swing rhythmically backwards and forwards; to be undecided, to vacillate

The system, conceived by scientists at the University of Michigan, is called Vivace, or 'vortex-induced vibrations for aquatic clean energy'...

Because the parts only oscillate slowly, the technology is likely to be less harmful to aquatic wildlife than dams or water turbines. And as the installations can be positioned far below the surface of the sea, there would be less interference with shipping, recreational boat users, fishing and tourism.
(THE TELEGRAPH,
29 NOVEMBER 2008)

...if it weren't for how Chardin has painted it, we wouldn't find this food so appetising. (Many still lifes don't whet our appetites.) And it's only because his pigment both conjures up these edible plums, and also lies bodily on the canvas's surface, that our desire can oscillate between the image of fruit and physical paint.
(THE INDEPENDENT,
6 FEBRUARY 2009)

According to mythology the god Bacchus taught man how to cultivate the vine and prepare wine from its fruit. Roman viniculturists hoping for a good harvest would hang a mask of the god from a tree in their vineyard to swing about in the breeze. The charm was known as an *ōscillium*, literally 'a little face', being a diminutive of *ōs*, a word that meant 'mouth' but was also sometimes applied to the whole face. In time *ōscillium* came to mean 'a swing' and as such was the source of the verb *ōscillāre*, 'to swing'. This was taken into English in the early eighteenth century as *oscillate*, initially a scientific term to describe the regular movement of a pendulum.

☛ *Or-*, the stem of *ōs*, 'mouth' is evident in:

orifice (16th cent): from Middle French, from Latin *ōrificium*, 'an opening', from *or-* and *facere*, 'to make'.
　oral (16th cent): from Late Latin *orālis*.
　oracy (1960s) a recent coinage modelled on *literacy*.
　usher (14th cent) is also from *ōs*, 'mouth'. The derivative *ōstium* meant 'entrance'. This gave *ōstārius*, 'entrance keeper', which became *ōstārius* in Medieval Latin and *user* in Anglo-French.

ostracism

exclusion from social contact or common privileges

Mr Beresford didn't even like him! Since the announcement of his sex change he had virtually been ostracised. After all the work he had put in towards organising the reception for the launch of the tilting carriages, he hadn't even been invited.
(DAVID NOBBS,
SEX AND OTHER CHANGES, 2004)

...comedy is about embarrassment, embarrassment leads to social humiliation, social humiliation leads to ostracism, ostracism, for social animals, is effectively death...
(THE GUARDIAN, 20 JUNE 2007)

The word comes from the Greek noun *ostrakismos*, 'banishment', which is derived from *ostrakon*, meaning 'a shard of pottery'. Every year the citizens of ancient Athens had the right to gather together and vote for the banishment of anyone whose power and authority was considered a threat to the equilibrium of the democratic state. People recorded their votes by writing a name on a fragment of pottery. A total of 6,000 votes had to be cast before the poll was declared valid. If a majority of these denounced one particular person he was banished for ten years, although he did not lose any property he might own.

The noun *ostracism* came into English in the sixteenth century, originally to refer to the classical practice. It was put to figurative use to denote 'exclusion' in general at the beginning of the seventeenth century.

☞ Proto-Indo-European *ost-* meant 'bone' and was responsible for several Greek words which denoted objects of a similar texture. *Ostrakon* was one of these. *Osteon*, 'bone', was a second. Its stem *osteo-* is found in a number of largely medical terms to do with the bones: *osteoarthritis, osteology, osteoid, osteopathy, osteoporosis*, etc. A third derivative was *ostreion*, which meant 'oyster'. This came into Middle English as *oystre* in the mid-fourteenth century, by way of Old French *oistre* and Latin *ostrea*.

· P ·

palaver
a trouble, a fuss, a hassle

*My nan looks as though she never guessed that her life could be filled with so much pain, so much discomfort, so much of what she would call a **palaver**.*
(TONY PARSONS,
ONE FOR MY BABY, 2001)

*I also take drugs. I've tried most things. My favourite is opium, though I've had it only once. It's really hard to get hold of and involves a **palaver** with a flame and a pipe.*
(SEBASTIAN FAULKS, ENGLEBY, 2007)

In Portuguese *palavra* (from Late Latin *parabola*, 'speech, talk') means 'word, talk' and was the term used by traders of that nation when they wanted to meet for a parley with the natives of the West African coast. Here the term was picked up by British sailors and appeared in written English as *palaver* in the early eighteenth century. Initially it meant 'negotiation', but was soon absorbed into colloquial speech to denote 'empty, idle chatter' or 'coaxing, cajoling talk' – a little of each doubtless characterised the original *palavras*. Although these meanings are still current, the term is perhaps more commonly used in its late nineteenth-century extended sense to refer to 'a fuss' or 'a wearisome, involved task or process'.

☛ Late Latin *parabola* meant 'allegory, speech, talk'. These senses evolved from Latin *parabola*, 'comparison', a borrowing of Greek *parabolē*, 'comparison, juxtaposition, analogy'.

Late Latin *parabola* gave Medieval Latin *parabolāre*, 'to talk'. From this Old French derived *parler*, 'to talk'. The feminine form of the past participle *parlée* was borrowed into English in the late fifteenth century as *parley*, originally meaning 'talk, debate', then 'negotiation'.

Parable is another word with Late Latin *parabola* in its history. It came into Middle English in the mid-thirteenth century via Old French *parabole*.

For another word from the same source, see PARLOUR.

pamphlet
a booklet; a tract, a treatise

He would drive back to Crampsford; he would complain to Mr and Mrs Allaby; he didn't mean to have married Christina; he hadn't married her; it was all a hideous dream; he would – But a voice kept ringing in his ears which said: 'You CAN'T, CAN'T, CAN'T.'
'CAN'T I?' screamed the unhappy creature to himself.
'No,' said the remorseless voice, 'YOU CAN'T. YOU ARE A MARRIED MAN.'
*He rolled back in his corner of the carriage and for the first time felt how iniquitous were the marriage laws of England. But he would buy Milton's prose works and read his **pamphlet** on divorce. He might perhaps be able to get them at Newmarket.*
(SAMUEL BUTLER,
THE WAY OF ALL FLESH, 1903)

*Her gaze was on him as he approached,
and when he was near enough she took a
pamphlet from her friend's pile and said,
'Would you like one? It's all about a
hydrogen bomb landing on Oxford.'*

*As he took it from her, her finger trailed,
surely not by accident, across the inside
of his wrist. He said, 'I can't think of
anything I'd rather read.'*
(IAN MCEWAN,
ON CHESIL BEACH, 2007)

Towards the end of the twelfth century
an erotic comic poem, written in Latin
and of unknown authorship, gained
great popularity in northern Europe.
It tells the story of Pamphilus (from
Greek *pamphilos*, 'beloved by all'), who
is infatuated with the virtuous Galathea.
He asks an old woman to act as a
go-between and entice Galathea to
her house. The bawdy content of
PAMPHILUS, SEU DE AMORE
('Pamphilus, or About Love') so tickled
the fancy of students at the University
of Paris that they were scolded for
neglecting their studies to read it.

At that time it was common for
brief works to be referred to by the
addition of the diminutive suffix *-et*. In
France, for instance, the translation of
Aesop's fables by Marie de France was
known as ISOPET. The same convention was applied to PAMPHILUS which
became PAMPHILET in Middle French
and PANFLET in Dutch. The poem was
certainly known in England, as both
Chaucer and Gower refer to it.

Records of the word *pamflet* in
Middle English to describe 'a short,
unbound written work', date from the
early fifteenth century, but the term
had appeared in Anglo-Latin in the
previous century. In PHILOBIBLON
(1344), for instance, the English
scholar Richard de Bury writes of
panfletos exiguos, 'slender pamphlets',
saying he would rather have a pamphlet
to read than a plump horse to ride.

pandemonium
hubbub, uproar, chaos

*When he was nearly parallel to the
spot, he indicated and turned. A riot,
a **pandemonium** of screeching brakes,
blaring horns, shouts, insults, and
curses ensued.*
(ANDREA CAMILLERI,
THE SCENT OF THE NIGHT, 2000)

*The traumatised dog shot off, squealing
from the attentions of a hissing cat,
who was beginning to realise that all
normality was draining from her life.
In accompaniment to the **pandemonium**
the front door bell rang, with three short
bursts. The undertakers had arrived.*
(MARY CAVANAGH,
A MAN LIKE ANY OTHER, 2007)

This word springs from the imagination of John Milton. In PARADISE
LOST (Book 1, 1667), he tells us that
Pandemonium is the capital of Hell,
where Satan presides over his council
of Evil Spirits:

*A solemn Councel forthwith to be held
    At Pandaemonium, the high Capital
        Of Satan and his Peers.*

Later in the poem *Pandemonium* is
described as the *citie and proud seate of
Lucifer*. Milton coined the name from
two Greek words: *pan-*, meaning 'all',
and *daimōn*, 'spirit'.

Other writers initially used Milton's
coinage as a name for Hell. Then, in
the second half of the eighteenth century, it was used to describe 'any
place of wickedness and lawlessness'.
Pandemonium was finally applied to the
'chaos and commotion' itself in the
first half of the nineteenth century.

pander

to satisfy, indulge or exploit another's desires or weaknesses

The battle to see which political party can out-pander the other on the subject of gasoline prices is embarrassing. If American consumers are having sticker shock at the pumps, it's because of a series of policy failures that stretch back decades. The last thing the country needs now is another irresponsible quick fix.
(NEW YORK TIMES, 28 APRIL 2006)

...the drink's £1.5 million relaunch with a lower alcohol content and sweeter taste has enraged several traditionalists who say the company is pandering to 'Londoners'. The re-branded drink is billed as 'slightly mellower'. But a number of landlords say it has met with such disapproval they are stockpiling remaining kegs of the old type.
(THE TELEGRAPH, 3 APRIL 2009)

Homer's ILIAD describes *Pandaros* (Latin *Pandarus*) as a distinguished and courageous archer in the Trojan army at the siege of Troy. Around 1335, the Italian writer Giovanni Boccaccio wrote IL FILOSTRATO, a story in verse about the love of Trolio, a son of Priam of Troy, for the beautiful young widow Criseide. In this story Pandarus is a close friend and contemporary of Trolio and cousin of Criseide, and he acts as a go-between to bring the young couple together. Boccaccio's work was the inspiration for Chaucer's celebrated narrative poem TROILUS AND CRISEYDE (c. 1385) in which Pandarus, this time introduced as Criseyde's uncle and guardian, acts on Troilus's behalf as before.

The fact that Chaucer depicted Pandarus as an older man with responsibilities towards his niece led, in the late fifteenth century, to the use of *pander* to denote 'one who arranges secretive, illicit love affairs, a pimp'. It was employed as a verb in the seven-teenth century with the dual senses 'to act as a pander' and 'to serve the baser designs of another'.

Pander to, with the weaker meaning 'to gratify or indulge another's whims', arose in the late nineteenth century.

parlour

a room in a house for entertaining, a sitting room; a salon, a shop, equipped for a particular purpose

'Just on your way?' he asked.
His question was almost justified by Winifred's proximity to the hat stand.
'I was. But now you're here, I'll stay for a bit. It seems ages since I saw you. Come into the parlour and sit down.'
Frederick could not imagine any other woman inviting him into his own parlour.
(ROY HATTERSLEY,
THE MAKER'S MARK, 1990)

I hear this from an undertaker who looks about nineteen. He...took me away, somehow, in a car or a taxi – whether I sat in the back or the front of it, I can not recall. But I know that I will remember this, the hinterland of the funeral parlour, suburban and pastel: a desk with a chair on either side and, up on a swivel stand, a laminated catalogue of coffins, all kinds and varieties of them, except, when I enquire for the sake of distraction, the eco-warrior's cardboard.
(ANNE ENRIGHT,
THE GATHERING, 2007)

Etymologically a *parlour* is 'a place for talking'. Middle English borrowed the term from Old French *parleur*, a derivative of the verb *parler*, 'to speak' (from Late Latin *parabolare*, 'to speak'). The *parlour* was a room in a medieval monastery or convent that could be used for private conversation or the reception of visitors. The earliest written record comes from the ANCRENE RIWLE (c. 1225), a devotional manual which offered guidance for the organisation and government of monastic communities.

In time, however, the word escaped from the cloisters. Medieval houses featured a hall which was originally used for all domestic activities. It was a busy area filled with smoke, heat and noisy bustle. Privacy was limited. By the second half of the fourteenth century the *parlour* was becoming a feature of domestic households, a quiet room where private conversation could be held (as in a monastery) and genteel pastimes pursued. This gradually evolved into the family sitting-room, still with the name *parlour*.

The word is today dialectally used in this sense but mainly survives in a number of compounds such as *parlour game*, *ice-cream parlour*, *beauty parlour*, *parlour politics* and *milking parlour*.

For a word with the same origin, see PALAVER.

peach
a soft juicy fruit with a downy skin

*Choose firm, but not hard, **peaches** with soft, velvety skins free from blemishes. The slightest bruise will cause rapid deterioration.*
(GOOD HOUSEKEEPING COOK BOOK, 2004)

See APRICOT.

pedigree
line of descent, ancestry

*There are some trees, Watson, which grow to a certain height, and then suddenly develop some unsightly eccentricity. You will see it often in humans. I have a theory that the individual represents in his development the whole procession of his ancestors, and that such a sudden turn to good or evil stands for some strong influence which came into the line of his **pedigree**. The person*

becomes, as it were, the epitome of the history of his own family.
(SIR ARTHUR CONAN DOYLE, THE RETURN OF SHERLOCK HOLMES, 1905)

*There were rumours…of a priest in one nearby town who had a way to hide Jews, and of a mayor in another hamlet who actually helped Jews get the papers they needed to pass as Aryans with the necessary **pedigree**.*
(CHRIS BOHJALIAN, SKELETONS AT THE FEAST, 2008)

A *pedigree* dog is a pure-bred animal with no trace of mongrel in it. Indeed, its line of descent will have been carefully recorded to prove it. Documentation is similarly available for the lineage of royalty and nobility. When medieval genealogists charted the ancestry of powerful families, the branching claw-like lines they used to mark the line of succession reminded people of a crane's foot, and so in Old French the diagram was called the *pie de grue*: *pie*, from Latin *pēs*, 'foot', and *grue*, from *grūs*, 'crane'). This became *pedegru* in Middle English. The spelling did not settle down as *pedigree* until the eighteenth century. The term began to be applied to an animal's line of descent in the early seventeenth century.

perfume
a liquid that gives off an agreeable odour; any pleasant scent

Perfume rose up from her, and when I moved in to spoon the potatoes on to her plate it seemed the scent was stronger. It rose up from below her throat down inside her flapping dress. She had her elbows on the table; her body was concave. She must have smeared the perfume with her fingers, rubbing it in like honey paste to enrich the skin.
(ROMESH GUNESEKERA, REEF, 1994)

*She stopped giggling, and then to my surprise she opened the passenger door and got in, bringing with her a tidal wave of heavy **perfume** that I found very unpleasant and stifling. It reminded me of my grandmother in old age, attempting to disguise the odours of incontinence.*
(LOUIS DE BERNIÈRES, THE PARTISAN'S DAUGHTER, 2008)

The source of this word is a now obsolete early Italian compound verb *parfumare*, 'to permeate with smoke', from Latin *per-*, 'through' and *fūmāre*, 'to smoke'. This was borrowed into French as *parfumer* and the derived noun *parfum* passed into English in the first half of the sixteenth century.

As the etymology suggests, *perfume* did not originally refer to the delicate scent of a rose or dab of fragrant oil, but denoted 'odoriferous smoke emitted by burning a substance'; this might be from incense or an oil warmed to make a room smell sweet, or it might be from herbs burnt for medicinal purposes or to disinfect a house after an infectious illness. In his CASTLE OF HELTH (1539), a popular medical book, Sir Thomas Elyot wrote: *If I lacked storax, I toke for a parfume the ryndes of olde rosemary and burned them, and held my mouth ouer the fume closunge myne eyes.*

From here the word was applied to any agreeable scent, such as that given off by flowers, and also to fragrances designed to be worn rather than burnt.

☛ Latin *fūmāre* derives from *fūmus*, 'smoke', which is ultimately responsible for English *fume* (15th cent) and *fumigate* (16th cent).

picnic
an outdoor meal

*The time that was finally settled on for the baby-welcoming was Labor Day. Another **picnic** lunch on the North Fork River was the plan, except that Hurricane Dennis moved through the area over the weekend and they changed it to an indoor event.*
(ANNE TYLER, BACK WHEN WE WERE GROWNUPS, 2001)

*I am getting ready to attend a 'block party' this evening. Chris and Peggy Ellis, for several years now, have graciously invited all the households in our neighborhood to monthly **picnics**. These are held on the vacant lot which is right behind my house.*
(NEVADA DAILY MAIL, 13 JUNE 2008)

When the French word *pique-nique* first appeared in the late seventeenth century, it referred to a fashionable party, not necessarily out in the open, where everyone brought along a share of the food. By the first half of the eighteenth century this way of socialising had spread to Germany and further. *Picnics* began to be enjoyed in England in the early nineteenth century, but already the entertainment was changing from a fashionable meal into an informal one, eaten outside and usually as part of a trip to the seaside or to the country. There is speculation that this change in picnic entertainment took place in England and subsequently influenced other countries, including France.

The origins of the French word *pique-nique* are unclear. It is supposed that the first element is from *piquer*, 'to pick', and that the second is either simply a reduplication (like English *flip-flop*) or a deliberate resuscitation of the recently defunct word *nique*, 'a trifle', to produce a rhyming term that literally meant 'pick a little of this and a little of that'.

pirate

a sea robber; someone who steals another's rights, copies another's work without permission; the copy so made

*Sometimes of a morning, as I've sat in bed sucking down the early cup of tea and watched Jeeves flitting about the room and putting out the raiment for the day, I've wondered what the deuce I should do if the fellow ever took it into his head to leave me... Young Reggie Foljambe to my certain knowledge offered him double what I was giving him, and Alistair Bingham Reeves, who's got a valet who had been known to press his trousers sideways, used to look at him, when he came to see me, with a kind of glittering, hungry eye which disturbed me deucedly. Bally **pirates**!*
(P G WODEHOUSE,
CARRY ON, JEEVES, 1925)

*The chances of anyone turning up in the corridor around midnight on 26 December were almost non-existent. She opened the door with a **pirate** copy of the company's card key which she had taken the trouble to make several years before.*
(STIEG LARSSON, THE GIRL WITH THE DRAGON TATTOO, 2008)

*These are the joyful faces of Captain Richard Phillips and his family as they are finally reunited after his **pirate** ordeal.*
Family members had feared they would never see the 53-year-old again after he was taken hostage by four pirates armed with AK-47 rifles on the cargo ship Maersk Alabama *a week ago.*
(DAILY MAIL, 18 APRIL 2009)

Peirātēs was a Greek term for 'a raider', derived from the verb *peiran*, 'to attempt, to attack' and the noun *peira*, 'an endeavour, an attack'. After it was borrowed into Latin as *pīrāta*, the noun developed the more specific meaning of 'one who commits robbery on the seas', and in this sense it was taken into English in the fifteenth

century. The poet John Lydgate gives an erroneous etymology in his FALL OF PRINCES (c. 1439), a translation from French of a work by the Italian poet Boccaccio: *Pirrus...was a rouere and robbed on the se... Off such robbyng he sclaundre & be diffame This woord Pirate off Pirrus took the name.*

The figurative application of *pirate* for 'one who reproduces the work of another for his own gain' arose in the second half of the seventeenth century. In those days it was the printed word that was snatched for profit. In a notice at the end of BROOKS' STRING OF PEARLS (1668), the author J Hancock refers to *Some dishonest Booksellers, called Land-Pirats, who make it their practise to steal Impressions of other mens Copies.* Later, in an edition of THE TATLER (1709), Steele and Addison complain that *these Miscreants are a set of wretches we authors call Pirates, who print any book...as soon as it appears...in a smaller volume and sell it (as all other thieves do stolen goods) at a cheaper rate.*

With the invention of radio, *pirates* began to rove the sound waves rather than the ocean waves, the term being applied to 'one who broadcasts programmes illicitly' in the early twentieth century. In more modern times, piracy extends to design, film and CD games.

See also BUCCANEER.

placebo

a remedy that brings psychological relief rather than a cure; an inactive substance given to a control group in an experiment

*A fruit-flavoured **placebo** pill that tricks small children into thinking they are getting medical treatment is to be launched in Britain despite concerns from childcare experts.*
Manufacturers of the sugar pills Obecalp – placebo spelled backwards – say it helps

soothe the pains of childhood without resorting to drugs with potentially harmful side-effects, but doctors fear it increases reliance on medication and could stop parents seeking help when necessary.
(THE GUARDIAN, 16 JUNE 2008)

*…the results of the randomised double blind controlled trial, the first of a skin care product, showed 70 per cent had significantly fewer wrinkles after 12 months of daily use compared to those using a **placebo**.*
(THE INDEPENDENT, 29 APRIL 2009)

In the Latin rite the first antiphon of Vespers in the Office for the Dead begins with the line *Placēbo Dominē in rēgiōne vivōrum*. It comes from Psalm 114: 9 and translates as 'I shall please the Lord in the land of the living.' Since at least the thirteenth century the service has been known by the first word of this anthem, *Placēbo*, 'I shall please' (from Latin *placēre*, 'to please').

From the fourteenth to the seventeenth centuries the word was used in a number of idioms such as *to play placebo* or *to be at the school of placebo*. These drew on the sense 'I shall please' and meant 'to flatter, to curry favour', so that *placebo* became synonymous with 'sycophant'.

By the eighteenth century this idiomatic sense was virtually obsolete, but during the second half of the same century the word was given a new lease of life when it was applied to a medicine which was designed to please; the value of the remedy might be in question, but taking it humoured the patient and might prove of some psychological help. Copper bracelets worn by sufferers from rheumatism probably work on this principle, although those who sell them say the metal draws acid from the body. Modern medicine has extended the use of *placebo* to refer to 'a harmless substance which is used as a control in an experiment to test new drugs'.

For a word with a similar etymology, see DIRGE.

plaudit
acclaim, approval

Not in the clamour of the crowded street,
*   Not in the shouts and **plaudits** of*
*   the throng,*
But in ourselves, are triumph and defeat.
(HENRY WADSWORTH LONGFELLOW,
THE POETS AND POETRY OF EUROPE,
1845)

*The décor is beige (a colour I normally detest, since it symbolises safety and mediocrity), but oddly enough, I loved it. And whoever does the flowers deserves some sort of **plaudit**.*
(EVENING STANDARD MAGAZINE,
3 DECEMBER 2008)

Valete et plaudite ('Farewell and give us your applause'), the Roman playwright Terence urges his audience at the end of EUNUCHUS (161 BC). The words were not just used by Terence but were the closing exhortation of many performances, as Quintilian confirms in his DE INSTITUTIONE ORATORIA (c. AD 80): *Quo veteres tragoediae comoediaeque clauduntur, Plaudite* ('That [phrase] with which old tragedies and comedies used to end, give us your applause').

The cry *plaudite* was the plural imperative of the Latin verb *plaudere*, 'to applaud'. The word first appears in English in the sixteenth century through the renewed interest in classical studies that characterised that period. From its earliest uses it appears not as an imperative but as a three-syllable noun (*plau-di-te*) meaning 'a round of applause'. During the early seventeenth century the final *e* first became mute and then was dropped, giving *plaudit*. Through the nineteenth century the word still meant 'applause' or some other audible form of praise or appreciation. Today, however, *plaudit* is usually 'a written or verbal expression of critical acclaim'.

☞ The Latin verb *plaudere*, 'to clap', is the source of other words which entered English in the sixteenth century. *Applause* (late 16th cent), for instance, derives from the Latin *ad-*, 'to' and *plaudere*, 'to clap', while *plausible* (16th cent) comes from the related Latin adjective *plausibilis* meaning 'deserving applause'. *Plausible* was originally used in the sense of 'worthy of praise or approval'. The modern meaning 'seemingly reasonable or valid', as in *a plausible argument*, also dates from the sixteenth century.

For another word from the same Latin source, see EXPLODE.

precocious
significantly more developed or advanced than the norm

*Entranced by the wild beauty of the setting, young Albia turned on me an expression she saved for when she knew indelicate issues were being discussed by adults who preferred her not to listen. Then she lost interest in being **precocious** and went back to admiring the grove-coloured hills and the lake.*
(LINDSEY DAVIS, SATURNALIA, 2007)

*Again we read of the shy, intellectually **precocious** son of a Scottish publisher – descended from crofters on the west coast of Scotland – and pushy American mother...*
(THE SPECTATOR, 10 JUNE 2009)

When Sir Thomas Browne in his PSEUDODOXIA EPIDEMICA or VULGAR ERRORS (1650) spoke of *precocious trees* he was using the word in a particular botanical sense. He goes on to explain that such plants *have their spring in the winter*. A *precocious* plant, then, is one which, like the forsythia or the apple, flowers or sets its fruit before it comes into leaf.

The surprising source of this word, given its early botanical application, is Latin *coquere*, which meant 'to cook' but was also used figuratively with the sense 'to ripen'. Thus *praecoquere*, which includes the prefix *prae-*, 'before', meant either 'to cook ahead of time' or 'to ripen early'. The derived adjective *praecox*, 'ripening early', was borrowed into English as *precocious* in the mid-seventeenth century.

By the last quarter of that century, *precocious* was being applied figuratively to 'something that develops prematurely' or to 'a person who, in one respect or another, has come into early maturity'. Thus a *precocious* child is one who has flowered before his or her time:

She was a very good baby and a precocious child who could read perfectly before she was four. My mother was horrified when Antonia picked up The Times *and started reading the leader article out loud. She accused me of teaching Antonia to read it parrot-fashion. I said, 'She's never seen it before, and of course she doesn't understand any of it. Who does?'*
(Lady Longford about her daughter, Lady Antonia Fraser, in THE SUNDAY TIMES, 18 DECEMBER 1994)

For another word from the same source, see APRICOT.

prestige

renown, status, admiration inspired by success or wealth

*Archaeology, the main source of prehistoric study, claimed extensive financial support from the state. Academic **prestige**, linked with opportunities for leading research expeditions, made the discipline an attractive and respected career choice.*
(YURI E BEREZKIN IN ANTIQUITY, 1 MARCH 2000)

*The army proclaimed Claudius Emperor, but the Senate objected and Claudius had little support in Rome. He needed a major victory to give himself **prestige**, backing and revenue.*
(PHILIP WILKINSON, WHAT THE ROMANS DID FOR US, 2000)

This word's origins lie with the skilful tricks and illusions of the juggler. These were known in Latin by the plural noun *praestigiae*. This was an altered form of unattested *praestrigiae*, a derivative of the verb *praestringere*, 'to bind fast, to blindfold' (from *prae-*, 'before', and *stringere*, 'to bind'). The sense was that the audience was blinded, dazzled by the conjuror's skill. From this French had *prestige*, meaning 'illusion, trick, deceit', a word which, like its Latin ancestor, was often used in the plural. It was borrowed directly into English in the second half of the seventeenth century, again regularly in the plural. Thomas Blount includes *Prestiges* in his GLOSSOGRAPHIA (1656), defining the term as *deceits, impostures, delusions, cousening tricks*.

In the early nineteenth century the word began to appear in the singular to denote 'dazzling success or reputation arising from past achievements or wealth'. This sense probably alludes to the blinding, almost magical, aura of success. Skeat quotes the comment that *prestige* is one of the rare examples of a bad word turned good. Nevertheless some people cannot shake off the suspicion that the glory invariably masks the true facts, just as the conjuror's sleight of hand hides the deceit. The Victorian historian Edward Augustus Freeman was certainly of this opinion: *Prestige, you know, I always like to have a pop at; I take it it has never lost its first meaning of conjuring tricks* (1881). Perhaps he is right to suggest that *prestige* is a mask that covers a baser reality.

For an example of a good word turned bad, see VILLAIN.

protocol

a code of etiquette for formal occasions; a preliminary draft of a treaty, convention, etc.

*Miriam has never called him – not since ringing the house about the lease expiring – and he doesn't call her. How can you have a sexual relationship with someone but not presume the liberty of a phone call? It is strange, and yet he feels to ring her would be to violate this **protocol** they seem to have established.*
(PHIL HOGAN, ALL THIS WILL BE YOURS, 2005)

*Mr Cowen needed the guarantees in the form of a '**protocol**' – the most legally watertight form of EU agreement. He said he could not reverse last year's Irish No to the treaty without the protocol.*
(THE TELEGRAPH, 19 JUNE 2009)

The Late Greek compound *prōtokollon* literally meant 'glued on at the beginning' (from *prōtos*, 'first' and *kolla*, 'glue'). In the Byzantine Empire it denoted the first leaf glued onto a roll of papyrus, which bore details of the manuscript's provenance and content. When the word came into English in the sixteenth century by way of Old French *prothocole* and Medieval Latin *prōtocollum*, it no longer referred to a flyleaf but to 'the outline of an agreement or negotiation that formed the basis of a subsequent legal document'. In the seventeenth century the word was specifically used in diplomatic contexts to denote 'the minutes or first draft made at a conference from which the final treaty or agreement is drawn up'.

In the late nineteenth century, French preoccupation with etiquette led them to apply *protocol* to the ceremonial procedures and formalities that surrounded such diplomatic negotiations and conferences. This paved the way for the adoption into English at the very end of the nineteenth century of the modern sense of the word, that of 'a strict code of conduct proper in a formal situation'.

The use of the word in scientific contexts began in the nineteenth century, when *protocol* denoted 'the original notes made in a clinical case or during an experiment'. By the middle of the twentieth century the word also signified 'detailed instructions of correct experimental procedure'.

For another word signifying a code of behaviour, see ETIQUETTE.

puny
weak, physically small

*Pound for pound, swallows might be the greatest migrants in the skies. Every February they gather in the flea-infested reed swamps of South Africa and feed themselves up to a still-**puny** 24g, before heading 6,000 miles north to Europe.*
(THE SUNDAY TIMES, 29 MARCH 2009)

*'I'm not going to sit trapped underground any more when I could cycle to work in half the time,' he announced one evening. 'I'll buy a fold-up bike and save myself a fortune on fares.' A week later, the fold-up bike arrived, a spindly model with tiny wheels and a **puny** frame; nothing to hint at the obsession to come.*
(THE TELEGRAPH, 17 JUNE 2009)

Old French had the word *puisné*, literally 'born after', to denote a 'younger child'. It was a compound of *puis*, 'after' (from unattested Vulgar Latin *postius*, 'after') and *ne*, 'born' (from Latin *nātus*, past participle of *nāscī*, 'to be born'). *Puny* was a phonetic rendering of *puisné* which arose in English in the sixteenth century. Both *puisne* and *puny* were current in English and both referred to someone who was either junior in age or, by extension, in rank; in 1609 Robert Cawdrey's alphabetical list of English words has *Puiney, younger borne*, while John Stockwood's *plaine and easie* English grammar book (1590) was specifically intended for *the Punies and Petits of the Grammar Schoole*.

In the seventeenth century *puisne* in particular was applied to an associate judge and remains part of legal vocabulary in modern English. *Puny*, on the other hand, was rarely used in this way, but by the late sixteenth century was developing a sense of 'small, weak, inferior', and with it often overtones of contempt.

Q

quarantine
a period of separation and isolation

*A winter sickness bug has struck at York Hospital, forcing bosses to **quarantine** a number of wards and shut down 21 patient beds.*
(YORK STAR, 18 DECEMBER 2008)

*A few years on, I had a letter from him from India, where he had gone to join the Ugandan Consulate and hadn't had the right jabs, so was in **quarantine**.*
(YASMIN ALIBHAI-BROWN,
THE SETTLER'S COOKBOOK, 2009)

In the fourteenth century, as sea trade between Europe and the countries of the eastern Mediterranean increased, so did the incidence of plague, which was borne on returning ships. In 1348, during the Black Death, the Venetian authorities began to demand a period of isolation before ships, cargoes or travellers were allowed to enter the city. Later, in 1403, Venice founded a quarantine station on an island in the lagoon. Since detention was for forty days, the period was known as *quarantina*, a word derived from Italian *quaranta*, 'forty' (from Latin *quadrāgintā*).

The system spread to other ports and was extended to cover other infections. Over time the required period of quarantine varied, but the word remained. Present British regulations for the isolation of imported animals, for example, stipulate a quarantine of six months. The earliest recorded use of the word in English, which shows that already the term could no longer be taken literally, occurs in Pepys' diary in the entry for 26 November 1663:

Making of all ships coming from thence…to perform their quarantine (for 30 days, as Sir Richard Browne expressed it…contrary to the import of the word; though, in the general acceptation, it signifies now the thing, not the time spent in doing it).

quarry
a site from which stone is extracted; the target of a hunt, prey

*A moment before I had been safe of all men's respect, wealthy, beloved…and now I was the common **quarry** of mankind, hunted, houseless, a known murderer, thrall to the gallows.*
(ROBERT LOUIS STEVENSON,
THE STRANGE CASE OF DR JEKYLL
AND MR HYDE, 1886)

*Everyone knew that those sent to Portland were given a pickaxe and ordered to break rocks in a **quarry**; leg-irons doubtless came into the reckoning as well.*
(JULIAN BARNES,
ARTHUR AND GEORGE, 2005)

Somewhere behind her, unseen and threatening, the dogs were gaining on her, excited by the promise of blood.
    *She was no longer the hunter, but the **quarry**.*
(KATE MOSSE, LABYRINTH, 2005)

Etymologically Old French *quarriere* is 'a place from which square blocks of stone are obtained'. The ultimate source of the word is Latin *quadrus*, meaning 'square', but in order to trace the development of the word it is necessary to supply a missing link. Although there is no written evidence, it is assumed that Old French once had the word *quarre*, derived from *quadrus*, to denote a 'square stone' and that *quarriere* was then formed from this unattested term. Middle English borrowed the word as *quarrer* (variant *quarey*) in the fourteenth century.

Quarry meaning 'game' is derived from a totally different source. In medieval times a reward was customarily offered to the hounds at the end of a successful hunt. It consisted of the dead animal's entrails spread out upon its hide. Similar titbits were also presented to hawks after a kill. In Middle English, the word for this gift was *querre* or *quirre*, from Anglo-French and Old French *cuiree*. This term was a variant of *couree*, 'intestines', from unattested Vulgar Latin *corāta*, 'entrails', from Latin *cor*, 'heart', perhaps influenced by *cuir*, the French for 'skin' or 'hide'. Later the word was applied to the quarry while it was still on the hoof or wing, so that it came to mean the 'animal pursued' rather than bits of it dead.

queue
a line of people

*'Bear up now, Dora,' she said. 'Israel will represent you. There's sure to be a crowd and it'll take a man of Israel's standing to get to the head of the **queue**.'*
(LAURIE GRAHAM,
THE UNFORTUNATES, 2002)

*I'd begun to feel ill at lunch time. I'd been standing in the dinner **queue**, my metal tray in one hand, when I suddenly realised that my stomach was tightening.*
(SUSAN FLETCHER, EVE GREEN, 2004)

Latin *cauda* is responsible for the modern French word *queue*, which means 'a tail'. English borrowed it from French in the sixteenth century as a

heraldic term denoting 'the tail of a beast', in particular a lion with a *queue fourchée*, 'double tail'. From the eighteenth century onwards *queue* was used for 'a pigtail', initially one at the back of a wig, and this sense is still current, though rare.

Not until the nineteenth century did *queue* come to denote 'a line of people waiting to be attended to'. The British have gained a reputation for the orderly way in which they form a line when waiting for service or public transport. It would seem from early uses of the word in this sense, however, that these manners were inspired by the French. In THE FRENCH REVOLUTION (1837), Thomas Carlyle writes that the *talent...of spontaneously standing in queue, distinguishes... the French People.* And almost four decades later Charles Davies describes *A long queue, like that outside a Parisian theatre* (UNORTHODOX LONDON, 1876). Indeed, the French expression *faire la queue*, literally 'to make the tail', means 'to queue up'.

The use of *queue* for a line of people is, appropriately enough, a British one. In America the word *line* is preferred.

quick
swift, rapid, speedy; living, alive

*This may be summer at its most somnolent but its days are still metred by the **quick** and the dead.*
As I sit in the shadow of a hedge a few feet away, there is a sudden frantic crashing of wings. A blackbird hurtles through a gap in the hedge followed a split-second later by a sparrowhawk.
(THE GUARDIAN, 24 AUGUST 2005)

'Actually I did just that the other day, Mma,' she said casually. 'I knew that you wouldn't mind.'

*Mma Ramotswe was **quick** to agree. 'Of course not. Of course not, Mma.'*
(ALEXANDER MCCALL SMITH,
THE GOOD HUSBAND OF
ZEBRA DRIVE, 2007)

*Both of them have perfect voices for radio, well modulated, firm but not sharp; both have minds stock full of information and yet are also **quick**-witted enough to be able to pick out what's most important and to talk about it in a way that we ordinary mortals can understand.*
(THE SPECTATOR, 30 JULY 2008)

Originally *quick* meant 'alive', coming from Old English *cwic(u)* and the unattested proto-Germanic form *kwikwoz*, 'lively'. From its earliest uses (dating back over a millennium), there has often been an implied contrast with the inanimate. A man's estate, for instance, might be divided into *quick* and *dead* goods, the quick being livestock. The contrast still lingers in the expression *the quick and the dead*, made familiar through older versions of the Bible and the Apostles' Creed. Again, *quick flesh* was 'living' flesh. Used as a noun since the sixteenth century, *the quick* denoted the 'most tender flesh' of the body, that which was most alive to pain – hence the idiom *to be cut to the quick*. Vigour, energy and, particularly, rapid movement are evidence of life and it is from these concepts that subsequent senses of *quick* emerged, including the present-day sense of 'swift,' which started to develop in the late thirteenth century.

American evangelist Billy Graham tells a story that plays upon the old and new senses of *quick*. To the question, *What types of people are there in New York?* the answer is: *Just two – the quick and the dead*.

quixotic
excessively idealistic and unrealistic

*When you fell in love at first sight, how long, let me ask, did it take you to become ready to fling every other consideration to the winds except that of obtaining possession of the loved one?... suppose your nature was **Quixotic**, impulsive, altruistic, guileless... how long under these circumstances do you think you would reflect before you would decide on embracing what chance had thrown in your way?*
(SAMUEL BUTLER,
THE WAY OF ALL FLESH, 1903)

*I never knew where I was with her, or what sort of treatment to expect at her hands, and this was, I suspect, a large part of her attraction for me, such is the **quixotic** nature of love.*
(JOHN BANVILLE, THE SEA, 2005)

*...there's Pirahã, an Amazonian language **quixotic** enough to have inspired at least one* New Yorker *article and much gnashing of teeth among linguists.*
(ELIZABETH LITTLE,
BITING THE WAX TADPOLE, 2007)

In 1605 the Spanish author Miguel de Cervantes published his novel DON QUIXOTE DE LA MANCHA, a satire on the chivalric literature that was popular at the time. The story tells of the exploits of an elderly gentleman who is so caught up in the idealism of the romances he reads that he feels compelled to roam the countryside righting wrongs. Don Quixote's over-active imagination totally transforms reality. He sees a flock of sheep as an army, for instance, and, in a particularly well-known episode, attacks windmills with his lance thinking they are giants.

Others attempted to cash in on the book's popularity by continuing the knight's adventures, and this goaded Cervantes into writing a second volume, which was published in 1615.

English translations appeared in 1612 and 1620; various other languages soon followed. Within a few years, references to the work started to appear in English literature. The line *Thy head is full of windmills*, for instance, occurs in Massinger and Dekker's THE VIRGIN MARTYR as early as 1622. The English idioms *to have windmills in one's head* and *to tilt at windmills* both originate in the story.

Since then a variety of words have been derived from the gentle knight's name to express 'fervent but impractical idealism'. *Quixotism* appeared in the 1680s, to be followed by *quixotly* and *quixoticism*. These are now obsolete, but the early nineteenth-century adjective *quixotic*, applied first to the hopelessly idealistic knight and subsequently to people or actions with a tendency towards capricious idealism, is current in modern English.

For another word originating in foreign literature, see GARGANTUAN.

· R ·

recipe

a list of ingredients and instructions for making a dish

With no Norman to talk to, the Queen now found she was conducting lengthier discussions with herself and putting more and more of her thoughts on paper, so that her notebooks multiplied and widened in scope. 'One recipe for happiness is to have no sense of entitlement.' To this she added a star and noted at the bottom of the page: 'this is not a lesson I have ever been in a position to learn.'
(ALAN BENNETT,
THE UNCOMMON READER, 2007)

Using surplus milk, they produced cheese to a new recipe that they devised themselves, that developed a unique aroma after a long and careful ageing process.
(THE TIMES, 13 DECEMBER 2008)

The word is the singular imperative form of the Latin verb *recipere*, 'to receive, to take'. The command *recipe*, 'take', often appeared at the top of a list of medicines required to cure a patient, the earliest record of the practice in English dating from the very beginning of the fifteenth century. The same convention was later applied to other similarly instructive lists, notably in cookery; the BABEES BOOK, a late fifteenth-century book of manners and etiquette for young pages, has *Recipe brede gratyd, & eggis*.

By the late sixteenth century *recipe* had begun to denote the prescription or the prepared medicine itself, and by the early eighteenth was also being more generally applied to 'a list of ingredients together with notes for making a preparation of some kind'; the Verney Letters archive – the personal history of an upper-class family covering several centuries – includes a letter from Sir Thomas Cave dated 5 October 1716 which says *Sister Lovett and I greatly admire the Ink you wrote last with,...but dare not wish for the Recipe it being no doubt a Secrett*. The word is first recorded as a culinary term towards the middle of the eighteenth century.

The recipe for Genoua-Bisket given in the entry for BISCUIT shows how the imperative 'take' was much used in cookery.

regatta

a meeting, social as well as competitive, for yachting and rowing races

The crew set to work in good earnest, inspired by the reward to be gained. There was not a sheet which was not tightened; not a sail which was not vigorously hoisted; not a lurch could be charged to the man at the helm. They worked as desperately as if they were contesting in a Royal yacht regatta.
(JULES VERNE, AROUND THE WORLD IN EIGHTY DAYS, 1873)

The oldest sailing regatta in the world, Cowes Week, started in near perfect conditions yesterday. It is 181 years old and shows every sign of continued growth, but there can be no doubt it has changed over the years. Little is known of its earliest

life, but what has been readily apparent is the way it has adapted to the wave of commercialism that is the tide in all sporting events.
(THE OBSERVER, 5 AUGUST 2007)

English travellers to Venice in the seventeenth century were sometimes fortunate enough to be present at a *regatta*, a colourful gondola race along the Grand Canal. One report of the period called the regatta *a costly and ostentatious triumph*. The word is probably from the Venetian dialect and literally means 'contention for mastery', being a derivation of the verb *rigattare*, 'to contend, to wrangle, to haggle'.

Not to be outdone, other countries also started to hold regattas. The first in England took place on the Thames on 23 June 1775 and caused great excitement in polite society. The PUBLIC ADVERTISER, 24 May, predicted that the *Regatta* would *keep at home many of our Nobility and wealthy Commoners*.

rehearse
to practise in advance of performance

*Jamie listened, eyeing her from time to time over the edge of his beer glass. He remained uneasy about the whole project, but he had to agree that she was well **rehearsed**.*
(ALEXANDER MCCALL SMITH, THE SUNDAY PHILOSOPHY CLUB, 2004)

*The Fury stretched out his hand and shook theirs and Gretel gave a careful, **rehearsed** curtsy. Bruno was delighted when it went wrong and she almost fell over.*
(JOHN BOYNE, THE BOY IN THE STRIPED PYJAMAS, 2006)

Old French *herce*, 'a harrow', 'a large rake', yielded the verb *hercer*, 'to harrow'. Sometimes lumpy ground would need harrowing a second time, and the term for this was *rehercer*. Over time this verb also developed the sense 'to repeat'. It was borrowed into Middle English as *rehercen* in the fourteenth century and meant 'to recite, to repeat aloud'. By the late sixteenth century the modern spelling had evolved and the word was being used as a theatrical term with the sense 'to practise a performance'. Early uses of *rehearse* and the derived noun *rehearsal* in this context occur in Shakespeare's A MIDSUMMER NIGHT'S DREAM (1590) when the 'mechanicals' Quince, Snug, Bottom, Flute, Snout and Starveling are busy preparing their 'comedy' *Pyramus and Thisbe*:

Pat, pat; and here's a marvellous convenient place for our rehersal. This green plot shall be our stage, this hawthorn brake our tiring-house; and we will do it in action, as we will do it before the Duke.

Come sit down, every mother's son, and rehearse your parts. Pyramus, you begin; when you have spoken your speech, enter into that brake; and so every one according to his cue.

For another word from the same source, see HEARSE.

remorse
deep regret at a wrong action

*So there you have the posish, and you can see why, as I left the dock a free man, **remorse** gnawed at my vitals. In his twenty-fifth year, with life opening out before him and all that sort of thing, Oliver Randolph Sipperley had become a jail-bird, and it was all my fault. It was I who had dragged that fine spirit down into the mire, so to speak, and the question now arose, What could I do to atone?*
(P G WODEHOUSE, CARRY ON, JEEVES, 1925)

*My own relief was so overwhelming that I was on a high of happiness and thanksgiving for several days. Yet even though the agony was over, I still found it hard to forgive myself for the ordeal I had put Victoria through. It took months for my **remorse** to fade.*
(JONATHAN AITKEN.
PRIDE AND PERJURY, 2000)

Remorse is very descriptive of the pangs of shame that continuously gnaw at the guilty conscience, for the word literally means 'a biting back'. It comes from the Latin verb *remordēre*, 'to vex, to torment', a compound of *re-*, 'again', and *mordēre*, 'to bite'. From the past participle of this verb Medieval Latin derived the noun *remorsus* and coined the phrase *remorsus conscientiae*, 'anguish of conscience'. This was borrowed into Old French as *remors de conscience* and from there into Middle English as *remorse of conscience* in the fourteenth century. The earliest record is in Chaucer's TROILUS AND CRISEYDE (c. 1385). This expression lingered until the early 1800s although, by the turn of the fifteenth century, *remorse* was already being used independently to convey exactly the same meaning.

rhubarb
a plant with reddish stalks which are eaten cooked and sweetened

*Here I learned to hate **rhubarb** and custard. Well, school rhubarb and school custard. I quite like it now, but I remember sitting hunched over one unappetising mound of red, green and yellow while my schoolmates played outside and a teacher stayed behind until the last morsel disappeared.*
(ALAN TITCHMARSH,
TROWEL AND ERROR, 2002)

Rhubarb is strictly a vegetable as it is the stem of a plant, but it is always eaten in sweet dishes.
(GOOD HOUSEKEEPING
COOKERY BOOK, 2004)

Rhubarb is a 'barbarous' plant native to China, where it was used as a purgative. It was put to similar use when it was imported into England. At one time the plant was cultivated on the banks of the Rha (now the Volga) for export to Europe and the lands of the eastern Mediterranean. Consequently, one of the two Greek terms for *rhubarb* was *rha*. The other, *rhēon*, became Latin *rheum*, which is now the botanical term for this family of plants. *Rha* was borrowed into Late Latin, still as *rha,* and from this Medieval Latin coined *rha barbarum*, literally 'barbarous rhubarb', which, influenced by the original Latin, then became *rheubarbarum*. This passed into Old French as *reubarbe* and from there into Middle English as *rubarbe* in the fourteenth century.

In the fifteenth and sixteenth centuries, rhubarb was not cheap. A character in John Heywood's play THE FOURE PP (1540) announces:

> *I haue a boxe of rubarde here*
> *Whiche is as deynty as it is dere.*

The spelling *rubarde* is an early, little used variant already waning when Heywood wrote it.

And, according to John Gerard's HERBALL (1597), there was nothing to beat the rhubarb imported from its original source:

> *The best Rubarbe is that which is brought from China fresh and newe... The second in goodnes is that which cometh from Barbarie [North Africa]. The last and woorst from Bosphorus and Pontus [modern Turkey].*

See BARBAROUS.

rigmarole
a complicated, wandering statement;
an unnecessarily complex set of
procedures

*At 10a.m. went on the box of Miss
Newton's brougham to the reopening of
Mansel Grange Church after a good
restoration. More than 25 clergy in
surplices. The Bishop preached in the
morning; the Archdeacon, Lord Saye and
Sele, in the afternoon. It was difficult to
say which was the worse sermon. The
former was a screed, the latter a* **rigmarole**,
*but the rigmarole was more appropriate
and more to the purpose than the screed.*
(FRANCIS KILVERT, DIARY,
26 FEBRUARY 1878)

*For Kate, the extension of a security pass is
the most significant and personal privilege
that she has been afforded to date. She has
in effect been given a key to the Royal
residences. Her visits need no longer be
heralded by William or his bodyguards
requesting her name be put on a list of
visitors held by the protection officer at
the gates. Nor need she go through the*
rigmarole *of presenting any identifying
documents other than her pass.*
(EVENING STANDARD,
18 AUGUST 2007)

Ragman was a popular game in the thirteenth century. It consisted of a set of
scurrilous character outlines written in
verse and inscribed on a scroll or
ragman roll. A string and seal were fastened to each verse. When the scroll
was rolled up, players would choose
one of the strings and then read aloud
the character description that chance
had allotted to them, often occasioning
great hilarity.

The source of the word *ragman* is
obscure. It may be of French origin; the
earliest English form is *rageman* (pronounced as three syllables with a hard *g*)
and *Rageman le bon*, 'Rageman the good',
is a character in a series of French verses

dating from 1290. There is, however, an
earlier recorded appearance of *Rageman*
in English. In 1276 it was given as a
nickname to a statute of Edward I by
which commissions of enquiry were set
up to investigate complaints of injustice.
The juries' returns were written on
parchment and bore pendent seals.
Their appearance suggested either a
'ragged man' or a game of 'ragman roll'.
Which came first – the statute or the
game? The word was subsequently
applied to other documents of similar
appearance, in particular to a charter of
1291 in which the Scottish nobility
pledged allegiance to Edward I.

Whatever the origins, it is considered that the game with its list of
characters influenced the figurative
application of both *Ragman* and
Ragman roll to any sort of 'inventory' or
'catalogue', especially a long register of
names. This is found from the fourteenth century; by the early sixteenth,
Scottish English records the use of
ragman for a 'long, unintelligible discourse', an application apparently suggested by the dislocated nature of a
long list. A similar use was developing
in England. Here, well over a century
after it had ceased to be used for 'a list',
ragman roll reappeared in the first half
of the eighteenth century as *rig-myrole*,
rigginonrowle, *rig-me-role* and finally *rigmarole* to describe 'a disconnected,
long-winded discourse', 'an elaborate,
contrived story' or, more generally,
rhetoric of this kind:

*Alfonso paused a minute – then begun
Some strange excuses for his late proceeding:
He would not justify what he had done,
To say the best, it was extreme illbreeding, –
But there were ample reasons for it, none
Of which he specified in this his pleading:
His speech was a fine sample, on the whole,
Of rhetoric, which the learn'd call rigmarole.*
(LORD BYRON, DON JUAN, 1818)

The history of *rigmarole* has developed still further in more modern times, for in the middle of the twentieth century its use was extended to apply to 'a long, complicated procedure', in other words 'a PALAVER'.

For other words originating in games, see HANDICAP and HAZARD.

rival
a competitor, an opponent

...there has survived in writing only the strange story that Thessalian women beat a rival to death with wooden tortoises in a shrine to Aphrodite.
(COLIN THUBRON,
THE HILLS OF ADONIS, 1968)

Even today you cannot visit South Georgia without hearing that name echoing from the sea and the ice. Destined to become Scott's great rival, both for sponsorship and for the attention of the public, Shackleton was a charismatic Anglo-Irishman who learned his craft as a mariner in the Merchant Marine.
(JONATHAN & ANGELA SCOTT,
ANTARCTICA, 2007)

Afterwards, Martha realized what had happened: the male humpback had spotted a rival. He had one thing on his mind – to see off the competition – and woe betide anything in his way.
(MICHAEL BRIGHT,
100 YEARS OF WILDLIFE, 2007)

Rival is a watery word, its source being the Latin noun *rīvus*, meaning 'a stream, a brook'. From this came the adjective *rīvālis*, which meant 'belonging to a brook'. This term was applied to those who 'belonged' to the brook in the sense that they lived on its bank and used it for their water supply. Before long *rīvālis* was used as a noun to mean 'one who shares a stretch of water with another', hence 'a near neighbour'. It is not difficult to imagine the kind of dispute that might arise over use of the stream – rerouting it for irrigation, accusations of pollution and the like. This notion of neighbours fighting for dominance was taken up by playwrights and poets, who then applied *rīvālis* in the context of love so that it came to mean 'a competitor in love, one who desires the same person as another'. *Rival* was taken into Middle French, initially with this latter sense, in the fifteenth century and into English in the last quarter of the sixteenth.

☞ *Derive* comes from Latin *dērivāre*, 'to draw off or divert water from its source' (from *de-*, 'away' and *rīvus*, 'brook'), and hence the figurative applications with the general sense 'to draw, obtain or receive from a source'. The word entered Middle English in the fifteenth century by way of Old French *deriver*.

For other words connected with a watercourse, though from a different source, see ARRIVE and RIVER.

river
a large stream of water flowing ultimately to the sea

*She by the **River** sate, and sitting there, She wept, and made it deeper by a teare.*
(ROBERT HERRICK, 1591–1674)

Never in his life had he seen a river before – this sleek, sinuous, full-bodied animal, chasing and chuckling, gripping things with a gurgle and leaving them with a laugh... All was a-shake and a-shiver – glints and gleams and sparkles, rustle and swirl, chatter and bubble.
(KENNETH GRAHAME,
THE WIND IN THE WILLOWS, 1908)

We caught a dozen handsome deep-bodied silver fish using a light net cast out into the current. The softness of the light, the weedy smell and the warm brown **river** *were captivating, quite unlike sea fishing. Alain, like all the river fishermen I met, was quiet, relaxed, content to watch the river flow.*
(RICK STEIN, FRENCH ODYSSEY, 2005)

River comes ultimately from the Latin noun *rīpa*, meaning 'riverbank'. From this the adjective *rīpārius*, 'belonging to a river bank', was derived to describe land or a dwelling place beside a river. It is assumed that in time the Vulgar Latin noun *rīpāria* evolved to denote land thus situated. The Spanish, Portuguese and Italian words deriving from this noun, *ribera*, *ribeira* and *riviera* respectively, all mean 'strand' or 'shore'. Initially the Old French term *riviere* had the same meaning, but this was then extended to refer to the watercourse as well. When Middle English borrowed the word in the second half of the thirteenth century it absorbed this dual meaning, although after the fifteenth century *river* ceased to refer to the 'bank'. In modern English, riverside buildings – castles and houses, pubs and tearooms – are described as being *on the river*, a throwback to the time when a *river* was also 'a shore'.

For other words about the river, see ARRIVE and RIVAL.

road
a surfaced route for the passage of vehicles

A republic was declared in Rome in 509 B.C., and all **roads** *have led here ever since. A very busy city of leisurely citizens, Rome serves up a jolt of big-city life with the warmth of a small provincial town.*
(PATRICIA SCHULTZ, 1,000 PLACES TO SEE BEFORE YOU DIE, 2003)

I saw a café with two old men playing chess on a plastic table on the roadside. I tried to assay a casualness I did not feel and kicked playfully at the countless carrier bags that blew like plastic dust devils haphazardly down the quiet, dirty, dusty **road**. *I sat down beside them. They looked up and nodded in greeting.*
(BOB GELDOF, GELDOF IN AFRICA, 2005)

A letter from one member of the Paston family to another in 1463 contains a report on the sorry condition of his horse, which had just been to the farrier's: *I sent your grey hors…to the ferror, and he seythe he shull never be nowght to rood nowthyr ryght good to plowe nor to carte.* Here, *road* does not mean 'way' but 'riding'. The word comes from the Old English verb *rīdan*, 'to ride', and its derivative *rād* which meant 'a riding, a journey on horseback'. *Road* is, therefore, a relative of the modern verb *to ride*.

In Old English the word also came to mean 'riding with hostile intent' and hence 'a raid'. The term *inroad*, recorded from the sixteenth century, reflects this; it meant 'a hostile incursion on horseback'. And the noun *raid* itself is a Scots variant of 'road'.

Both of the Old English senses persisted into the seventeenth century. In Shakespeare's HENRY VIII (1613) the usher Griffith, reporting the circumstances of Wolsey's death to Queen Katherine, tells how at first the cardinal was too weak to ride his mule but how *At last, with easie Rodes, he came to Leicester.* And as late as 1665 the legal and political writer Thomas Manley, in his book about the English wars with the Netherlands, writes that the English *assailed and made Incursions and Rodes upon all Spanish ships, and other places* (H GROTIUS DE REBUS BELGICIS).

The modern sense of 'a way made for the passage of people, horses and vehicles' began to emerge at the end of the sixteenth century. The earliest records of this are in the plays of Shakespeare, who was obviously comfortable using *road* in its old as well as its emerging sense.

robot
an automaton, a machine that automatically carries out the tasks of a human

*On their way there, they encounter the postgraduate Jim in a corridor, observing a small **robot**, about two feet high. It has three wheels, a rotating head with lenses for eyes, and a pair of mechanical claws.*
(DAVID LODGE, THINKS..., 2001)

*The surgeon holds a force-controlled handle at the tip of the **robot** and moves the robot around within the required region, whilst the robot actively constrains him to a safe and precise location.*
(THE INDEPENDENT, 3 JUNE 2009)

The modern nightmare of artificially created human beings that gradually develop reasoning and emotions before destroying their creators was the theme of R. U. R. (ROSSUM'S UNIVERSAL ROBOTS), written in 1920 by the Czech playwright Karel Capek. The play was performed in New York in 1922 and published in English translation in 1923.

Capek derived his word *Robot* from the Czech *robota*, which means 'forced labour, drudgery' (a *robotnik* is 'a serf'). *You see*, Capek wrote, *the Robots have no interest in life. They have no enjoyments.*

Robot also came to be used conversely: Capek's invention is applicable to people who spend their waking hours at repetitive tasks – on a production line, for instance. So in modern English a *robot* can be a passionless, dehumanised human as well as a highly sophisticated automaton.

The science of the design, building and application of such robots is known as *robotics* and was the coinage in the early 1940s of the American immigrant scientist Isaac Asimov, a well-known author of popular science and science fiction. In an essay entitled 'The Word I Invented', published in COUNTING THE EONS (1984), Asimov wrote:

I did not know at the time that it [robotics] was an invented term. The science of physics routinely uses the -ics suffix for various branches, as in mechanics, dynamics, electrostatics, hydraulics, and so on. I took it for granted that the study of robots was robotics. It wasn't until a dozen years later, at least, that I became aware that robotics was not listed in the second edition of Websters New International Dictionary *or (when I quickly checked) in any of the other dictionaries I consulted. What's more, when Websters's third edition was published, I looked up robotics at once and still didn't find it. I therefore began saying that I had invented the word, for it did indeed seem to me that I had done so.*

Asimov was also responsible for the noun *roboticist*, meaning 'an expert in the science of robotics'.

robust
strong, resilient, forceful

*I am better...but I intend to take care of myself. My mother often tells me I go at things too hard. Besides, I don't really get enough air and exercise – without which one can never be truly **robust**.*
(ANTHONY POWELL,
A BUYER'S MARKET, 1952)

*The more **robust** varieties of home-grown herbs can be dried successfully at home. Tie in bunches and hang in a cool airy place, covered with muslin to keep the dust off.*
(GOOD HOUSEKEEPING
COOKERY BOOK, 2004)

*Three-year-old Reagan was born in Uganda to a mother who has HIV, but he does not have the virus. His mother Alice has received counselling and support from World Vision and attended a successful Prevention of Mother to Child Transmission HIV programme. Reagan is a **robust**, healthy and talkative testament to the programme's success.*
(WORLD VISION CALENDAR, PHOTOGRAPH CAPTION FOR APRIL 2009)

Rōbus, from *ruber*, 'red', was an Old Latin word for a type of oak tree with very hard, reddish coloured wood. The mighty tree suggested great power and so *rōbus* (later *rōbur*) was also used to mean 'strength'. The adjective *rōbustus*, which is derived from it, therefore meant 'strong and solid as an oak'. The word was borrowed into English, possibly by way of French *robuste*, in the sixteenth century to describe a person who was 'vigorous and hardy', being of a sturdy constitution.

rostrum
a dais, a platform or stand for public speaking, conducting, auctioneering, etc.

*The moments before an auctioneer steps onto a **rostrum** are much like those of an actor. An auction is a drama that has to entertain its audience, and the auctioneer defines its success.*
(THE TIMES, 2 OCTOBER 2008)

The Mayor of the little [French] town of Vierville-sur-Mer, which peers down from the cliff above, was holding a ceremony in honour of the U.S. 29th Division who landed here. Anyone who has seen the opening scenes of Saving Private Ryan *will have an inkling of what happened to those men. It was a massacre. But eight survivors had made it back for this anniversary and, one by one, they came to the **rostrum** – some on sticks, some in wheelchairs – and recalled their stories.*
(DAILY MAIL, 8 JUNE 2009)

Rostrum in Latin meant 'beak, muzzle', being derived from the verb *rōdere*, 'to gnaw'. Metaphorically, it was applied to the prow of a ship, since the shape was considered reminiscent of a bird's bill.

The Romans had a colony at Antium (now Anzio on the west coast of Italy), a place notorious for its piracy. When it revolted, the Romans returned in force to re-establish the colony in 338 BC. Antium was deprived of all its ships and their 'beaks' were taken to the Forum in Rome where they were used to decorate the orators' platform. For this reason the stand, and the area in the Forum where it was situated, was known as the *rostra* (the plural of *rostrum*).

Rostra is found in English from the sixteenth century onwards in classical translations or with specific reference to the platform in Rome. Not until the second half of the eighteenth century was the singular form *rostrum* adopted into English to denote 'a platform set up for public speaking'.

☛ *Rōdere*, 'to gnaw', is evident in *corrode* (14th cent) and *erode* (17th cent), both meaning 'to gnaw away', and also in *rodent*, a nineteenth-century zoological coinage (from New Latin *Rodentia*, derived from *rōdent-*, the stem of *rōdēns*, present particple of *rōdere*).

· S ·

sack

a large bag made of coarse material; to plunder, to spoil; to dismiss

The four Greek bronze horses, stolen from Byzantium by the Venetians in 1204 when they persuaded Crusaders to **sack** *the city, were also removed – this time from the gallery of St Mark's basilica in Venice – and replaced with copies.*
(THE TELEGRAPH, 22 JULY 2001)

Paul Ince, the manager of Blackburn Rovers, rounded on his critics last night, accusing them of conspiring to get him **sacked** *because they are envious of his career as a successful player for Manchester United.*
(THE TIMES, 6 DECEMBER 2008)

But why, I thought, without muttering it out loud to the others, must the two things be mutually exclusive, a sense of humour, or wit, or playfulness, and a genuine socialism. Must we all be cloth **sacks** *and grow our own sandals to be taken seriously?*
(JILL DAWSON,
THE GREAT LOVER, 2009)

Sack in the sense of 'large oblong bag' is Semitic in origin; it derives from Hebrew *saq*, 'sackcloth', and has made its way into the languages of eastern and western Europe.

The sackcloth of the Old Testament was made of animal hair, especially that of a goat. It was usually black in colour and always coarse in texture. This cheap, hard-wearing cloth was both worn by herdsmen and used to make grain bags, so that *saq* was also applied to them: the word is used in this sense in Genesis 42, for instance, where Joseph tests his brothers by placing a gold cup in one of their sacks of grain.

The term was taken into Greek as *sakkos* and then into Latin as *saccus*, still meaning both 'sackcloth' and 'sack'. From here it was extensively borrowed into other languages. Old English had *sacc*, which became *sak* or *sack* in Middle English.

Sack with the sense 'pillage', 'spoil', dates from around the mid-sixteenth century and is a borrowing of French *sac*, which in turn comes from Italian *sacco*, 'plunder'. Many authorities consider that this Italian word and Italian *sacco* meaning 'bag' (from Latin *saccus*) are one and the same and suggest that its use in this context arose through the stuffing of spoil into sacks in order to cart it away. In support of this theory, the Italian and French expressions *mettere a sacco* and *mettre à sac* both mean 'to plunder' and have the literal sense 'to put in a bag'. The sixteenth-century English equivalent, a direct borrowing of the French, was *to put to sack* or *to put to/onto the sack*. The verb *to sack* also dates from the sixteenth century.

Sack in the sense of 'dismissal from one's occupation' has been current in English in the idiomatic phrases *to give someone the sack* and *to get the sack* since the nineteenth century, but *den zac krijen*, 'to get the sack', already existed in Middle Dutch and the idea was known in French from the seventeenth century. The usual explanation offered for the expression is that workmen would leave their tools in a bag at their place of work. If a master wanted to dismiss a labourer, he would hand over his sack of tools to show that he shouldn't come back.

☛ Latin *saccellus*, a diminutive of *saccus*, gave Old French *sachel*, 'a small bag'. This was borrowed into Middle English in the fourteenth century and denoted 'a small bag for carrying money or food for the day'. The spelling *satchel* dates from the second half of the sixteenth century, as does the sense 'small bag for carrying school books':

This done, thy setchell and thy bokes take,
And to the scole haste see thou make.
(F SEAGER, THE SCHOOLE OF VERTUE
AND BOOKE OF GOOD NOURTURE FOR
CHYLDREN, 1557)

Sachet is a French diminutive of *sac*, 'bag, sack', which was borrowed into English in the nineteenth century.

salad

a dish mainly of uncooked green vegetables

*They say **salad** helps you lose weight but I suspect that's only because you lose interest in eating anything at all halfway through the second lettuce leaf.*
(GOOD HOUSEKEEPING, APRIL 2009)

There is no menu – each street kitchen serves either pho *(noodle soup) or* bun cha *(char-grilled pork served with noodles and a green **salad**). We plump for the latter and it's tasty, although I avoid the salad. (My mum says the salad might be washed in local tap water, which will kill me.)*
(STEPHEN MERCHANT IN BALES
WORLD MAGAZINE, SUMMER 2009)

The salad is the glory of every French dinner and the disgrace of most in England (Richard Ford, GATHERINGS FROM SPAIN, 1846). It seems that the English cannot get anything right when it comes to food, not even in dishes where no cooking is required. The secret must lie in the dressing.

The Romans ate raw vegetables which they flavoured with salty dressings. The politician Cato enjoyed cabbage served in this way and the Emperor Tiberius had a passion for cucumbers. Apicius, a fourth-century cookery writer, gives a recipe for cucumber salad with a dressing of pepper, pennyroyal, honey, liquamen (a type of salty fish sauce rather like anchovy essence) and vinegar. The Roman fondness for salads extended into the winter months. For instance, Columella, who wrote on agricultural matters in the first century, preserved lettuce leaves by pickling them in brine and vinegar (Don and Patricia Brothwell, FOOD IN ANTIQUITY, 1969).

The probable Latin term for the salad dishes over which the Romans drooled reflects the saltiness of the dressings: *herba salāta*, literally means 'salted greens' (from unattested Latin *salāre*, 'to salt', from *sāl*, 'salt'). Vulgar Latin shortened the term, making a noun of *salāta*. This became *salada* in Provençal and *salade* in Old French, from where it was borrowed into Middle English. An early recipe from THE FORM OF CURY (1390) runs:

Salat. Take persel. sawge, garlec...waische hem clene...and myng hem wel with rawe oile, lay on vyneger and salt, and serue it forth.

The word, then, had entered the language but not, by popular repute, the culinary flair – although the Reverend Sidney Smith (1771–1845) seemed to know what he was doing:

*SIDNEY SMITH'S RECIPE FOR
SALAD:*
*To make this condiment, your poet begs
The pounded yellow of two hard-boiled eggs,
Two boiled potatoes, passed through
kitchen-seive,
Smoothness and softness to the salad give;
Let onion atoms lurk within the bowl,
And, scarce-suspected, animate the whole.
Of mordant mustard add a single spoon,
Distrust the condiment that bites so soon;
But deem it not, thou man of herbs, a fault
To add a double quantity of salt.
And, lastly, o'er the flavoured
compound toss
A magic soup-spoon of anchovy sauce.
Oh, green and glorious! Oh, herbaceous
treat!
'Twould tempt the dying anchorite to eat;
Back to the world he'd turn his
fleeting soul,
And plunge his fingers in the salad bowl!
Serenely full, the epicure would say,
Fate cannot harm me, I have dined today.*

☛ Other salty culinary terms deriving
from Latin *sāl*, 'salt', are:

salami (19th cent): Italian plural of
salame, 'salted pork', from *salare*, from
unattested Latin *salāre*, 'to salt'.

sauce (14th cent): Middle English
through Old French *sauce*, from Latin
salsa, feminine of *salsus*, 'salted'.

sausage (14th cent): Middle English
sausige, through Old Norman French
saussiche, from Late Latin *salsīcia*, from
Latin *salsīcius*, 'made with salt', from
salsus, 'salted'.

See also SALARY.

salary

remuneration for work, a wage, usually
paid monthly

*My mother's father, a good-hearted Irish
Catholic named Michael McGuire, had
worked the whole of his adult life as a hand
in the stockyards on a paltry **salary**.*
(BILL BRYSON, THE LIFE AND TIMES
OF THE THUNDERBOLT KID, 2006)

*Although we could afford to live on my
husband's wage alone, my **salary** means
I can buy a treat when I want to and give
more to the kids.*
(GOOD HOUSEKEEPING, APRIL 2009)

These days salt is plentiful and cheap
and therefore taken for granted. In
ancient times, however, this was not
the case. Salt, which was essential to
enhance the flavour of food and to preserve it, was a luxury and had to be
imported into many regions of the
Roman Empire. At one time Roman
soldiers were given a *salārium* (from
Latin *sāl*, 'salt'), an allowance with
which to buy salt. The word was then
applied to the soldier's pay and later
extended into civilian use. The expression *to be worth one's salt* (that is, one's
wages) derives from this ancient practice but, curiously, appears to date back
only to the early nineteenth century.
Salary came into Middle English in the
fourteenth century from Anglo-French
salarie and Old French *salaire*.

For other words derived from *sāl,* see
SALAD.

sandwich

two slices of bread with a filling
between

*At the restaurant, sitting on a high stool
before a pine counter, he choked over an
egg **sandwich** made with thick crumby
slices of a bread that had no personality
to it.*
(SINCLAIR LEWIS, OUR MR WRENN,
THE ROMANTIC ADVENTURES OF A
GENTLE MAN, 1914)

*Stellings has got a small first-floor flat in Arundel Gardens, Notting Hill, **sandwiched** between a bongo player and a junior anaesthetist.*
(SEBASTIAN FAULKS, ENGLEBY, 2007)

What else would a true Englishman put in his sandwich but cold roast beef? According to Pierre-Jean Grosley (LONDRES, 1770), who supplied an account of the origin of the word, this traditional fare, wedged between slices of toast, was offered to John Montagu 4th Earl of Sandwich (1718–92), a compulsive gambler who spent entire days at the tables without stopping for food or rest.

Grosley, a French man of letters and a travel writer, was in London in 1765 when he first came across the word, but it is recorded earlier in the journal of the writer Edward Gibbon. After a visit to the Cocoa Tree, a fashionable London club where men of society could gamble for very high stakes, Gibbon wrote in his journal for 24 November 1762:

I dined at the Cocoa Tree... That respectable body...affords every evening a sight truly English. Twenty or thirty...of the first men in the kingdom,...supping at little tables upon a bit of cold meat, or a Sandwich.

To be fair to the Earl's reputation, N A M Rodger, in his biography THE INSATIABLE EARL (1993), suggests that John Montagu was dedicated to the arts and to his political life and that his habit of eating sandwiches probably began in his office.

To trace the word back still further, the estimable Earl took his title from *Sandwich*, a town in Kent and one of the medieval Cinque Ports which defended the south-east coast. Situated about 3 km (2 miles) up the river Stour, Sandwich ceased to be a port in the sixteenth century when the harbour silted up. Its name derives from Old English *Sandwic*, meaning 'sand village'.

For a game played at the Cocoa Tree, see HAZARD. For the early history of the club, see CHOCOLATE.

sarcasm
sharp, wounding, bitter comment

*The blatant soldier often convulsed whole files by his biting **sarcasms** aimed at the tall one.*
(STEVEN CRANE,
THE RED BADGE OF COURAGE, 1895)

*'In English, tone – or, more properly, intonation – usually applies to an entire thought: we pitch our voices up at the end of a question or use a monotone to convey **sarcasm**. In Chinese, however, tone can change the meaning of the words themselves.*
(ELIZABETH LITTLE,
BITING THE WAX TADPOLE, 2007)

Sarcastic humour or comment is intended to wound. This is evident from the savage etymology of the word *sarcasm*. The Greeks had a verb *sarcazein*, derived from *sarx*, 'flesh', which literally meant 'to tear flesh' as an animal would. When they applied the term metaphorically, it had the sense 'to bite the lips in fury' and then 'to speak contemptuously'. From this came the noun *sarkasmos*, which meant 'a barbed comment', 'a biting taunt'. This was taken into Late Latin as *sarcasmus* and from there into English in the second half of the sixteenth century as a personification of a cutting, scoffing spirit, 'a figure called Sarcasmus'. In his ANATOMY OF MELANCHOLY (1621), Robert Burton writes: *Many are of so petulant a spleene, and haue that figure Sarcasmus so often in their mouths...*

In the first quarter of the seventeenth century English borrowed the word again, this time from French as *sarcasme*. It meant 'a biting remark' and so was often found in the plural as *sarcasmes* or *sarcasms*. *Sarcasm* as a general noun dates from the second half of the nineteenth century.

For a word from the same source, see SARCOPHAGUS. For a word with a similar meaning, see SARDONIC.

sarcophagus
an ornate stone coffin or tomb

*A grand piano stood massively in a corner; with dark gleams on the flat surfaces like a sombre and polished **sarcophagus**.*
(JOSEPH CONRAD,
HEART OF DARKNESS, 1902)

*Blomkvist looked around. A raised **sarcophagus** belonged to Alexandre Vangeersad, and four graves in the floor housed the remains of the earliest family members. More recently the Vangers had apparently settled for cremation.*
(STIEG LARSSON, THE GIRL WITH THE DRAGON TATTOO, 2008)

This is a word to make your flesh creep: Greek corpses were encased in stone coffins which had the reputation of devouring the contents.

Lithos sarkophagos was the name the Greeks gave to a type of limestone which they cut from quarries near Assus, a city in Troas, Asia Minor. The name is a compound made up of *sark-*, stem of *sarx*, 'flesh', and *-phagos*, 'eating', from *phagein*, 'to eat', and means, quite literally, 'flesh eating'.

In Philemon Holland's translation of Pliny's NATURAL HISTORY (1601) we discover the reputed properties of the stone. It seems that *within the space of forty daies it is knowne for certaine to consume the bodies of the dead which are bestowed therein*. Those laid to rest in a coffin made of or lined with the stone could therefore expect a speedy decomposition. Eventually the Greeks transferred the term *sarkophagos* from the stone to the coffins themselves.

The word, promoted by Holland's translation, came into English in the seventeenth century by way of Latin *sarcophagus*. The first references are to the stone only, and then subsequently to the ornate coffin.

☛ The Greek stem *sark-* is also evident in words such as *sarcoma* and *sarcoplasm*.

For another word from *sarx*, 'flesh', see SARCASM.

sardonic
cynically mocking, scornful

*After being granted immediate bail to await sentencing in June, I had to go down to the cells below the court for a few minutes in order to recover my house and car keys, which had been taken off me by a **sardonic** custody officer with the explanation: 'Just in case one of 'em's a skeleton key to the detention area – we do have people here who do that sort of thing.'*
(JONATHAN AITKEN,
PRIDE AND PERJURY, 2000)

'So...how does it feel, Bill?'
'How does what feel?'
'Being single. Being free. Having the world as your oyster.'
*He let out a **sardonic** laugh. 'Ginnie, I'm pushing sixty.'*
(SIMON BRETT, THE PENULTIMATE CHANCE SALOON, 2006)

A little bit of classical confusion surrounds this word. The ancient world was familiar with a poisonous herb which grew on the island of Sardinia. If eaten, it was supposed to cause facial spasms and contortions which looked like a bout of hideous laughter. Dryden's verse translation of Virgil (1697) refers to the horrible spectacle thus:

May I become...
Rough as a Burr, deform'd like him
who chaws
Sardinian Herbage to contract his Jaws.

The plant was known in Latin as *herba Sardonia*, 'Sardinian herb'. Greek already had a word *sardanios* which meant 'bitter' or 'scornful'. However, the similarity in sound and the association of a scornful expression with the leer of a person under the influence of the Sardinian herb brought about a substitution of *sardonios* (from Latin *Sardonia*) for *sardanios* in Late Greek. From this Greek confusion came the Latin expression *Sardonius rīsus*, 'bitter laugh'.

The first English borrowings – in the sixteenth century – refer to *Sardonian laughter* and *Sardonian smiles*, a translation of the Latin phrase. Robert Green, for instance, in his romance MENAPHON (1589) has the lines:

Haue you fatted me so long with Sardenian
smiles,
that...I might perish in your wiles?

During the sixteenth century the French term *sardonique* evolved from the unattested Latin adjective *sardonicus* (an alteration of *sardonius*) and this was borrowed into English as *Sardonick* in the seventeenth century. The modern spelling emerged in the early eighteenth century, discarding at the same time the capital letter that properly denotes an adjective of place in English.

The Latin *risus Sardonicus* has been retained as a medical expression to denote the involuntary and rather disagreeable grin worn, for instance, by sufferers of tetanus where the facial muscles are in spasm.

scandal

a public outrage, disgrace; malicious gossip

This morning [name rubbed out] came privately to church at 10.30 with [name rubbed out] to be churched after the birth of her son, which took place three months after her wedding. This has been a great **scandal** *and grief to us.*
(FRANCIS KILVERT, DIARY, SUNDAY, 5 OCTOBER 1873)

One should never make one's debut with a **scandal**. *One should reserve that to give an interest to one's old age.*
(OSCAR WILDE, THE PICTURE OF DORIAN GRAY, 1891)

But then, suddenly, towards the end of February, when 'House Full' notices were being placed nightly outside the St James's, Wilde's success was clouded by **scandal**, *and before long his fortunes were in steep and irreversible decline.*
(DAVID LODGE, AUTHOR, AUTHOR, 2004)

Greek had an old word, *skandalon*, 'a spring trap' (from proto-Indo-European *skand-*, 'to leap'), which was figuratively applied to mean 'a moral snare or stumbling block'. Late Latin borrowed it as *scandalum* and used it in ecclesiastical contexts to denote 'that which causes one to fall into sin', a meaning it retained when it was taken into Old French as *escandle*. From there the word followed two routes into English, one arriving at *scandal* and the other at *slander*.

Escandle was borrowed into early Middle English as *scandle* with the ecclesiastical sense of 'dishonour brought to the Christian faith by the unseemly conduct of its adherents'. Its appearance was brief, however, the only known written record being the ANCRENE RIWLE (c. 1225), a devotional manual for religious recluses. Then, in the second half of the sixteenth century, the word was re-adopted from the revised French form *scandale*.

Scandale had been introduced into French as a specifically religious term based on ecclesiastical Latin *scandalum* because the Old French *escandle* had gone astray – it had developed variants, one of which was *esclandre*, and the additional sense of 'calumny, malicious falsehood'. This variant also started to appear in Middle English from the late thirteenth century as *sclaundre* and *slaundre* and similarly denoted 'false reports maliciously spoken to injure a person's reputation' – in other words, *slander*.

scapegoat
a person who takes the blame for the shortcomings of others

Everyone in Rome had heard of the **Scapegoat**. *And as Hieronymus quickly discovered, once he began making the rounds, there was hardly a household in Rome that wouldn't admit him if he paid a call. He was a curiosity, don't you see? Exotic, mysterious – the famous Scapegoat of Massilia, the sacrificial victim who was never sacrificed.*
(STEVEN SAYLOR,
THE TRIUMPH OF CAESAR, 2008)

Because terrible things can happen does not mean all risk should be eradicated. To hear stories of children being denied enjoyable and educational activities because there is always the faintest chance of something going wrong is depressing. We can teach children to be vigilant and sensible without being frightened of their own shadows. But if parents expect teachers to exercise common sense, then they must play their part by not always looking for a **scapegoat** *when things go awry.*
(THE TELEGRAPH, 22 JUNE 2009)

The most solemn day of the Jewish religious calendar is that of Yom Kippur, the Day of Atonement when, in the Judaism of the Old Testament, animal sacrifices were offered to atone for sin and reconcile the people to God. On this day alone was the high priest permitted to bring the blood of sacrifice into the holy of holies, directly into the Lord's presence. First a bullock was sacrificed as a sin-offering for the priest and his house. Next two goats were presented before the Lord and lots were cast to determine which of them should be slaughtered as the sin-offering for the people. When this sacrifice was complete the high priest laid his hands upon the remaining goat and confessed all the sins of the people over it before finally casting the creature out into the desert, where it ran off, symbolically taking the sins of the people away with it.

This goat has been called the *scapegoat* since Tyndale's translation of the Pentateuch in 1530, *scape* being an archaic variant of *escape*, the unstressed initial vowel having been omitted. The term arises from Tyndale's rendering of a particular word, *Azazel*. This is found only in the directions given for the Day of Atonement in Leviticus 16. Tyndale, along with other translators before him, understood *Azazel* as meaning 'the goat that goes away', from '*ēz*, 'goat', and *āzāl*, 'departs' or 'escapes', hence his coinage *scapegoat* in verse 8 of this chapter:

And Aaron cast lottes ouer the. ii. gootes: one lotte for the Lorde, and another for a scape-goote.

This is not the only interpretation, however. Other scholars have deliberated long over *Azazel* and have come up with various alternative explanations. Some point to similarities with the Arabic verb *azala*, 'to remove', and say it is an infinitive with the sense 'in order to remove'. Others suggest it means 'a lonely place' or 'a precipice'. The translators of the New English Bible have taken this view. Their rendition of the same verse reads: *He shall cast lots over the two goats, one to be for the Lord and the other for the Precipice*. The majority considers that *Azazel* derives from '*āzaz*, 'to be strong' and '*ēl*, 'God' and is the name of a demon that prowled the wilderness. In support of their theory, they point out that wherever it is used the name counterbalances that of the Lord. The Revised Standard Version of the Bible (1952) is deemed correct in its translation: *Aaron shall cast lots upon the two goats; one lot for the Lord and the other lot for Azazel*.

While none of these interpretations changes the essential import of the passage, they do cast into doubt the correctness of Tyndale's *scapegoat* although, interestingly enough, the term has been chosen for the widely acclaimed New International Version (1973).

In English early uses of the word were strictly confined to religious comment. Not until the first half of the nineteenth century was it applied in secular contexts to denote one who, like the biblical scapegoat, shoulders all the blame for the misdeeds of others. Today, the word frequently appears in the press as the plaintive cry of politicians reprimanded or dismissed because of unpopular government policies.

For other words concerning sacrifices and offerings, see ANATHEMA and HOLOCAUST.

scavenger

a human or animal that searches through what others have discarded for useful items or food

The following list completes, I believe, the terrestrial fauna: a fly (Olfersia) living on the booby, and a tick which must have come here as a parasite on the birds; a small brown moth, belonging to a genus that feeds on feathers; a beetle (Quedius) and a woodlouse from beneath the dung; and lastly, numerous spiders, which I suppose prey on these small attendants and **scavengers** *of the water-fowl.*
(CHARLES DARWIN, THE VOYAGE OF THE BEAGLE, 1839)

To find the best trash, you have to stay close to the dump trucks and diggers. People get crushed or buried – especially children who are harder for the drivers to spot. It's even worse at night... **Scavenging** *on the dump is not the life the family envisaged.*
(HABITAT FOR HUMANITY NEWSLETTER, SPRING 2009)

In the Middle Ages the governing authorities of London, and many other English towns, protected their own merchants by imposing a tax upon goods offered for sale within their boundaries by any trader coming from outside. The tax was called the *scawage* in Anglo-French, becoming *scavage* in Middle English. The Anglo-French term was a variant of Old Northern French *escawage*, 'inspection', from *escauwer*, 'to inspect' (whose Germanic origins were also responsible for English *show*).

In Middle English the officers who collected the levy were known as *scavagers* but, in the sixteenth century, the variant form *scavenger* appeared and took precedence. (This insertion of an *n* in words ending in -*ger* occurred in other borrowed words from the late Middle English period onwards: *messenger*, *harbinger* and *passenger* among them.)

Back-formations

English commonly makes a verb from an existing noun. One of the ways this happens is by back-formation: a new word is created from another by the removal of what is perceived to be an affix.

For example, *burglar* was not formed, as one might suppose, from the verb *burgle* and the agent suffix *-ar*. On the contrary the verb, which appeared only in the second half of the nineteenth century, is a back-formation of *burglar*, a noun in use since the fifteenth century. The verb was simply created by the removal of the assumed suffix *-ar*. In the same way the verb *scavenge*, which dates back principally to the nineteenth century, is a back-formation of the late sixteenth-century noun SCAVENGER. Other examples of a similar kind are:

> EAVESDROP (17th cent) from *eavesdropper* (15th cent)
> *peddle* (mid-17th cent) from *pedlar* (14th cent)
> *swindle* (18th cent) from *swindler* (18th cent)
> *edit* (late 18th cent) from *editor* (mid-17th cent)
> *stage-manage* (1870s) from *stage-manager* (early 19th cent)

Many verbs are back-formations of other kinds of nouns: *injury* (14th cent) yielded *injure* (16th cent), and *enthuse* is a nineteenth-century American back-formation from *enthusiasm* (16th cent). To take a more modern example, most people would guess correctly that *televise* was derived from *television*. It is a back-formation modelled on verbs such as *revise* which end in *-(v)ise* and whose related nouns end in *-ision*, like *revision*.

Although most of the words which are formed in this way are verbs, nouns and adjectives are also created:

> *greed* (17th cent) from *greedy* (10th cent)
> *haze* (18th cent) from *hazy* (17th cent)
> *gullible* (19th cent) from *gullibility* (18th cent)

Other languages increase their stock of words in a similar fashion. English *democrat* (late 18th cent) is a borrowing from French *democrate*. This in turn is a back-formation of the adjective *democratique*, 'democratic'. Indeed, the word was modelled on the earlier *aristocrate*, a popular back-formation of *aristocratique* at the time of the French Revolution.

Occasionally old, forgotten words are resurrected as back-formations. Today only the negative forms of the words *uncouth*, *unkempt* and *unruly* are familiar. For humorous effect, however, some authors resuscitate, by a process of back-formation, the Old English and Middle English adjectives *couth*, *kempt* and *ruly*. See entries for UNCOUTH, UNKEMPT, UNRULY and NEGATIVE PREFIXES (page 287).

During the sixteenth century the *scavengers* were also given the extra responsibility of keeping the streets clean and, when the tax was no longer levied, they remained as street cleaners. The term for one who did this unappealing but necessary work was soon more widely applied to 'any person or creature who lives by what others discard'.

scruple
a moral hesitation over a course of action

While it was in progress, some of the Spaniards observed what appeared to be a door recently plastered over. It was a common rumour that Montezuma still kept the treasures of his father, King Axayacatl, in this ancient palace. The Spaniards, acquainted with this fact, felt no **scruple** *in gratifying their curiosity by removing the plaster.*
(WILLIAM HICKLING PRESCOTT,
THE HISTORY OF THE CONQUEST
OF MEXICO, 1843)

Anthony nodded, and said nothing for a few seconds. 'The fact is, we've been dodging the issue all day. And I know why. You have **scruples**, *and so do I.'*
(CARO FRASER,
A CALCULATING HEART, 2004)

A Scruple is a great trouble of mind proceeding from a little motive, wrote Jeremy Taylor in DUCTOR DUBITANTIUM (1660), his book of guidance on questions of morality and conscience. Latin *scrūpus*, which meant 'a rough pebble', was used metaphorically by the Roman statesman Cicero to denote 'a cause of uneasiness or uncertainty' over something. When the smallest pebble falls into a person's shoe it is the cause of great discomfort, just as a seed of doubt over a question of conscience brings mental torment. In time the Latin diminutive *scrūpulus*, 'small sharp stone', also acquired this figurative sense. This became *scrupule* in French and *scruple* when it was borrowed from there into English in the sixteenth century.

serendipity
the gift of making fortunate discoveries

THE LAWS OF **SERENDIPITY**
1 In order to discover anything, you must be looking for something.
2 If you wish to make an improved product, you must already be engaged in making an inferior one.
(ANON)

Maria didn't seem to know the other guests very well...she spent most of the pre-dinner drinks being amused by Bill. And when it came to eating, the **serendipity** *of the seating plan also put him next to her.*
(SIMON BRETT, THE PENULTIMATE
CHANCE SALOON, 2006)

This happy coinage to describe 'the knack of making fortunate and surprising discoveries' is from the pen of Horace Walpole, the eighteenth-century man of letters. In a letter to his lifelong correspondent Horace Mann, written on 28 January 1754, Walpole describes how he came to invent the word and what exactly he meant by it, explaining that Mann would *understand it better by the derivation than by the definition*:

I once read a silly fairy tale, called The Three Princes of Serendip; as their highnesses travelled, they were always making discoveries, by accidents and sagacity, of things which they were not in quest of: for instance, one of them discovered that a mule blind of the right eye had travelled the same road lately, because the grass was eaten only on the left side, where it was worse than on the right – now do you understand Serendipity?

The fairytale itself dates back to the mid-sixteenth century. It was written by an Italian, Christoforo Armeno and was included in a collection of stories based on travel.

On the other hand, *Serendip*, the name of the home of the three princes, has an ancient history. Around the year AD 150, the Graeco-Egyptian mathematician and geographer Ptolemy (c. AD 100-170) charted the first map of the island of Sri Lanka, which he called *Sila-Diva*. Several centuries later, Ptolemy's work was extensively referred to in the Islamic world and his maps greatly assisted Arab seafarers plying the trade route to China. These sailors came to refer to the island as *Sarandib*, which became *Serendip*, or *Serendib*.

Serendipity was not greatly used until the twentieth century. Since then it has become a favourite title of compilers of anthologies inviting their readers into a literary lucky dip. The journalist and critic Ivor Brown (1891–1974) mentions a *Serendipity* bookshop in Bloomsbury, London, a name that invites hopeful browsing. The word now has wide currency.

The derived adjective *serendipitous* dates from around the middle of the twentieth century.

Shrovetide
the three days before Ash Wednesday

A performance of the complete Petrushka... *brought the orchestra's wind and strings together again. Oramo was in his element, vividly energising the busy detail of the* **Shrovetide** *Fair, from the dancing bear to the hurdy-gurdy, and giving warmth to the folksy tunes Stravinsky later called his 'Russian export style'.*
(THE GUARDIAN, 4 NOVEMBER 2006)

In England the carnival season before Lent was known as Shrovetide. *Shrove* is the past tense of the verb *shrive*, meaning 'to hear confession and impose penance', so *Shrovetide* was a period of spiritual preparation for Lent. The word

PRECISE TIMING

It is unusual to be able to date very precisely the first use of a new word. Sometimes it can be done, however. *Sputnik*, for instance, entered the English language (and many others throughout the world) on the day it was launched in 1957.

TIME magazine is innovatory in its use of language and among the many words that have first seen the light of day in a specific issue and subsequently survived are: *heightism* (1971), *televangelist* (1973), *roadies* (1973), *petropolitics* (1973), *chillout* (1973), *megadisaster* (1976) and *superbug* (1977).

Of course, journalists are not alone in experimenting with language. Many others have done the same, and some of their neologisms have in due course gained acceptance. The poet Robert Browning, for instance, seems to have been the first to use *artistry* – in THE RING AND THE BOOK (1868–9).

See also SERENDIPITY.

became current, against competition from other terms such as *Fastens-eve* and *Fastingong*, in the early fifteenth century.

Spiritual preparation it may have been, but it was also a time of unruly festivities: city youths in the twelfth century played football (a violent and undisciplined game in those days) and held cock-fights; fifteenth-century children indulged in rowdy behaviour at school; satirical plays mocked ecclesiastical and other authorities; and pancakes were eaten to use up reserves of butter and eggs, which were among the foods forbidden during Lent. Tradition has it that in 1445 a woman in Olney, Buckinghamshire, was still busy making pancakes when the shriving bell rang. Anxious not to be late, she rushed into the church still clasping her pan. The annual pancake race, open only to women, is still run in Olney every Shrove Tuesday to commemorate the tardy housewife.

This quotation from THE INDE-PENDENT (16 February 1994) illustrates some Shrovetide customs that are still observed:

With its emphasis on the Church service which follows the race, Olney's lenten tradition is considerably more civilised than those of other parts of Britain. The competition in Jedburgh, Roxburgh, where its Shrovetide football game, originally played with the severed heads of English border raiders, is waged through the boarded up streets; another in Atherstone, near the Warwickshire border with Leicestershire, originated during the reign of King John in a fierce struggle for a bag of gold.

See also CARNIVAL and LENT.

silhouette

the outline of an object or person, filled with a uniform colour

*A widening band of light fell across us. I turned my manacled body and saw a sapphire blue vista through an opening door. There, **silhouetted** in grotesque outline was a slender, pinched body, short bandy legs, bulging ears on a head depressed between thick shoulders.*
(H G WELLS,
THE FIRST MEN IN THE MOON, 1901)

*I can remember what the back of her head looked like while she was writing, **silhouetted** against the soft light of the lamp; her hair, the slope of her shoulders. But not her face.*
(MARGARET ATWOOD,
MORAL DISORDER, 2006)

*Josephine knew that what she was about to see was an illusion, but the power of the image – a black **silhouette**, framed by burning torches fixed to the stonework at the back of the stage – was so great that she could not help but feel a stab of apprehension.*
(NICOLA UPSON,
ANGEL WITH TWO FACES, 2009)

In 1759 the new French Controller General of finances, Etienne de Silhouette, proposed a number of petty fiscal reforms aimed at reviving the French economy, which was suffering the strain of the Seven Years' War. The nation's table plate, for instance, was handed over to the mint and the purses of the nobility were squeezed when their pensions and privileges were reduced. Soon the phrase *à la silhouette*, meaning 'on the cheap', had been coined, a satirical stab at the minister's perceived penny-pinching. Another story says that this same phrase was used of men's suits – cut without pockets in order to ridicule Silhouette's stinginess.

Coincidentally, the mid-eighteenth century saw the growth of interest in outline portraiture. It is said that the simplicity of these unadorned portraits inspired society wags to call them *silhouettes*, a further reference to the minister's parsimony. However, Émile Littré, the compiler of the DICTION-NAIRE DE LA LANGUE FRANCAISE (1877), records a statement that the term arose because Silhouette himself made a hobby of the art. If so, one can imagine the barbed jokes at his expense: that the portraits were as cheap as the Controller's economies; that, adorning the walls of his chateau at Bry-sur-Marne, they saved him the expense of purchasing more costly works of art.

The unpopular minister resigned his post within nine months and would doubtless have sunk into obscurity had his name not become the rather attractive term for an outline. Its first recorded use in England is in 1798.

silly

foolish, without judgement; not meriting serious consideration

'Please,' called Sam. 'Could Scales tell the story today? He's got a very interesting family.'

'If Scales can tell a story, yes,' said Miss Green. 'I want to tidy my cupboard, but remember, although I shall be on the other side of the room with my back to you, I shall be listening, and if anyone's silly...'

'No one will be silly with me!' said Scales.
(JUNE COUNSEL,
A DRAGON IN CLASS 4, 1984)

I have memories of Dad doing silly dances with me when I was little and it was lovely to share a precious moment like that again.
(GOOD HOUSEKEEPING, JULY 2009)

Through its long history *silly* has undergone a startling change of meaning. It comes from unattested proto-West Germanic *sœli*, meaning 'happiness, luck'. The derived adjective was the unattested *sœliga*, 'happy', which became *gesœlig* in Old English. By the late twelfth or early thirteenth century, this had evolved into *seely* and meant 'blissfully happy, fortunate' and therefore 'blessed by God'.

Whether or not it is the nature of the fortunate or blessed to be innocent and artless, *seely* began to develop a further sense, that of 'helpless and defenceless' and hence 'deserving compassion'. These senses became common in the fifteenth century as *seely* gradually evolved into *silly*. And *silly* was not reserved for people. The epithet *silly sheep* arose at this time, *silly* being applied to animals that were regarded as defenceless:

The poor cillie Mouse crept out of her small caue.., thinkyng no harme.
(WILLIAM BULLEIN, A DIALOGUE
AGAINST THE FEVER PESTILENCE,
1564)

During the sixteenth century, however, *silly* began to take on pejorative connotations. Those who were helpless or meriting sympathy were often humble, unsophisticated and ignorant and so the word was used to describe those who were 'frail, insignificant' and 'untutored'; common or country folk, for instance. Hence *the sillie people* were 'the unlearned' and *the silly herdman* was 'an ignorant rustic'. Since such people were generally deemed deficient in wisdom or common sense, the word also started to develop a sense of 'foolish' towards the end of the sixteenth century and this prevailed to become the current modern meaning.

For other words that have undergone a complete change in meaning, see BUXOM and NICE.

sirloin

a choice cut of beef

Sirloin is another tender beef cut, sold boned and rolled for roasting, or cut into sirloin steaks.
(GOOD HOUSEKEEPING
COOKERY BOOK, 2004)

The recession appears to have dented our appetite for sirloin steak. Horizons, a market analyst, claims that chicken breast has overtaken sirloin as the most common item on restaurant menus. As cash-strapped consumers look to cut expenditure, eateries are changing menus to include more lower-priced items. Sirloin is clearly regarded as a luxury item.
(THE TIMES, 17 APRIL 2009)

DAYS OF THE WEEK

Monday for wealth,
Tuesday for health,
Wednesday the best day of all.
Thursday for crosses,
Friday for losses,
Saturday no day at all.

It is not known which ancient people first divided days into groups of seven, giving each of the days the name of one of the planets in the solar system, but it was through the Romans that this reckoning spread to Europe. For the Romans, most of the names of the days of the week not only represented the planets but honoured their deities as well. Most Romance languages absorbed the Latin titles for weekdays but renamed those of the weekend for Christian religious observance. The Germanic tribes, however, translated the titles, substituting the names of those of their own deities who most closely resembled the particular Roman gods.

Latin	Romance (eg Italian)	Old English
diēs sōlis (day of the sun)	*domenica* (Lord's day)	*sunnandæg* (day of the sun)
lūnae diēs (day of the moon)	*lunedi* (day of the moon)	*monandæg* (moon's day)
Martis diēs (day of Mars, god of war)	*martedi* (day of Mars)	*tiwesdæg* (day of Tiu, god of war)
Mercurii diēs (day of Mercury)	*mercoledi* (day of Mercury)	*wodnesdæg* (day of Woden or Odin – eloquent and swift, like Mercury)
Jovis diēs (day of Jove or Jupiter, god of the sky)	*giovedi* (day of Jove)	*thuresdæg* (day of Thor, god of thunder)
Veneris diēs (day of Venus, goddess of love)	*venerdi* (day of Venus)	*friged æg* (day of Frig, wife of Woden and goddess of married love)
Sāturnī diēs (Saturn's day)	*sabato* (Sabbath day)	*saterdæg*, contracted form of *sæternesdæg* (Saturn's day)

In his CHURCH HISTORY OF ENGLAND (1655), Thomas Fuller repeats the tradition that Henry VIII coined *sirloin* when he knighted a loin of beef. The ATHENIAN MERCURY (6 March 1694) also provides a detailed account:

King Henry VIII, dining with the Abbot of Redding, and feeding heartily on a Loin of Beef, as it was then called, the Abbot told the King he would give a thousand marks for such a Stomack, which the King procured him by keeping him shut in the Tower, got his thousand marks, and knighted the Beef for its good behaviour.

Another tradition credits James I with the jest. Jonathan Swift refers to it in POLITE CONVERSATION (1738):

Miss Notable: *But pray, why is it called a sirloin?*
Lord Smart: *Why you must know, that our king James I., who loved good eating, being invited to dinner by one of his nobles, and seeing a large loin of beef at his table, he drew out his sword, and in a frolic knighted it.*

The good monarch must have thought it a particularly witty act, for he evidently repeated it. Both Blackburn in Lancashire and Chingford in Essex have houses where the extempore ceremony is said to have taken place. John Roby in his TRADITIONS OF LANCASHIRE (1829–31) gives a detailed account of the first of these, at Houghton Tower in 1617.

Not to be outdone, Charles II also has his champions, doubtless because he is styled *the merry monarch*. Under the heading *Sir-Loin of Beef* the COOK'S ORACLE (1822) states:

This joint is said to owe its name to King Charles the Second, who dining upon a Loin of Beef…said for its merit it should be knighted, and henceforth called Sir-Loin.

This is obviously an old seventeenth-century joke centring on a play on words, but it has nothing to do with the word's etymology. In the sixteenth century English had *surloyn*, a borrowing of the postulated Old French *surloigne*, a variant of *surlonge*. This was a compound of *sur*, 'above' and *longe*, 'loin' (from Latin *super*, 'above' and *lumbus*, 'loin'), the joint being cut from the upper part of the rump. Records of the variant spelling *sirloin* date back to the 1630s. Subsequently Joseph Addison spells it thus in a 1712 edition of THE SPECTATOR, and Dr Johnson has an entry in his DICTIONARY (1755) under this spelling.

Although *sirloin* is now the only accepted form, the word was still commonly spelt with a *u* in the last quarter of the nineteenth century, and this spelling was robustly defended by Skeat, who says that *sirloin* is *an inferior spelling of surloin*. The tradition that the joint was knighted by one of our monarchs may be untrue, but it has probably been influential in the demise of *surloin* and the rise of *sirloin*.

slander
defamation of character

Included herewith you'll find all the documents pertaining to the lawful adoption of the child you actually accused me of having kidnapped. I, for my part, consider the matter settled. If you persist in pursuing it, let me warn you that I will sue you for slander.
(ANDREA CAMILLERI,
THE SCENT OF THE NIGHT, 2000)

See SCANDAL.

slippery
difficult to stand upright on or grasp; not to be trusted

*The cigar-makers, with seven of them in full evening-dress and two in dinner-coats, were already dancing on the waxy floor of Melpomene Hall... [Mr Wrenn] felt very light and insecure in his new gun-metal finish pumps now that he had taken off his rubbers and essayed the **slippery** floor.*
(SINCLAIR LEWIS, OUR MR WRENN, THE ROMANTIC ADVENTURES OF A GENTLE MAN, 1914)

*[Benjamin] Franklin also emerges as rather different from the genial grandfather of legend – a **slippery** character, who never forgot a slight and whose general benevolence stopped firmly short at his own family.*
(THE TELEGRAPH, 6 NOVEMBER 2005)

*The only thing the glue wouldn't stick to, interestingly, was a piece of plastic model; then it just became a **slippery** lubricant that allowed any two pieces of model to glide endlessly over each other, never drying.*
(BILL BRYSON, THE LIFE AND TIMES OF THE THUNDERBOLT KID, 2006)

Middle English probably took its verb *slip* from Middle Low German *slippen*, 'to slip, to slide'. This in turn came from the proto-Germanic base *slip-* and proto-Indo-European *sleib-*, 'slippery, slimy'. The Old English adjective *slipper,* which meant 'smooth and slippery', shares the same history. By the close of the sixteenth century, however, *slipper* was all but redundant, having been replaced by a smart new coinage, *slippery*.

The earliest written record of this word dates back to Miles Coverdale's translation of the Bible (1535), in which Psalm 34: 6 reads: *Let their waye be darcke and slippery*. Coverdale's translation was made not from original texts but from the Vulgate and Luther's Zurich Bible. Luther's rendering of the same verse has the German word *schlipfferig*, 'slippery'. It seems likely that Coverdale, influenced by this term, used it to rework the existing

English adjective *slipper*. *Slippery* became very productive figuratively and was applied in a wide variety of contexts: *a slippery character, the slippery ladder of ambition, the slippery slope, a slippery subject* and so on.

Slipper as a noun to describe a light indoor shoe that was easy to slide on and off dates from the fifteenth century and derives from the verb *to slip*. In the sixteenth century *slip-shoe* was also used. *Slipshod* began life as an adjective to describe a person wearing slip-shoes in the second half of that century. Later the word was also applied to people who slopped and shuffled about in shoes that had not been tied or were down at heel. In his poem 'Truth' (TABLE TALK, 1781), the poet William Cowper describes

The shivering urchin, bending as he goes,
With slip-shod heels, and dew-drop at his nose.

In the eighteenth century, those who shuffled about in shoes that were down at heel were generally regarded as rather slovenly, and so *slipshod* ceased to refer to the condition of a person's footwear and began to be used more generally to denote 'messy appearance' or 'careless work'.

See UPROAR for another word influenced by Luther's translation of the Bible.

slipshod

carelessly done; of messy appearance

An ordinary woman who wore the same frock twice in a fortnight would not be thought slipshod or negligent of appearances. But in the Queen…such repetitions signalled a dramatic falling away from her own self-imposed standards of decorum.
(ALAN BENNETT,
THE UNCOMMON READER, 2007)

…McDonald had a great-uncle who died under the general's evidently slipshod command at the Somme…
(THE INDEPENDENT,
4 NOVEMBER 2008)

See SLIPPERY.

sop

a trifling thing offered to appease someone or win them over; a morsel of food (bread) soaked in liquid

Whatever there might still be to learn of his history, it would only be peripheral, a sop to curiosity; there was nothing of himself, the man's own sheer and vital self, withheld.
(SALLY VICKERS,
MR GOLIGHTLY'S HOLDAY, 2003)

A few dishes still draw some fans, like the…small but tasty mussels bathed in a wine broth loaded with garlic and herbs (all this dish needed was a sop more interesting than humdrum supermarket-style French bread).
(NEW YORK TIMES, 8 OCTOBER 2006)

The unattested proto-Germanic base *sup-* was responsible for the Old English verb *soppian*, which meant 'to soak or dip bread in liquid'. *To sop* is rarely used today but is still evident in *sopping (wet)*, 'soaked through', and *soppy*, which meant 'saturated' in the nineteenth century and by the early twentieth also meant 'saturated with sentiment' and hence 'foolishly affectionate'.

The noun *sop* referred to the piece of soaked bread itself. The liquid it was dipped in could be anything: broth, milk, wine, honey or the dripping under the roast. In the second half of the seventeenth century *sop* also came to denote 'a bribe, a small token given to win over the recipient'. This sense arose from the idiomatic phrase *a sop to Cerberus*. Cerberus was the monstrous dog with three heads who guarded the entrance to Hades. In THE AENEID (29–19 BC), the epic poem by the Roman poet Virgil, Cerberus was given cake soaked in drugged honey so that Aeneas could visit his father in the Underworld.

☛ The proto-Germanic base *sup-* is also responsible for:

soup (17th cent): proto-Germanic *sup-* yielded the unattested verb *suppāre*, 'to soak', in Late Latin. The derived noun *suppa*, 'sop', became *sope*, 'a slice of bread soaked in wine or broth' in the Old French of the twelfth century. It was, however, common to serve broth ladled over chunks of bread and so, by the fourteenth century, *sope* denoted 'broth with bread'. *Sope* became *soupe* in modern French and was borrowed from there into English.

supper (13th cent): from Old French *super*, 'supper', a noun use of the verb *super*, 'to eat the evening meal', from proto-Germanic *sup-*. The English verb for 'to eat supper' is *to sup*, again derived from the same base.

sophisticated
refined, cultured; complex, advanced

*...this menu is what I would eat if I was a grander, more **sophisticated** person – probably without kids – in tribute to my grandmother's delusions of grandeur.*
(THE INDEPENDENT, 16 DECEMBER 2006)

Hundreds of thousands of mainline rail commuters today faced slow journeys because of leaves on the line...
*Network Rail, which is responsible for the tracks, today launched a multi-million-pound operation to tackle the problem. A spokesman said: 'Over the past two years we have cut delays caused by autumnal weather by over 60 per cent. Use of new and **sophisticated** technology, attention to detail and heavy investment in manpower and machinery has paid dividends.'*
(EVENING STANDARD, 13 OCTOBER 2008)

The sophists were a group of itinerant intellectuals who, in ancient Greece from the second half of the fifth century BC, offered instruction in ethics and rhetoric in return for a fee. Plato and Aristotle held a dim view of these teachers, claiming that they were not really interested in pursuing truth but simply in winning debates, and that their arguments were more often than not fallacious. Thus *sophistēs*, the Greek word for such a teacher (from *sophizesthai*, 'to play clever tricks', from *sophos*, 'clever'), came to denote 'a specious reasoner'. The derived adjective *sophistikos* was taken into Latin as *sophisticus*, and from this Medieval Latin made the verb *sophisticāre* with the sense 'to corrupt, to adulterate something'. The Middle English borrowing *sophisticate* appears in Sir John Maundeville's account of his travels (c. 1400), in which he writes of dishonest merchants bulking up their stocks of expensive pepper with an inferior ingredient before selling it on, and in the sixteenth century Andrew Boorde writes that *they the which do put any other thynge to ale...doth sofysticat theyr ale* (THE BREVIARY OF HEALTHE, 1547).

Used as an adjective in the early seventeenth century, the past participle *sophisticated* meant 'mixed with some impure substance', but it also developed a related sense, that of something being 'altered from its original simplicity'. By the same token, *unsophisticated* meant 'unadulterated, unaltered'. By the late seventeenth century *unsophisticated* was being used to describe 'a person who is natural, innocent and lacking in worldly experience'. It was not until the late nineteenth century, however, that *sophisticated* was applied in the contrary sense to 'someone who has lost their original naivety and is thus knowledgeable about society and the ways of the world'. The application of *sophisticated* to highly developed, advanced techniques or equipment is a development of this and dates from the middle of the twentieth century.

spice
powdered flavouring for food, obtained from plants; extra excitement

*Variety's the very **spice** of life,*
That gives it all its flavour.
(WILLIAM COWPER, THE TASK, 1785)

***Spices**, too, come into their own in winter cooking. Originally, their volatile oils helped to prolong the life of many foods, and they were essential in celebratory meals.*
(JILL NORMAN, WINTER FOOD, 2005)

'I have decided it is time I began work on my memoirs.'

*Maude looked at him speculatively. She was obviously wondering whether she would be in them, and if so whether she ought to **spice** things up a little. Do or say a few more unforgettable things.*

(MICHÈLE ROBERTS,
READER, I MARRIED HIM, 2004)

The Latin word *speciēs*, 'outward appearance, particular kind' (from *specere*, 'to look'), is responsible for both *species* and *spice* in English. A direct borrowing from Latin in the sixteenth century gave *species*; *spice* took a slightly longer route. In Late Latin *speciēs* with its notion of 'kind, sort' began to be used to refer to 'a particular sort of merchandise' and, more especially, to spices. In this sense it was borrowed into Old French as *espice* and into Middle English as *spice* in the thirteenth century. Since then its position has been secure, both in the basic sense of 'a flavouring for food' and in the parallel figurative senses that evolved, those of 'added enjoyment, excitement, zeal'.

☛ *Special* (13th cent) is a borrowing of Old French *especial*, from Latin *speciālis*, 'individual, of a particular kind', a derivative of *speciēs*.

See also GROCER.

spinster

an unmarried woman, often past normal marrying age and considered fussy and prim

*Colombo is one of the calmest places on earth... The asphalt avenues with their very occasional cars are graced, in the evening, by processions of saris whose colours are those of the pastel drawings of the English **spinsters** buried in the nearby cemeteries.*

(ANDRÉ MALRAUX,
ANTIMEMOIRES, 1967)

*Kathleen has always in the past been Myra's companion and confidante, and Myra must have assumed that she would remain a lifelong **spinster** and so be always available for consolation and companionship.*

(ALAN BENNETT,
UNTOLD STORIES, 2005)

In medieval times running sheep and shearing them was a man's work but washing, carding and spinning the wool was a woman's responsibility. In addition to providing for their own needs, many rural women took in raw wool and span extra yarn for the important weaving industry in order to augment their income. Women in medieval illustrations of domestic rural life are invariably pictured with their distaff, the cleft stick upon which the raw wool was held, whether they are feeding the chickens or stirring the pot. Indeed L F Salzman (ENGLISH LIFE IN THE MIDDLE AGES, 1926) tells how the occupation was so widespread that the implement became a symbol of a woman's work and, ultimately, of a woman herself. As a reflection of the status of the distaff, the medieval queens of France were buried with an ornate distaff at their sides.

A *spinster*, then, is literally 'a woman who spins'. Middle English *spynnester* is composed of the verb *spinnen*, 'to spin', and *-ster*, a suffix which in Old English denoted a female agent. *Spinnen* came from Old English *spinnan* and ultimately from the unattested proto-Indo-European root *spen-*, 'to draw out, to stretch'.

In the fourteenth century, the word *spinster* was added to women's names in civic lists and official documents to show their occupation. By the seventeenth century, however, *spinster* had become a recognised legal term to denote 'an unmarried girl or woman'. From then on it no longer belonged to the lower echelons of society but was applied across the social board with no consideration of rank. In registers and legal documents the term was simply appended to an unmarried woman's name; in his GLOSSOGRAPHIA (1656), a dictionary of hard words in current use, Thomas Blount defines *spinster* as *the onely addition for all unmarried women, from the Viscounts Daughter downward. This use is still heard in churches when the banns of marriage are read aloud by law in the weeks preceding the ceremony: Janet Perkins, spinster of this parish.*

In POOR RICHARD'S ALMANACK (1733) Benjamin Franklin summarises centuries of history in one short verse:

> *When great Augustus ruled the World*
> *and Rome,*
> *The Cloth he wore was spun and wove*
> *at Home,*
> *His Empress ply'd the Distaff and the*
> *Loom.*
> *Old England's Laws the proudest Beauty*
> *name,*
> *When single, Spinster, and when married,*
> *Dame,*
> *For Housewifery is Woman's noblest Fame.*
> *The Wisest household Cares to Women yield*
> *A large, a useful and a grateful Field.*

By the eighteenth century a somewhat derogatory shadow had been cast over *spinster*: it was popularly used of an unmarried woman who no longer seemed to have any prospects of conjugal bliss and had become, or was destined to be, an old maid. Even today *spinster* conjures up the image of a rather fussy maiden lady; it is not a term to apply to an unmarried career woman.

☛ Spiders also spin and this is reflected in their name. It comes from *spīthra*, an Old English derivative of the unattested noun *spinthron*, from *spinnan*, 'to spin'. This gave Middle English *spither* or *spithre* and modern English *spider*.

The suffix *-ster* has a long history. In some periods and in some regional varieties, it has meant 'a female agent'. It was replaced in this sense by the French import *-stress*, as in *seamstress*, *songstress*, etc. From the sixteenth century onwards, surviving words ending in *-ster* and new coinages have not been so gender specific. *Gamester*, *jokester*, *tipster*, *youngster* and many more are no longer necessarily female.

spoil

to damage something; to deteriorate; to overindulge (a child)

*Tons of **spoilt** food and potentially millions of rands in lost revenue – this is the devastating impact of a power failure that has hit Bedfordview and surrounding Ekurhuleni areas.*
(PRETORIA NEWS, SOUTH AFRICA, 2 MAY 2007)

*With a three-strand narrative that reveals the perspectives of Jimmy, his sceptical wife Liz and their 12-year-old daughter Anne Marie, it has just enough humour to make the family compelling, and some delicate touches of insight – usually from Anne Marie – that raise it above a suburban comedy. A too-neat conclusion does not **spoil** its gentle wit.*
(REVIEW OF 'BUDDHA DA' BY ANNE DONOVAN, IN THE INDEPENDENT, 20 MARCH 2009)

*As a mother of three young children, Claire Malpass doesn't get much time to **spoil** herself, so her mum Pamela Parry put her forward for a makeover.*
(THE SENTINEL, 21 APRIL 2009)

When an animal was killed in ancient times the Latin word for its stripped skin or hide was *spolium*. The noun was then used figuratively to denote 'the armour and possessions stripped from a slain enemy by his victor' (hence *the spoils of war*). The derived Latin verb *spoliāre* thus meant 'to despoil, to strip a defeated enemy'. It was taken into Old French as *espoillier* and from there into Middle English as *spoil* in the early fourteenth century.

Besides being a term of war, *spoil* could also denote 'to seize goods by violence'. By the fifteenth century the verb might also mean 'to rob someone of a quality or talent' and by the sixteenth the sense 'to mar or destroy the effectiveness of something' had evolved. The related sense 'to harm someone's character through over-indulgence' (particularly applied to a child) dates from the late seventeenth century. At first this use was evidently regarded as an every-day colloquialism, for in his novel TOM JONES (1749) Henry Fielding writes of a gentleman whose sole surviving child is *one daughter, whom in vulgar language, he and his wife had spoiled*. The sense 'to deteriorate, to go off' also dates from the late seventeenth century.

stamina
physical or mental endurance

*Plunging into an icy Norwegian fjord was just the start of a **stamina**-sapping 16-hour endurance test for a former Exeter School pupil turned army officer.*
(WESTERN MORNING NEWS, 30 AUGUST 2008)

*The presidency is increasingly a job for the young and fit. The hours are long, the stakes are high, and the pressures immense. Obama has demonstrated physical and mental **stamina**. He'll need both.*
(CAPITAL TIMES, 26 OCTOBER 2008)

The ancients believed that when a person was born the Fates span a thread to measure the length of their life. Thus the thread was also an indication of a person's constitution; only accident, violence or disease could cut life short. The Latin word for such a thread, and also for a thread in the warp of a fabric, was *stāmen*, a term that can be traced back to unattested proto-Indo-European *stāmen*, from stā-, 'stand'.

Stāmina is the Latin plural of *stāmen*. When the word was taken into English its senses reflected the classical pre-occupation with the threads of life. In the middle of the seventeenth century *stamina* meant 'the original constitution of something, the basic elements'. From the early eighteenth century the notion of 'vital capacities dictating the length of life' had been adopted, and finally, also in the eighteenth century, came the sense of 'vigour, the strength to overcome debilitating illness or fatigue'.

It was Pliny the Elder, the Roman natural philosopher, who thought that the male fertilising part of the lily resembled a thread and applied the word *stāmen* to it. The adoption of the word into modern botany was, however, the inspiration of Adriaan van den Spiegel (1578–1625), a Flemish anatomist and botanist.

staple
a major trading commodity of a country; a basic food regularly consumed by people in a particular country; a U-shaped metal fastener

*Take a sheet of A4 paper and cut in half giving you two A5 sheets. Holding the paper landscape-wise, take the top right corner and bring it down to meet the bottom left. You will form a cone shape, which can be just turned up at the bottom and secured with a **staple**.*
(THE TIMES ONLINE, 8 JUNE 2006)

*Prices for fresh seasonal foods are noticeably keener this year, though it is possible to make them yet more affordable with the addition of economical **staples**, such as butter beans, couscous, farro (whole wheat) and green lentils.*
(THE TELEGRAPH, 11 JUNE 2009)

Staples were originally towns selected by the Crown as exclusive trading centres for particular goods destined for export. The idea was to bring the flow of trade under royal control and ensure that the duties were paid to the Exchequer. The system arose in the reign of Edward II (1307–27) and over the years applied to goods such as tin, lead, leather, woollen cloth and wool, the chief of these in the fourteenth century being raw wool destined for the weavers in Flanders. In 1363, during the reign of Edward III, the town through which all wool exports had to pass was Calais, which at the time belonged to the English crown and became known as The Staple. Here 26 wool merchants were incorporated as the Company of the Staple and enjoyed a monopoly in that commodity. This came to an end in 1558 when Calais was retaken by the French.

The word *staple* originated in the unattested proto-Germanic *stapulaz*, 'pillar'. This became *stapel* in Middle Dutch and meant both 'pillar' and 'market'. The assumption is that the sense 'marketplace' emerged from stalls being placed beneath a roof supported by pillars. *Stapel* was borrowed into Old French as *estaple*, 'market', and from there into Middle English as *staple*: They may bey Wolle...atte the Stapull of Calais (ROLLS OF PARLIAMENT, 1423).

By the early seventeenth century, the word was being transferred from the trading place to the stock on sale or the basic food consumed by people in a particular community. Captain John Smith, who was among the early settlers in Virginia and subsequently explored more of the north-eastern coast of America, wrote that *the main Staple...is fish* (A DESCRIPTION OF NEW ENGLAND, 1616), and in his historical allegory DONDA'S GROVE (1640), James Howell describes corn,

wine and salt as *three rich staples*.

The word *staple* denoting 'a loop of metal' also comes from *stapulaz*, which was taken into Old English as *stapol* and meant 'post, pillar'. Its application to 'a U-shaped metal fastener' dates from the late thirteenth century but how this sense developed is a mystery.

starboard

the right-hand side of a ship, looking forward

I wrestled with the drinks cabinet, concealed inside a ship's wheel set on a wooden column. To unlock the little door at the front and get at the booze you had to steer to port, then do a quick flip to **starboard**.
(MICHÈLE ROBERTS,
READER, I MARRIED HIM, 2004)

An old and carefully maintained Kelvin engine pushed us along...and we were soon out of the Holy Loch and turning south down the firth, with skipper Michael giving our 15-year-old son a turn at the wheel and explaining the dangers around us: ferries to port and **starboard**, *a container ship dead ahead, an infamous reef off the starboard bow.*
(THE GUARDIAN, 13 JUNE 2009)

It might be supposed that this nautical term for the right-hand side of a ship originated in ancient methods of navigating by the stars. In fact *starboard* evolved from the Old English *stēorbord*. Early Germanic ships were steered not by a rudder at the stern, but by a special paddle called a *stēor* (ultimately from the unattested proto-Germanic noun *steurō*, 'steering'), which was dropped over the right-hand *bord* or 'ship's side'.

The term *larboard* (*laddeborde* in Middle English) – the left-hand side of the ship to which the steersman had his back – was modelled on the earlier *starboard*. *Ladde* is thought to derive from *laden*, 'to load'. When quays were built to make the loading of vessels easier, ships had to be moored with the steering paddle free and cargo was therefore always taken over the left board. The later term *port* (Old English from Latin *portus*, 'harbour, haven') is thought to have arisen in the late sixteenth century for the same reason, the left-hand side of the vessel being the one that was presented to the port or harbour. Gradually the use of *port* superseded that of *larboard* since the former was less easily confused with *starboard*. On 22 November 1844, this Order was issued from the Admiralty in England:

The word 'Port' is frequently… substituted…for the word 'Larboard', and as…the distinction between 'Starboard' and 'Port' is so much more marked than that between Starboard' and 'Larboard', it is their Lordships direction that the word 'Larboard' shall no longer be used.

Less than fifteen months later, the US Navy put out a Department Notice in very similar terms.

In modern times, of course, much nautical vocabulary has been applied to aircraft, so that *starboard* and *port* now also refer to the right and left sides of a plane.

☛ Other nautical terms ultimately from proto-Germanic *steurō*, 'steering', are:

steer (OE): Old English *stēor*, from unattested proto-Germanic *steurjan*.

stern (13th cent): Middle English *sterne*, probably from Old Norse *stjörn*. This formerly denoted the 'steering equipment' of a ship, but now refers simply to the 'back part of a vessel'.

stark
sharp, clear; harsh, bare

*How did he keep from going **stark** raving mad during his four hours of daily commuting? 'I would just think about all the great things in life that we have and enjoy them,' Peerce said.*
(ORLANDO SENTINEL, 20 FEBRUARY 2006)

*At this age [50s and 60s], divorce doesn't necessarily occur because the couple have problems – it's more that one of them might want a relationship with someone else. If so, there's a **stark** choice to be made, with serious repercussions on the rest of their family, and it's very sad. But it's a very emotional choice for the person leaving too, because they see it as their last chance of happiness.*
(THE INDEPENDENT, 30 AUGUST 2008)

*As the clouds parted to unveil the **stark** landscape of the Galapagos Islands, the doubts began to re-emerge. Why had we spent so much money to come to a place that looked more like the dark side of the moon than a tropical island? Why were we taking part in what has been described by some as an organized assault on one of the world's greatest natural treasures?*
(TORONTO STAR, 10 JANUARY 2009)

This word has cognates in the other Germanic languages where the sense is 'strong'. Old English had *stearc*, which meant 'strong, stiff, rigid, unyielding' and became a well-used adjective in Old and early Middle English. It might describe the hardness of a person's heart or of his character; or it could be applied to the severity of one's circumstances or the cruelty of a punishment. It carried the sense of 'strong' or 'stout' in describing a structure, a weapon, a person or an authority. *Stark* also meant 'stiff in the body', through weariness, cold or old age.

In the early fifteenth century *stark* began to denote 'utter, absolute', the sense evolving from that of 'rigid, unyielding'. From here, towards the end of the century, it began to be used as an intensive adverb meaning 'absolutely, entirely', hence *stark blind, stark drunk, stark (staring/raving) mad*.

Contrary to appearances, however, the phrase *stark naked*, 'completely naked', has a different origin. It was coined in the thirteenth century as *start-naked*, where *start* (*steort* in Old English) denoted 'an animal's tail'. Thus the phrase literally meant 'tail naked', that is with the bottom half also exposed. The substitution of *stark* for *start* took place in the sixteenth century, making the expression rather less colourful.

stark naked
totally naked

*Have you ever found yourself doing the ironing at three o'clock in the morning, glass of Scotch at hand, **stark naked** and singing at the top of your voice? Not me, of course – but behaving oddly in the privacy of your own home is a birthright.*
(THE GUARDIAN, 20 MAY 2009)

See STARK.

station
a stopping place along a train or bus route where passengers board or alight; social rank

*...a big, rather gloomy old **station** built for busier and grander times and a plaque on the wall whose chilling inscription commemorates the thousands of people who, in 1940 and 1941, were packed into cattle-wagons here and shipped out on a one-way ride to the Gulag camps in Siberia.*
(MICHAEL PALIN, NEW EUROPE, 2007)

*Elgar's emergence as a widely known musician in the late 1890s had the effect of a dam breaking. For years, he had struggled against indifference and disbelief when trying to stake a claim as a composer of worth. Sensitive, thin-skinned and downright chippy, it took marriage to an older woman – and one, as the Victorians put it, well above his **station** – to make him believe he should persist, and could succeed.*
(THE TELEGRAPH, 23 MAY 2007)

In classical Latin the noun *statiō* meant 'a standing still'. It was derived from the verb *stāre*, 'to stand', and might be applied to the firm posture of a man preparing to fight, for instance. Later it also had the more concrete sense of 'a place where people or things stay', hence 'a post, a station, a residence', and then 'a job, a position'. The word came into Middle English via French *station* in the fourteenth century.

During the sixteenth century *station* was used for 'a temporary stopping place on a journey', then during the eighteenth it began to be applied in the United States to 'a routine stopping place' for passengers on coach journeys; a place where they could stretch their legs and take meals and where the horses were changed for the next leg of the journey. James Hall, one of the earliest authors to write about the American frontier, describes one such station in THE LEGEND OF KENTUCKY (1833):

And every here and there a station...a rude block-house, surrounded with palisades, afforded shelter to the traveller, and refuge, in time of danger, to all within its reach.

The earliest recorded mention of a *railway station* dates from 1830, with reference to the Liverpool and Manchester railway.

The adjective *stationary* dates from the seventeenth century and comes from Latin *statiōnārius*, 'belonging to a military station', a derivative of *statiō*, 'a standing still'.

See also STATIONER.

stationer

a person selling writing materials

*...I'm here in Smythson of Bond Street looking for a Schiaparelli pink Fashion Diary which I fancy...The Fashion Diary seems to be the iconic product that has turned what had been a grand and venerable **stationer** (stationer of choice to Charles Dickens, Sigmund Freud, polar expeditions, maharajahs, kings and all the rest) into a hip-hop stationer, sought after by the new royalty of stage and screen – Gwyneth Paltrow, Steven Spielberg, Madonna and their ilk.*
(THE TIMES, 20 DECEMBER 2002)

*The red post box in the wall of the building is indicative of the miniature post office that once existed here. Gordon has a wonderful anecdote about the teacher breaking off from teaching lessons to serve locals their stamps and **stationery** from what was then a serving hatch rather than a shop.*
(YORKSHIRE LIVING, APRIL 2009)

Latin *statiōnārius* meant 'belonging to a military station' and was a derivative of *statiō*, 'a standing still' (see STATION for more details). Medieval Latin used this noun to distinguish a tradesman who had an established shop from an itinerant vendor. In Middle English the borrowed term *staciouner* was applied particularly to booksellers. Most of these were itinerant, but there were permanent bookshops at the universities where the governing bodies would license trustworthy vendors to trade.

Over time *stationer* came to be applied loosely to anyone who was connected with the book trade, or who sold other requirements for study

such as paper and pens. In his GLOSSOGRAPHIA (1656) Thomas Blount attempts correction:

Stationer...is often confounded with Bookseller, and sometimes with Book-binder, whereas they are three several Trades; the Stationer sells Paper and Paper-Books, Ink, Wax, etc. The Book-seller deals onely in printed Books, ready bound; and the Bookbinder binds them, but sells not. Yet all three are of the Company of Stationers.

Despite Blount's efforts, it was not until the eighteenth century that *stationer* was applied solely to 'a vendor of paper and writing materials'.

The derived noun *stationery* dates from the early eighteenth century. It has the appearance of an adjective and came about through the shortening of a combination such as *stationery ware*.

stepchild

a son or daughter by one's spouse and a previous partner

*Having been an only child, Cinderella was initially excited at the idea of having **stepsisters**. However, she became bitterly disappointed at discovering they were apt to be as cruel as their mother.*
(LAURA JAMES,
TIGGER ON THE COUCH, 2007)

*Britain today is heaving with women coping with the complications of families that include children, **stepchildren** and step-siblings with ex-husbands and in-laws thrown in for good measure.*
(THE TIMES, 3 JANUARY 2009)

The whole range of step-relationships is based on an Old English prefix *stēop,-* which is connected to the Old High German verb *stiufen*, 'to bereave'. *Stēop-* had the sense 'deprived of parents', and so the Old English compounds *stēop-bearn* (stepbairn) and *stēopcild* (stepchild) originally meant 'orphan' and then 'a child, by a former marriage, of one's spouse'. More recently, the *step*-combinations have also been applied to new family relationships formed not through bereavement but through divorce and remarriage.

sterling

connected with British currency, usually the pound; of high quality, first class

But elephants are far from cheap in India, where they are becoming scarce… When therefore Mr Fogg proposed to the Indian to hire Kiouni, he refused point-blank. Mr Fogg persisted, offering the excessive sum of ten pounds an hour for the loan of the beast to Allahabad. Refused. Twenty pounds? Refused also. Forty pounds? Still refused. Passepartout jumped at each advance; but the Indian declined to be tempted. Yet the offer was an alluring one, for, supposing it took the elephant fifteen hours to reach Allahabad, his owner would receive no less than six hundred pounds **sterling**.
(JULES VERNE, AROUND THE WORLD IN EIGHTY DAYS, 1873)

'Oh, Jo, I do feel bad. You know I do –'
   'Well, how do you think I feel! I'll tell you: discarded. Like a bit of old carpet that did **sterling** *service for years and then is dragged off to the local tip!'*
(KATIE FFORDE, GOING DUTCH, 2007)

Most commodities are priced in US dollars, so some of the impact of cost deflation is offset by currency appreciation, which makes ingredients more expensive in **sterling** *terms.*
(THE TIMES, 6 DECEMBER 2008)

The earliest attested reference to *sterling* in Middle English is from the late thirteenth century. However, there are earlier Anglo-Latin, Old French and Medieval Latin examples. The word is probably an English one and derives from the unattested late Old English *steorling*, meaning 'a little star' (a combination of *steorra*, 'star', and *-ling*, a diminutive suffix), a reference to the tiny star evident on the early silver pennies from the reign of William Rufus onwards (c. 1087–1100).

Over the centuries, however, alternative etymologies have been suggested. Silver coins from the reign of Edward the Confessor (1042-66), for instance, bore an emblem of four birds, giving rise to the suggestion that the word derived from Old English *stærlinc*, 'starling'.

Another favourite theory, now discredited, held that the coin was first minted by the Easterlings, Hanse merchants and money-lenders with whom England traded, and that it bore their name. There is, however, no evidence to support this and the OED points out that it is also highly unlikely that a word would be shortened by the loss of a stressed initial syllable: *easterling* reduced to *sterling*.

The term *pound sterling* was originally *pound of sterlings*, a clear reference to 'a pound weight of silver pennies'. It took 240 pennies to make an English pound. *Sterling* was used to denote 'English currency' from the early seventeenth century.

The widely recognised qualities of silver were figuratively attributed to people of sound character from the seventeenth century onwards: *The nephew…is a young man of sterling worth, and Spanish gravity* (Washington Irving, THE ALHAMBRA, 1832).

For notes on another currency, see DOLLAR.

stickler

a person very insistent on discipline, rules, accuracy, etc.

*Her parents ('the young ones') live below, and Chloe thinks it is very silly that they insist on paying rent. Though she feels she has to take it ('you know what a **stickler** my mother is') she secretly pays it into an account in their own name.*
(MAUREEN FREELY,
ENLIGHTENMENT, 2007)

*As well as apparently being a **stickler** for being referred to by his full title, Sir Ben Kingsley appears decidedly sniffy when it comes to the talents of fellow performers.*
(DAILY EXPRESS, 2 JANUARY 2009)

Sticklers are people who insist on a particular point or scruple. They may be sticklers for punctuality, politeness, form, etiquette or shiny shoes. In the sixteenth century, a *stickler* was 'an umpire', someone who presided over a contest or tournament to guarantee fair play or to come between combatants where necessary. It has been claimed that the name derived from *stick*, the suggestion being that this was the weapon the stickler was often forced to resort to when parting quarrelsome contestants. However, an earlier form, *stightler*, existed in the fifteenth century, showing that the noun derived rather from the Middle English verb *stightlen* (14th cent), which meant 'to arrange, to control, to prepare, to govern'. According to Skeat, the verb was often applied to the work of a steward given the responsibility of making arrangements and overseeing events. *Stightlen* in turn was from Old English *stihtan*, 'to set in order'.

One might conjecture that umpires were generally despised for their nit-picking; certainly, the history of *stickler* takes a downward turn from the second half of the sixteenth century, when the word was found in political contexts to denote 'one who is actively involved in a matter', often with the implication that such a person was a meddler. By the first quarter of the seventeenth century a *stickler* had also become 'an adversary, an opponent given to raising objections'. Towards the middle of that same century the term was combined with *for* to give the modern sense 'one who advocates a principle, one who insists on something (petty)'.

See also UMPIRE.

sycophant

an obsequious flatterer

*I would open the door from the bedroom, a preposterous figure in a dressing-gown, blink, pause, then withdraw again with a mumbled apology. But in that brief instant she would have turned to me with a smile and a look quite different from that reserved for her **sycophantic** retinue.*
(GRAHAM SWIFT, EVER AFTER, 1992)

*If ever you are at some important function and all the **sycophants** are trying to grab their two minutes with the boss, spend half an hour chatting to the boss's partner instead, and you'll be the only one they'll talk about on the way home.*
(JOHN O'FARRELL, AN UTTERLY
IMPARTIAL HISTORY OF BRITAIN, 2007)

The literal meaning of Greek *sukophantēs* is 'fig-shower' (from *sukon*, 'fig' and *phantēs*, 'shower', from *phainein*, 'to show'). Sycophants in ancient Greece were those who ingratiated themselves by informing against others. There is, however, no evidence from classical texts to support the theory, commonly held since at least the sixteenth century, that the term first applied to those who informed against the illegal exportation of figs from Attica.

More probable by far is the suggestion that fig relates to an obscene gesture of the 'Up yours!' variety, which originated in ancient times, was once common in England and still prevails in southern Europe. The gesture, which is illustrative of the female genitals, is made by thrusting one's thumb between the first two fingers or into the mouth. It takes its name from *sukon*, 'fig', which the Greeks used euphemistically for 'vulva'. Metaphorically speaking, a sycophant was making this gesture of triumphant contempt at those he was informing against.

When the word first entered English by way of Latin *sȳcophanta* in the first half of the sixteenth century, it had the ancient sense of 'tell-tale, informer' but swiftly came to mean 'flatterer, toady, one who curries favour'.

☞ *Phainein*, 'to show', is responsible for a number of English words, such as:

Epiphany (14th cent): 'the manifestation of Christ to the Gentiles': from Greek *epiphaneia*, 'manifestation', from *epiphainein*, 'to manifest', from *epi-*, 'on, to', and *phainein*, 'to show'.

phase (19th cent): from *phases* (plural), from New Latin *phasis*, from Greek *phásis*, 'any of the cyclical aspects or appearances of the moon or planets'.

phenomenon (17th cent): from Late Latin *phaenomenon*, from Greek *phainomenon*, from *phainesthai*, 'to appear', passive of *phainein*.

Phainein was also the source of the Greek derivative *phantazein*, 'to make visible'. From this came the noun *phantasma*, 'spectre, apparition', *phantasma* in Latin. By way of Old French it was taken into Middle English as *fanto(s)me* in the thirteenth century. The spelling *phantom* was revised after the Latin in the seventeenth century.

A second common word from the same Greek derivative is *fantasy*, which came into English in the fifteenth century.

For another word with a similar meaning, see TOADY.

T

tabby
a cat with brindled fur

Rebecca took a bite from her piece of candy, which looked more like some kind of novelty toilet soap. As soon as she could get her teeth unstuck, she asked her aunt, 'Is that Percival?'
*She meant the cat – a fat gray **tabby**. 'Why, no, dear,' Ida said, 'that's Daisy. Percival died last Christmastime.'*
(ANNE TYLER, BACK WHEN WE WERE GROWNUPS, 2001)

*On the kitchen shelf he had rows of empty jam jars and topless fish tins in which were screws, nails and bits of cut string. He had a **tabby** cat called Susan who dozed in his chair beneath the antimacassar.*
(SEBASTIAN FAULKS, ENGLEBY, 2007)

Attābī was a watered silk fabric which, from medieval times, was manufactured in *Al-'attābīya*, a quarter of Baghdad from which it took its name. The district itself had once been the home of Prince *Attāb*, and was called after him. The silk, which was imported into Europe, was known as *atabis* in Old French. This became *tabis* in French, the word passing from there into English in the first half of the seventeenth century. In English *tabby* was a general term for 'silk taffeta', originally striped but later also watered; Nathan Bailey defines it as *a Sort of Silk, waved or watered* in his ETYMOLOGICAL ENGLISH DICTIONARY of 1727.

Tabby was first used to describe a brindled cat in the late seventeenth century, the allusion being to the streaked fabric. In his NEW ACCOUNT OF EAST INDIA AND PERSIA (1698), John Fryer describes a tiger as being *of a light Yellow, streaked with Black, like a Tabby Cat*. By the second half of the eighteenth century, *tabby* was also being used as a noun: *The civet varies in its colour, being sometimes streaked, as in our kind of cats called tabbies*, wrote Oliver Goldsmith in A HISTORY OF THE EARTH AND ANIMATED NATURE (1774).

Also in the eighteenth century *tabby* began to be applied humorously to elderly SPINSTERS who were perceived as having some of the spiteful characteristics of a cat, a use which sadly drifted into oblivion in the late nineteenth century.

tabloid
a (popular) newspaper of small format

*I stood on the church steps wearing black Prada from head to toe, smiling weakly (with, I liked to think, a hint of allure still) and shaking hands with the many guests. The **tabloids** called me brave and brokenhearted. It couldn't have been better.*
(JULIAN CLARY, MURDER MOST FAB, 2007)

*Prince Harry, the third in line to the throne, and his girlfriend Chelsy Davy have decided to end their five-year relationship, it was confirmed by royal sources last night after reports in **tabloid***

newspapers. *Inevitably, the separation was said to have been amicable and they remain friends.*
(THE OBSERVER, 25 JANUARY 2009)

On 14 March 1884, the London-based drug company Burroughs, Wellcome and Co registered *Tabloid* as a trademark for the medicines they prepared and compressed into tablet form. There was nothing new in drugs presented in this way, but the small firm had the advantage of new machinery capable of turning out copious quantities of first-class tablets.

Mr Wellcome needed a trade name for marketing purposes and *Tabloid* was coined by adding the suffix *-oid*, meaning 'resemblance, similarity' (from Latin *-oīdēs*, from Greek *-oeidēs*, 'having the form of', from *eidos*, 'shape'), to the existing term *tablet*. *Tablet* itself had come into Middle English in the fourteenth century by way of Old French *tablete*, a diminutive form of *table*. At first it referred to 'a small flat slab' of clay, stone or marble, which could be written or carved upon, but its use was extended in the second half of the sixteenth century to 'small compact cakes of compressed medication or soap'.

To the annoyance of Burroughs Wellcome, *Tabloid* was seized upon and was soon being used by other chemists. The verdict of a High Court action to confirm the company's right to use the word exclusively for 'compressed medicines' reveals how the term had escaped into general use (now without the initial capital letter) to refer to 'a compacted form' of anything at all, from tea to rocks:

The word Tabloid has become so well-known…in consequence of the use of it by the Plaintiff firm in connection with their compressed drugs that I think it has acquired a secondary sense in which it has been used and may legitimately be used so long as it does not interfere with their trade rights. I think the word has been so applied generally with reference to the notion of a compressed form or dose of anything.
(MR JUSTICE BYRNE, REPORTS ON PATENT AND TRADE MARK CASES XXI, 20 NOVEMBER–14 DECEMBER 1903)

Since the early twentieth century even the news has been compressed. The word is common in the world of journalism, a *tabloid* being a popular newspaper of small format which offers concentrated easy-to-read articles and news stories. This is still current, although the twenty-first century has seen the publication of serious broadsheet newspapers in tabloid format if not tabloid content.

taboo
a prohibition, a forbidden thing

By the second half of the 1950s, the extent of royal coverage had become so monumental, and the tone so cloying, as to invite a reaction. I remember well when it happened. One morning in 1957 Kingsley Martin came into my office at the New Statesman *and slapped down on my desk an article he had just been sent by Malcom Muggeridge: 'Read that. It's a crackerjack (his favourite term of praise). The best article I have ever read.' This was Muggeridge's famous piece on the 'Royal Soap Opera', which first broke the* **taboo** *on criticising royalty.*
(PAUL JOHNSON, WAKE UP, BRITAIN!, 1994)

The biggest problem is that many men have not been educated about the warning signs of testicular cancer. They might think that they are over-reacting to a dull pain, which could be a symptom of something more serious. My aim is to help break down any **taboos** *surrounding the disease and, at the same time, raise awareness.*
(GOOD HOUSEKEEPING, APRIL 2009)

Taboo came into English through Captain James Cook's accounts of his voyages in the South Seas (1777). It is a borrowing of the Tongan adjective *tabu*, a term of prohibition to indicate that a particular article, word or action had been declared sacred and was consecrated uniquely for royal or religious purposes, or was forbidden to a particular section of the community. Cook described it thus:

Not one of them would sit down, or eat a bit of any thing... On expressing my surprize at this, they were all taboo, as they said; which word has a very comprehensive meaning; but, in general, signfies that a thing is forbidden. Why they were laid under such restraints, at present, was not explained.
(VOYAGE TO THE PACIFIC OCEAN, 1777)

Pronouncing *taboo* was not confined to Tonga, however. The practice prevailed throughout the islands of the Pacific where various forms of the word are found: the Maori, for instance, have *tapu* and the Fijians *tambu*.

Strictly the stress should fall on the first syllable. English, however, accentuates the final syllable and uses the term as a noun, an adjective and sometimes as a verb. A common use today is in the phrase *taboo words*. These are any expressions that allude too directly to sensitive subjects such as copulation, death, old age, sweat and any number of other topics that are viewed as embarrassing and for which people therefore resort to euphemisms.

For another Polynesian word that entered English through Captain Cook's writings, see TATTOO.

tadpole
the larva of a frog or toad

*A spawn of children cluttered the slimy pavement, for all the world like **tadpoles** just turned frogs on the bottom of a dry pond.*
(JACK LONDON,
THE PEOPLE OF THE ABYSS, 1903)

*Brown-headed Kingfishers...don't really hunt fish: they are members of the subfamily Daceloninae, forest kingfishers, which hunt insects and small reptiles. I have seen them catch both fish and **tadpoles**, but neither make up a large part of their diet.*
(CHARLIE HAMILTON JAMES,
KINGFISHER: TALES FROM THE
HALCYON RIVER, 2009)

The poem FROG (1981) by Mary Ann Hoberman mentions three names that have been given to the larva of the frog or toad: *pollywiggle, pollywog* and *tadpole*. *Tadpole* is the generally accepted term; *pollywiggle* and *pollywog* (sometimes *polliwog* or *pollywoggle*) are both old dialectal words in English and *pollywog* is current in the United States. *Pol* (or *polle*), a Middle English word meaning 'head', is a common element in each, since the creature gives the appearance of being nothing more than a large head with a slim tail attached. The French word *têtard* (from *tête*, 'head', Old French *testard*) is based on the same observation. While the dialectal terms also focus on the frantic wiggle of the tail, the initial element in *tadpole* is *tadde*, a Middle English word meaning 'toad'. The entire word, therefore, means 'toad head'.

As for *toad*, well, the Old English word was *tadīga* but further back than this it is impossible to go; the origin of the word is lost in time.

☛ Modern English *poll*, 'the casting or recording of votes', is more literally 'a head count'. It has been in use since the seventeenth century.

tailor

a person who makes suits, jackets, etc. for men, usually to special order

'Why are women so fond of raking up the past? They're as bad as tailors, who invariably remember what you owe them for a suit long after you've ceased to wear it.'
(SAKI, REGINALD, 1904)

Here [Hoi An, Vietnam] you turn up at a tailor's shop at noon with your favourite dress or suit, choose fabric, return at 4pm for a fitting, suggest improvements, then, as you head out for cocktails by the river at dusk, you collect your new duds, usually better than the original.
(THE TIMES, 30 MAY 2009)

This word goes back to the Latin noun *tālea*, an agricultural word which meant 'a cutting from a plant'. From this, Vulgar Latin derived the unattested verb *tāliāre*, 'to cut', which in turn gave *tāliātor* to denote 'a cutter'. This noun became *tailleur* in Old French and generally denoted 'a person who cuts'; a *tailleur de bois*, for example, was 'a wood-cutter' and a *tailleur d'images* 'a sculptor'. The *tailleur d'habits*, then, was the 'cutter out of clothes' (Medieval Latin had the similar term *tāliator vestium*), although by the thirteenth century this artisan was already simply referred to as the *tailleur*. The word came into Middle English in the fourteenth century by way of Anglo-French *taillour* and meant 'a person who makes clothes'.

The adjective *tailor-made* dates from the second half of the nineteenth century and was initially used of plain, well-cut women's clothing. Towards the end of that century it was used with the sense 'made for a particular purpose'. Nowadays even human beings can be *tailor-made*:

The birth of the first British baby genetically screened before conception to be free of a breast cancer gene means that the tailor-made child (blue eyes; high IQ, anyone?) is undoubtedly round the corner – rapidly followed by a life customised by science to meet our personal 'needs'.
(GUARDIAN. CO.UK, 12 JANUARY 2009)

☛ Also derived from Latin *tālea* are:

detail (17th cent): from French *détail*, from Old French *detail*, 'a piece cut off', from *detailler*, 'to cut in pieces', from the intensive prefix *de-*, 'entirely', and *tailler*, 'to cut', from Vulgar Latin *tāliāre*.

retail (14th cent): from Old French *retaille*, 'a piece cut off', from *retaillier*, from *re-*, 'back', and *taillier*, 'to cut, to trim', from Vulgar Latin *tāliāre*.

For another word from the same source, see TALLY.

talent

a natural ability, a gift for something

Suppose I want to play music but seem to have no obvious talent. Never mind: there are music shops selling instruments, tuning forks, metronomes and 'How To' books by the score. And scores by the score.
(STEPHEN FRY,
THE ODE LESS TRAVELLED, 2005)

Where does artistic talent come from? It's a question I've been forced to think about long and hard since my son Otto, who is seven, has developed a skill for drawing that seems to have come from nowhere but himself. Drawing is one of the many disciplines for which I have no aptitude.
(THE GUARDIAN, 21 JUNE 2008)

Greek *talanton* denoted 'a unit of weight or money'. When Latin borrowed the term as *talentum*, it also gave it the figurative sense of 'will, inclination', so that, when the word first came into Middle English in the late thirteenth century via Old French *talent*, it was with the sense of 'desire, appetite for something'.

FABRICS

Fabrics are often named for their place of manufacture, giving rise to a number of quaint or exotic-sounding words:

Calico (16th cent): a hard-wearing cotton cloth. In the sixteenth century it was known as *Calicut-cloth* after the town in Kerala on the southwest coast of India, now known as Kozhikode, from which it was exported.

Cambric (16th cent): a fine cotton or linen fabric made in Cambrai, France. It took its name from *Kameryk* (Latin *Camaracum*), the Flemish name for the town, and this was borrowed into English as *cameryk* and corrupted to *cambric*.

Cretonne (19th cent): this heavy, printed-cotton furnishing fabric takes its name from *Creton*, the Normandy village where it originated.

Damask (14th cent): this richly patterned cloth was called *pannus de damasco*, 'cloth of Damascus', in Medieval Latin, since it was exported to Europe from that Syrian city.

Denim (late 17th cent): the name is a corruption of *serge de Nîmes*, a term given to a type of serge fabric that was woven in the French town of Nîmes. English often referred to it as *serge de Nim* before further corrupting the term by isolating the two last words and blending them together to form *denim*.

Hessian (19th cent): this loosely woven cloth made of jute, which was used to make sacks and wrap bales, takes its name from the West German state of *Hesse* where it was made.

Lawn (15th cent): this word for fine cotton or linen cloth is probably a corruption of *Laon*, a linen-weaving town in northern France.

Muslin (17th cent): This fine, semi-transparent cotton cloth was originally manufactured in the Iraqi town of *Al-Mawsil*. The Arabs called it *mūslin*, 'cloth of Mosul', and this word was borrowed into Italian as *moussolina*, into French as *mousseline* and into English as *muslin*.

Poplin (18th cent): came into English via the French *papeline*, from Italian *papalina*. This is a feminine form of the adjective *papalino*, which means 'papal'. The cloth was described as *papalina* because it was made in Avignon, which had been a papal city in the fourteenth century.

Satin (14th cent): is probably a borrowing of Arabic *zaitūnī*, 'of Zaitun', which came into English as *satin* by way of Middle French: *satin*, *satanin*, *zatanin*, *zatany*. According to Marco Polo, Zaitun was a great oriental sea port of the thirteenth century. It is generally identified as modern Tsinkiang in southeast China.

Worsted (13th cent): This closely woven woollen cloth still bears its original Middle English name which derives from *Worthstede*, now known as Worstead, the Norfolk parish where it was first produced.

continued overleaf

FABRICS *continued*

Other fabrics are named for their appearance or colour:

Chintz (17th cent): a colourful glazed cotton fabric. When brightly painted calico was first imported into Britain, English took the singular *chint* from the Hindi word *chīnt* – a derivation from the Sanskrit *chitra*, meaning 'of many colours' – to refer to the cloth. Vendors describing their wares would speak of their silks, satins, brocades and *chints*. The unfamiliar plural was subsequently taken by the public to be a singular noun and supplanted the earlier *chint*. It is unclear why in the second half of the eighteenth century *chints* became *chintz*.

Chino (20th cent): this twilled fabric is used for sportswear and uniforms. The term originated in the United States, being an American Spanish word meaning 'toasted', a reference to the light golden-brown colour of the original fabric.

Corduroy (18th cent): it is tempting to devise a French etymology for this ribbed cotton fabric, linking it with *corde du roy*, 'king's cord'. Instead its derivation is rather less attractive, probably coming from a combination of *cord* and an obsolete term for a type of woollen fabric, *deroy* or *duroy*.

Gingham (17th cent): this cotton cloth made up of dyed yarn and woven into stripes or checks originally came from Malaya, where it was known as *ginggang*, meaning 'striped'. It was imported into Europe by the Dutch, who retained the Malay word *gingang*.

Lace (16th cent): a delicate fabric with its open pattern in the weave. The word *lace* (also *laas* or *las*) had various meanings in Middle English, but its figurative meaning of 'a trap', 'a snare' best reflects its ancient origin. It came into English by way of Old French *laz* or *las*. This in turn derived from an unattested Late Latin term *lacium* and from Latin *laqueus*, meaning 'a noose', 'a snare'. From this history, it is possible to see how the sense 'thread' or 'string' came about and passed into Middle English. Medieval clothing was fastened with cords and these, too, were referred to as *laces*. The transference of the term to a fabric made of intricately woven threads took place in the mid-sixteenth century.

Velvet (14th cent): a heavy fabric with a downy pile, originally made of silk. The word has its origins in *villus*, a Latin word meaning 'shaggy hair'. This gave *villūtus* in Medieval Latin and *velu*, 'hairy', in Old French. The noun *veluotte* derived from this and passed into Middle English as *veluet*.

Some fabrics are named for the raw material used in their manufacture:

Flannel (14th cent): a soft fabric, originally of wool, now also of cotton. Latin *lāna*, 'wool' is akin to *gwlān*, the Welsh word for 'wool'. From this Welsh derived *gwlanen*, 'woollen cloth'. Middle English *flanen*, 'sackcloth', is a corruption of this. The association of the Welsh with the cloth may have given rise to the use of *flannel* as an informal term for 'wordy, insincere talk'. In Shakespeare's THE MERRY WIVES OF WINDSOR (1598) Falstaff, when scolded by the Welsh parson, Hugh Evans, declares, *I am dejected; I am not able to answer the Welsh flannel.*

Linen (Old English): this is cloth made from the flax plant, and that fact is reflected in its name. Its origins lie in an ancient Indo-European word for 'flax' which gave an unattested Germanic form *līnam*. The derived Germanic adjective *līnīn* meant 'made of flax' and this was borrowed into Old English as *līnen* or *linnen*.

And still others have an etymology that defies any category:

Chiffon (18th cent): this sheer silky fabric is etymologically nothing more than a bit of old rag and the term, though French, has English origins. Old English had *cipp*, 'a beam', from which Middle English acquired *chip*, 'a fragment cut off'. This was borrowed into Old French as *chipe*, from which came the variant *chiffe*, 'old rag'. In Modern French *chiffon* is a 'rag' or 'duster'. A *chiffonier*, 'a type of ornamental cabinet', is etymologically nothing more than a cupboard for storing rags.

Serge (14th cent): the name for this worsted twill cloth probably ultimately derives from *sī*, the Chinese word for 'silk'. The Greeks traded with an oriental people whom they named *Sēres*, 'the silk people'. From this Late Latin had *sērica lāna*, 'wool of the Seres', in other words 'silk'. Vulgar Latin had the unattested form *sērica*, which was taken into Old French as *sarge* and from there into Middle English.

Silk (9th cent): the name of this fabric, woven from threads produced by the silkworm, probably originates in *sī*, the Chinese word for 'silk'. Some etymologists hold that the Old English form *sioloc*, which gave Middle English *silk*, came from Latin *sēricum*, 'silk', a borrowing of Greek *sērikos*, 'silken', from *Sēres*, 'the oriental people from whom silk was obtained' (see *serge* above). Others argue that *sī* was picked up by the Slavic and then the Germanic peoples before passing into English.

Taffeta (14th cent): the origins of this stiff silk fabric are Persian. The Persian verb *tāftan* meant 'to weave', the derived adjective *tāftah* meaning 'woven'. This was borrowed into Turkish as *tafta* and into Old Italian as *taffettà*. It came into Middle English as *taffeta* by way of Old French *taffetas*.

Tweed (19th cent): the word was originally a trademark, a misspelling of *tweeled* – that is 'twilled' in Scottish dialect – that arose through confusion with the name of the river *Tweed*.

However, in the Bible, one of Jesus's parables (Matthew 25: 14–30) tells of a man about to embark on a long journey who calls his three servants to him and entrusts each one with a sum of money, measured in talents. Two of the servants invest their *talents* and make the money grow. The third, however, buries his in the earth. When the master returns he praises the two faithful servants but the one who has wasted his money is punished.

In the fifteenth century, based on the teaching of this parable, *talent* came to denote 'any particular God-given gifting of mind or body intended for self-improvement or to bless others'. By the seventeenth century, the word was being used free from any religious overtones to denote 'a special aptitude for something'.

tally
a reckoning, a score, an account

All told, more than 10,000 athletes competed on the world stage, in most cases purely for love of competition and pride of country. And no matter where the Olympics are held, that is more meaningful than any medal tally.
(BOSTON HERALD, 24 AUGUST 2008)

Classified as Critically Endangered, and considered one of the world's rarest parrots, the encouraging news of the rediscovery of this male comes with good news about the species' breeding progress, with the egg tally *for this year's breeding season currently standing at 37.*
(ARKIVE.ORG WEBSITE, FEBRUARY 2009)

Centuries ago merchants and tradesmen used *tallies* as invoices and receipts. The word derives from Latin *tālea*, an agricultural term meaning 'cutting' or 'twig', and came into Middle English as *taly* or *talye* through Norman French *tallie* and Medieval Latin *talia*. A *tally*

was a simple wooden rod with notches cut across one of its faces to represent the amount of money owed or received. The rod was then split in two lengthways, both parties in the transaction receiving half. Brought together, the halves corresponded exactly and were legal proof of the debt incurred or payment made.

Tallies were still tendered as receipts by the British Exchequer until the reign of George III (1760–1820) and the elmwood sticks were stored in the Palace of Westminster. In 1826, however, the Court of Exchequer was abolished and in 1834 William IV gave orders that the tallies should be burned. Bundles of them were taken to the furnaces beneath the Lords' chamber, but their blaze was so intense that the flues caught fire and almost all of the Palace burnt down. It took three decades to finish rebuilding the new Houses of Parliament.

For another word from the same source, see TAILOR.

tantalise
to teasingly offer something but not actually provide it

Their success, in other words, wasn't due to some mysterious process known only to themselves. It had a logic, and if we can understand that logic, think of all the tantalising *possibilities that opens up.*
(MALCOLM GLADWELL, THE OUTLIERS, 2008)

Princess Di's former butler Paul Burrell leaves the inquest into her death with his credibility in tatters. Under cross-examination, he is forced to admit that the 'big secret' he tantalisingly *mentioned in one of his books was just the well-known fact that Diana was thinking of moving abroad.*
(THE WEEK, 20 DECEMBER 2008)

Tantalus, the mythical king of Phrygia, deeply offended the gods. He stole food from Zeus's table and revealed the gods' secrets. As a punishment he was consigned to Hades, where he was condemned to stand up to his chin in water whose level receded each time he tried to slake his raging thirst. Fruit trees grew at the edge of the pool, their boughs overhanging the water, but each time he stretched out his hand to pluck a ripe fruit the branches raised it just beyond his reach.

Tantalise, 'to torment someone by showing or promising things and then withdrawing them', was derived from the king's name in the late sixteenth century, when the story was widely known.

The nineteenth century discovered a new fascination for Tantalus. There was a *Tantalus-cup*, a novelty siphon encased within the figure of a man whose chin came up to the bend of the siphon. Like Tantalus in the fable, the figure stood chin-high in water but was unable to drink. And there was the *tantalus* or *tantalus-stand*, a receptacle for the display of spirit-decanters. Although not appearing to be so, the decanters were locked into the stand – seemingly available but in fact unobtainable.

In 1802 a Swedish chemist, Anders Ekeberg, named a new element he had discovered *tantalum*. He was, he said, following a custom which favours names from mythology. Certainly that had been the case in Sweden just ten years before when Torbern Bergman had given *hartshorn* the name *ammonia* on the same grounds. Ekeberg's choice was apt because when tantalum is immersed in acid it is unable to absorb any of it or be saturated by it, just as King Tantalus was incapable of imbibing water.

The passion for mythological names was unabated. In 1801, an English chemist named Charles Hatchett had discovered a metallic element that he called *colombium*. It was found in the mineral that came to be called *tantalite*, from *tantalum*. However, since *colombium* and *tantalum* were very closely related in their chemical properties, the German chemist Heinrich Rose in 1844 renamed colombium *niobium*. In Greek mythology *Niobe* was the daughter of Tantalus.

For another term that originates in the myths of the ancient world, see AMMONIA.

tart
a flat open-topped pastry containing (often) a sweet filling; a promiscuous woman

*The menu is very un-ladies-who-lunch, it being almost wholly meaty, with mains of steak or sausages or lamb rump or ham hocks, the only alternatives being fish pie or a cheese and onion **tart**.*
(THE SPECTATOR, 5 FEBRUARY 2005)

*There was always one girl who was designated the 'company **tart**'. She was the one who managed to avoid the long, grim train journeys when the chorus girls were on tour. A man would be sure to take her to the next town by car. These girls most impressed Jean [Rhys]: their savoir faire, their disregard for the opinions of others.*
(THE SUNDAY TIMES, 26 APRIL 2009)

Tarts in the late fourteenth century had a variety of fillings, sweet or savoury, and were just like pies with a top crust. By the sixteenth century, however, the fillings were usually sweet and the pastry case open without a crust on the top. A sixteenth-century cookery book, A PROPER NEWE BOOKE OF COKERYE, has the following recipe for the pastry case:

*Take fyne floure and a cursey of fayre water
and a dysche of swete butter and a lyttel
saffron, and the yolckes of two egges and
make it thynne and as tender as ye maye.*

Middle English *tarte* was a borrowing
of Old French *tarte*. This was possibly
a variant of *tourte*, 'a kind of bread', a
word from Latin *torta*, 'round bread
(twisted)', the feminine of *tortus*,
'twisted', from *torquēre*, 'to twist'.

In the nineteenth century *tart* was
used figuratively as a term of endear-
ment for a girl or woman. In John
Hotten's DICTIONARY OF MODERN
SLANG, CANT AND VULGAR
WORDS (1859) it is defined as *a term
of approval applied by the London lower
orders to a young woman for whom some
affection is felt*. Hotten goes on to say
that *the expression is not generally
employed by the young men, unless the
female is in 'her best'*. Some authorities
suggest that *tart* in this context was a
shortening of *sweetheart*. Others point
out that a piece of nineteenth-century
slang for 'a sweetheart' or 'a mistress'
was *jam tart*, a term that was often also
reduced to *jam*:

*There were three bits of jam stepping out of
the tram,
So we tipped them a wink in a trice.*
(BROADSIDE BALLAD, C. 1886)

Whatever the origin, *tart* swiftly
descended the morality ladder until, by
the end of the nineteenth century, it
denoted 'a promiscuous woman', 'a
prostitute'. John Farmer and William
Henley described the word's fall thus:

Tart (common). *Primarily a girl, chaste
or not; now (unless loosely used) a wanton,
mistress, 'good-one'.*
(SLANG AND ITS ANALOGUES PAST
AND PRESENT, 1890–1904)

The verb *to tart up*, meaning 'to titivate'
or 'to smarten oneself up', dates from
the 1930s.

The etymology of the adjective *tart*
is difficult. Old English had *teart*, which
meant 'severe, painful' and was used to
describe suffering, discipline or punishment. This sense has been obsolete
since the early seventeenth century.
The sense 'sharp to the taste' appeared
in the late fourteenth century. The figurative use describing sharp, cutting
words or speech dates from the beginning of the seventeenth century.

tattoo
a signal on a drum or bugle; a
permanent picture or design on
the body

*…Lewis had a **tattoo** on his biceps – a
green band of barbed wire on his white
Welsh flesh, that led him to wear short
sleeves whatever the weather. This tattoo
was his trademark. It made him stand out
in a crowd…*
(SUSAN FLETCHER, EVE GREEN, 2004)

*A cheetah explodes towards camera, its
feet beating a blistering **tattoo** on the
dry earth, while a solitary leopard climbs
higher into a tree, smooth as silk.*
(JONATHAN & ANGELA SCOTT,
STARS OF BIG CAT DIARY, 2009)

When tavern keepers in Holland heard
the bugle or drum recalling the soldiers
to barracks, they would turn off the
taps on their casks to discourage soldiers from lingering over their drink.
The signal was known as *taptoe*, a
Dutch compound of *tap*, 'tap', and *toe*,
'shut, closed'. The word was borrowed
into military English in the seventeenth century and variously spelt as as
taptow, *taptoo* or *tattoo*. It was a signal
for the soldiers to repair to their quarters for the night:

*If anyone shall bee found tiplinge or
drinkinge in any Taverne, Inne, or Alehouse
after the houre of nyne of the clock at night,
when the Tap-too beates, hee shall pay
2s. 6d.*

(COLONEL HUTCHINSON'S ORDERS,
1644)

In the eighteenth century the drum
signal formed the basis of an entertainment when it was embellished by
military marches and music performed by torchlight. The *Edinburgh
Tattoo* is still performed and televised
annually.

Also during the eighteenth century
the word was used for 'a regular beating
or rapping, as of a drum'. Jack
London gives this vivid description
of a seaman's death in THE SEA
WOLF (1904):

*The captain, or Wolf Larsen, as men called
him, ceased pacing, and gazed down at the
dying man. So fierce had this final struggle
become that the sailor paused in the act of
flinging more water over him, and stared
curiously, the canvas bucket partly tilted
and dripping its contents to the deck. The
dying man beat a tattoo on the hatch with
his heels, straightened out his legs, stiffened
in one great, tense effort, and rolled his
head from side to side. Then the muscles
relaxed, the head stopped rolling, and a
sigh, as of profound relief, floated upward
from his lips.*

Tattoo in the sense 'a design on the
body made by puncturing the skin and
inserting indelible dyes' has a totally
different etymology. It is a borrowing of
tatau, a Polynesian or Tahitian word for
this process. *Ta* means 'a mark, a
design'. *Tattoo* was introduced into
English by Captain Cook's record of his
voyages on the South Seas in 1769. In
his JOURNAL DURING HIS FIRST
VOYAGE, he writes:

*Both sexes paint their Bodys, tattow,
as it is called in their Language. This
is done by inlaying the colour of Black
under their skins, in such a manner as
to be indelible.*

It is perhaps surprising that a word was
not coined in English before this time,
as the practice to which it refers is very
ancient and widespread. The Authorised
Version of the Bible (1611, more than
150 years before Captain Cook's
voyage) renders Leviticus 19: 28 as *Ye
shall not make any cuttings in your flesh for
the dead, nor print any marks upon you.*
One of the best modern versions of
scripture, the New International Version
of 1973, translates this as *Do not cut your
bodies for the dead or put tattoo marks on
yourselves.* The practice that Leviticus
refers to dates back to the divine revelation given to Moses at Sinai, very early
indeed in recorded history.

Tattooing among West Indians and
Central Americans was commented on
by Columbus; travellers also found it
in some North American tribes and
among Eskimos. Nor was the practice
unknown in England. There is the
legend that in 1066 the body of King
Harold was identified by his sister
Edith on the battlefield of Hastings by
the tattoo on his neck. Since it had
been the practice of Saxons so to mark
their soldiers as an aid to identifica-
tion, there may be some truth in the
story.

For another word introduced into
English by Captain Cook's voyages,
see TABOO.

tawdry
showy, cheap, of poor quality

*It is the biggest Indian reservation on the
eastern United States and it was packed
from one end to the other with souvenir
stores selling **tawdry** Indian trinkets, all
of them with big signs on their roofs and*

sides saying: Moccasins! Indian Jewelry! Tomahawks! Polished Gemstones! Crappy Items of Every Description!!
(BILL BRYSON,
THE LOST CONTINENT, 1989)

*'Don't be ridiculous,' he said. 'You do not want to be alone. We're part of each other now, you know we are, it's stupid to deny it. What are you trying to make out this is, some **tawdry** fling?'*
(MARGARET FORSTER, KEEPING THE WORLD AWAY, 2006)

Some remarkable characters are commemorated in the commonest words. St Etheldreda (c. 630–679) – also known as St Audrey, a corruption of her Latinised name (from Old English *Aethelthryth*) – was one of five daughters of Anna, King of the East Angles in Suffolk. Each one of the sisters became a saint. Audrey had two, apparently unconsummated, marriages, first with Tonbert and then with Egfrith. The latter was some 15 years her junior and, after a decade of marriage, he pressed her for his conjugal rights. Reluctantly he granted her a dissolution of their marriage, so that she could maintain her virginity. At first, in AD 672, she entered the convent at Coldingham; in the following year she founded a religious community at Ely. (The Norman cathedral now stands on the site of the abbey she built.) The rest of her life was spent in a severe regime of penance and prayer.

According to the Venerable Bede's ECCLESIASTICAL HISTORY (AD 731), St Audrey died of a tumour in her throat, an affliction she looked upon as just punishment for earlier vanity because, in her youth, she had had a penchant for wearing fine necklaces.

St Audrey was well loved and her shrine became a popular visiting place for pilgrims. On 17 October each year, her saint's day was marked with a holiday and a fair at Ely. Here were sold laces and fringes for wearing about the neck in her honour. These were known as *St Audrey's laces*, often corrupted to *Tawdry laces* or *tawdries*. Ardent suitors would sometimes buy them to woo their sweethearts. An old ballad pleads:

> *One time I gave thee a paper of pins,*
> *Another time a tawdry lace;*
> *And if thou wilt not grant me love,*
> *In truth I'll die before thy face.*

Some sweethearts, however, were more demanding than others:

> *It was a happy age when a man might have wooed his wench with a pair of kid leather gloves, a silver thimble, or with a tawdry lace; but now a velvet gown, a chain of pearl, or a coach with four horses will scarcely serve the turn.*
> (BARNABY RICH, MY LADY'S LOOKING-GLASS, 1616)

These quotations show that tawdry laces were worn by rich and poor alike. Nicholas Harpsfield, Archdeacon of Canterbury in the reign of Mary Tudor (1553–58), says that the necklaces were *formed of thin and fine silk* (HISTORIA ANGLICANA ECCLESIASTICA, printed 1662). However, in POLY-OLBION, a topographical poem of England and Wales (1612), Michael Drayton calls them *a kind of necklace worn by country wenches*. Certainly those offered at the saint's fair were of the cheap-and-cheerful variety, produced to please the country girls and suit their purses. Not surprisingly, then, by the end of the seventeenth century *tawdry*, used as both a noun and an adjective, was applied to any form of inexpensive and showy finery. Nowadays the noun is obsolete.

tea

the dried leaves of a specific shrub, used to prepare an aromatic drink

'Is there ony hot watter?' asked Mrs Gregson.
'Plenty o' that,' said the red-faced man.

*'Teem it in t' big urn,' said Mrs Gregson, 'an' squeeze th' **tay-bag**. It'll be thick enoof for th' choir lads.'*

'Couldn't we brew a fresh lot?' asked the vicar's wife.

'We could,' said Mrs Gregson, 'but they wouldn't know th' difference. We allus keep it a bit thin. It's better for their kidneys.'

'It's a shame,' said Mrs Pyot. 'There's plenty as likes strong tay.'

(T THOMPSON,
LANCASHIRE BREW, 1935)

*Being interviewed for casual labour on the building site, a candidate was asked by the foreman: 'Can you make a decent cup of **tea**?'*

'Oh yes,' came the reply.

'Can you drive a fork-lift truck?' asked the foreman.

A little disconcerted, the job-seeker scratched the back of his head and inquired: 'Just how big is this teapot then?'

(DAILY MAIL, 23 APRIL 1994)

*Papa ignored her and poured his **tea**, and then he told Jaja and me to take sips. Jaja took a sip, placed the cup back on the saucer. Papa picked it up and gave it to me. I held it with both hands, took a sip of the Lipton tea with sugar and milk, and placed it back on the saucer.*

'Thank you, Papa,' I said, feeling the love burn my tongue.

(CHIMAMANDA NGOZI ADICHIE,
PURPLE HIBISCUS, 2004)

Tea is prepared from the leaves and leaf buds of the shrub *Camellia sinensis*. A Chinese legend dates the discovery of the beverage to the third millennium BC. It tells how falling leaves from a camellia tree drifted into a pot of water which the legendary emperor Shen-Nung had set to boil, filling the air with their fragrance. Tea was first drunk in China for its medicinal properties and then for pleasure so that, by the sixth century AD, there was a thriving tea trade in eastern Asia.

In the early seventeenth century the Dutch, who traded extensively in the East, started to import shipments of a herb which the Chinese infused in hot water to make a drink, and which was known as *te* in the Amoy dialect. Under this name, in the 1630s, the Dutch introduced it into France, where it was known as *thé*, and in the early 1650s into England, where it was originally called *tay*, a form still current in some northern dialects (see the first quotation above). *Tay* persisted until the second half of the eighteenth century but was finally ousted by *tea* (sometimes *tee*), a form which arose within a few years of the product's appearance in England.

In his diary for 25 September 1660, Samuel Pepys records sending for *a cup of tee (a China drink) of which I never had drunk before*. Pepys does not say what he thought of his first cuppa. It is to be hoped that he enjoyed it, for he was a man of modest means and it must have cost him dear. Tea was an extremely expensive commodity, being a monopoly of the East India Company. As such, however, it was fit for a king – in 1664 Charles II was delighted by a presentation of two pounds of tea. It was another century before cheaper illegal cargoes were brought in from the continent and the beverage could be enjoyed by all classes.

Although the Dutch were responsible for introducing the English to their national drink, they were not the first to bring news of the Chinese herb into Europe. The Portuguese were establishing colonies and trading links in the East at about the same time. They first arrived in Macau, for instance, in 1513 and from there started officially to trade with China in 1553. It was in the late 1550s that they first made mention of tea, calling it *chá*, a word they borrowed from the Mandarin *ch'a*. When tea became known in Europe several lan-

A TASTE OF INDIA

British involvement in India began largely with the mercantile activities of the East India Company, which was incorporated in 1600. There was severe competition between the British, the French and the Dutch to challenge the Portuguese, the first Europeans to trade in India, and it was not until the mid-eighteenth century that Britain predominated. A century later, the East India Company had assumed political rule throughout much of the subcontinent. This continued until 1858, when the British government took over until India gained independence in 1947. British influence on the region was obviously great; there was also considerable impact in the other direction. With regard to language specifically, English has gained a number of words, including:

bungalow (17th cent): first recorded as *bungale* in the second half of the seventeenth century, the word comes from Gujarati *bangalo*, meaning 'of Bengal'. It therefore denoted a 'Bengali-style house', that is, a flimsy one-storey construction with a thatched roof.

chutney (19th cent): the Hindi word for this spicy relish is *chatni*. An early recipe for it recorded in English lists *cocoa-nut, lime-juice, garlic, and chillies* among its ingredients.

curry (late 16th cent): from the Tamil word *kari* meaning 'sauce'.

dinghy (late 18th cent): the Hindi word *dēṅgī* or *dīṅgī* was a diminutive of *dēṅgā*, 'boat', and referred to a small open native boat.

---

guages also adopted the term, which even travelled overland to Russia, becoming the modern Russian *chai*. Spanish, for instance, had *cha* and Italian *cia*. These became obsolete in favour of words based on *te*. Modern Portuguese, however, retains *chá* and it lingers on in English where it has gradually degenerated into a jocular slang term, *a nice cuppa cha*.

For other seventeenth-century taste sensations, see CHOCOLATE and COFFEE. See also CADDY.

teetotaller
one who abstains from alcoholic drink of any kind

*She talked about the poor blighter as if he wasn't there. Not that Motty seemed to mind. He had stopped chewing his walking-stick and was sitting there with his mouth open. 'He is a vegetarian and a **teetotaller** and is devoted to reading. Give him a nice book and he will be quite contented.'*
(P G WODEHOUSE,
CARRY ON, JEEVES, 1925)

*He is a non-smoking **teetotaller**, which I assume indicates a rich and varied, possibly even tumultuous past, and we get on very well.*
(SIMON GRAY,
THE LAST CIGARETTE, 2008)

The eighteenth and nineteenth centuries saw a marked increase in the consumption of strong alcohol in Britain. Rum flowed in from the West Indies, and Dutch gin, which had been introduced by William of Orange in the late seventeenth century, was in cheap and abundant supply. By the mid-eighteenth century it was not uncommon for a city dweller to drink a pint of gin a day. Generally speaking, *dungaree* (17th cent): the *Dungrī* district of Bombay gave its name to a stout coarse fabric that was manufactured there. This became *dungaree* in English. In the nineteenth century the name *dungarees* was applied to hardwearing trousers made of this or similar material. (For other Indian cloth imports, see FABRICS, page 263).

jungle (18th cent): the Hindi word *jāṅgal* (from Sanskrit *jāṅgala*, 'desert') originally referred to 'uncultivated land, bush'. Anglo-Indian use then applied the term to uncultivated areas that were covered with dense vegetation. By the mid-nineteenth century the word was being applied to similar areas in other parts of the world and had also gained its figurative applications.

kedgeree (17th cent): Hindi *khichrī* was a dish of rice and spiced pulses to which European cookery added fish and eggs.

shampoo (18th cent): the term was taken into Anglo-English as a verb and referred to giving someone a relaxing massage. It is a borrowing of Hindi *chāmpo*, which came from *chāmpnā* meaning 'to massage, to press'. Its modern uses as a verb meaning 'to wash the hair' and as a noun denoting the cleansing agent itself are recorded from the 1860s.

It is not surprising that many borrowings cluster round the practicalities of life: a building to live in, food, features of the landscape and products from the country. There are specialist dictionaries on Anglo-Indian words and phrases which record the mutual influence of the two languages.

---

however, heavy drinking was frowned upon only when it led to rowdy or unsocial behaviour. It was not until the beginning of the nineteenth century – when two doctors, one American and one Scottish, published papers in their respective countries suggesting that alcohol could seriously damage health – that real concern about this menace grew. By now there were large numbers of taverns and gin palaces in every big town, especially in the poorer areas, where those who were ground down by poverty and hard work sought to forget their condition through drink. This pattern was repeated on the other side of the Atlantic. It was time to recognise alcohol abuse as a serious problem.

The first temperance society was founded in Saratoga, New York, in 1808, but it was another twenty years or so before the movement really flourished in Britain. Credit for the word *tee-total*, which served as a rallying cry in both Britain and America, is claimed by both countries.

According to the British story, the word's origin has nothing to do with *tea* as an accepted beverage. The *tee* element is a repetition of the first letter of *total* and is therefore an intensifier. In the early days of the movement some reformers were content to preach abstinence from spirits only. Others disagreed, saying that only total abstinence would do. One of this band was Richard (Dicky) Turner, an artisan of Preston, Lancashire, who, *contending for the principle at a temperance meeting about 1833, asserted that 'nothing but te-te-total will do'* (STAUNCH TEETOTALLER, January 1867). The word had immediate appeal. The 1834 issues of his local temperance paper, the PRESTON TEMPERANCE ADVOCATE, are full of testimonies of *tee-total abstainers* who have signed the *tee-total pledge*. Mr Turner became something of a celebrity for his clever coinage. Even his tombstone proclaims the fact. The inscription reads:

Beneath this stone are deposited the remains of Richard Turner, author of the word Teetotal as applied to abstinence from all intoxicating liquors, who departed this life on the 27th day of October 1846, aged 56 years.

Possibly a stimulus to Turner's linguistic inventiveness was the word *teetotum*. This was a type of top or spinner, with letters written on the sides. The way it fell decided how the players in the game proceeded. The toy had been in use for over a hundred years by Turner's time and may have been known to him.

The American case for coinage rests on two strands of evidence. Firstly, there is an 1832 example of *teetotally* as an emphatic adverb:

These Mingoes…ought to be essentially, and particularly, and tee-totally obflisticated off of the face of the yearth.
(JAMES HALL, LEGENDS OF THE WEST)

This particular use has no reference to abstinence from strong drink, however, and is surely just a Kentucky backwoodsman repeating a colloquialism to intensify his point.

The second piece of evidence is put by the Reverend Joel Jewell in a letter to the editors of the CENTURY DICTIONARY (1891). The Reverend became the secretary of a temperance society in Hector, New York. The society had a policy of partial abstinence but in January 1827 it decided to introduce a new pledge for those who wished to make a stronger commitment. The initials that the two pledges bore distinguished them: *O P* signified 'old pledge' and *T* indicated 'total abstinence', so that the new word

emerged from the continuous repetition of *T, Total* However, while there is no contemporary evidence to support this claim, letters of the period show that the total abstinence movement in America came later than and was influenced by the work in Preston – an indication, perhaps, that Dicky Turner can rest in peace. Certainly American lexicographers of the 1840s (Webster and Worcester) and medical professionals ascribed to him the word's origin.

For an entry a teetotaller would shun, see ALCOHOL.

temper
a person's disposition; a tendency to become angry; to adjust

He is well known for possessing an incendiary **temper***. But never has Gordon Ramsay launched such a scathing attack on his fellow TV chefs.*
He accused Antony Worrall Thompson of having 'more chips on his shoulder than McDonald's', said Ainsley Harriott was more a comedian than a chef, and has accused Raymond Blanc of having a temper 'like a rottweiler'.
(EVENING STANDARD, 19 MAY 2003)

There is no disputing he demonstrates a level head and an even **temper** *but, in interview terms, you wouldn't call this goalkeeper a safe pair of hands just yet. There is an honesty about McGregor which always means he has the potential to drop himself in it.*
(THE SUNDAY TIMES, 4 DECEMBER 2005)

Tempering *the effects of Sydney's harsh light and the glare of the water has been a priority. 'I like soft, quiet light to come home to,' says Jeffery, who has painted the walls in watery blues and greens, and hung windows with layers of light-filtering curtains and blinds.*
(THE GUARDIAN, 11 FEBRUARY 2006)

The BOKE OF ST ALBANS (1486) was a collection of essays on topics such as hunting printed by the St Albans Press. In one of the essays the reader is urged to *take Oyle of spayne* [olive oil] *and tempere it with clere wyne.* Similarly, in his TREATYSE OF THE PESTILENCE (1544), Thomas Phaer advises that *in a hote season it is good to temper ye said wine with a litle rose-water.* The earliest sense of the verb *to temper* in English was 'to make something suitable for purpose by mixing it with something else'. It had come into Old English as *temprian,* from Latin *temperāre,* 'to apportion, to moderate in due measure', a word allied to *tempus,* 'fit season, time'.

When the noun *temper* was derived from the verb in the fourteenth century it denoted 'a mixture of proper proportions'. In the early seventeenth century, its use was extended to refer to a person's 'mental composure', to keeping one's mix of emotions in proper balance. In the eighteenth century, when this was successfully managed, a person was said to have a *good temper*; failure to keep one's composure resulted in an *ill* or *bad temper.* It was from this notion that *temper* in the sense 'a tendency to angry outbursts' evolved in the nineteenth century. In WALKER REMODELLED. A NEW CRITICAL PRONOUNCING DICTIONARY OF THE ENGLISH LANGUAGE (1836), Benjamin Smart described the development of *temper* thus: *...from the original sense, calmness, moderation; by a special application of the latter derivative senses, heat, irritation.*

temple

a building set apart for the worship of a god

Higher up are the ruins of a Byzantine church built from the stones of a **temple** *to Adonis, stained grey and brown as the wind has found or overlooked them.*
(COLIN THUBRON, THE HILLS OF ADONIS, 1968)

The original Ruby Pier entrance had been something of a landmark, a giant arching structure based on a historic French **temple***, with fluted columns and a coved dome at the top.*
(MITCH ALBOM, THE FIVE PEOPLE YOU MEET IN HEAVEN, 2003)

Whenever a Roman politician had a difficult decision to make, he would consult an augur, a man skilled in divining the will of the gods by observing nature. The *templum* was 'a section of the sky marked out by augurs for their observation of the stars or of birds'. The augur would look at the type or number of birds to cross the *templum* and note their flight patterns before making his prediction.

Templum is probably related to Greek *temein,* 'to cut', and was borrowed directly into Old English as *tempel,* becoming *temple* in Middle English under the influence of Old French *temple.*

The Latin verb *contemplārī,* 'to examine portents with care', was formed from the intensive prefix *con-* and *templum* to denote the work of the augurs in the temple. The word was then applied more generally with the sense 'to observe carefully'. It was taken into English as *contemplate* at the end of the sixteenth century with the sense 'to meditate upon'.

For other words involving signs and portents in ancient Rome, see AUSPICIOUS and CONSIDER. See also DISASTER and INFLUENCE.

thrill

(to give or feel) intense excitement or pleasure

*Tombstoning, the adrenalin-fuelled practice in which **thrill**-seekers throw themselves off cliffs into the sea, is fast becoming big business. The popularity of the extreme sport – in which jumpers attempt to achieve the maximum depth possible by entering the sea feet first with arms crossed and legs together – is soaring, despite a recent spate of deaths.*
(THE OBSERVER, 19 AUGUST 2007)

*Sergei Prokofiev has a claim to be the most popular classical composer of the 20th century. Everybody has **thrilled** to the grandeur of his 'Montagues and Capulets', endlessly pillaged for TV adverts and walk-on music for pop bands and football teams. And the strange toy-soldier march from his* The Love for Three Oranges *is lurking in most people's memory too.*
(TELEGRAPH.CO.UK, 28 APRIL 2009)

This word came about in the fourteenth century through a process called metathesis, whereby letters, sounds or syllables in a word are changed around to give a new form of that word. Old English *brid*, for example, became *bird* in modern English. The term responsible for Middle English *thrill* was Old English *thīrlian*, 'to pierce with a sharp instrument', from *thīrl*, 'hole'.

At the very beginning of the fourteenth century *thrill* also meant 'to pierce', but in the late sixteenth and early seventeenth centuries it took on the figurative sense of 'to stab through with sudden intense emotion'. The earliest records of this new application are in Shakespeare's plays. In KING LEAR (1605), for instance, a messenger brings Lear the news that the Duke of Cornwall is dead, killed by one of his servants as he tried to put out Gloucester's eyes: *A Seruant that he bred, thrill'd with remorse, Oppos'd against*

the act. The sense 'to give or feel great pleasure' seems to date from the early twentieth century.

For other information on *thīrl*, see WINDOW and also the notes on *nostril* at the end of that entry.

toady

a flatterer, a hanger-on

*'He [Sir Simon Rattle] is at his peak now,' says [Helen] Wallace. 'He's doing the things he wants to do, still pushing forward, and never **toadying** to popular taste. He continues to produce difficult programmes, not always that attractive, but highly unusual and unconventional.'*
(THE INDEPENDENT, 24 JULY 2004)

*It feels strange suddenly to be regarded as a royal **toady**. I have written critically about Charles both in the past and in this most recent piece. But for the Diana devotees, there is nothing so disgusting as a positive appraisal of the Prince's second wife. The public remains implacably opposed to Camilla becoming Queen.*
(THE TIMES, 27 APRIL 2006)

Charlatans were tricksters, quack doctors who travelled from place to place selling miracle cures for all ills. They relied upon their clever, persuasive patter to sell their wares. This is reflected in the origin of the word *charlatan*, which is a borrowing of Italian *ciarlatano*, a derivation from the verb *ciarlare*, 'to babble', 'to chatter'.

These itinerant quacks also demonstrated proof of the efficacy of their medicines in order to persuade the gullible public to buy them. In the seventeenth century they were often accompanied by a toad-eater, an accomplice who would apparently eat a toad. The crowd, believing toads to be poisonous, would gasp with horror as the creature was swallowed and again with amazement as the charlatan effected his cure. The toad-eater was completely dependent upon his master for his livelihood and performed the trick out of self interest. In the eighteenth century his role gave rise to the figurative application of *toad-eater* as a 'flatterer' and 'parasite'. The term was reduced to *toady* in the first half of the nineteenth century, the verb *to toady*, meaning 'to fawn', dating from the same period.

For a synonym, see SYCOPHANT.

toast
a grilled piece of bread, crisp and brown; to drink to someone's health and happiness

Toast, now, was a different kettle of fish: toast fingers, with a boiled egg, was something which Mr Golightly was partial to...
(SALLY VICKERS,
MR GOLIGHTLY'S HOLIDAY, 2003)

*He was the one, rather than Violet, who became excited by the news of the engagement and arranged the lunch at the Randolph and proposed half a dozen **toasts**. It crossed Edward's mind, barely seriously, that he was rather too keen to give his daughter away.*
(IAN MCEWAN,
ON CHESIL BEACH, 2007)

Etymologically this culinary term has to do with the effect of the burning sun upon the earth. The Latin verb *torrēre* meant 'to dry, to parch'. The past participle was *tostus*, from which Vulgar Latin derived the unattested verb *tostāre*, 'to brown with heat'. From this the Romance languages took their words for 'toast'. Old French had the verb *toster*, 'roast, grill', which passed into Middle English in the fourteenth century. The noun *toast* was derived from it in the fifteenth.

From at least the fifteenth century it was common to serve wine or ale with a piece of spiced toast in it. In

Shakespeare's THE MERRY WIVES OF WINDSOR (1598), Falstaff, at the Garter Inn, commands his follower Bardolph, *Fetch me a quart of Sacke, and put a toast in 't*. The toast served to flavour the drink.

In the seventeenth century this practice gave rise to a figurative application in which *a toast* was a lady, usually an admired society beauty, who was said to flavour the wine like spiced toast and to whose health a company was invited to drink. In his comedy THE WAY OF THE WORLD (1700), William Congreve writes of the bitterness of one who is *More censorious than a decayed Beauty, or a discarded Toast*. Sir Richard Steele, writing in THE TATLER (4 June 1709), gives the following account of the origin of this use:

Many wits of the last age will assert that the word, in its present sense, was known among them in their youth, and had its rise from an accident at the town of Bath, in the reign of king Charles the Second. It happened that, on a public day, a celebrated beauty of those times was in the Cross Bath, and one of the crowd of her admirers took a glass of the water in which the fair one stood, and drank her health to the company. There was in the place a gay fellow half fuddled, who offered to jump in, and swore, though he liked not the liquor, he would have the toast. He was opposed in his resolution; yet this whim gave foundation to the present honour which is done to the lady we mention in our liquors, who has ever since been called a toast.

The application of *toast* to 'drinking a person's health' may or may not originate in this story, but certainly comes from the practice of serving drink with spiced grilled bread.

☛ *Torrid* comes from *torridus*, a Latin adjective derived from *torrēre*, 'to parch'. It was used to translate the

Latin term *zona torrida*, 'torrid zone', from the fourteenth century, but became an adjective in its own right meaning 'parched, burning' in the early seventeenth century. Later senses developed from the idea of 'hot in passion', whether the passion of ardent zeal or lust.

Surprisingly, *torrent* is also from the verb *torrēre*, 'to parch'. The derived adjective *torrēntem* meant 'hot, boiling, raging', and when used as a noun denoted 'a raging stream of water'. The word came into English in the sixteenth century by way of French *torrent*.

tobacco

leaves of the tobacco plant dried and prepared for smoking

*[Virginia Woolf's] cigarettes were made from a special **tobacco** called My Mixture. Mr Woolf bought it for her in London and, in the evenings, they used to sit by the fire and make these cigarettes themselves. It was a mild sweet-smelling tobacco, and she would not have any other cigarettes, though sometimes she smoked a long cheroot which she enjoyed very much.*
(R J NOBLE, RECOLLECTIONS OF VIRGINIA WOOLF, 1975)

*Wisps of blue exhaust glowed in front of every headlight; the exhaust grew so fat and thick it could not rise or escape, but spread horizontally, sluggish and glossy, making a kind of fog around us. Matches were continually being struck – the drivers of autorickshaws lit cigarettes, adding **tobacco** pollution to petrol pollution.*
(ARAVIND ADIGA, THE WHITE TIGER, 2008)

Tabaco was a New World crop that the Spanish brought back with them from the Indies in the sixteenth century. The word was then borrowed directly into a number of other European languages: *tabaco* (Portuguese), *tabac* (French), *tabak* (German, Dutch, Russian). The English spellings *tabaco* or *tabacco* were common until the early seventeenth century.

The OED chronicles the debate on the rather disputed origin of the word. A Spanish writer, Oviedo, says that it is of Haitian origin. His HISTORY OF THE INDIES (1535) states that *tabaco* was the name given to a pipe through which the Indians smoked dried plant leaves and that the term was erroneously transferred to the plant itself by the Spaniards. However, according to Las Casas, another Spaniard who wrote a history of the region in 1552, *tabaco* was the Indian term not for a pipe but for a tight roll of leaves, rather like a cigar in form and use.

Which account is correct? It is not known for sure, but a learned paper in the AMERICAN ANTHROPOLOGIST (1889) presents evidence that members of a tribe of South American Indians may have come to northern Haiti towards the end of the fifteenth century. They used a pipe called a *taboca*, similar to the one described by Oviedo, for inhaling various hallucinatory plant substances. Possibly Oviedo muddled the pipe and the rolled-up leaves, the similarity between *taboca* and *tabaco* being the cause of his error.

The Spaniards knew that the indigenous peoples of the Indies and Central America used tobacco in their religious rituals, but they were not averse to smoking it themselves. By 1558 tobacco was being grown in Spain, as well as imported, to feed the new habit. It did not catch on in England, however, until, according to tradition, it was introduced to the English court by Sir Walter Raleigh. Raleigh certainly popularised the habit and was a con-firmed addict, understandably needing a final smoke to calm his nerves before his execution in 1618. One ballad composer had this to say about the subsequent widespread use of the weed:

> *Though many men crack,*
> *Some of ale, some of sack,*
> *And think they have reason to do it;*
> *Tobacco hath more,*
> *That will never give o'er,*
> *The honour they do unto it.*
> *Tobacco engages*
> *Both sexes, all ages,*
> *The poor as well as the wealthy;*
> *From the court to the cottage,*
> *From childhood to dotage,*
> *Both those that are sick, and the healthy.*

James I detested tobacco, which he referred to as *that most filthy weed*, but royal disapproval was not enough to prevent the government from protecting the Virginian tobacco trade. England, as the ballad proclaimed, was hooked.

See also CIGAR.

tour, tourist

a trip or journey taken for pleasure; a person taking such a journey

*From experiences like these I learned that camel meat's not bad, and that serendipity really is the best **tour** guide.*
(PATRICIA SCHULTZ, 1,000 PLACES TO SEE BEFORE YOU DIE, 2003)

*This **tour** was not helping her in the least. If anything, the more she travelled, the more she saw, the more anxious about her future she became, and he did not know what to do with her.*
'Charlotte,' he said, 'perhaps it is time to go home. Rome will keep for another day.'
(MARGARET FORSTER, KEEPING THE WORLD AWAY, 2006)

*A procession of mules cross us on the rocky paths, some laden with gravel for building, others with straw or shopping – ten different brooms poking out from the panniers at different angles – and one hefting a very ample **tourist**, a gaggle of giggling guides in her wake.*
(THE TIMES, 20 JUNE 2009)

When *tour* was first borrowed from Old French in the early fourteenth century, it had none of the pleasurable connota-tions it has today. It meant 'a turn of duty or work, a shift', a sense retained in the modern phrase *tour of duty*. The term originated in Greek *tornos*, 'a tool for drawing a circle, a lathe'. This passed into Latin as *tornus* and from there into Old French as *tour*, 'one's turn, a turning'. Not until the mid-sev-enteenth century did *tour* begin to denote 'a travelling round to visit various places'.

In the late eighteenth century the noun *tourist* was coined to describe in particular someone who toured around for pleasure. The word is a combination of *tour* and the suffix *-ist*, 'a person who does a specified thing'. Although travel was becoming easier it was still a slow process, and tours were necessarily long. During the eighteenth century it became fashionable for the sons of the British elite to take the *Grand Tour* of Europe, visiting sites of cultural interest with a tutor. That, at least, was the idea. In practice the young men would often sample riotous living for a few months before sinking back into everyday routine at home. Today's youngsters, of course, embark on the almost obligatory 'gap year' for their taste of freedom.

☛ Greek *tornos*, 'lathe', is also responsible for the verb *to turn*. When the word was borrowed into Latin as *tornus*, the verb *tornāre*, 'to turn on a lathe, to round off', was derived. This passed into Old English as *thyrnan*, *turnian*, initially meaning 'to rotate'.

Vulgar Latin derived the unattested verb *tornidiāre*, 'to wheel around, to turn', from Latin *tornus*, 'lathe'. This passed into Old French as *torneier*, 'to tourney, to tilt', the reference being to the way the horses wheeled around for a new charge. The derived noun *torneiement*, 'tournament', was borrowed into Middle English in the late thirteenth century. *Tournament* was applied to 'a contest in any game of skill' in the second half of the eighteenth century.

travel

to journey from one place to another (by transport); to visit another country for business, curiosity, enjoyment, etc.

Travel is fatal to prejudice, bigotry and narrow mindedness, and many of our people need it sorely on these accounts.
(MARK TWAIN,
THE INNOCENTS ABROAD, 1869)

Supermarket shoppers in the next decade will be able to pick fruit and vegetables from plants still growing on the shelves, according to a report into the future of retailing... Currently, produce out of season takes about three or four days to **travel** *from field to supermarket shelf, but under the futuristic plan the plants would be grown in hydroponic pods.*
(TELEGRAPH.CO.UK, 16 MAY 2009)

Late Vulgar Latin of the sixth century had the noun *trepālium* to denote a particular instrument of torture. Ducange, the seventeenth-century French philologist who composed a glossary of Medieval and Late Latin terms, suggested that this was a kind of rack upon which martyrs were tortured. Whatever its form, that the device consisted of three stakes or beams is evident from its etymology, *trepālium* being a compound of the Latin words *tres*, 'three', and *pālus*, 'stake'. The

derived verb *trepāliāre* meant specifically 'to torture on the *trepālium*', and more generally 'to torture, to torment'.

When this word passed into Old French as *travailler*, its reflexive sense was 'to afflict or weary oneself, to cause oneself trouble', hence the subsequent intransitive sense 'to toil, to labour'. The derived noun *travail* thus meant 'painful effort, wearisome toil' (modern French has *travail*, 'work') and in this sense it was borrowed into Middle English around the middle of the thirteenth century. Modern English retains the word *travail* with the sense 'strenuous mental or physical toil'.

The word had not been long in Middle English, however, before it began to denote 'journey'. This is probably explained by the considerable effort any journey demanded in the early fourteenth century. *Travail* and *travel* are, therefore, the same word, the latter coming about through a mere shift in stress, and the two forms were used interchangeably well into the eighteenth century. In his SERMONS (c. 1770), John Jortin wrote of one who *wrought with labor and travel night and day*, while in BOSCOBEL (1660), Thomas Blount writes of one whose feet were *much galled with travail*.

treacle

molasses, the thick, dark syrup produced in the refining of sugar

These palms are, for their family, ugly trees. Their stem is very large, and of a curious form, being thicker in the middle than at the base or top. They are excessively numerous in some parts of Chile, and valuable on account of a sort of **treacle** *made from the sap.*
(CHARLES DARWIN,
THE VOYAGE OF THE BEAGLE, 1839)

*When that young man had caught her from
stone to stone as she passed over the ford at
Bolton, she was almost ready to give herself
to him. But then had come upon her the
sense of sickness, that faint, overdone flavour
of sugared sweetness, which arises when sweet
things become too luscious to the eater. She
had struggled to be honest and strong, and
had just not fallen into the pot of **treacle**.*
(ANTHONY TROLLOPE,
LADY ANNA, 1846)

*I ate nice things, and when I was presented
with something green or simply bland, like
the occasional frond of Seventies lettuce for
Sunday tea or a bowl of Ready-Brek in
winter, I smothered it – the former with
salad cream, the latter with **treacle**.*
(ANDREW COLLINS,
WHERE DID IT ALL GO RIGHT?, 2003)

*Romeo was played by John Abwole, a
graceful, idealistic young black man with
treacly eyes.*
(YASMIN ALIBHAI-BROWN,
THE SETTLER'S COOKBOOK, 2009)

The Greek term *thēriakē antidotos* meant
'an antidote for the bite of venomous
creatures'. This was often shortened to
thēriakē, a word derived from *thērion*,
'wild or venomous animal', a diminutive
of *thēr*, 'wild beast'. When the Romans
came across Greek texts describing anti-
dotes to stings and bites of creatures
such as snakes, spiders and scorpions,
they borrowed the word as *thēriaca* and
worked upon the recipes, eventually
coming up with an antidote to poisons
that included opium and the cured flesh
of a viper. Old French borrowed the
Latin word as *triacle* and from there it
was taken into Middle English.

In the fourteenth century, then,
triacle was an ointment containing
venom to destroy venom. It was also a
soothing salve. Some translations of the
Bible – the Great Bible of 1539, for
instance – used *treacle* or *triacle* as a rendering for 'balm': *Is there no treacle at*
Gilead? (Jeremiah 8: 22). Later the term
more generally denoted 'an efficacious
remedy' for the healing of diseases.
Some plants held to have medicinal
qualities had *treacle* incorporated into
their local country names: rue, valerian
and garlic, for instance, were all generally known as *countryman's treacle* in
various counties.

Naturally any remedy that was
intended to be swallowed was more
palatable if it was sweetened; sugar syrup
proved a useful agent for this, so that by
the end of the seventeenth century
treacle denoted not only 'a sovereign
remedy' but also 'a syrup, molasses'.

Figuratively, *treacle* – or, more commonly its adjective *treacly* – often
denotes 'cloying sentimentality':

*The digital camera has been responsible
for a mass premature obsolescence and
it's time somebody pointed it out. In our
family, the children who had the good
fortune to be born before its invention
enjoy the warm, treacly feeling of seeing
their baby photos dotted about the house;
the ones born after have so far lived
without trace.*
(THE TELEGRAPH, 26 JANUARY 2009)

It is not only in the context of *treacle*
that the idea surfaces of incorporating
something of the animal by which one
has been bitten into a remedy.
Sixteenth- and seventeenth-century
medical treatments regularly recommended putting a hair from a dog that
had bitten you into the wound, to
assure healing. From this came the subsequent saying *Take the hair of the dog
that bit you*, in the sense of having a
drink the following morning of the
same beverage that had caused the
hangover the night before.

For another sticky confection, see
MARMALADE.

trivial
unimportant, insignificant, slight

*Habitual attitudes and behaviour often
receive reinforcement from external
circumstances. To take a **trivial** example,
anyone who has attempted to give up
smoking comes to realize that the wish for
a cigarette often depends upon cues from
the environment which recur at intervals.
Finishing a meal; sitting down to work at
a familiar desk; reaching for a drink after
work is over – such trivial reinforcing
stimuli are well known to everyone who
has struggled with the habit.*
(ANTHONY STORR, SOLITUDE, 1988)

*With immense self-control, she managed to
keep her voice steady, her look calm. 'Okay.
If you're going to be stupid about it, fine.'
She turned and left the room.*

*Roger sat at his desk without moving
for some moments. Those **trivial** words
summed it all up. The way she regarded
everything, including him.*
(CARO FRASER,
A CALCULATING HEART, 2004)

The Latin noun *trivium* meant, 'a fork in
the street, a place where three roads
meet' (from *tri-*, 'three' and *via*, 'way').
People invariably bump into one another
and exchange gossip at a busy crossroads
and so the derived adjective *triviālis*,
which literally meant 'belonging to the
crossroads', carried the sense 'common-
place, ordinary'. When trivial was borrowed into English in the late sixteenth
century, therefore, it meant 'ordinary,
everyday, common', senses that soon
developed into 'unimportant, trifling'.

Trivial was not new to the sixteenth
century, however. Medieval learning
had been divided into seven liberal
arts. Four of these – music, arithmetic,
geometry and astronomy – were regarded as the higher disciplines and
were known as the *quadrivium*, literally
'the four roads' (from *quadri-*, 'four',
and *via*, 'way'). The remaining three –
grammar, rhetoric and logic – were the
lower disciplines and comprised the
trivium, 'the three roads'. When *trivial*
first appeared in Middle English in the
fifteenth century, therefore, it was used
to describe anything to do with the
trivium and its subjects. The fact that
the adjective referred to the lower
disciplines, together with growing
disregard for antiquated medieval
scholarship, possibly further influenced
the derogatory use of *trivial* in the late
sixteenth century.

·U·

umpire
an arbiter, judge, referee

*A black spot happened to cross the eye of
the ancient **umpire** just as the baker put
all his feet and legs and pads in front of
a perfectly straight ball, and, as he
plaintively remarked over and over again,
he had to give the batsman the benefit of
the doubt, hadn't he? It wasn't as if it
was his fault that a black spot had crossed
his eye just at that moment.*
(A G MACDONELL,
ENGLAND, THEIR ENGLAND, 1933)

*All too often he would stand at the crease,
watch a disrespectful bowler arrive in a
whirl of arms, feel a thud on his pads, glare
down the pitch at the **umpire**, and hear,
from twenty-two yards away, the regretful
judgement, 'Very sorry, Sir Arthur.' A
decision against which there was no appeal.*
(JULIAN BARNES,
ARTHUR AND GEORGE, 2005)

*The problem of where to store these bananas
was a real one, involving lengthy discussion
with a ballboy and, eventually, the
intervention of the **umpire**, who suggested a
shelf in the shade of the official's chair.*
(THE TIMES, 24 JUNE 2009)

Modern English is familiar with an
umpire as 'one who enforces rules and
fair play' in certain sports such as
cricket, baseball or tennis. Originally,
however, an *umpire* was a person who
was chosen as an arbitrator in any circumstances where the services of a fair
and impartial moderator were required.
The first attested use of *umpire* in a
sporting context is with reference to
wrestling in 1714, some three hundred
years after its use as 'judge, arbiter'.

The word originated in Old French as
nonper or *nomper*, literally 'non-peer',
that is 'not equal', 'a third, and therefore
impartial, party' (from *non*, 'not' and *per*,
'equal', from Latin *pār*, 'equal'). It was
borrowed into Middle English as
noumpere in the mid-fourteenth century.
However, the initial *n* was wrongly
understood to belong to the indefinite
article, so that by the early fifteenth
century *an oumpere* had become current.
Spellings such as *umpere*, *umpeer* and
umpyre followed, *umpire* becoming finally
established around the end of the seventeenth century.

☛ Also from Old French *per* and Latin
pār, 'equal', comes English *peer* (early
14th cent) meaning 'one's equal'.
Studies in child development are much
concerned with *peer pressure* (c. 1957) –
pressure to conform put on children
and teenagers by others in their *peer
group* (c. 1943). In the cases where
one's equal was a fellow nobleman,
the term *peer* came to mean 'lord'. It is
particularly found today in the phrase
peers of the realm (1707).

Pār is also evident in *compare* (14th
cent), while its derivative *paria*, 'equal
things', is the source of English *pair*
(13th cent), through Old French *paire*.

For details of an old game where an
umpire was required, see HANDICAP.
See also MIND YOUR INDEFINITE
ARTICLE (page 284).

MIND YOUR INDEFINITE ARTICLE

A few common English words, at some stage in their development, lost an initial letter *n* to the indefinite article. *Apron*, for instance, was originally spelt *napron*, being a fourteenth-century borrowing of Old French *naperon* (a diminutive of *nape*, 'tablecloth'). Modern French retains *napperon* for 'tablemat', but in English *a napron* became *an apron*. The error was already in evidence by the mid-fifteenth century but not until the end of the sixteenth was the initial *n* lost for ever.

Another borrowing from Old French, *noumpere*, suffered the same fate in the fifteenth century, eventually to emerge as UMPIRE. But the error was indiscriminate and attacked English words as well. Old English *nædre*, 'snake', became *naddre* in Middle English but between 1300 and 1500 lost its initial *n* to the indefinite article to become *adder*.

Sometimes the error was reversed. The entry for IDIOT shows how, in the sixteenth century, the word was sometimes spelt as *nidiot*, the initial *n* having been transferred from the end of the indefinite article. This form gave rise to the variant *nidget*, which persisted into the nineteenth century.

The various forms through which Old English *efeta* passed to emerge as *newt* are difficult to account for, but in the fifteenth century an *n* was transferred to the intermediate form *ewt*.

Nickname has a similar history. Middle English had *ekename*, that is 'an additional name', until around the mid-fifteenth century, when the form *nekename* began to appear.

Such misinterpretations are not unique to English, however. The long and complicated history of OMELETTE is marked by a similar error in French – this time involving the definite article.

---

uncouth
unrefined, uncultured, ill-mannered

*He collected his loot, thank you very much, and with it he did what a lot of newly rich men do: he bought a football club. At Newcastle United he seems to be having more fun than he could ever have imagined. Ashley likes nothing better than standing on the terraces among the **uncouth** fans...*
(THE SPECTATOR, 13 FEBRUARY 2008)

*Adolf Hitler's '**uncouth**' personal conduct, including biting his nails during meals, has been exposed in secret intelligence papers. The documents paint a picture of Hitler based on information from one of his wartime aides, who describes the Nazi leader as a solitary*
man *'of extremely few but intense emotions' and 'shocking' table manners.*
(BELFAST TELEGRAPH,
19 FEBRUARY 2009)

English has retained a number of adjectives whose negative form is current while the positive has become either obsolete or rare. *Uncouth* is one of these. The Old English adjective *cūth* (*couth*) meant 'well-known, familiar', being a derivative of the verb *cunnan*, 'to know'. Originally, then, its negative, *uncūth* (*uncouth*), meant 'unknown', 'unfamiliar'. The adjective *couth* barely managed to survive into the eighteenth century but then reappeared as a back-formation of *uncouth* in the late nineteenth, often in humorous contexts. It remains rare and today is used rather self-consciously: *The backlash is something rightwing people do. Like 'kempt hair' and 'couth behaviour', references to a 'left-wing backlash' are rare indeed* (THE GUARDIAN, 10 January 2005).

Uncouth, on the other hand, remained a well-used word. It developed various shades of meaning over the centuries, all seemingly stemming from the notion that what is unknown and unfamiliar is also strange, suspect and therefore ultimately unacceptable. The Anglo-Irish satirist Jonathan Swift, tongue in cheek, applied it to the Scots' way of talking:

There are some people who think they sufficiently acquit themselves and entertain their company with relating of facts of no consequence, nor at all out of the road of such common incidents as happen every day; and this I have observed more frequently among the Scots than any other nation, who are very careful not to omit the minutest circumstances of time or place; which kind of discourse, if it were not a little relieved by the uncouth terms and phrases, as well as accent and gesture, peculiar to that country, would be hardly tolerable.

(HINTS TOWARDS AN ESSAY ON CONVERSATION, 1710)

The modern senses 'awkward, clumsy' developed in the sixteenth century and 'crude and unrefined' in the eighteenth.

☛ *Unruly* is another example of a negative form that has outlasted the positive. It is of more recent coinage and quite transparent in its meaning and origin. The adjective *ruly* now survives only as a back formation of *unruly*. It was coined around the turn of the fifteenth century and meant 'obedient to rule', 'orderly'. *Unruly*, meaning 'ungovernable', 'disorderly' dates from the same period.

See also UNKEMPT, UNWIELDY and NEGATIVE PREFIXES (page 287).

unkempt

dishevelled, uncombed; neglected, uncared for

*Ikmen took a moment to look at the Heper house. Made entirely of wood, it stood upon a considerable plot of ground, which had its wild **unkempt** existence between a petrol station and a row of ugly shops which had been built in the 1970s.*
(BARBARA NADEL, HAREM, 2003)

*We sat in the shade of a leafy tree and I enjoyed the slight **unkemptness** of the grass – the French don't really have lawns round their houses, just grass.*
(RICK STEIN, FRENCH ODYSSEY, 2005)

This term ultimately goes back to unattested proto-Indo-European *gombhos*, which probably meant 'tooth'. This produced West Germanic *kambaz*, 'comb', which gave the Old English noun *camb*. The comb is therefore named for its teeth. The verb *to comb* was derived from the noun in the late fourteenth century. In the mid-sixteenth century the participle *combed* was combined with the prefix *un-*, 'not', to give *uncombed*, an adjective applied to untidy hair and tangled wool.

Unkempt and *uncombed* both mean the same thing and are relatives. *Kambaz* had spawned the derivative *kambjan*, 'to comb', which became *cemban*, in Old English. This evolved into the Middle English form *kemb*, 'to comb' (which was then superseded by *comb*). From this was derived *unkembed*, 'uncombed', which was used from the fourteenth to the nineteenth centuries. The variant *unkempt* is a contracted form found from the late sixteenth century onwards.

At first, however, *unkempt* was applied to language and not to hair or appearance. In his SHEPHEARDS CALENDER

(1579), Edmund Spenser laments *howe my rymes bene rugged and unkempt*, and in the FAERIE QUEENE (1590) he writes of *vncourteous and vnkempt* words. Not until the eighteenth century, when it supplanted *unkembed*, was *unkempt* used in its literal sense of 'uncombed'. Having established itself, in the following century it went on to develop the wider sense of 'neglected, uncared for' with regard to the whole appearance, not just the hair.

Unkempt is one of those words that is much more common with a negative prefix. The adjective *kempt*, however, has been around for nearly a thousand years, but was little used up to the second half of the nineteenth century. It may well have come back into use because of the rise of *unkempt* in the general sense of 'scruffy' around that time. *Kempt* originally referred to well-combed hair or wool, but it now enjoys the extended sense 'well-tended':

The strangest thing about turning 60 is remembering how antique people of 40 used to look when I was 20. Now I feel rather young and have to remind myself to act my age, whatever that means. One of the things it does mean is that I should try to be a little more kempt than comes naturally to me.
(VOGUE, JULY 2007)

See UNCOUTH and UNWIELDY for other words that begin with a negative prefix. See also NEGATIVE PREFIXES (opposite).

unwieldy
difficult to handle, unmanageable

*[Roger] Kennedy's prose is often **unwieldy**. In one particularly egregious example, discussing the demand for cotton fabric in antebellum America, he writes: '[Southern ladies] wore neoclassical cotton frocks, scandalous from the point of view of Abigail Adams in their neoclassical susceptibility to the caress of every breeze and their*

Hellenistic revelations of the contours beneath and the withdrawal of their bodice-lines to the very frontier of decent coverage.'
(REVIEW OF 'MR JEFFERSON'S LOST CAUSE' BY ROGER KENNEDY, IN THE BOSTON GLOBE, 26 JANUARY 2009)

*Other off-road cars are indeed too large and **unwieldy** to make much sense in urban areas but the Range Rover – dicky throttle response in the diesel aside – never feels like it's too big or unmanageable.*
(THE SUNDAY TIMES, 15 MARCH 2009)

The verb *to wield* can be traced back to an unattested proto-Germanic base *walth-*, 'to possess power'. Originally, in Saxon times, *to wield* meant 'to rule, govern, command', but by the eleventh century an extended sense, 'to manage a tool or weapon with skill', was emerging. Both senses are still current today; one can *wield* power and authority as well as a weapon, a tool or even a pen.

The derived Middle English adjective *wieldy*, now rarely used, meant 'strong, vigorous, capable of handling a heavy weapon'. Its opposite, *unwieldy*, coined in the fourteenth century, therefore meant 'weak and feeble in body', through age, perhaps, or infirmity: *A toothless, old, impotent, and unweldie woman* (Reginald Scot, THE DISCOVERIE OF WITCHCRAFT, 1584).

In the sixteenth century *wieldy* was also applied to the object wielded, to give the sense 'easily handled or controlled'. It might refer to a horse, a boat or a weapon:

When you break a colte, you firste beate him for his wildnes, and afterward being weldy do cherish your hobby.
(BRIAN MELBANCKE, PHILOTIMUS, 1583)

NEGATIVE PREFIXES

It seems that some words have bias to the negative – they prefer to appear with a negative prefix and look odd without it.

UN	IN
uncouth	inalienable
ungainly	incessant
unkempt	indelible
unruly	indomitable
unscathed	ineffable
untoward	inept
unwieldy	inestimable
unwonted	inexorable
	innocent
DIS	innocuous
disabled	inordinate
disconsolate	insatiable
disgruntled	insufferable
dismayed	inviolate
dishevelled	
disparate	

P G Wodehouse is one writer to break this rule for humorous effect:

He spoke with a certain what-is-it in his voice, and I could see that, if not actually disgruntled, he was far from being gruntled.
(THE CODE OF THE WOOSTERS, 1938)

See also the entries for UNCOUTH, UNKEMPT and UNWIELDY.

In the Choice of a Sword, we take care that it be weildy.
(SIR ROGER L'ESTRANGE, SENECA'S MORALS BY WAY OF ABSTRACT, 1693)
Its opposite, *unwieldy*, duly followed suit with the sense 'difficult to control or handle', because of the object's size or shape:

A ship that by reason of the biggenesse is vnwildie.
(SIR THOMAS ELYOT, DICTIONARY, 1552)

For other words that begin with a negative prefix, see UNCOUTH and UNKEMPT. See also NEGATIVE PREFIXES (above).

upholsterer

a person who stuffs chairs and sofas and covers them with fabric

'What are you growing there?' The **upholsterer** *lugs an armchair up the walkway to the house but his quick eyes are on the land.*
'Olives and grapes,' I answer.
'Of course, olives and grapes, but what else?'
(FRANCES MAYES,
UNDER THE TUSCAN SUN, 2003)

*You can also decorate your green garlands
with spray-painted bows. Scrim – the very
loosely woven cloth, thinner than sacking,
that **upholsterers** use on chair seats –
makes excellent filigree bows.*
(THE INDEPENDENT,
20 DECEMBER 2008)

*It's the story of an **upholsterer**, a battered
old armchair, an angry Irishman, a
shooting, a lost leg and a reconciliation
that saw two men find God.*
(SUNDAY MIRROR, 10 MAY 2009)

The verb *to uphold*, a compound of *up*
and *hold*, once had the now obsolete
sense 'to keep in good repair'. In the
fourteenth century, a person who
repaired and dealt in second-hand articles of clothing or furniture was known
as an *upholder*, the *-er* suffix indicating
'someone involved with the specified
occupation'. In his SURVEY OF
LONDON (1598), the Elizabethan
chronicler and antiquary John Stow
describes a lane which *in the raigne of
Henry the sixt, had ye for the most parte
dwelling Fripperers or Upholders, that solde
olde apparell and housholde stuffe.*

During the early fifteenth century
upholder was challenged by *upholdster*,
an alternative formed by adding the
suffix *-ster*, 'one who is associated with
an activity'. By the second half of that
century, however, *upholster* was taking
hold, the pronunciation of the *d* after
the *l* proving too difficult.

The next twist came in the early
seventeenth century when the suffix *-er*
was reinstated, this time quite need-
lessly, on the end of *upholster* to form
upholsterer. By this time, the word had
come to specify 'a tradesman skilled in
stuffing chairs and sofas and covering
them with fabric'.

The noun *upholstery* to denote 'an
upholsterer's work or materials' dates
from the mid-sixteenth century. The verb
to upholster dates from the mid-nineteenth
and is a back-formation of *upholsterer*.

uproar
commotion, hubbub; outcry,
controversy

*I went down to Greenway Lane Farm by
the quiet meadows fragrant with the incense
of evening prayers. How sweet and still and
pure after the noise and dust and crowd
and racket of the town, the fine and smart
dresses, the tawdry finery, the flaunting
ribbons and the **uproar** of the cheese
market where the band was thundering
and the dancers whirling. Here the sweet
flowers were blossoming and the only
sound was the birds singing very quietly.*
(FRANCIS KILVERT, DIARY,
WHIT MONDAY, 25 MAY 1874)

*But later, in bed, I became anxious. Never
before had I heard the wind quite so violent
in Fairacre... I pulled the bedclothes up
round my ears, thanked heaven that I was
a schoolteacher and not a sailor, and slept
amidst the **uproar**.*
(MISS READ,
THE FAIRACRE FESTIVAL, 1968)

*Before taking office, Clinton added to his
troubles by casually mentioning that he
wanted to lift the ban on gays in the
military. The ensuing **uproar** persisted into
the first months of his administration.*
(THE WEEK, 6 DECEMBER 2008)

Appearances can be deceptive. *Uproar*, in
spite of its form and meaning, does not
derive from the same source as *roar*. *Roar*
is an old imitative word: Old English had
rarian, which has parallels in early
German and Dutch words. *Uproar*, on
the other hand, is a borrowing of Dutch
oproer. This is a compound of *op*, 'up',
and *roeren*, 'to stir, to move', so that *oproer*
literally means 'a stirring up', and hence
'mutiny, insurrection, disorder'.

Uproar was introduced into English
by William Tyndale, a leader of the
Reformation in England, who had plans
to translate the Bible into English.
These met with considerable opposi-

tion, however, and so he undertook the task in Germany. Here he made his translations of the New Testament (1526) from the original Greek, but also drew upon the work of other translators. One of these was Martin Luther, who used the related German word *aufruhr* when referring to certain scenes of confusion in the original text. Tyndale's work reflects this use, for where Luther has *aufruhr*, Tyndale has *uproar*. He renders Acts 21: 38, for instance, as: *That AEgipcianwhych...made an vproure, and ledde out into the wildernes about iii. thousande men.*

When Miles Coverdale made his translation of the Bible nine years later, in 1535, he drew not on the original texts but on the Vulgate Bible and Luther's and Tyndale's renditions, so that *uproar* features in his text also. Such was the impact of these versions of the Bible in the vernacular that *uproar* became a familiar word from the 1540s onwards. Besides its sense of 'commotion and disorder', it developed the related meaning of 'deafening clamour and outcry', which was obviously influenced by *roar*. The early English spelling was either *uprour(e)* or *uprore* but, by the end of the sixteenth century, *uproar* had made an appearance, about the same time that the spelling of *roar* also settled into its modern form.

For another instance of a word influenced by an etymologically unrelated word, see BLINDFOLD. For other words that entered English through Bible translation, see SCAPEGOAT and SLIPPERY.

urchin
a poor, ragged child

*He went on to paint more ingratiating pictures, in which **urchins** seem to have been hired to smile at the viewer or chuckle sweetly at the antics of dogs.*
(THE OBSERVER, 18 FEBRUARY 2001)

*The Doge's cook spots an **urchin** stealing and takes him on as an apprentice.*
(REVIEW OF 'THE BOOK OF UNHOLY MISCHIEF' BY ELLE NEWMARK, IN THE TIMES, 18 JUNE 2009)

Urchin, *hurcheon* and *irchin* are three variants, all meaning 'hedgehog'. Their source was Latin *ēr*, 'hedgehog'. From this Latin derived *(h)ērīcius*, 'hedgehog', which became unattested *hēriciō* in Vulgar Latin and *herichon* in Old Northern French. Middle English borrowed the word as *(h)irchon* towards the end of the thirteenth century. THE ROMAUNT OF THE ROSE (c. 1400), a translation of a French courtly love poem, describes a fellow whose hair was grown *like sharp vrchouns*, and in THE CHRONICLES OF ENGLAND (1480) William Caxton describes one poor man whose body was *stykked as full of arewes as an vrchone is full of prikkes*.

The figurative application of *urchin* to 'a poor, ragged child' dates from the sixteenth century, the term becoming more frequent in the late eighteenth with the advent of the industrial revolution: *He sent an urchin (I do not mean a hedgehog...but a boy, commonly so called)* (William Cowper, LETTER TO MRS THROCKMORTON, 10 May, 1790).

Urchin was applied to the small, hedgehog-like sea creature with the soft body and spiny shell at the very beginning of the seventeenth century.

utopia

an ideal state, a country of
unattainable perfection

I know perfectly well I'll be called a
utopian. *It's true! And I say: Why not?*
We must have utopias so that one day they
may become realities. Less than a century
ago, social security, unemployment benefits,
and paid vacations were utopias; today
we have them and everyone takes it for
granted. The same is true for everything:
what for the moment seems unattainable
will be tomorrow's reality.
(EMILIE CARLES,
TR. AVRIEL H GOLDBERGER,
A WILD HERB SOUP, 1991)

God forbid we should ever achieve some
kind of prelapsarian ***utopia*** *on earth*
because then you would have to live your
life instead of just complaining about it.
(KATE ATKINSON,
ONE GOOD TURN, 2006)

Swirling around the greatest American
writers of this period is a credulous
optimism that must have seemed naive
and dangerous to them. They heard others
say ***Utopia*** *was achievable – just go off*
and form a farming community with a
few good friends.
(SHELLEY COSTA BLOOMFIELD,
THE EVERYTHING GUIDE TO EDGAR
ALLAN POE, 2007)

Sir Thomas More was a leading scholar
and humanist in Renaissance England.
He numbered Erasmus, Colet and Lily
amongst his friends and at court was
greatly favoured by Henry VIII. In
1516 More published a political work
written in Latin and entitled UTOPIA,
the name he gave to an imaginary
island where a perfect form of government and society had been achieved.
The work is divided into two parts:
Book One is a discourse on the economic, legal, social and moral failings
of contemporary Europe; Book Two
details the perfection of Utopia, where
principles dear to the humanists, such
as education for all, religious tolerance
and community of goods, are given full
rein and result in a state that is happy,
stable and just. More was too much of
a realist to imagine that such perfection
was ultimately possible or had ever
been reached: he coined *Utopia* from
Greek *ou*, 'not', and *topos*, 'place' so
that the island was literally called
'nowhere'.

The work was widely acclaimed. It
was translated into French, German,
Italian, Spanish and, in 1551, English.
And so, in all these languages, *Utopia*
describes ideal, albeit unattainable,
political or social reform. The cynicism
of our modern age has meant that
utopian is now often a term of condemnation; the implication is that whatever
is so described may be praiseworthy but
is quite impractical and unrealistic.

Possibly More might be heartened
to hear that Utopia now officially exists
– it is the place on Mars where the
Viking II spacecraft landed in 1976.

vaccine

a substance containing antigens which is injected into the bloodstream to protect a person against a specific disease

*Hopes of a **vaccine** for cancer received a boost yesterday following trials of a new therapy which successfully blocked tumour growth in animals. The experimental vaccine protected animals from cancer for up to five months, and stopped tumours growing bigger in those which already had the disease.*
(THE GUARDIAN, 23 MAY 2006)

*The NHS has a stockpile of more than £500 million of the Tamiflu anti-viral drug which has proved effective on patients in Mexico, and scientists are working on developing a **vaccine** against the new strain, said Mr Johnson.*
(PRESS ASSOCIATION, 27 APRIL 2009)

Smallpox was once dreaded; epidemics were frequent, the mortality rate was high and survivors were left badly scarred, although safe in the knowledge that they were now protected from re-infection. The observation that cow-hands and milkmaids who had been infected with the less serious disease of cowpox also seemed to have later immunity from smallpox is sometimes attributed to a Dorset farmer, Benjamin Jesty, although it appears that there was quite a tradition to this effect among country folk. Dr Edward Jenner's interest and subsequent research into the rumour are undisputed, however.

The culmination of Jenner's investigations came in 1796 when he inoculated an eight-year-old boy, James Phipps, with matter from cowpox pustules and afterwards inoculated him with smallpox. The boy remained healthy. Jenner was then able to demonstrate that matter drawn from a vesicle on the boy's body was effective in inoculating others. In this way resistance to the disease could be passed on.

Jenner published his findings in 1798. Initially they were not well received and met with fierce opposition until a number of eminent physicians and surgeons declared their confidence in Jenner's work. In 1853 vaccination against smallpox was made compulsory in Britain. Nevertheless the order was often ignored, while outrageous rumours circulated among the uneducated that vaccinated patients risked becoming like cows themselves. The case was cited of a youngster from Peckham who displayed bovine behaviour, moving on all fours, mooing and butting. An entry in Francis Kilvert's diary dated 27 February 1871 reads:

Clyro Petty Sessions. Fifteen people summoned for neglecting to have their children vaccinated, but they got off by paying costs.

The following year the order was enforced.

Vaccine entered English as an adjective derived from Latin *vaccīnus*, 'belonging to a cow', from *vacca*, 'cow'. The coupling *variolae vaccinae* to denote 'cowpox' appeared in the title of

Jenner's seminal work, INQUIRY INTO THE CAUSE AND EFFECTS OF THE VARIOLAE VACCINAE (1798). Thereafter the adjective *vaccine* frequently appeared in medical journals in phrases such as *vaccine disease*, *vaccine matter*, *vaccine virus* and *vaccine inoculation*. The latter was the source of the verb *vaccinate* and the noun *vaccination*, both of which were coined at the beginning of the nineteenth century. Initially *vaccination* referred uniquely to the preventative treatment of smallpox. Later, in honour of Jenner's pioneering work, the French micro-biologist and chemist Louis Pasteur (1822–95) applied the term more widely to the prevention of other diseases by inoculation. The earliest recorded use of *vaccine* standing alone as a noun to denote 'matter for inoculation' dates from 1846.

vanilla

flavouring obtained from the orchid's dried pods

Vanilla has a fabulous tropical scent and a wonderful aroma, sweet smelling and utterly alluring. I once visited the market at Marigot on the island of St Martin in the Caribbean to look at the local produce. The sight, scent and aroma of the vanilla, sold in bunches by market traders that day, will stay with me for the rest of my life.
(PAUL GAYLER,
FLAVOURS OF THE WORLD, 2002)

*I ate this dish on the island of La Réunion in the Indian Ocean. It was here that the French planted **vanilla** at the beginning of the 19th century, but the plants were sterile until a young slave, Edmond Albius, found a way to fertilise the flowers by hand. Since then, vanilla vines all over the world have been fertilised in the same way.*
(JILL NORMAN, WINTER FOOD, 2005)

Vanilla pods come from a species of climbing orchid indigenous to the tropics of Mexico. The Aztecs used them with other ingredients such as chilli water and powdered flowers to enhance the flavour of their chocolate drink. When the conquering Spaniards adapted the chocolate recipe to their taste, they replaced the chilli with nutmeg and cinnamon, but retained the vanilla and took pods home with them to Spain.

The Spanish avoided the difficult Aztec word *tlixochitl* with some justification and instead called the pod *vainilla*, 'little sheath', with an eye to its elongated shape. *Vainilla* was a diminutive form of *vaina*, 'sheath', which in turn came from Latin *vāgīna*, meaning 'sheath, scabbard'.

Vanilla came into English in the seventeenth century along with the recipe for chocolate which, for almost a century, had been jealously guarded by the Spanish. In 1662 the court physician Henry Stubbe published THE INDIAN NECTAR, OR A DISCOURSE CONCERNING CHOCOLATA in which he praised the beneficial qualities of chocolate, saying that *they added...the Vaynillas [to the chocolate]...to strengthen the brain.*

☛ The Romans used the term *vāgīna* as a euphemism for the 'female genital canal', hence English *vagina* (17th cent).

See also CHOCOLATE. For other words based on imagined likenesses see HEARSE, LIZARD, LOBSTER and MUSCLE.

vault
an arched roof; to leap over

The Scotsman, *open in front of her on the table, reported a bank robbery that had gone wrong when the robbers had inadvertently locked themselves in the* **vault**.
(ALEXANDER MCCALL SMITH, FRIENDS, LOVERS, CHOCOLATE, 2005)

The priest became apoplectic. The long sash window would screech upwards, banging at the top of its rise, and the thin figure, hand on ledge, would **vault** *from the opening in a blurred flurry of black soutane, clutching his priest-skirts and flying across the ground towards the startled boy, screaming at him to get off the holy turf.*
(BOB GELDOF, GELDOF IN AFRICA, 2005)

These homonyms are from the same source but took different paths into Modern English.

The Latin verb *volvere* meant 'to roll, to turn round'. Its feminine past participle *volŭta* evolved in Vulgar Latin into the unattested noun *volta*. This meant 'a turn, a bend' and was therefore applied to 'an arched roof, a vault'. Middle English borrowed the word from Old French *vaute, voute* in the fourteenth century. The spelling with *l* began to appear in the fifteenth century and was established by the late seventeenth.

Vault with the sense 'to leap (with the aid of the hands or a pole)' came into English from Middle French *volter* in the sixteenth century. The French verb was a borrowing of Italian *voltare* which meant 'to turn a horse with a bound' – a manoeuvre that the Anglo-Italian lexicographer John Florio (1553–1625) was later to describe as one that *cunning riders teach their horses* – and hence 'to spring, to bound'. The Italian term was derived from unattested Vulgar Latin *volvītare*, from Latin

volvere, 'to turn'. Unusual uses of the noun *vault* in English include the copulation of rutting male deer:

It is a pleasure, to beholde them when they goe to Rutte and make their vaute.
(GEORGE TURBERVILLE, THE NOBLE ARTE OF VENERIE OR HUNTING, 1575)

and the art of mounting a horse without using the stirrups:

Vault *is also used for the Manages practis'd on the wooden Horse, to learn to mount and unmount with Ease and Expedition.*
(EPHRAIM CHAMBERS, CYCLOPAEDIA, 1728)

For other words from Latin *volvere*, see VOLUME.

vegetable
a plant grown to be eaten; a person who leads a monotonous existence or who is reduced to inactivity through illness

He [my father] spent the last three years of his life as a **vegetable**, *after having 11 strokes in nine minutes. Then my mother died and it was almost as if I didn't have to protect anyone any more and my father could no longer do me any harm.*
(CLARISSA DICKSON WRIGHT IN THE GUARDIAN, 13 FEBRUARY 2003)

…I have a politically incorrect problem that is so shameful I can only whisper it to you. I don't really like **vegetables**. *I like meat. I may possibly eat a potato but after that what I really want is, well, more meat.*
(GOOD HOUSEKEEPING, APRIL 2009)

The origin of this word is full of life. The Latin verb *vegēre* meant 'to be lively'. The derived adjective *vegetus*, 'lively, active', was responsible for a new verb *vegetāre*, 'to enliven', whose Late Latin derivative *vegetābilis* meant 'animating' and hence 'full of life', and was used to describe vegetating plants. And so, when Middle English acquired the adjective as *vegetable* at the beginning of the fifteenth century, by way of Old French, it meant 'having the growing properties of plants'. The poet Andrew Marvell (1621–78) used the word figuratively in this sense when he wrote:

> My vegetable love should grow
> Vaster than empires and more slow.
> (TO HIS COY MISTRESS)

Vegetable appeared as a noun in the second half of the sixteenth century, when it simply denoted 'a plant'. Not until the mid-eighteenth century was it applied to 'a plant grown for human consumption'.

The adjective *vegetable* was first used to describe a 'wearisome existence' in the nineteenth century. In his HISTORY OF NAPOLEON BONAPARTE (1854), the American writer J S C Abbot writes of *pauper peasantry* who were *weary of a merely vegetable life* and were *glad of any pretext for excitement*. By the early twentieth century, the noun *vegetable* was being used figuratively to denote 'a person who leads a monotonous existence' or 'one who, particularly through mental problems, is reduced to passivity'.

The word *vegetarian*, which was irregularly coined in the first half of the nineteenth century, should really have been *vegetablearian*, the suffix *-arian* denoting 'belief, advocacy'. The new noun was much publicised by the Vegetarian Society which was founded in Ramsgate, Kent, in 1847.

The term *vegan* to denote 'one who abstains from all food of animal origin' was invented by Donald Watson, founder of the Vegan Society, in 1944. He took the *veg* of *vegetable* and added the suffix *-an*, 'a believer in'. He had this to say about the launch of his magazine and his new word:

'Vegetarian' and 'Fruitarian' are already associated with societies that allow the 'fruits' of cows and fowls, therefore...we must make a new and appropriate word... I have used the title 'The Vegan News'. Should we adopt this, our diet will soon become known as the vegan diet, and we should aspire to the rank of vegans.
(VEGAN NEWS, 2 NOVEMBER 1944)

ventriloquist

someone appearing not to speak, yet producing the speech for a dummy, another person, etc.

The wizard spent his early life in Omaha. On reaching maturity he became a **ventriloquist** *and claims to have been trained by a 'great master'. He boasts of being able to imitate any kind of bird or beast and uses his ability to project his voice in order to present a deceptively intimidating image of himself.*
(LAURA JAMES,
TIGGER ON THE COUCH, 2007)

It's not hard to be a little freaked out by Andrew Lawrence. Morbidly pale and piercingly pink-eyed, with bizarrely angular features, he raspingly says of himself: 'If you stuck a bow-tie on me, I'd look like a **ventriloquist's** *dummy.' And he's right.*
(THE TELEGRAPH, 4 AUGUST 2008)

According to the etymology, a *ventriloquist* is 'one who is skilled in speaking from his belly'. The word came into English in the mid-seventeenth century from Late Latin *ventriloquus*, 'belly-speaker', a compound of Latin *venter*, 'stomach' and *loquī*, 'to speak'. The Late Latin term was modelled on the Greek word *eggastrimuthos* (*engastrimyth* in English), which was similarly derived.

Ancient texts contain many hints of the use to which ventriloquism was put to deliver oracles and the like. Both Aristophanes and Plato mention Eurycles of Athens, a well-known *engastrimyth* of the fifth century BC, saying that he delivered oracles by means of a *daemon*, 'a demon', living deep within that moaned from his belly.

The Christian Church, however, would not tolerate divination. Ventriloquism was regarded as a device of sorcery or evidence of possession by an evil spirit and was punishable by death. In the early fifteenth century, the French magician Meskyllene was executed for touring with a box which uttered judgements and predictions. In the reign of King Francis I of France (1494–1547), the valet de chamber Louis Brabant used his skills as a ventriloquist to secure the hand of a beautiful heiress and a considerable fortune by imitating voices of the deceased. Elizabeth Barton, the Holy Maid of Kent (1506–34), was one of the few ventriloquists whose trances, for a time at least, were sanctioned by the church. The Archbishop of Canterbury, Thomas Cranmer, described one of these episodes thus:

When she was brought thither and laid before the image of our Lady, her face was wonderfully disfigured, her tongue hanging out and her eyes being in a manner plucked out and laid upon her cheeks; and so, greatly disordered.

Then there was a voice heard speaking within her belly, as it had been in a tun, her lips not greatly moving; she all that while continuing by the space of three hours in a trance.

Not until the eighteenth century did *ventriloquism* in the modern sense of 'throwing one's voice', rather than speaking from deep within, emerge as entertainment, and that provoked comment that the term was inappropriate, *since they appear more frequently to speak...from the roof or distant corners of the room, than from their own mouths or their own bellies* (ENCYCLOPEDIA BRITANNICA, 1797).

☛ Latin *loquī*, 'to speak' is the source of:

colloquy (16th cent) and *colloquial* (18th cent): from Latin *colloquī*, 'to speak together, to converse'.

eloquent and *eloquence* (14th cent), *elocution* (16th cent): from Latin *eloquī*, 'to speak out'.

loquacious (17th cent): from Latin *loquāx* (stem *loquāc-*), from *loquī*, 'to speak'.

Latin *venter* is the source of:

ventral (18th cent): from Latin *ventrālis*, 'of the stomach'.

ventricle (15th cent): from Latin *ventriculus*, diminutive of *venter*.

victim
somebody who is killed, harmed or taken advantage of

*Music may be used to treat heart attack and stroke **victims** after Italian scientists found it can affect blood pressure.*
(THE TELEGRAPH, 22 JUNE 2009)

Young offenders will soon be picking litter, scrubbing graffiti or pulling weeds in your town – and officials want you to decide exactly what tasks they will do. Under the Community Payback scheme teenagers will have to carry out menial duties, improving neighbourhoods they may once have terrorised as a form of community service...
*[Mike Grimshaw, restorative justice officer, said] 'It's a scheme which benefits everyone involved – one of the ideas behind it is that if the kids are speaking to **victims** then they are less likely to re-offend.'*
(SCUNTHORPE EVENING TELEGRAPH, 27 JUNE 2009)

This word is a direct borrowing of Latin *victima*, which denoted 'a person or animal offered as a religious sacrifice' and may be allied to Germanic *weihan*, 'to consecrate'. Its earliest appearance in English is in a religious work, MONS PERFECCIONIS (1497) by Bishop John Alcock.

After Elizabeth I came to the throne in 1558, Protestantism was gradually reinstated in England and a large number of Catholics crossed the Channel to live in France. English academics joined the new Catholic University of Douai where, in 1569, William Allen founded a seminary for English Catholic priests preparing to return to England following the assumed successful invasion by Spain. Here the first Catholic translation of the Bible into English was made. The New Testament appeared in 1582 from Rheims, where the college had a temporary home. The work was a translation of the Latin Vulgate and the translators in Rheims were the first to use the word *victim* freely in English.

Victim began to be more generally applied to 'one who is killed or tortured by another' in the second half of the seventeenth century. The weaker sense denoting 'one who suffers hardship or is treated badly' arose in the second half of the eighteenth century.

villain

a rogue, a criminal

*[Miss Long] was infatuated and would not listen to those friends who told her that he was a **villain** and only wanted her money... At length Lady Catherine gave way and consented to the marriage, which Miss Long never ceased to regret, for her husband treated her in the most brutal manner and squandered the estate.*
(FRANCIS KILVERT, DIARY,
FRIDAY, 12 DECEMBER 1873)

*What puzzled me about **villains** was why, when they were masquerading as respectable citizens, their essential no-goodness wasn't as obvious to people on the screen as it was to me in the stalls.*
(ALAN BENNETT,
UNTOLD STORIES, 2005)

*The biggest surprise is that his previously one-dimensional **villain** of a father turns out to have been quite complex and emotional after all; looking at his son, we shouldn't really be taken aback.*
(REVIEW OF 'JOHN LENNON: THE LIFE'
BY PHILIP NORMAN, IN THE TIMES,
29 NOVEMBER 2008)

This is an instance of public opinion making corrupt endings of honest beginnings. A Roman *vīlla* was 'a country estate' and the Vulgar Latin term for a 'farm estate worker' was the unattested noun *vīllānus*. In the early fourteenth century, when the word came into Middle English as *vilein* or *vilain* by way of Old French, it denoted 'a peasant or serf who, under the feudal system, was bound to serve a lord in exchange for the right to hold a parcel of land'. Such social inferiors were generally despised by those of a higher class. Low birth meant base instincts and hence a lack of moral judgement and a natural inclination to wrongdoing. Interestingly the two Middle English variants *vilein* and *vilain* eventually parted company, the former retaining the meaning of 'serf' and the latter taking on the derogatory overtones of 'scoundrel'.

In English the Latin adjectival suffix *-ānus* is very commonly found in the slightly different guise of *-an*. It means 'of, coming from, pertaining to', as in *urban*: 'belonging to a city', *Roman*: 'coming from Rome', *Lutheran*: 'pertaining to Luther'.

For other words for scoundrel, see CAD and BLACKGUARD.

viper
a type of poisonous snake

*Of reptiles there are many kinds: one
snake...from the size of the poison channel
in its fangs, must be very deadly. Cuvier, in
opposition to some other naturalists, makes
this a sub-genus of the rattlesnake, and
intermediate between it and the **viper**. In
confirmation of this opinion, I observed a
fact, which appears to me very curious and
instructive... This Trigonocephalus has...in
some respects the structure of a viper, with
the habits of a rattlesnake.*
(CHARLES DARWIN,
THE VOYAGE OF THE BEAGLE, 1839)

*With the speed of a **viper**, he snatched her
wrist across the table. 'Don't even think
about blackmailing me!'*
*'I'm not blackmailing you, I'm promising
you I will do this!' she replied, her face set
hard and determined against the pain
inflicted by his hands.*
(BARBARA NADEL, HAREM, 2003)

*Every house had up to a dozen storks' nests
on its flat roof. Schliemann discovered that
the birds were useful because they killed
vipers and the noisy frogs that infested
the local marshland.*
(NICK MCCARTY, TROY, 2004)

Vipers are ovoviparous creatures; the
eggs hatch inside the female, and the
young are then nourished by the yolk
before being born alive. In ancient
times it was believed that the live
young, impatient to be born, ate their
way out of the female's side at birth, so
killing her. This fable is borne out in
the etymology of the word *viper*. Latin
vīpera, 'viper, snake', is a contracted
form of the unattested *vīvipera*, a compound of *vīvus*, 'alive, living', and
parere, 'to give birth, to produce'. Latin
vīpera passed into Old French as *vipere*
and from there into English in the early
sixteenth century.

The most efficacious cure for the
viper's bite was a compound containing
its flesh (see TREACLE), but the flesh
on its own was also greatly valued for its
medicinal and nutritive properties.

At the end of the sixteenth century
a figurative use of *viper* emerged when
it was applied to a vindictive, spiteful
person. In similar vein, and at the same
time, the phrase *a viper in one's bosom*
became current. This alludes to the old
fable of the viper nurtured in a person's
bosom that turns and poisons its host.

☛ *Vīvus* comes from the verb *vīvere*,
'to live'. This verb is apparent in many
other words denoting life, living,
liveliness and survival:

convivial (17th cent): from Latin
convīvālis, 'belonging to a feast', from
convīva, 'one who enjoys a feast with
other guests', from *convīvere*, 'live
together'.
    revive (15th cent): from Late Latin
revīvere, 'to live again'.
    survive (15th cent): from Old French
survivre, from Late Latin *supervīvere*,
from *super-*, 'over', and *vīvere*, 'to live'.
    vital (14th cent): from Old French
vital, from Latin *vītālis*, from *vīta*, 'life'.
    vivacious (17th cent): from Latin
vīvāx, 'lively', from *vīvere*, 'to live'.
    vivid (17th cent): from Latin *vīvidus*,
'lively'.
    vivisection (18th cent): a compound
of Latin *vīvus*, 'alive', and *sectiō*, 'a
cutting', from *secāre*, 'to cut'

Latin derived the noun *parēns*, 'parent',
from *parere*, 'to give birth'. Its stem
parent- was responsible for *parent*
in Old French and then English
(15th cent).

volume

a large book or one that is part of a set; a large amount of something; the loudness of a sound

The following day continued in much the same fashion. When he wasn't working at the bottom of the garden or listening to Tony Bennett at double the usual **volume** *he was following her from room to room.*
(MARK HADDON,
A SPOT OF BOTHER, 2006)

Other figures show that footwear and leather accounted for the largest increase in the **volume** *of sales between February and April. The largest drop was in food, beverages and tobacco.*
(BELFAST TELEGRAPH, 17 JULY 2007)

With encyclopaedias of Scotland and Ireland already published (in 1994 and 2003, respectively) it is a wonder that it has taken the proud Welsh nation so long to put itself on the map with a weighty and authoritative **volume**, *published simultaneously in Welsh and in English.*
(THE INDEPENDENT,
15 FEBRUARY 2008)

In ancient times books were papyrus sheets which were glued together to form a long roll. The book roll, which averaged over 11 metres (35 ft) in length, was attached to rods to keep it stiff and was accessed by unrolling it with the right hand while re-rolling the section that had been read with the left. The roll's subject matter was written on a label, a *titulus*, source of our word *title*, and hung upon the scroll.

The word for such a book roll was *volūmen*, a derivative of *volvere*, 'to roll'. It was borrowed into Middle English by way of Old French *volume* in the fourteenth century, when it denoted both 'a parchment roll' and 'a book'. In the sixteenth century the word was applied to 'a book that forms one part of a larger work'. *Volume* then denoted the large size of a book and, in the seventeenth century, this sense was generalised to refer to the 'bulk or quantity' of anything at all.

The word's application to 'the quality and strength of sound' seems to have begun in the late eighteenth century, and was initially used of voices. In his COMPLETE DICTIONARY OF MUSIC (1801), Thomas Busby defines *volume* as *a word applied to the compass of a voice from grave to acute; also to its tone, or power: as when we say, 'such a performer possesses an extensive or rich volume of voice'*.

☛ Latin *volvere*, 'to roll', is evident in other English words:

convolution (16th cent): from Latin *convolvere*, 'to roll together'.

convolvulus (16th cent): from Latin *convolvere*, 'to roll together, to roll around'. The common variety of this plant is popularly known as *bindweed*. Both words describe its habit of climbing by twisting itself around a support.

devolve (15th cent) and *devolution* (16th cent): from Latin *devolvere*, 'to roll down'.

revolt (16th cent): from French *révolter*, from Italian *rivoltare*, from unattested Vulgar Latin *revolvitāre*, from Latin *revolvere*, 'to roll back'.

For another word from Latin *volvere*, see VAULT.

wanton

excessive and pointless; capricious, wilful, arbitrary; immoral, lewd, lascivious

*I discovered that a lot of imported drainage pipes for the settlement had been tumbled in there. There wasn't one that was not broken. It was a **wanton** smash-up.*
(JOSEPH CONRAD, HEART OF DARKNESS, 1902)

*Alternatively, they acquiesce and collapse. Go all **wanton** and girly, and lie back with their arms and legs in the air like immobilised ladybirds, desperate to catch the first man who falls on them.*
(MARY CAVANAGH, A MAN LIKE ANY OTHER, 2007)

*A new scheme to buy a share of houses from people who would otherwise face repossession is more contentious. The details need to be worked out with care so that **wanton** recklessness will not be rewarded. But in principle it should be possible to get it right, and keeping people in their homes is a justifiable use of public funds.*
(THE GUARDIAN, 3 SEPTEMBER 2008)

A lack of firm discipline in the formative years is at the etymological heart of this word. The Middle English adjective *wantowen*, 'ill-bred, undisciplined', is made up of the prefix *wan-*, meaning 'lacking, wanting', and *towen*, which came from Old English *togen*, the past participle of *tēon*, 'to pull, to draw along', and therefore 'to bring up, to educate, to take in hand'. The other side of the coin was the Middle English ad-

jective *welitowen*, which meant 'well brought up'.

Not surprisingly, from its earliest uses *wanton* often described unruly children. Indeed, in the sixteenth and seventeenth centuries, the word was employed as a noun to denote 'a spoilt brat': *I am enforced to thinke...that thy parents made thee a wanton with too much cockering* [pampering] (John Lyly, EUPHUES AND HIS ENGLAND, 1580).

From the seventeenth to the nineteenth centuries the adjective often singled out cruel boys, inspired by Shakespeare's use in KING LEAR (1605):

As flies to wanton Boyes are we to th' Gods,
They kill us for their sport.

But the Middle English adjective also described unruly, rebellious people in general, its many subsequent shades of meaning springing from the basic notion of lack of discipline and self-control which manifests itself in thoughtless excess. By the end of the thirteenth century, for instance, lustful, unchaste women and lewd behaviour in general also came within its scope. Francis Bacon epigrammatically puts it thus: *Nuptial love maketh mankind; friendly love perfecteth it; but wanton love corrupteth, and embaseth it* ('Of Love', ESSAYS, 1625).

More popular works were free with the adjective. It is hardly surprising that it is found repeatedly in John Cleland's FANNY HILL (1748–9). Here is one instance:

*Then his touches were so exquisitely
wanton, so luxuriously diffus'd and
penetrative at times, that he had made me
perfectly rage with titillating fires.*

From the seventeenth century *wanton*,
applied to cruelty, neglect or destruction,
had the sense 'gratuitous, arbitrary'. The
British historian and politician James
Bryce gives a nice example of this use in
THE AMERICAN COMMONWEALTH
(1888): *Tyranny consists in the wanton and
improper use of strength by the stronger.*

wedlock

matrimony, the state of marriage

*Live fast, die young, Louise used to joke,
but it was hard to move fast when you were
hampered by linen chests and silver napkin
rings, not to mention having voluntarily
shackled yourself to one man for the rest of
your life. Was this what they meant by
wedlock?*
(KATE ATKINSON, WHEN WILL THERE
BE GOOD NEWS?, 2008)

*Under normal circumstances, a respectable
public figure like Cicero would hardly boast
that his daughter was about to give birth
out of **wedlock**. But circumstances were no
longer normal.*
(STEVEN SAYLOR,
THE TRIUMPH OF CAESAR, 2008)

The two elements of this word seem to
suggest the permanency of the marriage bond, that one is 'locked' into
the marriage relationship. In fact
Middle English *wedlock* comes from the
Old English term *wedlāc*, where *wed(d)*
meant 'a pledge' and *-lāc* was a suffix
with the sense of 'carrying out' or
'putting into action' the noun that
preceded it. Thus the word had the
sense 'giving a solemn promise or
vow'. The suffix *-lāc* appears in a
number of Old English compounds –
rēaflāc, for instance, was 'robbery' and
feohtlāc 'warfare' – but, of these, only

wedlock remains. Written references to
wedlock date from the late eleventh
century. Initially it meant 'the marriage vow'. Its application to 'the state
of marriage' dates from the early thirteenth century.

Because of its importance to the
fabric of social life, the state of wedlock
finds eloquent expression in the greatest
writers:

*Boweth youre nekke under that blissful yok
Of soveraynetee, noght of servyse,
Which that men clepeth spousaille
or wedlock*
(CHAUCER, 'THE CLERKES TALE',
CANTERBURY TALES, 1387)

Shakespeare recognises the pain or the
pleasure wedlock can bring:

*For what is wedlock forced but a hell,
An age of discord and continual strife?
Whereas the contrary bringeth bliss,
And is a pattern of celestial peace.*
(HENRY VI, PART ONE, 1592)

The term is somewhat old-fashioned to
modern ears but remains familiar
through the words of the marriage service
in the BOOK OF COMMON PRAYER
that date back to 1549 (*Forasmuche as N
and N haue consented together in holye wed-
locke...*), and also through the thirteenth-
century expressions *born in* and *born out of
wedlock*, to denote legitimate and illegitimate offspring. However, modern forms
of the marriage service and an end to
the taboo of illegitimacy may well mean
the days of this lone surviving compound
are numbered.

☛ *Wedding* is the gerundive of the
verb *wed*, 'to pledge' and hence 'to
marry'. Originally, it meant 'the act
of marrying' and then 'the state of
wedlock', but around the end of the
thirteenth century began to be applied
as a noun to the marriage ceremony
itself. *Wed* comes from unattested
proto-Germanic noun *wathjam*, 'vow'.

window

an opening in a wall to admit light and air and afford a view; a period of time during which an activity can take place

*Perhaps she knew with her intelligence that the chains she forged only aroused his instinct of destruction, as the plate-glass **window** makes your fingers itch for half a brick; but her heart, incapable of reason, made her continue on a course she knew was fatal.*
(W SOMERSET MAUGHAM,
THE MOON AND SIXPENCE, 1919)

*I know that I'll raise eyebrows by including unconventional destinations such as Calcutta and Madagascar, arduous choices that some travelers might avoid, but I consider them deeply moving and insightful **windows** into the human experience.*
(PATRICIA SCHULTZ, 1,000 PLACES TO SEE BEFORE YOU DIE, 2003)

*If you were born in the late 1840s, you missed it – you were too young to take advantage of that moment. If you were born in the 1820s, you were too old – your mind-set was shaped by the old, pre-civil war ways. But there was a narrow nine-year **window** that was just perfect.*
(MALCOLM GLADWELL,
THE OUTLIERS, 2008)

Window derives from an Old Norse word *vindauga* and was introduced into English by the Vikings. It is a compound of *vindr*, 'wind', and *auga*, 'eye', and is literally, therefore, 'an eye to admit the wind'. It was adopted into Middle English in the first half of the thirteenth century, gradually replacing the existing Old English word *eagthyrel*, (eyethurl), literally 'eyehole', and hence 'window' (from *eage*, 'eye', and *thyrl*, 'hole'). Two different manuscripts of the early Middle English book of devotions the ANCRENE WISSE or ANCRENE RIWLE (c. 1225), written by a chaplain for three sisters, contain

both the last recorded mention of *eagthyrel* and the first of *window*.

But the acceptance of *window* was not plain sailing from then on; it had to jostle for prominence with *fenester*, an Old French borrowing first recorded in 1290 and still in use in the mid-sixteenth century. Indeed, Edward Hall, in his chronicle THE UNION OF THE NOBLE AND ILLUSTRATE FAMELIES OF LANCASTRE AND YORKE (1548), found himself unable to decide in favour of one term over the other as he struggled to make his meaning clear: *In the Fenestres and wyndowes were images resemblynge men of warre.* By the end of the century, however, *window* was established and had royal approval, for Elizabeth I, in her pursuit of religious tolerance, declared she did not wish *to open windows into men's souls.*

The open window has played a significant role in the literature of romance. Romeo, most famously, woos Juliet at her balcony; Cyrano de Bergerac does the same to Roxanne; Belvile (in Behn's THE ROVER, 1677) stations himself at Florinda's chamber window. Few, however, can have been as direct as Diana to Bertram in Shakespeare's ALL'S WELL THAT ENDS WELL (1604):

When midnight comes, knock at my chamber window;
I'll order take my mother shall not hear.
Now will I charge you in the band of truth,
When you have conquer'd my yet maiden bed,
Remain there but an hour, nor speak to me.

The 1950s and '60s saw a period of intense interest in space exploration fuelled by the Space Race between the Soviet Union and the United States. The expression *launch window* was coined in America in the 1960s to refer to 'a period when atmospheric conditions and planetary activity permit the launch of a spacecraft'. On 18 October 1967 the NEW YORK TIMES reported that *The Soviet and American vehicles flew to Venus close together because both were fired during one of the periodic 'windows' for such shots.* This particular use of *window* gave rise to the more general *window of opportunity* in the 1970s. *Window* is now regularly used to denote 'a brief interval during which an activity can take place'.

☛ In modern English the Old English *thyrel* survives in *nostril* (Old English *nosthyrel*, from *nosu*, 'nose' and *thyrel*, 'hole') and as *thirl* in some northern dialects to denote 'an opening'.

Fenester (from Old French *fenestre*, from Latin *fenestra*, 'window', probably related to Greek *phainein*, 'to show') is found in the modern English noun *defenestration*, usually only with reference to the historical Defenestration of Prague (1618), and its derived verb *defenestrate*, 'to throw out of a window', which is confined to humorous contexts.

See VIKING CONQUESTS (opposite).

wit
natural intelligence; a gift for intelligent humour

When strolling through US customs, he once announced: 'I have nothing to declare but my genius.' So Oscar Wilde would probably not have been surprised to be named as Britain's greatest-ever **wit**.
(EVENING STANDARD,
15 OCTOBER 2007)

See WITNESS.

witness
someone who gives evidence about something seen or heard; someone who observes an event or activity

'We are concerned about what Mr Aitken will do when he is abroad. We are concerned about the number of foreign **witnesses** *in this case, and that he might interfere with them,' he said. This was a new theory about the criminality of my character. In the manner of Lord Lucan, the defendant Aitken would not merely vanish but would also 'interfere with' the foreign witnesses.*
(JONATHAN AITKEN,
PRIDE AND PERJURY, 2000)

Grace was a **witness** *to Jackson's abuse of prescription drugs. She said he took a mixture of them – in her words, 'he always ate too little and mixed too much'.*
(THE SUNDAY TIMES,
28 JUNE 2009)

The unattested proto-Indo-European base *weid-* had the sense 'to see, to perceive', and therefore 'to know', and was responsible for the Old English word *wit*. Originally *wit* denoted 'that part of the mind that is attentive to thought and feeling' and hence 'intellect, reason'. Thus the phrase *to be at one's wits' end*, which dates from the fourteenth century, means 'to be perplexed, to have reached the end of one's capacity to reason out a situation'. The modern sense 'a gift for clever, humorous remarks' dates from the sixteenth century.

The Old English word *witnes* literally meant 'the state or condition of knowing', being composed of *wit* and the suffix *-ness*, 'state, the condition of being'. Its original sense was 'knowledge, wisdom', but it also came to mean 'knowledge gained through being an observer of an event' and hence 'testimony'. Finally, in Old English, *witnes* came to denote 'one who bears testimony', the sense which has survived into modern English.

VIKING CONQUESTS

The period of Viking invasion and settlement in England dates from the middle of the eighth century to the beginning of the eleventh. It began with short, swift coastal raids, followed in the 860s by large-scale attacks which brought much of eastern England under Viking control. The Saxon king Alfred the Great (871-c. 900) secured Wessex against the invaders through battle and negotiation, and his successors succeeded in regaining much of the eastern territory. Then, in 991, came a new Scandinavian invasion. Years of marauding and pillaging ended in 1014 with the seizure of the throne by the Danish king Canute (Cnut). There followed a quarter-century of Danish rule.

Throughout these centuries of upheaval and invasion, large numbers of Scandinavians settled in England, integrating themselves into communities in their adopted country. This assimilation left English with a store of Old Norse words. The language already spoken in England (brought in by earlier invasions of Angles, Saxons and Jutes – see EARLY LATIN INFLUENCES, page 94) was from the same Common Germanic source as that spoken by the Vikings and so they shared many everyday words. It is, therefore, sometimes difficult to tell whether a word was already in English before the Vikings or was introduced by them.

Sometimes it is possible to distinguish, however. One group of words that came in with the Danes has an *sk* pronunciation: *sky, skin, skirt, whisk*, etc., whereas that *sk* sound in Old English words had usually softened to a *sh* pronunciation (written *sc*), as in *ship, fish*. This led to pairs in which a Germanic root gave two different products through separate development: Old English *scyrte* produced *shirt*, while Old Norse *skyrta* became *skirt*. Their Common Germanic root was *skyrta*. Similarly, the *g* and *k* sounds in words such as *leg, get, girth, egg, anger, bag, cake, take, kid, meek* and *link* indicate an Old Norse origin.

woman
a grown female human being

*This book appears to be primarily about two things: love and surely the **woman**'s lot, for Laura is unquestionably the victim of a male-dominated Victorian society...*
(REVIEW OF 'LAURA BLUNDY' BY JULIE MEYERSON, IN THE SPECTATOR, 8 APRIL 2000)

*As Alexander McCall Smith watched a cheerful **woman** in Botswana efficiently wring the neck of a chicken, he knew he'd found his muse. Inspired, the Scottish law professor created Mma Precious Ramotswe,* *the spirited heroine of the No. 1 Ladies' Detective Agency, first published by a small Scottish press in 1998.*
(U.S. NEWS & WORLD REPORT, 28 APRIL 2003)

In Old English *man(n)*, a Germanic word of undetermined origin, originally meant 'a human being' and could be applied to a person of either sex. The words *wer* and *wīf* were used to distinguish between 'a male person' and 'a female' respectively. Old English then put *wīf* and *man* together to give the compound noun *wīfman*, 'a female human being', and this gradually replaced *wīf*. During the tenth century *wīfman* lost its medial *f* and became *wimman*. Similarly the plural of *wīfman* was *wīfmen*, and this became *wimmen*, the pronunciation which persists in English to this day. The early thirteenth century saw the emergence of *wummon*, which was an easier pronunciation after an initial *w*, and the late thirteenth and early fourteenth centuries record *womman* and *woman*.

As for *wīf*, the earliest records show that it began to denote 'a wife' in the ninth century, this use becoming more common in the Middle English period as its reference to 'a woman' declined. Chaucer's Wife of Bath (c. 1387) was a woman who had had five husbands, but *an old wives' tale* is a story with no truth in it recounted by an old woman.

See HUSBAND.

world

the earth and its inhabitants; the state of existence; a planet; a sphere of interest or activity

*Nothing is more certain than that **worlds** on worlds, and spheres on spheres, stretch behind and beyond the actually seen.*
(EDWARD CARPENTER, THE DRAMA OF LOVE AND DEATH, 1912)

*It was the **world** which Isabel's father had come from, but from which he had wanted to free himself. He had been a lawyer, from a line of lawyers. He could have remained within the narrow world of his own father and grandfather, a world bounded by trust deeds and documents of title, but as a student he had been introduced to international law and a world of broader possibilities.*
(ALEXANDER MCCALL SMITH, THE SUNDAY PHILOSOPHY CLUB, 2004)

'We're all going to Hell, I expect. I'll wager there is no Heaven.'
'Maggie, don't say that!' Maisie cried.

'Well, maybe there's a Heaven for you, Miss Piddle. You'll be awfully lonely there, though.'
'I don't see why there has to be just the one or t'other,' Jem said. 'Can't there be something that's more a bit of both?'
*'That's the **world**, Jem,' Maggie said.*
(TRACY CHEVALIER, BURNING BRIGHT, 2007)

*Midnight. I am sitting on the terrace in a white plastic chair, the sort of white plastic chair you see in bars and cafés across the **world**, and staring at this yellow pad with a kind of angry listlessness.*
(SIMON GRAY, THE LAST CIGARETTE, 2008)

English *world*, Dutch *wereld* and German *Welt* share a common origin, an unattested proto-Germanic compound of *wer*, 'man', and *ald*, 'age', which meant 'the age of man'. Initially, then, Old English *w(e)oruld* denoted 'the course and experience of human life'. The primary modern sense of 'the earth' developed from the ninth century. The application to 'one's realm of activity and interest' dates from the sixteenth century.

worry

to trouble, distress; to bother, annoy, pester

*...that good dog, more thoughtful than its master, had, it seemed, been watching the old gentleman in his sleep...and he still attended on him very closely, **worrying** his gaiters in fact, and making dead sets at the buttons.*
(CHARLES DICKENS, THE CRICKET ON THE HEARTH, 1845)

*'What do you think the corporal's going to do?' Anna asked him, her voice buoyed by little eddies of **worry**, when he had finished telling her about Manfred.*
(CHRIS BOHJALIAN, SKELETONS AT THE FEAST, 2008)

*My four children are all taller than me now. They have relationships, secrets, whole other lives of which I know nothing. They lock their doors. They tell me not to **worry** and not to pry.*
(GOOD HOUSEKEEPING, APRIL 2009)

Worry is a violent verb coming from the unattested West Germanic *wurgjan*, which meant 'to strangle, to choke', from the proto-Indo-European root *wergh-*. In Old English this became *wyrgan* and in Middle English *worien* or *wirien*, 'to throttle'. In the late fourteenth century the term was also applied to dogs and, in those days, to wolves, which had the habit of seizing their prey by the throat in order to kill it. This use is still current – farmers have the right to shoot any dog which *worries* their sheep.

Later uses appear to arise from the dog's tenacity as it chokes its victim. In the sixteenth century *worry* was used with the sense 'to harass aggressively'. When this sense was employed in a lighter vein in the following century, it took on the modern meaning, 'to pester, to plague, to annoy' – by repeated demands, for instance, or constant talk: *You worry me to death with your chattering* (Charles Dickens, THE OLD CURIOSITY SHOP, 1840).

In a similar way concerns and fears work away unrelentingly in our imaginations to make us anxious and so, in the nineteenth century, *worry* came to mean 'to cause anxiety'. For William Hazlitt it was the *small pains* that plagued. They are, he says, *more within our reach; we can fret and worry ourselves about them'* (TABLE TALK, 1822). Anthony Trollope, on the other hand, wrote of the persistence of fear: *Men, when they are worried by fears...become suspicious.*
(THE LAST CHRONICLE OF BARSET, 1867)

write

to form letters and symbols on paper or other surface with an instrument such as a pen or pencil

*Once the late Sinclair Lewis arrived at Harvard, drunk as usual (alcoholism is our main occupational disease) to talk about **writing**. 'Hands up, all those who want to be writers!' he yelled. Everyone's hand went up. 'Then why the hell aren't you at home writing?' he asked, and staggered off the platform.*
  I begin with this anecdote because it illustrates a simple but profound truth: a writer is a person who writes.
(JOHN BRAINE,
WRITING A NOVEL, 1974)

***Write** down a list of at least twenty words. When you've done that, settle down and once more see how many rhymes you can come up with for each word.*
(STEPHEN FRY,
THE ODE LESS TRAVELLED, 2005)

*Like my teenage self (another diarist and secret would-be novelist), Cassandra often **wrote** for so long that her hand ached. And her questions about writing were my questions. Where do writers write best? How does a writer manage to find time to write about her life whilst still living it? What is the best way to convey a setting or describe an object? How does one write about things that are happening right now?*
(RUTH SYMES IN SLIGHTLY FOXED, AUTUMN 2008)

In today's highly literate and technological society it is difficult enough to imagine a time when books and records had to be written out by hand, let alone cut out of material, but that is the ultimate meaning of the verb *to write*. The Old English term *writan* meant 'to write by cutting', as one might score marks into bark or engrave characters into stone. Ultimately it goes back to unattested proto-Germanic *wrītan*, 'to cut, to scratch'.

It is thought that early inscriptions among Germanic tribes were scratched upon beechwood tablets, or that the bark of beech trees was used, since the unattested proto-Germanic words for *book* and *beech* appear to be connected: *bōks*, 'writing tablet' and source of 'book' in many Germanic languages, is probably akin to *bōkā*, 'beech'.

Derivatives of these two words in modern Germanic languages also demonstrate the similarity: German, for instance, has *Buch*, 'book' and *Buche*, 'beech', while Dutch has *boek* and *beuk*. The modern English words *book* and *beech* come via Old English *bōc*, 'written account', and *bēce*, 'beech', respectively.

yacht

a light, fast boat, usually propelled by sails and used for pleasure or racing

*Then I found the place where the **yachts** were, all pretty and elegant, with their little flags and their wires slapping, rising and falling on the water. I sat down on my case and it made me feel happy just looking at the boats, and the sunlight on the water, sparkling.*
(LOUIS DE BERNIÈRES,
THE PARTISAN'S DAUGHTER, 2008)

*With its twin engines and helicopter decks, this luxury **yacht** does not look like the most environmentally friendly way to see the Caribbean. But the Prince of Wales's decision to charter the* Leander *for his official 11-day tour to Trinidad and Tobago, St Lucia and Jamaica is an attempt to cut his carbon footprint.*
(EVENING STANDARD,
9 FEBRUARY 2008)

English regard for Dutch nautical prowess is evident from the large number of words and idioms to do with ships and sailing that the English borrowed from their rivals across the Channel in the sixteenth and seventeenth centuries. In the sixteenth century the Dutch designed a swift, light sailing vessel known as a *jaghte*, a shortened form of the compound *jaghtschip*. This literally meant 'a ship for chasing', being a compound of *jagt*, 'a hunting' (from *jagen*, 'to chase, hunt'), and *schip*, 'a ship'. Some say that the craft, as its name implies, was designed to pursue illegal shipping off the Dutch coast.

Others claim that the vessel was simply named for its speed.

When the exiled English king Charles II sailed from Amsterdam at the time of his Restoration in 1660, it was on a yacht presented to him by the Dutch East India Company. This first royal yacht was named the MARY after the king's sister. Charles and his brother James, Duke of York, had other yachts built and in 1662 raced the ANNE and the KATHERINE on the Thames from Greenwich to Gravesend and back for a £100 wager. This royal endorsement made yachting fashionable and orders from wealthy gentlemen kept the boatyards busy. Surprisingly, however, it was not until the second half of the eighteenth century that yacht racing was organised to any degree.

The speedy Dutch vessel attracted international attention and the word was extensively borrowed into the languages of neighbouring countries. An early spelling in English, *yeagh* (1557), demonstrates the difficulty writers here had in adapting the unfamiliar guttural *gh* of the foreign word. There is great variation in spelling throughout the seventeenth century: *yoath, yolke, yaugh, zaught, jacht, yach* and *yott* are just a few examples, until *yacht* was finally settled upon in the mid-eighteenth century.

For another conveyance which attracted international attention, see COACH.
For another Dutch nautical borrowing, see ALOOF. For an entry about yacht racing, see REGATTA.

yen
a powerful yearning

...since the shops are packed with gorgeous little dresses – many of which are already discounted in the sales – anyone with a yen for frothy frocks should make the most of the festive season.
(THE TELEGRAPH, 20 DECEMBER 2006)

Flamboyant and irascible, he had the ear of the prime minister, a yen for a tipple and a highly developed eye for wallpaper costing £300 a roll.
(THE GUARDIAN, 11 MAY 2007)

During the eighteenth century, there was a trade imbalance between Europe and China. Although the demand for Chinese goods in Europe was high, China had set up restrictions on imported merchandise. Britain began to send opium to China from India, realising that its addictive qualities would create a growing demand. In 1773 the British East India Company gained a monopoly on Indian opium and worked out illegal ways of importing it into China in defiance of a Chinese ban on the drug as a harmful substance.

In the mid-nineteenth century, many Chinese emigrated to the United States to work as labourers on the railways and in the mining industries. Their number inevitably included opium addicts, those afflicted by the *yinyan*, the 'craving for opium' (from *yin*, 'opium', and *yan*, 'craving'). This term passed into American informal speech as *yen-yen*. In DARKNESS AND DAYLIGHT (1891), an account of temperance, mission and rescue work in New York, Helen Campbell quoted one Chinese woman as saying, '*I've got the yen-yen (opium habit) the worst way...and must have my pipe every night.*' Before long the phrase was reduced to *yen*, and by the early twentieth century was being applied more generally to denote 'a powerful longing or yearning' of any sort.

·Z·

zany

way out, eccentric, bizarre

'We interview over 1,000 senior executives a year and never hesitate to point out – politely – the need for some sartorial adjustment when required. One man appeared for interview wearing a zany waistcoat: he said it was his hallmark. Nobody had ever pointed out that in fact this was a big disadvantage, because new colleagues would notice the waistcoat rather than focus on what value he was adding.'
(THE SPECTATOR, 12 JULY 2007)

The writer's achievement here was to tap into the zany spirit of Tuscan humour to deliver a Pinocchio who swings alarmingly between lies and candour, generous sentiment and cruel mockery, good intentions and zero staying power.
(REVIEW OF 'THE ADVENTURES OF PINOCCHIO' BY CARLO COLLODI, IN THE NEW YORK REVIEW OF BOOKS, APRIL–MAY 2009)

John, and its variants, was a common name in all Christian countries and was therefore frequently used to refer to the man in the street generally, or to a fool or simpleton in particular. French, for example, has *Gros Jean*, and *Jack* is commonly used in this way in English. Venetian and Lombardic dialects transformed the Italian name *Gianni* (the short form of *Giovanni*, 'John') into *Zanni*. This variant became the name of a character in the *commedia dell'arte*, a servant who imitates his master in a farcical way. *Zanie* came into English, possibly through French, in the second half of the sixteenth century.

Shakespeare wrote of *Zanies* in both LOVE'S LABOUR'S LOST (1588) and TWELFTH NIGHT (1601), and Ben Jonson describes *a Zanito a Tumbler, That tries trickes after him to make men laugh* in EVERY MAN OUT OF HIS HUMOUR (1599). The meaning was extended in the seventeenth century to refer to 'a person who generally acts the fool to keep others amused' but all uses of the word as a noun are now obsolete.

Zany's appearance as an adjective in the first quarter of the seventeenth century was short-lived, but it re-emerged in the second half of the nineteenth with the sense of 'clownishly bizarre, crazy', the very meanings it still has today.

zest

gusto, enthusiasm; the outer skin of citrus fruits, used to flavour food

Zest. *Originally the tough outer skin of the walnut, but now used to denote the outer skin of citrus fruits, especially of lemon and orange, which contains the essential flavouring oils.*
(TOM STOBART, THE COOK'S ENCYCLOPAEDIA, 1980)

She has a rare zest for life, a passion for looking at things, for knowing what is going on. She has a magical attraction for young people who adore her enthusiasm.
(JULIA NEUBERGER, MOTHERS BY DAUGHTERS, 1995)

A pan-seared sea bass, crisply cooked and served with punchy gremolata (garlic, parsley and lemon zest) is 'pleasant enough', if not 'particularly striking'.
(THE WEEK, 29 NOVEMBER 2008)

Zest is a refreshing word with a hint of mystery. Many modern recipes call for the addition of citrus zest, that is, the brightly coloured layer in orange, lemon or lime peel that contains the flavoursome oil. These days an effective little gadget called a *zester* can be purchased to pare it away. Even tonic water now comes ready flavoured with the zest of lemon or lime – the gin is all that is needed.

Not surprisingly it was the French who introduced this taste sensation into British cookery in the seventeenth century. They called it *zest* (*zeste* in modern French), but no one has been able to discover how they derived this energetic word. The fact that French also applied the term to the membrane or film within a walnut that divides the kernel into four parts has lead to fanciful attempts to connect it with the Latin *schistus*, 'divided'.

In French *zest* has remained a culinary term, but the British have been more imaginative, so that, by the beginning of the eighteenth century, it was also figuratively used to denote 'something that adds spice or sparkle to an enjoyment'. Mrs Manley, in one of her scurrilous memoirs (1709), informed the world that *Monsieur St Amant lov'd nothing so tenderly as he did the Baron...he was the Zest to all his Pleasures*. Towards the end of the eighteenth century *zest* had also come to mean 'great enthusiasm, keen pleasure'. In MARTIN CHUZZLEWIT (1844), Dickens describes the midwife Sarah Gamp as one who *went to a lying-in or a laying-out with equal zest*.

zigzag
a sharply angled line which alternates in direction

On the eve of the First World War, he [Meidner] painted a series of pictures explicitly titled Apocalyptic Landscapes, *showing the city, shattered and consumed. The streets rock. The houses judder. The sky breaks up in* zigzags *and shoots out in firestorms.*
(THE INDEPENDENT, 26 JUNE 2009)

As the crowd zig-zagged to left and right, eventually striking off in different directions to stake a claim on a patch of turf or fimd a more sheltered position against one of the rocks, Josephine could not help but think that this was the strangest entrance to a theatre she had ever encountered.
(NICOLA UPSON,
ANGEL WITH TWO FACES, 2009)

This word is German in origin. It is not known how it was coined, but its sound and the repetition of its two elements are suggestive of an abrupt change in direction. Skeat suggests the reduplication of the German word *Zacke*, 'sharp point'. Indeed, the German word *zickzack* was applied to trenches constructed in a zigzag pattern to prevent enemy fire from sweeping along them. The term was taken from German into French in the late seventeenth century and borrowed from there into English at the beginning of the eighteenth. In the early twentieth century *zigzag* was used as a military slang word on both sides of the Atlantic to denote 'drunk'.

zodiac

a band of the celestial sphere which is divided into twelve parts, each with a distinctive sign

BOSSTROLOGY: THE TWELVE
BOSSES OF THE ZODIAC
Have you ever wondered what makes your
boss tick? A new book gives a revealing
insight into the different types of bosses,
according to their star signs. Read here to
find out how to deal with your boss, and
take our quiz to find out what kind of boss
you would make.
(MAIL ONLINE, 2 OCTOBER 2004)

With a century of different propaganda
it would probably be perfectly possible to
get armies to march on the basis of, say,
which sign of the **zodiac** *they had been*
born under. 'The crisis in the Lebanon
deteriorated further today, when a leading
Sagittarian moderate was assassinated
by a member of the Gemini militia.'
(JOHN O'FARRELL, AN UTTERLY
IMPARTIAL HISTORY OF BRITAIN, 2007)

In astrology the *zodiac* was the name given to an imaginary zone in the skies through which the sun appears to move during the course of the year. In ancient times astrologers divided the zone into twelve areas, each containing a major constellation. Ancient and medieval astrologers predicted events by observing the position of the sun, moon and other known planets in relation to each other.

The constellations were given names, all of which are still familiar through the popularity of 'star' columns in newspapers and magazines. Many of these names relate to animals – Taurus the Bull, Cancer the Crab, Leo the Lion and so on. The Greek for 'animal' was *zōion*, whose diminutive *zōidion* denoted 'a carved figure of an animal' and thence 'a sign of the zodiac'. *Zōidion* yielded the adjective *zōidiakos* and the heavenly band that contained the twelve signs was known as the *zōidiakos kuklos*, 'zodiac circle'. The term was abbreviated to *zōidiakos*, with the adjective becoming a noun. This passed into Latin as *zōdiacus* and, from there, the word and its associated superstition were taken into the Romance languages. Middle English *zodiac* was borrowed from Old French *zodiaque* in the fourteenth century.

For another word deriving from *zōion*, see ZOO.

zoo

a place where usually wild animals are kept for breeding and showing to the public

Thursday morning she took the children
to the **zoo***, where they spent some time*
commiserating with the dusty, panting lions.
(ANNE TYLER, BACK WHEN WE WERE
GROWNUPS, 2001)

Isaac remembered how, when he had first
arrived, so many of them used to dawdle on
the Promenade, watching the internees from
what they perceived to be a safe distance,
like spectators at a human **zoo***.*
(DAVID BADDIEL,
THE SECRET PURPOSES, 2004)

Zoo is derived from the Greek *zōion*, which meant 'animal'. From this the modern Latin word *zōologia* was coined to describe the study of animals in terms of their usefulness to medical science. When this was adopted into English as *zoology* in the seventeenth century it denoted 'the natural history of animals', as distinct from *botany*, 'the study of plants'.

The derived adjective *zoological* appeared in the early nineteenth century. In 1826 it was incorporated into the name of the Zoological Society of London, which was founded *for the advancement of Zoology and Animal Physiology, and for the introduction of new and curious subjects of the animal kingdom.* In 1829 the *Zoological Gardens*, the Society's collection of animals in Regent's Park, London, were opened to the public. Within two years, however, the gardens were popularly referred to as *the Zoological* and by the 1840s their name had been clipped to *zoo*. The names of similar animal collections opening in other cities and rejoicing in the cumbersome title *Zoological Gardens* immediately met the same fate – a new word had evolved.

For another word deriving from *zōion*, see ZODIAC.

• **bibliography** •

All lexicographers must admit to a dependence on the work of others. We are no exception. We owe a huge debt of gratitude to the many dictionaries and general reference sources that we have consulted. It would have been quite impossible to produce this book without the *Oxford English Dictionary*, for example, and there are many other standard dictionaries of British and American English (and of French, Spanish, Latin, Greek, etc.) that we have referred to regularly. Then there are more specifically dictionaries of etymology, such as Skeat's, that have aided us immensely. And given the historical nature of this book, dictionaries from previous centuries have been a rich source, notably Dr Johnson's *Dictionary of the English Language*, Grose's *Dictionary of the Vulgar Tongue*, Halliwell's *Archaic Words* and Nares' *Glossary of Words, Phrases, Names and Allusions*. Books about language have ranged from the encyclopedias on language, to textbooks such as Baugh and Cable's splendid *History of the English Language* and Hughes' *Words in Time*. Contemporary specialist dictionaries on slang, jargon, abbreviations, eponyms, etc. have also figured significantly in our researches, as have journals on language such as *Notes and Queries, American Notes and Queries* and *Verbatim*.

Ayto, J (1990). *Dictionary of Word Origins*. London, Bloomsbury.

Baugh, A C and T Cable (1993). *A History of the English Language*. London, Routledge.

Beeching, C L (1989). *A Dictionary of Eponyms*. London, Clive Bingley.

Crystal, D (1987). *The Cambridge Encyclopedia of Language*. London, Cambridge University Press.

Crystal, D (2004). *The Stories of English*. London, Penguin.

Dunkling, L (1994). *The Guinness Book of Curious Words*. Enfield, Guinness.

Greimas, A J (1968). *Dictionnaire de L'Ancien Français*. Larousse, Paris.

Grose, F (1785). *A Classical Dictionary of the Vulgar Tongue*. London, S Hooper.

Harper, D (2001). *Online Etymology Dictionary*.

Halliwell, J H (1850). *Archaic Words*. London, John Russell Smith.

Hoare, D (1883). *Exotics or English Words from Latin Roots.* London, Hodges, Smith & Co.

Hughes, G (1988). *Words in Time.* Oxford, Basil Blackwell.

Johnson, S (1755). *Dictionary of the English Language.* London, Robert Dodsley.

Lewis and Short (1880). *A Latin Dictionary.*

Merriam-Webster (1991). *New Book of Word Histories.* Springfield, Massachusetts, Merriam-Webster.

Nares, R (1822) *Glossary of Words, Phrases, Names and Allusions.*

Oxford English Dictionary online (2009).

Room, A (1991). *Dictionary of Word Origins.* Lincolnwood, Illinois, National Textbook Company.

Skeat, W W (1897). *Etymological Dictionary of the English Language.* Oxford, Oxford University Press.

Walsh, W S (1892). *A Handy Book of Literary Curiosities.* Philadelphia, Lippincott.

• index •